# BUSINESS
# DATA
# SCIENCE

# BUSINESS
# DATA
# SCIENCE

Combining Machine Learning and Economics to Optimize,
Automate, and Accelerate Business Decisions

## MATT TADDY

New York   Chicago   San Francisco   Athens   London   Madrid
Mexico City   Milan   New Delhi   Singapore   Sydney   Toronto

1  2  3  4  5  6  7  8  9   QVS   24  23  22  21  20  19

ISBN:      978-1-260-45277-8
MHID:        1-260-45277-8

e-ISBN:  978-1-260-45278-5
e-MHID:    1-260-45278-6

This publication is designed to provide accurate and authoritative information in regard to the subject matter covered. It is sold with the understanding that neither the author nor the publisher is engaged in rendering legal, accounting, securities trading, or other professional services. If legal advice or other expert assistance is required, the services of a competent professional person should be sought.

> —*From a Declaration of Principles Jointly Adopted by a Committee
> of the American Bar Association and a Committee of Publishers
> and Associations*

Library of Congress Cataloging-in-Publication Data

Names: Taddy, Matt, author.
Title: Business data science : combining machine learning and economics to
    optimize, automate, and accelerate business decisions / Matt Taddy.
Description: 1 Edition. | New York : McGraw-Hill Education, 2019.
Identifiers: LCCN 2018052621 | ISBN 9781260452778 (hardback) | ISBN 1260452778
Subjects: LCSH: Decision making—Econometric models. | Machine learning. |
    BISAC: BUSINESS & ECONOMICS / General.
Classification: LCC HD30.23 .T324 2019 | DDC 658.4/033—dc23
LC record available at https://lccn.loc.gov/2018052621

McGraw-Hill Education books are available at special quantity discounts to use as premiums and sales promotions or for use in corporate training programs. To contact a representative, please visit the Contact Us pages at www.mhprofessional.com.

*For Kirsty, Amelia, and Charlie.*

# CONTENTS

# PREFACE

## What Is This Book About?

Over the past decade, business analysis has been disrupted by a new way of doing things. Spreadsheet models and pivot tables are being replaced by code scripts in languages like R, Scala, and Python. Tasks that previously required armies of business analysts are being automated by applied scientists and software development engineers. The promise of this modern brand of business analysis is that corporate leaders are able to go deep into every detail of their operations and customer behavior. They can use tools from machine learning to not only track what has happened but predict the future for their businesses.

This revolution has been driven by the rise of big data—specifically, the massive growth of digitized information tracked in the Internet age and the development of engineering systems that facilitate the storage and analysis of this data. There has also been an intellectual convergence across fields—machine learning and computer science, modern computational and Bayesian statistics, and data-driven social sciences and economics—that has raised the breadth and quality of applied analysis everywhere. The machine learners have taught us how to automate and scale, the economists bring tools for causal and structural modeling, and the statisticians make sure that everyone remembers to keep track of uncertainty.

The term *data science* has been adopted to label this constantly changing, vaguely defined, cross-disciplinary field. Like many new fields, data science went through an over-hyped period where crowds of people rebranded themselves as data scientists. The term has been used to refer to anything remotely related to data. Indeed, I was hesitant to use the term *data science* in this book because it has been used so inconsistently. However, in the domain of professional business analysis, we have now seen enough of what works and what doesn't for data science to have real meaning as a modern, scientific, scalable approach to data analysis. *Business data science* is the new standard for data analysis at the world's leading firms and business schools.

This book is a primer for those who want to gain the skills to operate as a data scientist at a sophisticated data-driven firm. They will be able identify the variables important for business policy, run an experiment to measure these variables, and mine social media for information about public response to policy changes. They can connect small changes in a recommender system to changes in customer experience and use this information to estimate a demand curve. They will need to do all of these things, scale it to company-wide data, and explain precisely how uncertain they are about their conclusions.

These super-analysts will use tools from statistics, economics, and machine learning to achieve their goals. They will need to adopt the workflow of a data engineer, organizing end-to-end analyses that pull and aggregate the needed data and scripting routines that can be automatically repeated as new data arrives. And they will need to do all of this with an awareness of what they are measuring and how it is relevant to business decision-making. This is not a book about *one of* machine learning, economics, or statistics, nor is it a survey of data science as a whole. Rather, this book pulls from all of these fields to build a toolset for business data science.

This brand of data science is tightly integrated into the process of business decision-making. Early "predictive analytics" (a precursor to business data science) tended to overemphasize showy demonstrations of machine learning that were removed from the inputs needed to make business decisions. Detecting patterns in past data can be useful—we will cover a number of pattern recognition topics—but the necessary analysis for deeper business problems is about *why* things happen rather than *what* has happened. For this reason, we will spend the time to move beyond correlation to causal analysis. This book is closer to economics than to the mainstream of data science, which should help you have a bigger practical impact through your work.

We can't cover everything here. This is not an encyclopedia of data analysis. Indeed, for continuing study, there are a number of excellent books covering different areas of contemporary machine learning and data science.[1] Instead, this is a highly curated introduction to what I see as the key elements of business data science. I want you to leave with a set of best practices that make you confident in what to trust, how to use it, and how to learn more.

I've been working in this area for more than a decade, including as a professor teaching regression (then data mining and then big data) to MBA students, as a researcher working to bring machine learning to social science, and as a consultant and employee at some big and exciting tech firms. Over that time I've observed the growth of a class of generalists who can understand business problems and also dive into the (big) data and run their own analyses. These people are kicking ass, and every company on Earth needs more of them. This book is my attempt to help grow more of these sorts of people.

The target audience for this book includes science, business, and engineering professionals looking to skill up in data science. Since this is a completely new field, few

---

1. For example, Hastie et al. [2009] is the foremost modern statistics reference, and James et al. [2013] is a less advanced text from a similar viewpoint, while Bishop [2006] and Murphy [2012] are surveys from the machine learning community.

people come out of college with a data science degree. Instead, they learn math, programming, and business from other domains and then need a pathway to enter data science. My initial experience teaching data science was with MBA students at The University of Chicago Booth School of Business. We were successful in finding ways to equip business students with the technical tools necessary to go deep on big data. However, I have since discovered an even larger pool of future business data scientists among the legions of tech workers who want to apply their skills to impactful business problems. Many of these people are scientists: computer scientists, but also biologists, physicists, meteorologists, and economists. As machine learning matures into an engineering discipline, many more are software development engineers.

I've tried for a presentation that is accessible to quantitative people from all of these backgrounds, so long as they have a good foundation in basic math and a minimal amount of computer programming experience. Teaching MBAs and career switchers at Chicago has taught me that nonspecialists can become very capable data scientists. They just need to have the material presented properly. First, concepts need to be stripped down and unified. The relevant data science literature is confused and dispersed across academic papers, conference proceedings, technical manuals, and blogs. To the newcomer it appears completely disjointed, especially since the people writing this material are incentivized to make every contribution seem "completely novel." But there are simple reasons why good tools work. There are only a few robust recipes for successful data analysis. For example, make sure your models predict well on new data, not the data you used to fit the models. In this book, we'll try to identify these best practices, describing them in clear terms and reinforcing them for every new method or application.

The other key is to make the material concrete, presenting everything through application and analogy. As much as possible, the theory and ideas need to be intuitable in terms of real experience. For example, the crucial idea of "regularization" is to build algorithms that favor simple models and add complexity only in response to strong data signals. We'll introduce this by analogy to noise canceling on a phone (or the squelch on a VHF radio) and illustrate its effect when predicting online spending from web browser history. For some of the more abstract material (e.g., principal components analysis), we will explain the same ideas from multiple perspectives and through multiple examples. The main point is that while this is a book that uses mathematics (and it is essential that you work through the math as much as possible), we won't use math as a crutch to avoid proper explanation.

The final key, and your responsibility as a student of this material, is that business data science can only be learned by doing. This means writing the code to run analysis routines on real messy data. In this book, we will use R for most of the scripting examples.[2] Coded examples are heavily interspersed throughout the text, and you will not be able to effectively read the book if you can't understand these code snippets. You *must* write

---

2. See www.r-project.org. We use R because it is among the most commonly used languages for data science, it has many comprehensive prepackaged statistics and econometrics routines, and it is easy to read for those who are not computer scientists. However, in practice, a business data scientist will need to be able to read and make small changes in a bunch of languages—Python, Julia, SQL, and perhaps Scala or Java for those closer to the raw data. A good trick is to learn one language well (probably R) and then pick up what you need as you go.

your own code and run your own analyses as you learn. The easiest way to do this is to focus on adapting examples from the text, which are available on the book's website at taddylab.com/bds.

I should emphasize that *this is not a book for learning R*. There are a ton of other great resources for that. When teaching this material at Chicago, I found it best to separate the learning of basic R from the core analytics material, and this is the model we follow here. As a prerequisite for working through this book, you should do whatever tutorials and reading you need to get to a rudimentary level. Then you can advance by copying, altering, and extending the in-text examples. You don't need to be an R expert to read this book, but you need be able to read the code.

So, that is what this book is about. This is a book about how to *do* data science. It is a book that will gather together all of the exciting things being done around using data to help run a modern business. We will lay out a set of core principles and best practices that come from statistics, machine learning, and economics. You will be working through a *ton* of real data analysis examples as you "learn by doing." It is a book designed to prepare scientists, engineers, and business professionals to be exactly what is promised in the title: business data scientists.

Matt Taddy
Seattle, Washington

## Standard Usage for Some Common Notation

$\leq$ . . . . . . . .less than or equal to

$<$ . . . . . . . .less than

$\ll$ . . . . . . .much less than

$=$ . . . . . . . .equal to

$\approx$ . . . . . . . .roughly equal to

$\propto$ . . . . . . . .proportional to

$\perp\!\!\!\perp$ . . . . . . .independent from

$\mathbb{E}$ . . . . . . . .expected value (average)

$p(A)$ . . . . . .probability of $A$

$f(x)$ . . . . . .generic function of $x$

$\mathbb{E}[A\,|\,B]$ . . . .expectation for $A$ given $B$

$\mathbb{1}_{[A]}$ . . . . . . .indicator equals 1 if $A$
else 0

$\log(a)$ . . . .logarithm of $a$ with base $e$

$e$ . . . . . . . .Euler's number $\approx 2.71828$

$df$ . . . . . . .model degrees of freedom

lhd . . . . . .likelihood of the
observed data

dev . . . . . .deviance, where where
dev $\propto$ $-2\log$ lhd

MLE . . . . .maximum likelihood
estimate

OLS. . . . . .ordinary least squares,
i.e., the MLE for linear
regression

$n$ . . . . . . .number of observations

$p$ . . . . . . . .either data dimension or
a random variable (as in
$p$-value)

$y$ . . . . . . . .response of interest

$x$ . . . . . . .inputs to a regression

$\beta$ . . . . . . .linear regression
coefficients

$\varepsilon$ . . . . . . .independent additive
errors in regression

$\gamma$ . . . . . . .the causal treatment
effect

$\Sigma$ . . . . . . .covariance matrix

$\lambda$ . . . . . . .penalty weight

$\sum_{i\in S}a_i$ . . . . .sum of $a_i$ values for $i$ in
the set $S$

$\prod_{i=1}^{n}a_i$ . . . .product of $a_i$ values for $i$
from 1 through $n$

 Throughout the book, a black diamond denotes sections or subsections that are more advanced and abstract. The main content of the book does not require understanding of this material.

# Introduction

## A Tale of Two Plots

Consider the graph in Figure I.1. This shows seven years of monthly returns[1] for stocks in the S&P 500 index. Each dashed line denotes an individual stock's return series. Their weighted average—the value of the S&P 500—is marked with a bold black line. The thin black line shows returns on three-month U.S. treasury bills.

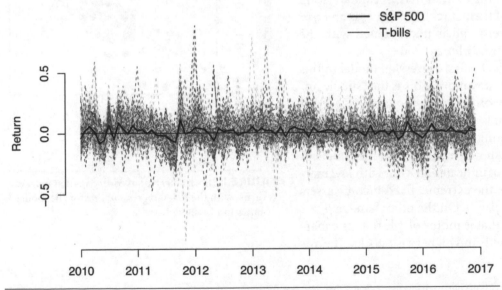

**FIGURE I.1:** A fancy plot: monthly stock returns for members of the S&P 500 and their average (the bold line). *What can you learn?*

---

1. A return is the difference divided by prior value: $(y_t - y_{t-1})/y_{t-1}$.

This is a fancy plot. It looks cool, with lots of different lines. It is the sort of plot that you might see on a computer screen in a TV ad for some online brokerage platform. *If only I had that information, I'd be rich!*

But what can you actually learn from Figure I.1? You can see that returns do tend to bounce around near zero.[2] You can also pick out periods of higher volatility (variance) where the S&P 500 changes more from month to month and the individual stock returns around it are more dispersed. That's about it. You don't learn *why* these periods are more volatile or when they will occur in the future. More important, you can't pull out useful information about any individual stock. There is a ton of *data* on the graph but little useful information.

**INSTEAD OF PLOTTING RAW DATA,** let's consider a simple *market model* that relates individual stock returns to the market average. The capital asset pricing model (CAPM) regresses the returns of an individual asset onto a measure of overall market returns:

$$r_{jt} = \alpha_j + \beta_j m_t + \varepsilon_{jt}. \tag{I.1}$$

The *output* $r_{jt}$ is equity $j$ return at time $t$ (actually the excess return[3]). The *input* $m_t$ is a measure of the average return—the "market"—at time $t$. You can take $m_t$ as the return on the S&P 500, which weights companies according to their market capitalization (the total value of their stock). Finally, $\varepsilon_{jt}$ is an *error* that has mean zero and is uncorrelated with the market: $\mathbb{E}[\varepsilon_{jt}] = 0$ and $\mathbb{E}[m_t \varepsilon_{jt}] = 0$.

Equation I.1 is the first regression model in this book. You'll see many more. This is the "simple linear regression" (or ordinary least squares [OLS]) that should be familiar to most readers. The Greek letters define a line relating each individual equity return to the market, as shown in Figure I.2 for example. A small $\beta_j$, near zero, indicates an asset with low market sensitivity. In the extreme, fixed-income assets like T-bills have $\beta_j = 0$. On the other hand, a $\beta_j > 1$ indicates a stock that is more volatile than the market, typically growth and higher-risk stocks. The $\alpha_j$ is

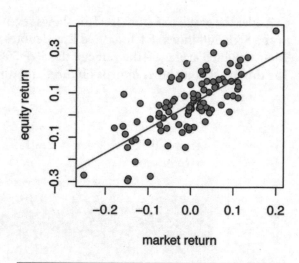

**FIGURE I.2:** A *scatterplot* of equity against market returns, with the fitted *regression line* for the model of Equation I.1 shown.

---

2. The long-term average is of course reliably much greater than zero. See, for example, Carvalho et al. [2017].

3. Most finance modeling works on units of *excess returns*: an asset's rate of return minus a measure of the "risk-free rate"—in other words, what you would have made by holding low-risk debt. A common measure of the risk-free rate is the return on U.S. Treasury bills (T-bills)—say, $u_t$ at time $t$. You work with $r_{jt} = (y_t - y_{t-1}) / y_{t-1} - u_t$, the return on equity $j$ at time $t$ minus the T-bill returns. Similarly, the market returns are the S&P 500 returns minus $u_t$. Since $u_t$ is small, this makes little difference, and the detail is often omitted.

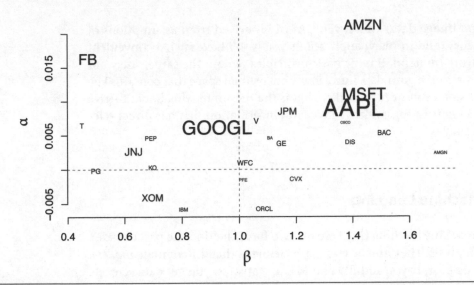

**FIGURE I.3:** Stocks positioned according to their fitted market model, where $\alpha$ is money you make regardless of what the market does and $\beta$ summarizes sensitivity to market movements. The tickers are sized proportional to market capitalization. This plot is an example of the information visualization strategy that I will try to emphasize throughout: business data science is all about distilling your decision problems into a small number of variables that can be compared in a few simple plots.

free money: assets with $\alpha_j > 0$ are adding value regardless of wider market movements, and those with $\alpha_j < 0$ destroy value.

Figure I.3 represents each stock "ticker" in the two-dimensional space implied by the market model's fit on the seven years of data in Figure I.1. The tickers are sized proportional to each firm's market capitalization. The two CAPM parameters—$[\alpha, \beta]$—tell us a huge amount about the behavior and performance of individual assets. This picture immediately allows you to assess market sensitivity and arbitrage opportunities. For example, over this period both Amazon (AMZN) and Microsoft (MSFT) have similar market sensitivity, but Amazon has generated much more money independent of the overall market. Facebook (FB) exhibits remarkably low market sensitivity while generating a large $\alpha$. Some of the older technology firms, such as Oracle (ORCL) and IBM, appear to have destroyed value over this period (negative $\alpha$). Such information can be used to build portfolios that maximize mean returns and minimize variance in the face of uncertain future market conditions. It can also be used in strategies like pairs-trading,[4] where you find two stocks with similar $\beta$ and buy the higher $\alpha$ while selling (*shorting*) the other.

CAPM is an old tool in financial analysis, but it serves to illustrate what we strive toward in business data science. An interpretable model translates raw data into information that is directly relevant to decision-making. The challenge in data science is that the data you'll be working with will be larger and less structured (e.g., it

---

4. Ganapathy Vidyamurthy. *Pairs Trading: Quantitative Methods and Analysis.* John Wiley & Sons, 2004.

will include text and image data). Moreover, CAPM is derived from assumptions of efficient market theory, and in many applications you won't have such a convenient simplifying framework on hand. But the basic principles remain the same: you want to project the information in your data into a low-dimensional space that contains key insights for the decisions you need to make. That is the reason for this book: to give you the tools to quickly turn messy data into useful information that has direct relevance to business policy.

## Big Data and Machine Learning

Big data (BD) and machine learning (ML) are the two forces behind the past decade's revolution in data analysis. They are the two main elements that differentiate *modern* data analysis from its past. If you add BD and ML to statistics, you get data science. If you also add some economics and econometrics, plus a focus on business-relevant problems and decision-making, you get business data science. In this section, we'll dive into both BD and ML and see why they are such game-changers.

WHAT DOES IT MEAN FOR DATA TO BE BIG? The term *big data* has its origin in computer engineering. In that context, it refers to data that is so large that it cannot be loaded into memory or even stored on a single machine. This is where you need tools such as Hadoop and Spark and *distributed* algorithms that can compute data summaries across multiple independent machines. The bigness of the data here is primarily driven by $n$, the number of events or observations being logged. It is a big volume of data.

This type of *big*—distributed-data big—certainly plays an important role in business data science. In any data-intensive firm there will be data engineers who spend much of their job creating the "pipes" that turn the massive distributed raw data into digestible aggregations and slices. A business data scientist needs to be able to work with these engineers to *collaborate* in the cooking process—the process of deciding what variables to track and how they should be calculated.

Although this book touches on some distributed data concepts (e.g., MapReduce algorithms and scalable computing), we will focus on the analysis layer that uses data from these pipes: statistical modeling and inference. There is a different notion of big data in this layer: the data *dimension* is big. This is data of high complexity. For example, online browsing behavior data might include visit counts across websites, and this yields a high-dimensional dataset (the dimension is the number of websites, which is large). As another example, for text analysis, the dimension of your models will depend upon the size of the vocabulary—the number of unique words in a corpus. And in all of these settings, you will observe the data across different people at different times and locations. This creates additional dimensions of complexity.

The two notions of big here—volume and complexity—tend to get wrapped together. This is for good reason: you need a large volume of data to learn anything about complex models. Or, turning it around, if you are trying to learn a simple *low-dimensional* target, then there is no reason to spend money storing and manipulating large amounts of data.[5] Moreover, a main driver of the big volume of data today is the digitization of business and society: we shop, talk, share, and live on computers and online. This creates massive amounts of data that has little *structure*, including raw logs of user actions, natural text from communications, and (increasingly) image, video, and sensor data. The high volume of data is arriving in inherently complex and messy high-dimensional formats.

In previous generations, the end goal of a data engineer would have been to *normalize* this messy data and fit summary statistics into a data table with standardized entries. Today, it is unrealistic to expect a fixed table structure to have long-term utility. Instead, data engineers work to build pipes of semistructured data: you have well-defined variables, but there are a huge (and potentially increasing) number of them. Web browser and text data are good examples: you'll get pipes of URLs or words, but as the data grows in volume, you'll be seeing never-before-visited URLs and never-before-spoken words added to your data dimension.

Analysis for this type of data requires a new toolset. In classical statistics, it is common to assume a world where you have data of fixed small dimension and increasing volume. This is the basis for, say, the hypothesis testing rules that you might have learned in a college statistics course. But these techniques do not work when the *dimension* of the data is big and always growing bigger as you get more *volume* of data. In this more complicated setting, you cannot rely upon the standard low-dimensional strategies such as hypothesis testing for each individual variable (*t-tests*) or choosing among a small set of candidate models (*F-test*). You'll also not be able to rely on standard visualization strategies and diagnostics for checking model fit and specification. You need a whole new set of tools that are *robust* in high dimensions: tools that give good answers even if your data seem impossibly complex.

MACHINE LEARNING is the field that thinks about how to automatically build robust predictions from complex data. It is closely related to modern statistics, and indeed many of the best ideas in ML have come from statisticians (the lasso, trees, forests, and so on). But whereas statisticians have often focused on *model inference*—on understanding the parameters of their models (e.g., testing on individual coefficients in a regression)—the ML community has been more focused on the single goal of maximizing *predictive performance*. The entire field of ML is calibrated against "out-of-sample" experiments that evaluate how well a model trained on one dataset will predict new data. And while there is a recent push to build more transparency into machine learning, wise practitioners avoid assigning structural meaning to the

---

5. For example, basic statistics tells you that $\bar{y} = \Sigma_i y_i / n$ is a good estimate of the mean for a random variable $y$. It has standard error equal to the sample standard deviation of $y$ divided by $\sqrt{n}$. You just need to make $\sqrt{n}$ big enough so that your standard errors are within tolerance for the application at hand.

parameters of their fitted models. These models are black boxes whose purpose is to do a good job in predicting a future that follows the same patterns as in past data.

Prediction is easier than model inference. This has allowed the ML community to quickly push forward and work with larger and more complex data. It has also facilitated a focus on automation: developing algorithms that will work on a variety of different types of data with little or no tuning required. There has been an explosion of general-purpose ML tools in the past decade—tools that can be deployed on messy data and automatically tuned for optimal predictive performance.

To make this discussion more concrete, consider the linear regression model

$$y_i \approx x_{i1}\beta_1 + x_{i2}\beta_2 + \ldots x_{ip}\beta_p. \tag{I.2}$$

Suppose that you estimate this model using a dataset of $n$ observations, $\{x_i, y_i\}_{i=1}^n$, to get the $p$ fitted parameters $\hat{\beta}_j$ and predicted response, say, for the next observation:

$$\hat{y}_{n+1} = x_{n+1,1}\hat{\beta}_1 + x_{n+1,2}\hat{\beta}_2 + \ldots x_{n+1,p}\hat{\beta}_p. \tag{I.3}$$

For example, each $x_{ij}$ could be a binary 0/1 indicator for whether web browser $i$ visited website $j$, and the response, $y_i$, could be the amount of money that user $i$ spends on your e-commerce website. The big data paradigm discussed earlier has big $n$ but also big $p$, perhaps even $p > n$. In other words, you see a lot of web browsers but also a lot of different websites.

Both statisticians and machine learners have been studying these "big $p$" problems over the past 20 years but with subtly different goals. Statisticians have largely concentrated on understanding how close $\hat{\beta}_j$ from Equation I.3 is to the "true" $\beta_j$ from Equation I.2 and on closing this "estimation error" gap. This type of model inference is difficult and indeed impossible for large $p$ unless you make a ton of assumptions about the way the world works. A lot of effort has been spent trying to understand how estimators perform in narrow and incredibly difficult scenarios.

In contrast, the machine learners have been less worried about closing this estimation gap. In most settings an ML practitioner wouldn't want to assume the model in Equation I.2 is actually "true." Instead, the machine learner just wants to make $\hat{y}_{n+1}$ as close as possible to the true $y_{n+1}$. This single-minded focus frees them to worry less about the structure of the model on the right side of Equation I.2 and allows rapid experimentation on alternative models and estimation algorithms. The result is that ML has seen massive success, to the point that you can now expect to have available for almost any type of data an algorithm that will work out of the box to recognize patterns and give high-quality predictions.

Of course, prediction has its limits. ML algorithms learn to predict a future that is mostly like the past. In the previous example, ML will discern what web traffic tends to spend more or less money. It will not tell you what *will* happen to the spending if you *change* a group of those websites or perhaps make it easier for people to browse the web (e.g., by subsidizing broadband). This limitation is most explicitly emphasized in the economics literature, where one characterization of it is named the *Lucas critique* in honor of Robert Lucas from the University of Chicago. Lucas won his Nobel Prize for work in macroeconomics, including work that argued against the then common practice of using past correlations of macroeconomic variables to guide policy-making (e.g., lower inflation accompanies higher unemployment, so you can drop interest rates to create jobs). Instead, he argued that unless you model the macroeconomy *structurally*—as derived from an economic theory foundation—then you cannot properly understand how individual policy changes will affect the full system.

So, prediction doesn't solve everything. However, structural analysis relies upon having strong prediction capabilities. You need to use domain structure to break complicated questions into a bunch of prediction tasks, that is, into a bunch of tasks that can be solved with "dumb" off-the-shelf ML tools. Good data science is all about figuring out what you can outsource as a prediction task and reserving your statistical and economic efforts for the tough structural questions. This typically involves a mix of domain knowledge and analysis tools, which is what makes the business data scientist such a powerful figure. The ML tools are useless for policy-making without an understanding of the business problems, but a policy-maker who can deploy ML to solve the many prediction tasks that they face will be able to automate and accelerate their decision processes.[6]

Some of the material in this book will be focused on pure prediction and pattern recognition. This is especially true in the earlier chapters on regression, classification, and regularization. However, in later chapters you will use these prediction tools as parts of more complicated structural analyses, such as understanding subject-specific treatment effects, fitting consumer demand functions, or as part of an artificial intelligence system. Throughout, we'll mention the limits of individual tools and recommend how they should be deployed. We'll also quantify the uncertainty around the predictions. This book will cover a ton of ML prediction tools, but you'll use them as part of larger systems with goals beyond pure prediction.

## Computation

To learn from this book, you need to be able to write and understand computer code. I'm not asking you to write object-oriented C++, to build a portable application with statically typed Scala, or to engineer production-quality software. You don't need to be a software engineer to work as a business data scientist. But you do need to be able

---

6. A currently active area of data science is combining ML tools with the sort of counterfactual inference that econometricians have long studied. This merges the ML and statistics material with the work of economists. See, for example, Athey and Imbens [2016], Hartford et al. [2017], and the survey in Athey [2017]. We cover this material in later chapters.

to read and write in a high-level *scripting* language—in other words, flexible code that can be used to describe recipes for data analysis.

The ability to interact with computers in this way—by typing commands rather than clicking buttons or choosing from a menu—is a basic data analysis skill. Having a script of commands allows you to rerun your analyses for new data without any additional work. It also allows you to make small changes to existing scripts to adapt them for new scenarios. Indeed, making small changes is how I recommend you work with the material in this book. The code for every in-text example is available online, and you can alter and extend these scripts to suit your data analysis needs.

The languages for data science and machine learning are getting progressively "higher level," meaning that you can do more with short statements and that grittier programming issues (e.g., memory allocation, data partitioning, optimization) are being solved automatically in the background. Some of the most exciting advances along these lines are in the area of deep learning, the type of general-purpose ML that powers the current rise in artificial intelligence technology (see Chapter 10). For example, Gluon wraps (i.e., provides higher-level functionality around) MXnet, a deep learning framework that makes it easier and faster to build deep neural networks. MXnet itself wraps C++, the fast and memory-efficient code that is actually compiled for execution. Similarly, Keras is an extension of Python that wraps together a number of other deep learning frameworks, such as Google's TensorFlow. These and future tools are creating a world of friendlier interfaces for faster and simplified machine learning.

In the examples for this book, all of your analysis will be conducted in R. This is an open-source high-level language for data analysis. R is used widely throughout industry, government, and academia. Microsoft produces an official enhanced version of R, and it and other companies sell enterprise products for managing data analysis. This is not a toy language used by a small group of professors or for teaching purposes—R is the real industrial-strength deal.

For the fundamentals of statistical analysis, R is tough to beat: all of the tools you need for linear modeling and uncertainty quantification are mainstays in R.[7] We've also found it to be relatively forgiving with the novice programmer. A major strength of R is its ecosystem of contributed packages. These are add-ons that increase the capability of "core" R. For example, almost all of the ML tools that you will use in this book are available via packages. The quality of the packages is more varied than it is for R's core functionality, but if a package has high usage, you can be confident that it works as intended.

You can run R in many ways. There is a dedicated graphical user interface (GUI) for whatever operating system you use. This is the program you will work with if you access R through the icons that arrive when you download and install R.[8] Alternatively, you can operate R through a *notebook* environment like that provided by

---

7. The only other language that could work for a book like this is Python (with the `pandas` package). Both are great, and most data scientists use both.
8. See `cran.r-project.org`.

Project Jupyter.[9] The notebooks mix code with Markdown, a user-friendly language for producing nice-looking HTML (websites), such that you can combine notes, code, and results in a single document that is viewable through any web browser. Finally, since R just works with text commands, you can run it through any command prompt or terminal on your computer. For example, see Figure I.4.

There are many great places to learn the basics of R. If you search simply *R* on Amazon, you will find a huge variety of resources for learning R. There are also many great tutorials available online, and many of them are free. You don't need to be an expert in R to read and learn from this book; you just need to be able to understand the fundamentals and be willing to mess around with the coded examples. Remember to use help (type ?function for help on a given function), print often to

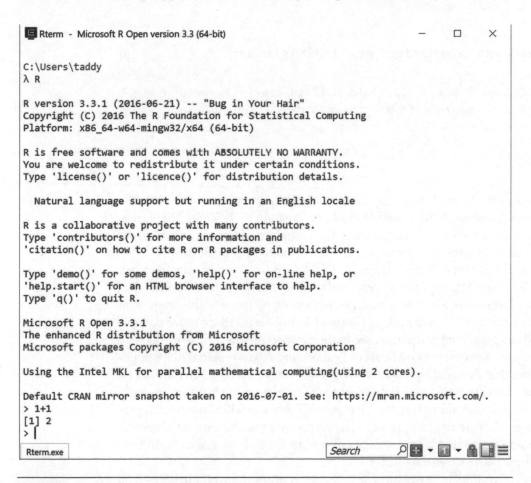

**FIGURE I.4:** R on Windows in cmder.

9. See jupyter.org. This mix of capabilities and content is especially valuable when learning, and I recommend you try a notebook interface. You can also find notebooks tuned specifically for R from R Studio, which is a company producing a variety of R-friendly tools.

see what your objects contain (to print variable A, you just type A or print(A)), and search the Internet when confused (Stack Overflow is a great source of information). The learning curve can be steep initially, but once you get the hang of it, the rest will come fast.

At its most basic, R is just a fancy calculator. Everything is based on assigning names.[10] For example, here's a simple R script with variables and some basic arithmetic:

```
> A <- 2
> B <- 4
> A*B
[1] 8
```

You can also work with *vectors* (and matrices) of multiple numbers:

```
> v <- c(2,4,6) # c(x,y,z,...) is used to create a vector
> v[1:2] # a:b indexes 'from a through b'
[1] 2 4
> v[1]*v[2]
[1] 8
```

Throughout this book, you'll see many snippets like the previous one. The # symbol denotes a comment, and we'll often use this to add explanation to the code. These commented snippets are a tool for demonstrating the actual execution of data analysis routines. Full code scripts and data are available at http://taddylab.com/BDS.

R is not perfect, and it is not the best language for all purposes. Python provides a better workspace for many ML applications, especially those involving unstructured data like raw text. For large-scale ML, you should probably work with one of the deep learning frameworks referenced earlier, such as Gluon or Keras. Similarly, massive datasets are often stored in specialized distributed computing environments. Frameworks such as Spark, which you can access via the Scala or Python language, are essential for building the data pipes that slice and aggregate this information. To execute ML routines on this type of truly massive data, you might want to consider purpose-built frameworks like Spark.ML. If you work for a large firm, it is possible that you will need to learn proprietary languages that are designed to suit your company's specific data management needs. And it is almost inevitable that at some point you will need to write an SQL query to "pull" data from a structured database.

This illustrates an important point: *No language is the best for all purposes.* You might imagine that you can learn a single programming language and never need to

---

10. R actually has two ways to assign variables. <- works pretty much the same as =. The former is preferred because = is used both for function arguments and for variable name assignment, but people write fine code using either.

figure out any others. Unfortunately, computing technology is too dynamic for this to be true. Anyone working with data will need to continue learning and updating their computational (and methodological) skills.[11] Thus, when choosing the language for this book (and for MBA classes at the University of Chicago), the question was simple: What language is best for learning data science? After some thought and experimentation, we landed on R.

**R CAN READ ALMOST ANY DATA FORMAT.** In this book, you will work mostly with .csv files containing *comma-separated values*. These are simple text files organized like a spreadsheet where the values (cell entries) are separated by commas. See the example in Figure I.5. The first row is a *header*, with column titles, and the remaining rows contain data entries.

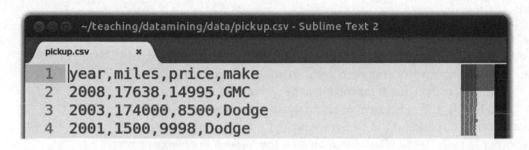

**FIGURE I.5:** The top of pickup.csv.

This format of data storage is called a *flat file* because it has only two dimensions: data observations (rows) and variables (columns). The data is stored in a simple text file, and in general you can choose any type of value *delimiter* (tabs, pipes [|], and spaces are alternatives to commas). In this book, you will work with the .csv format because it is common and the default text file representation for Microsoft's Excel software. Indeed, you can open any .csv file using Excel, and this is what your computer will likely default to using if you double-click the file icons.[12]

Flat files are not a good format for data storage and management. Companies do not store their data in flat files. Instead, they typically make use of a mixture of storage platforms for both structured and unstructured data. The structured data, consisting of well-defined variables, will live in a traditional *relational* database

---

11. Again, the best way to learn is usually by doing, making small changes to existing scripts and then extending your skills. This often happens naturally: you will need to use a tool that is written in a language that you don't know, and you'll learn just enough to get done what you need. After doing this enough times, you become proficient. The key is to look for examples when you are starting out.

12. Beware of Excel making changes to your data (e.g., by automatically formatting numbers or by trimming rows). Data that has been corrupted and resaved by Excel is a common source of frustration when working through the examples in this book.

containing a number of interconnected tables. This is the type of data that you access with a version of Structured Query Language (SQL):

```
select apple_id, apple_price from grocerylist
where apple_col = green
```

The flavor of SQL that you use will depend upon the brand of database you are accessing; examples are Microsoft SQL, Oracle, Teradata, or SQLite. It is possible to run analysis on the databases themselves, and R has interfaces that allow you to pull data directly from the database into your workspace. However, a more typical workflow will have data pulled from the database using a SQL query (aggregated and sliced according to your specific needs) and then written into a flat file for later analysis. Many of the data examples for this text were originally pulled from a database in this way.

Unstructured data, especially large unstructured data, will be stored in a *distributed file system* (DFS). These are systems that join together many machines over a network. Your data is broken into *blocks* that are stored on different machines, and the DFS provides mechanisms for working with such *partitioned* data. In this way, the DFS allows you to manipulate data that is far too big to be stored on a single computer. These are the systems that facilitate Internet-scale analysis—the processing of previously unimaginable amounts of data. One DFS framework that you might have heard of is Hadoop. Another heavily used DFS is Amazon's S3, the backbone of storage on Amazon Web Services (AWS).

This is the true big data. There are a variety of analysis platforms for wrangling and analyzing distributed data, the most prominent of which is Spark. When working at this scale, you need to make use of specialized algorithms that avoid having all of the data in a computer's *working memory* at a single time. For example, the MapReduce framework consists of algorithms that can prepare and group data into relatively small chunks (Map) before performing an analysis on each chunk (Reduce). We will introduce this sort of *distributed computing* in later chapters, and tools such as R spark and Microsoft's R server are making it relatively easy to adapt the methods you learn in this book to distributed computing environments. Although this text does not cover distributed computing in detail, almost all of the methods we introduce here are *scalable*. In other words, they will work quickly even on datasets that occupy a large percentage of your working memory, and they do not rely on inherently serial algorithms that are impossible to adapt to distribution.

Regardless of where your data come from and how much wrangling was required before analysis, at some point you will be working with a dataset that is (or could be) represented in a flat file and is small enough (or could be broken into small enough pieces) to fit into your computer's memory. At this point, all you need to do is read the data into R.

R has the `read.csv` function for reading data from `.csv` files into your workspace. A common newbie challenge is figuring out how to find your data. R has the concept of a *working directory*, and you need to connect from there to where you store your data. One easy strategy is to create folders for storing both your data and analysis scripts.[13] When you open R, you then just move its working directory to that folder. There are many ways to change your working directory. From the GUIs or RStudio there will be menu options, and you can always set an explicit path with the command setwd. After this is set correctly, just give read.csv the name of your data.

```
> trucks <- read.csv("pickup.csv")
> head(trucks)
  year   miles  price   make
1 2008   17638  14995    GMC
2 2003  174000   8500  Dodge
3 2001    1500   9998  Dodge
4 2007   22422  23950    GMC
5 2007   34815  19980    GMC
6 1997  167000   5000    GMC
```

Here, trucks is a dataframe, which is a matrix with names. I have used head to print the first six entries of the matrix. You can use index names and numbers to access the data.

```
> trucks [1,] # the first observation
  year  miles   price  make
1 2008  17638   14995   GMC
> trucks [1:3,] # the first three observations
  year   miles  price   make
1 2008   17638  14995    GMC
2 2003  174000   8500  Dodge
3 2001    1500   9998  Dodge
> trucks [1:3,1] # first three of the first variable (year)
[1] 2008 2003 2001
> trucks year [1:3] # same thing
[1] 2008 2003 2001
> trucks [1:3, 'year'] # same thing again
[1] 2008 2003 2001
```

The values in this dataframe each have a "class": price, year, and miles are continuous, while make is a factor (i.e., a categorical variable). These are the two most common data classes.

---

13. In general, it pays to keep your code and data organized. I *strongly* recommend that you use a version-control platform to keep track of your changes, collaborate with others, and share your work (especially important if you hope to get a job in data science). I and many others use GitHub.

You can also call functions on the data:

```
> nrow(trucks)
[1] 46
> summary(trucks) ## summary of each variable
      year            miles            price            make
Min.    :1978   Min.    :  1500   Min.    : 1200   Dodge :10
1st Qu. :1996   1st Qu. : 70958   1st Qu. : 4099   Ford  :12
Median  :2000   Median  : 96800   Median  : 5625   GMC   :24
Mean    :1999   Mean    :101233   Mean    : 7910
3rd Qu. :2003   3rd Qu. :130375   3rd Qu. : 9725
Max.    :2008   Max.    :215000   Max.    :23950
```

Among these functions are a number of convenient plotting capabilities.[14] For example, in the following code, we quickly visualize the trucks data with a histogram (for the distribution of a single variable), some boxplots (for comparing a continuous variable to a factor), and a scatterplot (for continuous versus continuous comparison).

```
> hist (trucks$price) ## a histogram
> plot (price ~ make, data=trucks) ## a boxplot
> plot(price~miles, data=trucks, log="y", col=trucks$make) ##
  in color
> ## add a legend (colors 1,2,3 are black, red, green)
> legend ("topright", fill=1:3, legend=levels (trucks$make))
```

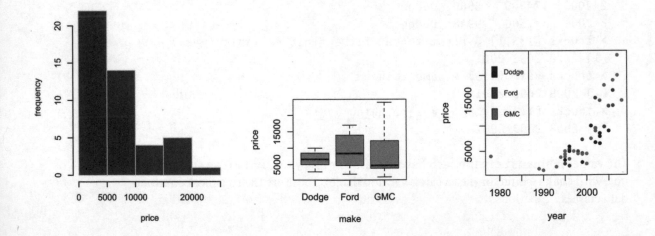

---

14. One advantage of R is that it makes it easy to create professional-quality graphs.

You can also fit *statistical models*, such as a regression for the log price of pickup trucks as a function of make, mileage, and year.

```
> fit <- glm(log(price) ~ make + miles + year, data=trucks)
> summary (fit)

Call:
glm(formula = log(price) ~ make + miles + year, data = trucks)

Deviance Residuals:
    Min        1Q     Median        3Q       Max
-0.91174   -0.22547   0.01919   0.20265   1.23474

Coefficients:
              Estimate Std. Error t value  Pr(>|t|)
(Intercept) -1.518e+02  2.619e+01  -5.797  8.41e-07 ***
makeFord     1.394e-01  1.780e-01   0.784   0.43780
makeGMC      1.726e-01  1.582e-01   1.091   0.28159
miles       -4.244e-06  1.284e-06  -3.304   0.00198 **
year         8.045e-02  1.306e-02   6.160  2.56e-07 ***
---
Signif. codes: 0 '***' 0.001 '**' 0.01 '*' 0.05 '.' 0.1 ' ' 1

(Dispersion parameter for gaussian family taken to be 0.1726502)

    Null deviance: 23.3852 on 45 degrees of freedom
Residual deviance: 7.0787 on 41 degrees of freedom
AIC: 56.451

Number of Fisher Scoring iterations: 2
```

Here, glm stands for "generalized linear model" and the ~ symbol is read as "regressed onto." This function is the workhorse of Chapter 2, and you will become familiar with its use and interpretation.

Essentially, this is all there is to it! The many functions you can apply to data are what make R such a great analysis tool. If you can read and understand the previous snippets, you are in good shape to start reading the rest of this book. In the coming chapters, we will build an expanded functionality and understanding of the methods behind these functions. But your basic workflow will remain as it is here: read data and apply functions to get results. Once you realize how powerful this way of working can be, you will never look back.

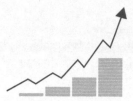

# Uncertainty

## 1

The real world is messy. Recognizing this mess will differentiate a sophisticated and useful analysis from one that is hopelessly naive. This is especially true for highly complicated models, where it becomes tempting to confuse signal with noise and hence "overfit." The ability to deal with this mess and noise is the most important skill you need to learn to keep from embarrassing yourself as you work and learn with data.

In any analysis, you have targeted unknowns and untargeted unknowns. The former are built into the model as parameters to be estimated, and you use these estimates explicitly in your decision-making processes. The latter are variously represented as error terms and distributions or, in a fully nonparametric analysis, as an unknown data-generating process.[1] These untargeted unknowns are a *nuisance*. You don't care about them directly, but they need to be accounted for if you want to infer the targeted parameters. The distinction here is application specific—one analyst's nuisance is another's target. But it is impossible to accurately model everything simultaneously, so you need to choose your targets carefully and treat them seriously.

This chapter introduces the statistician's concept of uncertainty, the framework we use to characterize what you know in terms of probabilities. In much of data science and machine learning, we seek to design models that perform well in the presence of uncertainty and do so via regularization (see Chapter 3) and other model stabilization tools. In other cases, it is necessary to do full accounting of uncertainty and assign probability distributions to important parameters. Real-world applications require a mix of both stability and uncertainty quantification, and to understand any of these techniques you need a clear understanding of the basics of uncertainty.

---

1. Parametric analysis quantifies uncertainty conditional on an assumed true model, while nonparametric analysis allows for model misspecification. See Chapters 5, 6, and 9 (and the material in this chapter on the bootstrap) for examples of nonparametric inference.

Uncertainty quantification is one of the more difficult and abstract subjects in data science. Many readers may wish to skip ahead to Chapters 2–4 and return once more warmed up.

## Frequentist Uncertainty and the Bootstrap

We need to start by reviewing the basics of *frequentist* uncertainty. This is the sort of uncertainty that has been taught in introductory statistics for decades, and it is characterized by a thought experiment: "If I were able to see a new sample of data, generated by the same processes and scenarios as my current data, how would my estimates change?"

We'll begin with a simple analysis of the online-spending activity for 10,000 households over a single year. In addition to their total U.S. dollars spent online, each row of the dataset contains some basic information about a single household, such as whether they have any children, whether they have access to broadband Internet, and their race and ethnicity and region.

```
> browser <- read.csv("web-browsers.csv")
> dim(browser)
[1] 10000       7
> head(browser)
  id anychildren broadband hispanic  race region spend
1  1           0         1        0 white     MW   424
2  2           1         1        0 white     MW  2335
3  3           1         1        0 white     MW   279
4  4           0         1        0 white     MW   829
5  5           0         1        0 white      S   221
6  6           0         1        0 white     MW  2305
```

Figure 1.1 shows the sample of spend values.

Consider the unconditional mean for the variable spend: the average amount of money spent online annually by households in the United States. You can estimate this mean—say, $\mu_{spend} = \mathbb{E}[spend]$—with its *sample average*.

```
> mean(browser$spend)
[1] 1946.439
```

Here, you don't think that $\mu_{spend}$ is *exactly* equal to $1946.439; rather, this is a good guess and the truth is ideally *near* to this value.

How near? Let's review some basic statistics. Suppose you have *n independent* random variables: $\{x_i\}_{i=1}^n$. In terms of our current example, this is saying that each household

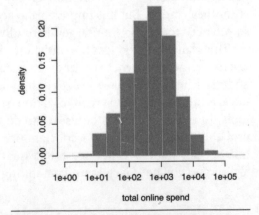

**FIGURE 1.1:** Household spending. Notice that the distribution is roughly normal on the *log scale* (look at the *x*-axis).

spends a specific amount without consideration of what the other households in the sample do online. The sample mean is then

$$\bar{x} = \frac{1}{n} \sum_{i=1}^{n} x_i. \tag{1.1}$$

The variance of this statistic can be calculated as

$$\mathrm{var}(\bar{x}) = \mathrm{var}\left(\frac{1}{n} \sum_{i=1}^{n} x_i\right) = \frac{1}{n^2} \sum_{i=1}^{n} \mathrm{var}(x_i) = \frac{\sigma^2}{n}. \tag{1.2}$$

Here, $\sigma^2 = \mathrm{var}(x) = \mathbb{E}[(x - \mu_{\mathrm{spend}})^2]$ is the variance of a randomly drawn household's online spending. Note that you are able to move $\mathrm{var}(\cdot)$ inside the sum only because of independence. So, we can estimate the variance for $\bar{x}$ here as follows:

```
> var(browser$spend)/1e4 # since we have 10,000 households
[1] 6461.925
```

This implies a standard deviation around $\sqrt{6462} \approx 80$.

The ever-important *central limit theorem* (CLT) states that the average of independent random variables becomes normally distributed (i.e., Gaussian or as a "bell curve") if your sample size is "large enough." Assuming $n = 10{,}000$ is large enough, the end result is that the sample average for online spending is normally distributed with mean 1946 and standard deviation 80. We write this as $\bar{x} \sim N(1946, 80^2)$. Figure 1.2 plots the distribution.

What is this distribution? It is our best guess at the *sampling distribution*. It captures the uncertainty described by the thought experiment: "If I was able to get a *new* sample of observations, from the same *data-generating process*, what is the probability distribution on the new sample average?" This is what is referred to as frequentist uncertainty. It is the sort of uncertainty you have seen in basic statistics classes. For example, consider this common description of a confidence interval:

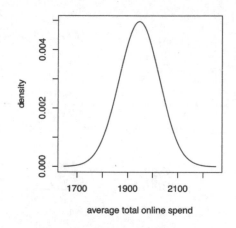

**FIGURE 1.2:** Sampling distribution for $\bar{x}$. This picture tells us that if we got a new sample of 10,000 households, we'd expect the new sample average spending to be around $1946 \pm $160.

> *The poll predicts that 49% of eligible voters would currently vote yes; this number is accurate within ±3 percentage points 19 times out of 20.*

This statement describes how an estimated total vote changes under the thought experiment of repeatedly polling a different random set of voters. Similarly, the familiar hypothesis-testing logic—"reject if $p$-value is less than 0.05"—corresponds to a rule that rejects a null hypotheses mean $\mu_0$ if it falls too far into the tails of the sampling distribution in Figure 1.2.

**THE BOOTSTRAP** is a computational algorithm for constructing sampling distributions. We will use the bootstrap because the *theoretical* sampling distributions that are relied upon for much of classical statistics—Gaussian distributions derived from the CLT, as in Figure 1.2—are not valid for the complex settings encountered in business data science. The need for a different approach arises mostly because there are stages of model building that aren't considered in the classical formulas (e.g., variable selection, computational approximation), and the uncertainty in these steps needs to be propagated through to your final analysis. In addition, when the number of model parameters is large relative to the number of observations, the CLT will give a poor representation of real-world performance.

Instead of relying on theoretical approximation, the bootstrap uses *resampling from your current sample* to mimic the sampling distribution. Recall our definition for the sampling distribution: it is the distribution on an estimator—say, $\hat{\beta}$—that we get by re-estimating $\beta$ on each of multiple datasets of size $n$ from the population. Figure 1.3 illustrates this process.

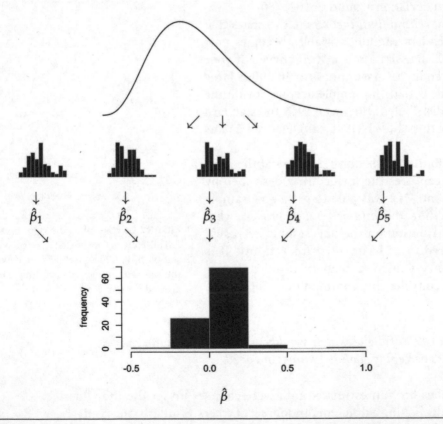

**FIGURE 1.3:** Illustration of the sampling distribution. Each middle-row histogram is a sample from the population, and the bottom histogram is the distribution of resulting estimates $\hat{\beta}$.

The bootstrap in Algorithm 1 mimics the process in Figure 1.3 by replacing samples from the population with *resamples* from your sample.[2] The *with-replacement* sampling here is essential. It implies that each observation can be chosen more than once for inclusion in the resampling. For example, if we are sampling with-replacement five items from the set {1, 2, 3, 4, 5}, possible resamples would include {1, 1, 3, 3, 4} and {2, 2, 2, 3, 5}. Using the common analogy of "drawing balls out of a bucket," we are putting the ball back in after each draw. This type of sampling is what introduces *variability* in our resamples: in this example, without-replacement sampling would *always* yield the set {1, 2, 3 , 4, 5}.

---

**ALGORITHM 1**  **The Nonparametric Bootstrap**

Given data $\{z_i\}_{i=1}^n$, for $b = 1 \ldots B$:

- Resample *with-replacement* $n$ observations $\{z_i^b\}_{i=1}^n$.

- Calculate your estimate, say, $\hat{\beta}_b$, using this resampled set.

Then $\{\hat{\beta}_b\}_{b=1}^B$ is an approximation to the sampling distribution for $\hat{\beta}$.

---

The resulting "bootstrap sample" can be used for all of the same purposes as your usual theoretical sampling distribution. For example, an approximate standard error—the standard deviation of your sampling distribution—can be approximated by the standard deviation of this bootstrap sample:

$$\text{se}(\hat{\beta}) \approx \text{sd}(\hat{\beta}_b) = \sqrt{\frac{1}{B}\sum_b (\hat{\beta}_b - \hat{\beta})^2}. \tag{1.3}$$

Here, $\hat{\beta}$ (without subscript) is the estimated parameter you get using the full original sample. So long as the estimator is *unbiased*, which means that $\mathbb{E}[\hat{\beta}] = \beta$, then you can use this standard error to build your usual 95% confidence interval:

$$\beta \in \hat{\beta} \pm 2\text{sd}(\hat{\beta}_b). \tag{1.4}$$

Revisiting our online spending example, we can write a simple bootstrap for the sampling distribution.

---

2. There are many different types of bootstrap, and we cover here only a couple main algorithms. See Davison and Hinkley [1997] for a practical guide to the full world of bootstrapping.

```
> B <- 1000 # number of bootstrap samples
> mub <- c() # a vector to contain the sampled means
> for (b in 1:B) {
+     samp_b <- sample.int(nrow(browser), replace=TRUE)
+     mub <- c(mub, mean(browser$spend[samp_b]))
+ }
> sd (mub)
[1] 80.23819
```

At the end of this loop, we are left with a set of $\bar{x}_b$ values `mub`, each corresponding to a different data resample. Note that the `replace=TRUE` flag yields with-replacement sampling on the observation indices.

```
> sort(samp_b)[1:10]
[1] 1 1 2 2 4 4 5 7 8 9
```

Figure 1.4 shows the resulting bootstrap estimate of the sampling distribution. We see that it matches closely with the theoretical Gaussian sampling distribution that is implied by the central limit theorem (and the bootstrap standard deviation of 80 matches the theoretical standard error). This makes sense: we have a large sample ($n = 10,000$) and are targeting a simple statistic ($\bar{x}$), so the CLT applies and the theoretical distribution is correct. The advantage of the bootstrap is that it will work in many settings where this theory is unavailable or incorrect.

The bootstrap works by replacing the population distribution with the *empirical data distribution*—the distribution that you get by placing probability $1/n$ on each observed data point. Figure 1.5 illustrates this approximation in comparison to Figure 1.3: we've simply swapped a distribution for a histogram.

How close is the bootstrap-estimated sampling distribution to the truth? It depends upon how well your observed sample represents the population distribution. In general, dimension matters: you can bootstrap a low-dimensional statistic (like $\bar{x}$) but should not expect to use resampling to learn a sampling distribution in more than two to three dimensions. For example, you can bootstrap the distribution for individual regression coefficients. You can also use the results to estimate the sampling covariance between pairs of coefficients, but you will need a lot of data to get reliable answers and should be cautious about the reliability of your estimates.

As a more complex example, consider linear (least-squares) regression for log spending as a function of whether the household has broadband Internet and any children. We will fit parameters of the following regression model:

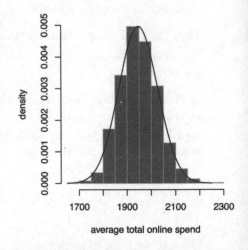

**FIGURE 1.4:** The bootstrapped sampling distribution (histogram) for household online spending, with the theoretical sampling distribution from Figure 1.2 overlaid.

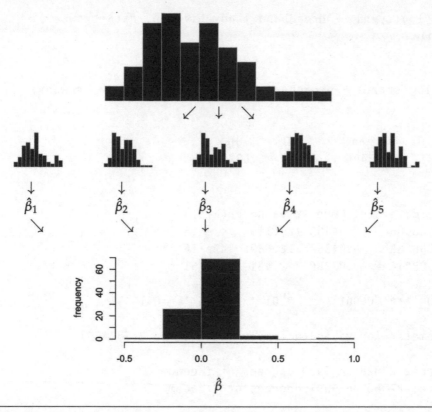

**FIGURE 1.5:** An illustration of the bootstrap approximation to a sampling distribution. Compare to Figure 1.3. Now, each of the middle-row histograms is a with-replacement resample from your observations, and the bottom histogram is the distribution of resulting estimates.

$$\log(\text{spend}) = \beta_0 + \beta_1 \mathbb{1}_{[\text{broadband}]} + \beta_2 \mathbb{1}_{[\text{children}]} + \varepsilon. \tag{1.5}$$

Here, the indicator functions $\mathbb{1}_{[\text{broadband}]}$ and $\mathbb{1}_{[\text{children}]}$ create binary dummy variables that are one for households with broadband or kids, respectively, and zero otherwise. The error term here, $\varepsilon$, contains all variation in log spending that is not explained by the regression inputs.

> Logarithm in this book is always base $e$ so that $\log(a) = b \Leftrightarrow e^b = a$. Variables that move multiplicatively with each other—e.g., as in "households with broadband access spend 75% more online"—are often modeled as linear on the log scale. See Chapter 2 for details.

To fit this regression in R, we use the `glm` command for "generalized linear models." This can be used to fit the linear regression model in Equation 1.5 (which could also be fit using R's `lm` command) and it is also capable of fitting nonlinear models such as logistic regression. To use `glm`, you simply give R the regression formula and data frame:

```
> linreg <- glm(log(spend) ~ broadband + anychildren, data=browser)
> summary(linreg)

Call:
glm (formula = log(spend) ~ broadband + anychildren, data = browser)

Deviance Residuals:
     Min        1Q    Median        3Q       Max
 -6.2379   -1.0787    0.0349    1.1292    6.5825

Coefficients:
             Estimate Std. Error t value Pr(>|t|)
(Intercept)   5.68508    0.04403 129.119   <2e-16 ***
broadband     0.55285    0.04357  12.689   <2e-16 ***
anychildren   0.08216    0.03380   2.431   0.0151 *
---
Signif. codes: 0 '***' 0.001 '**' 0.01 '*' 0.05 '.' 0.1 ' ' 1

(Dispersion parameter for gaussian family taken to be 2.737459)

      Null deviance: 27828 on 9999 degrees of freedom
Residual deviance: 27366 on 9997 degrees of freedom
AIC: 38454

Number of Fisher Scoring iterations: 2
```

There is a lot to unpack here, and we'll discuss the glm output in more detail in Chapter 2. But if you focus on the coefficients, you can see that there are "estimates" $\hat{\beta}_j$ with "standard errors" se($\hat{\beta}_j$). These are the centers and standard deviations of the theoretical sampling distributions for those estimators. These sampling distributions should be approximately Gaussian under the CLT. For example, a 95% confidence interval for the broadband coefficient is as follows:

```
> 0.55285 + c(-2,2)*0.04357
[1] 0.46571 0.63999
```

To get a bootstrap estimate of the sampling distribution, we just repeat the same regression on with-replacement resamples of the original data:

```
> B <- 1000
> betas <- c()
> for (b in 1:B){
```

```
+       samp_b <- sample.int(nrow(browser), replace=TRUE)
+       reg_b <- glm(log(spend) ~ broadband + anychildren,
   data=browser[samp_b,])
+       betas <- rbind(betas, coef(reg_b))
+ }
> betas [,1:5]
     (Intercept)   broadband   anychildren
[1,]     5.728889   0.5736488   0.02465046
[2,]     5.672288   0.5457318   0.06641667
[3,]     5.612364   0.6175716   0.09134826
[4,]     5.677401   0.5712354   0.07893055
[5,]     5.650967   0.5743827   0.08233983
```

Each row of the matrix betas is a single draw from the *joint* distribution over our three regression parameters. We can calculate the sampling correlation between broadband and child coefficients:

```
> cor(betas[,"broadband"], betas[, "anychildren"])
[1] -0.01464454
```

There is little correlation between these two coefficients; in other words, the estimated spend-broadband relationship is roughly independent from the estimated spend-children relationship.

We can also compare the *marginal* (single-variable) sampling distribution for coefficients to the theoretical ones. Figure 1.6 shows the results for the broadband coefficient. Once again, the theoretical and bootstrap distributions are similar to each other. However, in this case, the two sampling distributions are measuring two different thought experiments about uncertainty in $\hat{\beta}_1$. In the theoretical case, we are imagining new spend$_i$ draws for *the same* [broadband$_i$, anychildren$_i$] inputs that are in the original sample. This is called a *fixed design* setup. In the bootstrap case, we are imagining that both the inputs and outputs are drawn anew from the population, in other words, that we are drawing a new sample of households. This is called a *random design* setup. In Figure 1.6, we can see that the distinction makes little difference here; however, with higher-dimensional inputs, it will cause the two distributions to diverge from each other.

Finally, consider the *multiplicative* effect of broadband on spending, $\exp[\hat{\beta}_1]$. This is a *nonlinear* transformation of $\hat{\beta}_1$, and in general you will not know the distribution of an estimator after such transformations. However, we can simply exponentiate the resampled $\hat{\beta}_{1b}$ to get the distribution for the transformed

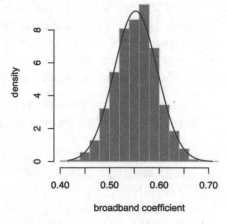

**FIGURE 1.6:** Bootstrapped sampling distribution (histogram) for the broadband regression coefficient $\hat{\beta}_1$ from Equation 1.5, with the theoretical sampling distribution N(0.55, 0.044²) overlaid.

estimator. Figure 1.7 shows the results: houses with broadband spend 60% to 90% more online.

The bootstrap is not perfect. There are a variety of settings where it "breaks." This can happen if the empirical data distribution is a poor approximation to the population or if the statistic you are targeting requires a lot of information about the entire population distribution. For example, we tend to not trust bootstraps for high-dimensional parameters because the joint sampling distribution is a function of all the population cross-variable dependencies. Or, when the data population has heavy tails (i.e., it includes some rare large values), you will have trouble bootstrapping the mean because the extreme values have an outsized influence on your distributional estimate.[3]

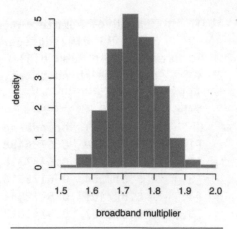

**FIGURE 1.7:** Bootstrapped sampling distribution for the multiplicative effect of broadband on spending: $\exp[\hat{\beta}_1]$. Note that in this special case, since $\hat{\beta}_1$ is close to normally distributed, $\exp[\hat{\beta}_1]$ has a *log-normal distribution.*

However, in general the bootstrap is a reliable tool for uncertainty quantification. I recommend you use it regularly. As a rule, you can bootstrap a low-dimensional statistic unless there is something strange about your data. In cases where the bootstrap fails, it is usually the case there are also no good theoretical standard errors. When this happens, we can look to alternative versions of the bootstrap. For example, instead of resampling from the original data, you can use a *parametric* bootstrap to generate new data for each bootstrap sample by drawing from a fitted model.[4]

Consider the marginal distribution for online spending from our earlier example. There, we used the formula in Equation 1.2 to calculate the standard error for the mean of online spending as around $80. Using a parametric bootstrap, we would instead repeatedly draw data from estimates of an assumed model—say, $x \sim N(\hat{\mu}, \hat{\sigma}^2)$—and use the standard deviation of the resulting sample means as an estimate of the standard error.

```
> xbar <- mean(browser$spend)
> sig2 <- var(browser$spend)
>
> B <- 10000
> mub <- c()
> for(b in 1:B){
+    xsamp <- rnorm(1e4, xbar, sqrt(sig2))
+    mub <- c(mub, mean(xsamp))
+}
> sd(mub)
[1] 79.70425
> sqrt(sig2/1e4)
[1] 80.3861
```

---

3. Matt Taddy, Hedibert Lopes, and Matt Gardner. Scalable semi-parametric inference for the means of heavy-tailed distributions. *arXiv:1602.08066*, 2016b.
4. See also the section on uncertainty quantification in Chapter 3, where the parametric bootstrap is used to provide inference for lasso algorithms.

Here, the results end up matching nearly exactly the earlier theoretical standard errors and the results from the nonparametric bootstrap. However, the parametric bootstrap makes a big assumption that we didn't require for our other procedures: we've assumed that the data is normally distributed. The parametric bootstrap approximates the population distribution by using our estimate of a specific model. This allows it to work for higher-dimensional parameter targets—since we have a full probability model, we don't need as much data to learn the population distribution—but our results will be sensitive to how well this model represents reality.

Throughout the book, a black diamond denotes material that is more advanced and abstract. The main content of the book does not require understanding of this material.

◆ WE CLOSE THIS SECTION WITH AN ADVANCED TOPIC: USE OF THE BOOTSTRAP WITH *BIASED* ESTIMATORS—that is, for procedures that produce $\hat{\beta}$ where $\mathbb{E}[\hat{\beta}] \neq \beta$. You might not have previously encountered such estimators because, in a perfect world, bias is to be avoided. However, in business data science the world is not perfect, and you are often willing to introduce a little bit of bias in exchange for less noise in your estimation (e.g., see Chapter 3). If you are worried that your estimator might be biased, then you should replace Algorithm 1 with the slightly more complex bootstrap algorithm that targets confidence intervals directly (i.e., it avoids the intermediate step of calculating standard errors).

Algorithm 2 resembles closely our earlier bootstrap. The difference is that it targets the distribution for errors—how much larger or smaller the estimates are than the target—rather than the distribution for the estimates themselves. In this algorithm, the sample estimate $\hat{\beta}$ is your stand-in for the true (unknown) $\beta$. If the $\hat{\beta}_b$ values tend to be larger than $\beta$ using your estimation procedure, then you should assume that $\hat{\beta}$ is, in expectation, larger than $\beta$. Note that the bottom end of the interval in Equation 1.6 is defined by subtracting the largest (95th percentile) errors while the top end subtracts the smallest errors.

---

**ALGORITHM 2** | **Nonparametric Bootstrap for Confidence Intervals**

Given data $\{z_i\}_{i=1}^n$ and full sample estimate $\hat{\beta}$ for parameter $\beta$, for $b = 1 \ldots B$:

- Resample *with-replacement* $n$ observations $\left\{ z_i^b \right\}_{i=1}^n$.
- Calculate your estimate, say, $\hat{\beta}_b$, using this resampled set.
- Calculate the *error*, say, $e_b = \hat{\beta}_b - \hat{\beta}$.

Then $\{e_b\}_{b=1}^B$ is an approximation to the distribution of errors between estimates and their target. To get the 90% confidence interval for the true $\beta$, you would calculate the 5th and 95th percentiles of $\{e_b\}_{b=1}^B$—say, $t_{0.05}$ and $t_{0.95}$—and set your interval as

$$[\hat{\beta} - t_{0.95}, \hat{\beta} - t_{0.05}]. \tag{1.6}$$

...ice, recall that the sample variance, $s^2 = \sum_i (x_i - \bar{x})^2 / n$,

...e population variance, $\sigma^2 = \mathbb{E}[(x - \mu)^2]$. You can show[5]

... of $s^2$, which demonstrates that $\mathbb{E}[s^2] \neq \sigma^2$:

$$ ] = \mathbb{E}[(x - \mu)^2] - \mathbb{E}[(\bar{x} - \mu)^2] = \sigma^2 - \sigma^2/n. \tag{1.7} $$

This is ... t it is common to use $\sqrt{s^2 n / (n-1)}$ as an unbiased estimate of the sample s... deviation. Consider estimating the standard deviation of online spending using only a subsample of 100 browsers.[6]

```
> smallsamp <- browser$spend[sample.int(nrow(browser), 100)]
> S <- sd(smallsamp) # sample variance
> S
[1] 7572.442
> sd(browser$spend)
[1] 8038.61
> s/sd(browser$spend)
[1] 0.9420089
```

We find that the small sample standard deviation, $s$, is more than 5% smaller than the full sample standard deviation (which, with 10,000 observations, is close to the true $\sigma$). You can use the CI bootstrap of Algorithm 2 to obtain a confidence interval for $\sigma$ that is based on $s$ but corrects for this bias.

```
> eb <- c()
> for (b in 1:B){
+       sb <- sd(smallsamp[sample.int(100, replace=TRUE)])
+       eb<- c(eb, sb-s)
+ }
> mean(eb)
[1] -407.8306
```

Note that the mean of the bootstrap errors, $B^{-1} \sum_b e_b = -408$, is nowhere close to zero. This indicates that we are working with a biased estimator. But when these errors are subtracted from our full sample estimator $s$, we are effectively *subtracting this bias*. That is, we have been able to estimate the bias and correct for it. For example, the mean of $s - e_b$ is now relatively close to the full sample standard deviation (our best guess at $\sigma$).

---

5. Fill in all the steps of this derivation as a good exercise for contrasting population and sample expectation.
6. The subsample $n = 100$ is small enough that this bias will matter. At the full sample, as for most applications in this book, $n$ is so big that this bias makes little difference and you don't need to worry about it.

```
> mean (s-eb)
[1] 7980.273
> sd(browser$spend)
[1] 8038.61
```

Moreover, the resulting 90% confidence interval is centered around $\sigma$:

```
> tvals <- quantile(eb, c(0.05, 0.95))
> tvals
        5%        95%
-4667.349 3161.858
> s - tvals[2:1] # 90% CI
4410.584 12239.792
```

Although this is the first chapter of this book, bootstrapping is a fairly advanced topic. Don't worry if this material feels a bit unintuitive. One of the reasons that we introduce it at this early stage is that it gives you a way to *simulate* from sampling distributions and hence to actually observe uncertainty in practice. I encourage you to do this simulation while working through the rest of the book; it will help you to understand the stability of the algorithms and what to expect when you apply them in the real world.

## Hypothesis Testing and False Discovery Rate Control

Looking again at the output of the regression, there are two columns beyond the Estimate and Std. Error values that characterize the sampling distribution.

```
Coefficients:
              Estimate Std. Error t value Pr(>|t|)
(Intercept)    5.68508    0.04403 129.119  <2e-16 ***
broadband      0.55285    0.04357  12.689  <2e-16 ***
anychildren    0.08216    0.03380   2.431  0.0151 *
```

What do t value and Pr(>|t|) mean? Why the ***? Most readers will recognize these as the artifacts of *hypothesis testing*.

Pr(event) is how R denotes a probability function that maps from an event to its probability. We write this as p(event). We overload notation and use the same "p" symbol for both probability mass functions (for discrete events) and for probability density functions (for continuous events).

A hypothesis test is a tool for deciding between two qualitatively different realities. One option will be the *null* hypothesis, which should be your "safe bet." It is the status quo or stable option and typically corresponds to setting a parameter equal to zero. The *alternative* hypothesis will be a set of possible values. When you "reject the null" in favor of the alternative, you will end up working with the sample estimate for some parameter.

The decision between null and alternative hypotheses is based upon a *sample statistic* that measures the distance between the null reality and your sampled parameter estimates. For a test of the null hypothesis $\beta = 0$ versus the alternative hypothesis $\beta \neq 0$, your test statistic is $z_\beta = \hat{\beta}/\text{se}(\hat{\beta})$. It tells you how far away your sample estimate is from zero as measured in standard errors (i.e., standard deviations of the sampling distribution). This is what is labeled as t value in the regression output, but we'll call it a *z statistic*.[7]

A hypothesis test translates this test statistic into a probability called a *p*-value that represents how rare, or strange, your sample would be *if* the null hypothesis is true. This *p*-value gives you the probability of seeing a larger test statistic than what you've observed. Or, from another perspective, it is the proportion of times that you would wrongly reject your safe null if the test statistic you've observed is enough to lead you to adopt the alternative.

In the regression example, the *p*-value is $p(|Z| > |z_\beta|)$ where $Z \sim N(0, 1)$. The normality of $Z$ comes again from the central limit theorem: the standard deviation is equal to 1 because we've divided by the standard error, and the center at 0 is our null hypothesis assumption. As illustrated in Figure 1.8, the *p*-value measures the probability mass in the tails past your observed test statistic.

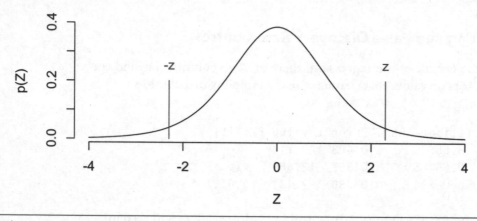

**FIGURE 1.8:** Illustration of a normal test statistic. For the "two-sided" alternative $\beta \neq 0$, the *p*-value is the volume in the tails out past either *z* or –*z*.

Finally, the usual testing procedure is to choose a cutoff $\alpha$ for your *p*-value *p* and conclude "significance" (a true nonzero regression coefficient) for $p < \alpha$. This is justified as giving only $\alpha$ probability of a false positive (concluding a real regression

---

7. Most introductory statistics books spend a lot of time differentiating between *z* and *t* statistics, the former having a normal distribution and the latter Student's *t* distribution. In this book, the sample sizes are large enough that things will be approximately normally distributed whenever such a distinction arises. When distributions are non-normal, they won't be Student's *t* either, and you'll rely upon bootstrapping.

relationship where none exists). For example, in a regression, you might conclude that $\beta \neq 0$ only if its $p$-value is less than the accepted risk of a false discovery for each coefficient. If your tolerance for this risk is 1%, implying $\alpha = 0.01$, then for the online spending regression you'd conclude a nonzero bandwidth effect ($2e-16$ is $2/10^{16}$, or practically zero) but decide to keep $\beta_{\text{anychildren}} = 0$ in your working model.

**THE PROBLEM OF MULTIPLICITY** breaks this seemingly simple relationship between $p$-values and reliability. Under the usual testing procedure, $\alpha$ is for a single test. If you repeat many tests, about $\alpha \times 100\%$ of the true-null signals (e.g., regression coefficients that correspond to nonexistent relationships) should erroneously pop up as significant. This can lead to strange results when you are looking for rare true signals in a haystack of spurious noise.

Imagine a regression estimation problem where 5 out of 100 coefficients have a real relationship with the result. We would say here that the true coefficient set is *sparse*: most of the $\beta_j$ are zero. In the best-case scenario, when you run hypothesis tests, you find all of these five true signals (i.e., there are no false negatives). Let's assume you do find all five and test the remaining 95 with an $\alpha = 0.05$ significance cutoff. In that case, you expect that you will erroneously conclude significance for 5% of the useless 95 variables, leading you to include $4.75 \approx 5$ spurious regressors in the final model. The end result has you using a model with ten inputs, but in truth 50% of them are junk that is unrelated to your response variable! Such false discoveries are worse than useless: they add noise to your model and reduce the quality of your predictions.

This situation, where a high proportion of "discoveries" are false positives, gets worse with decreasing signal-to-noise ratios. For example, if you have one true signal out of 1000 hypothesis tests with an $\alpha = 0.05$ cutoff, then you will have around $0.05 \times 999 \approx 50$ false discoveries. Your false discovery (FD) proportion will be around $50/51 \approx 98\%$. This might sound extreme, but having far fewer than 1/1000 true signals is the norm in applications like digital advertising, where a true signal is the rare existence of a website in browser history that indicates future purchasing intent.

In general, you have

$$\text{FD Proportion} = \frac{\text{\# false positives}}{\text{\# tests called significant}}$$

as a measure of the amount of spurious noise you have introduced into the model through false discovery. The FD proportion is a property of the fitted model. You can't know it: either you've made mistakes or you haven't. However, you can control its expectation, the *false discovery rate*:

$$\text{FDR} = \mathbb{E}[\text{FDP}] = \mathbb{E}\left[\frac{\text{\# false positives}}{\text{\# tests called significant}}\right].$$

This is the multitest aggregate analog of the probability of a false positive from a single test. Because probability is just expectation for a binary random variable, the

FDR for a single test is equal to the probability of a false positive—what we called $\alpha$ earlier.

Just as we used an $\alpha$-cutoff procedure to control false positives in single tests, you can ensure that FDR $\leq q$ for some chosen $q$-cutoffs (e.g., 0.1 is common). The Benjamini–Hochberg (BH) algorithm[8] controls your FDR by defining a cutoff on ranked lists of $p$-values.

---

**ALGORITHM 3**  **Benjamini–Hochberg (BH) FDR Control**

For $N$ tests, with $p$-values $\{p_1 \dots p_N\}$ and target FDR $q$:

- Order your $p$-values from smallest to largest as $p_{(1)} \dots p_{(N)}$.

- Set the $p$-value cutoff as $p^* = \max\left\{ p_{(k)} : p_{(k)} \leq q\dfrac{k}{N} \right\}$.

The *rejection region* is then the set of all $p$-values $\leq p^*$, and this ensures that FDR $\leq q$.

---

Note that $p_{(k)}$ denotes the $k$th order statistic.

The BH procedure is easiest to understand visually. Consider a new online spending regression with our set of covariates expanded to include race, ethnicity, and region:

```
> spendy <- glm(log(spend) ~ .-id, data=browser)
> round (summary(spendy)$coef,2)
            Estimate Std. Error  t value  Pr(>|t|)
(Intercept)     5.86       0.16    36.34      0.00
anychildren     0.09       0.03     2.54      0.01
broadband       0.52       0.04    11.93      0.00
hispanic       -0.18       0.04    -4.30      0.00
raceblack      -0.25       0.18    -1.41      0.16
raceother      -0.41       0.31    -1.32      0.19
racewhite      -0.21       0.15    -1.36      0.17
regionNE        0.26       0.05     4.98      0.00
regionS         0.01       0.04     0.13      0.90
regionW         0.18       0.05     3.47      0.00
> pval <- summary(spendy)$coef[-1, "Pr(>|t|)"]
```

8. Y. Benjamini and Y. Hochberg. Controlling the false discovery rate: A practical and powerful approach to multiple testing. *Journal of the Royal Statistical Society, Series B*, 57:289–300, 1995.

In the last line of code, we extract the *p*-values for the nine regression coefficients (excluding the intercept). In Figure 1.9, these values are plotted against their rank from smallest to largest. The line on Figure 1.9 has slope 0.1/9, which corresponds to the BH cutoff line for $N = 9$ and $q = 0.1$. The recipe in Algorithm 3 is now simple: find the largest *p*-value that is below this line and call it and all smaller *p*-values "significant." These five points are shown in Figure 1.9; you expect that around $q = 0.1$ of them (0 to 1 of the values) are false positives.

◆ **WHY DOES THE BH ALGORITHM WORK?** The explanation requires a bit of probability theory. First, you know that *p*-values *from true null signals are uniformly distributed.* To see this, consider a random *p*-value $p(Z)$ corresponding to a test statistic $Z$ drawn from the null hypothesis distribution. The cumulative distribution function for $p(Z)$ is then $p(p(Z) < p(z))$ for any $p(z) \in (0, 1)$. This implies that

$$p(p(Z) < p(z)) = p(|Z| < |z|) = p(z) \qquad (1.8)$$

such that a null *p*-value is a random variable $U$ where $p(U < u) = u$. This is the definition of a uniform random variable—in particular, a U(0, 1) random variable, with density shown in Figure 1.10.

The second thing to know is that the order statistics for a sample of $N$ independent uniforms all have expectation $\mathbb{E}[p_{(k)}] = k/(N + 1)$. This fact comes from the uniforms being, on average, evenly spaced between zero and one. Thus, in expectation, $N$ *p*-values from the null should follow a line of slope $1/(N + 1)$, as shown as black dots in Figure 1.11. The lighter triangles in the same figure show the observed *p*-values from the spending regression. These observed *p*-values are (except for $p_{(9)}$, the largest) all *smaller* than you'd expect for draws from the null U(0, 1) *p*-value distribution. That is, they offer some measure of evidence *against* the null hypotheses.

The gap between observed *p*-value order statistics and the null line of slope $1/(N + 1)$ gives a measure of how much non-null signal is in the data. But how big of a gap is "significant"? The BH algorithm says that if the *p*-values live below a line with slope $q/N$, then they can be called significant with an FDR that is no larger than $q$. The simple proof for this assumes *independence between tests* and (see Figure 1.12). Unfortunately, independence between tests is an unrealistic

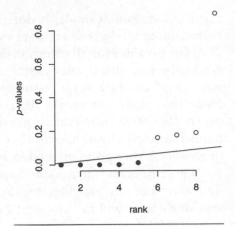

**FIGURE 1.9:** The BH algorithm for FDR control in your spending regression with nine covariates. The nine *p*-values are plotted against their rank, and the line has slope 0.1/9. The five *p*-values below this line are "significant," and a procedure that defines significance in this way has an FDR of 10%.

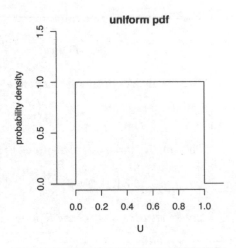

**FIGURE 1.10:** The probability density function for a U(0, 1) uniform random variable, defined via $p(U < u) = u$ for $u \in [0, 1]$.

assumption. For example, it doesn't hold in the multiple regression example: if you remove a variable from the regression, the $p$-values for all other coefficients will change. This is a big reason why, in later chapters, we will resort to alternative methods such as the lasso for variable selection. In the meantime, you can view the BH algorithm as giving you a decent (but often conservative) guess at your FDR. If you are handed a stack of $p$-values and little extra context, the BH procedure is your go-to method for quantifying the FDR.

One of the main points of this chapter is that you make many decisions whenever you interact with data. Life is not resolvable into single tests, and the problem of multiplicity will be ever-present. We introduced multiplicity with a story about how given $\alpha$ ($p$-value cutoffs) can lead to big FDR: $\alpha \rightarrow q(\alpha)$. With the BH procedure, we've reversed the mapping. BH is a recipe for the $\alpha(q)$ that will give you whatever FDR $q$ you want: $q \rightarrow \alpha(q)$. In either case, FDR is *the* way to summarize risk when you have many tests. You'll never think about testing the same again!

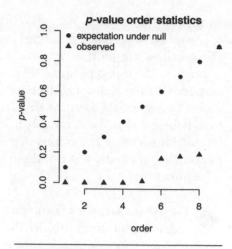

**FIGURE 1.11:** Expected uniform order statistics $\mathbb{E}[p_{(k)}]$ and their rank $k$. For comparison, we also show the $p$-value order statistics from Figure 1.10.

---

$N$ is the total number of tests, $N_0$ is the number that have true nulls, $R(u)$ is the number of $p$-values $\leq u$, and $r(u)$ is the number of these that correspond to true nulls.

The FDP for a $p$-value cutoff of $u$ is

$$FDP(u) = \frac{r(u)}{R(u)}.$$

The BH algorithm chooses a cutoff $u^*$ such that

$$u^* = \max\left\{u : u \leq q\frac{R(u)}{N}\right\}.$$

This implies that $1/R(u^*) \leq q/(Nu^*)$. Hence the FDR at cutoff $u^*$ is

$$FDR(u^*) = \mathbb{E}\left[\frac{r(u^*)}{R(u^*)}\right] \leq \mathbb{E}\left[\frac{r(u^*)}{Nu^*}\right] = q\frac{N_0}{N} \leq q,$$

since $\mathbb{E}[r(u)/u] = N_0$ for the $N_0$ independent uniform $p$-values from the true null tests.

---

**FIGURE 1.12:** Proof that the FDR (i.e., expected FD proportion, or FDP) for the BH procedure is less than $q$.

FOR A LARGER FDR EXAMPLE, we'll consider an application in statistical genetics. The approach known as GWAS, for "genome-wide association studies," involves scanning large DNA sequences for association with disease. The hope is that a number of DNA locations can be identified as promising for exploration and lab experimentation.

Since this experimentation is expensive, it is crucial that you understand the FDR—in this case, the expected failure rate for further exploration—when reporting the list of promising locations.

Single-nucleotide polymorphisms (SNPs) are paired DNA locations that vary across chromosomes. The allele that occurs most often is major (symbolized $A$), and the other is minor ($a$). For example, a common SNP summary is minor allele frequency (MAF).

$$MAF: \quad AA \rightarrow 0 \quad Aa/aA \rightarrow 1 \quad aa \rightarrow 2. \tag{1.9}$$

In this context, a simple GWAS asks the question, "Which SNP MAF distributions vary with disease?" Significant dependence between MAF and disease status marks that location as promising for exploration.

Willer et al. [2013] describe meta-analysis of GWAS for cholesterol levels. We'll focus on the "bad" LDL cholesterol. At each of 2.5 million SNPs, they fit the simple linear regression

$$\mathbb{E}[LDL] = \alpha + \beta AF.$$

Here, AF is allele frequency for the "trait increasing allele" (you can think of this as essentially the MAF). Willer et al. have 2.5 million SNP locations, implying 2.5 million tests of $\beta \neq 0$ and thus 2.5 million $p$-values.

This set of $p$-values is plotted in Figure 1.13. Recall that $p$-values from the null (in this case, $\beta = 0$ and no disease–AF association) are uniformly distributed. The histogram in Figure 1.13 looks *almost* uniform, except for a small spike near zero of *extra small p*-values. The $p$-values in this spike, which look smaller than what you'd get from a true null distribution, are the only hope for discovery.

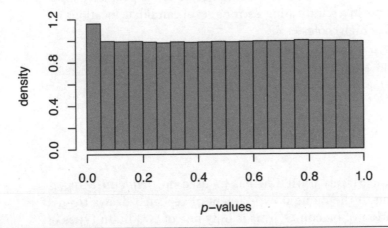

**FIGURE 1.13:** Cholesterol GWAS $p$-values: Which are significant?

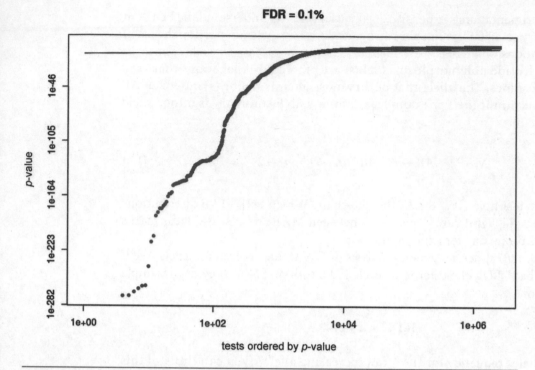

**FIGURE 1.14:** Visualization of the BH procedure for our cholesterol GWAS with $q = 0.001$. The line defining our rejection region is plotted, with slope $0.001/N$, and the roughly 4000 $p$-values below that line are significant with FDR < 0.001.

Application of the BH algorithm in this case is illustrated in Figure 1.14. Although the distribution in Figure 1.10 looks nearly uniform, there is a lot of signal among the smallest $p$-values. Out of the 2.5 million total tests, we find around 4000 $p$-values are significant at the tiny FDR of $q = 10^{-3}$, or 0.1%. That implies we can expect only about four of these 4000 are false positives, indicating a strong set of candidate locations for exploring the genetic roots of high cholesterol.

Association is not causation. Many genetic factors may be, for example, also correlated with social or economic factors that influence diet and health.

## Bayesian Inference

All of the discussion of uncertainty until now has focused on *frequentist* uncertainty—that corresponding to the thought experiment of repeated draws from a hypothetical fixed population of outcomes. This is only one of two main types of uncertainty. The other is *Bayesian uncertainty*, which characterizes probabilities over models and parameters by appealing to the idea of subjective beliefs rather than repeated trials.[9]

Decision-making on this basis is referred to as *Bayesian inference*. A full treatment of Bayesian methods and ideas is beyond the scope of this book. For that, I refer you to the now-classic reference of Gelman et al. [2014] as well as the shorter primer by Hoff [2009]. However, although we will not deal in detail with explicit Bayesian inference, this way of thinking about uncertainty underlies much of what we cover in the text. Indeed, compared to frequentism, Bayes plays an as large or larger a role in the practice of business data science. Much of contemporary machine learning is driven by ideas from Bayesian inference, and formal decision theory—quantification of risks and expected rewards—is inherently Bayesian. A basic understanding of the Bayesian framework will help you to understand how these methods are developed and why they work.

Bayesian inference is the mathematical framework of beliefs. It formalizes the process of "If you believe $A$ and you then observe $B$, you should update your beliefs to $C$." This is sometimes referred to as *subjective probability*, but you don't need anyone to hold these specific beliefs for the framework to be valid. Rather, Bayesian inference provides a framework for combining *assumptions* (and a degree of confidence in those assumptions) with evidence. When those assumptions are clear, then Bayesian inference is completely transparent: you know all of the inputs to your decision process, and the relative weight placed on data versus prior knowledge is explicit.

Mechanically, Bayesian inference works through a combination of prior distributions and likelihoods. As we detail in the next chapter, the likelihood is the probability of the data you have observed *given* a fixed set of model parameters—say, $p(X|\Theta)$ for data $X$ and parameters $\Theta$ and where | denotes "given" or "conditional upon." The *prior distribution*, $\pi(\Theta)$, is the probability distribution over $\Theta$ *before* you have observed any data. This choice of prior is an assumption that you are bringing to your analysis, as is the model that defines your likelihood. The *posterior* distribution—the probability distribution on your parameters after observing data—is then available via Bayes rule:

$$p(\Theta|X) = \frac{p(\Theta|X)\pi(\Theta)}{p(X)} \propto p(\Theta|X)\pi(\Theta). \qquad (1.10)$$

Here, recall that $\propto$ stands for "proportional to." The *marginal likelihood*,

$$p(X) = \int p(\Theta|X)\pi(\Theta)\,d\Theta,$$

is the probability of the data under the assumed likelihood model after averaging all possible values of $\Theta$. Since it doesn't depend upon $\Theta$, the nominal target of inference, $p(X)$ is mostly a nuisance for Bayesian inference. The computational strategy of estimating Equation 1.10 via Markov chain Monte Carlo (MCMC)[10] is a successful attempt to circumvent

---

9. Check out Hacking [1975] for a fantastic investigation into the concepts of probability and the origins of frequentist and Bayesian schools.
10. Alan E. Gelfand and Adrian F.M. Smith. Sampling-based approaches to calculating marginal densities. *Journal of the American Statistical Association*, 85 (410):398–409, 1990.

the need to explicitly calculate p($X$). This strategy is largely responsible for the explosion of Bayesian inference during the 1990s and 2000s.

A good way to get an intuition for Bayesian inference is to play around with *conjugate models*. These are prior and likelihood combinations such that, as you accumulate data, the posterior distribution remains in the same family as the prior. The mechanics of posterior updating can be written out and made explicit. One intuitive example is the beta-binomial model where you have binomial trials with constant success probability $q$. The prior distribution for $q$ is a beta distribution:

$$\pi(q) = \text{Beta}(q; \alpha, \beta) \propto q^{\alpha-1}(1-q)^{\beta-1}\mathbb{1}_{[q \in (0,1)]}. \tag{1.11}$$

For example, the Beta(1, 1) prior yields $\pi(q) = \mathbb{1}_{[q \in (0,1)]}$, the familiar uniform distribution. Again, note that the $\propto$ symbol means "is proportional to" and in Equation 1.11 we are ignoring a normalizing constant that ensures $\int_0^1 \pi(q)\,dq = 1$ for all $\alpha, \beta > 0$.

Each binomial realization can be viewed as a combination of Bernoulli trials (e.g., tosses of a weighted coin) where $x = 1$ with probability $q$ and $x = 0$ with probability $1 - q$. Under a Beta($a$, $b$) prior distribution on $q$, the *posterior* distribution for $q$ after a single Bernoulli realization for $x$ becomes

$$p(q|x) = \text{Beta}(a_1 = a + x, \ b_1 = b + 1 - x). \tag{1.12}$$

Updating in this manner over $n$ trials, $a_n$ can be interpreted as the number of observed "successes" and $b_n$ the number of observed "failures" out of $n$ trials. As you run more trials (i.e., you flip the coin more times), these parameters grow, and your uncertainty about $q$ decreases. For example, since the mean of a Beta($\alpha$, $\beta$) distribution is $\alpha / (\alpha + \beta)$, under a Beta(1, 1) prior a single successful trial yields a mean of $\mathbb{E}[q|x_1] = 2/3$. An additional successful trial yields $\mathbb{E}[q|x_1, x_2] = 3/4$. Figure 1.15 illustrates beta-binomial

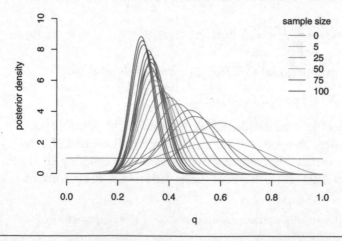

**FIGURE 1.15:** Posterior density functions for $q$, the success probability in a series of Bernoulli trials (coin tosses), as a function of the sample size (number of tosses) under a Beta(1, 1) prior. The "true" probability is 1/3.

posterior updating across a number of simulated binomial trials, moving from the flat uniform prior to a Gaussian-like peak around the true probability of 1/3 after 100 trials.

As this example illustrates, Bayesian inference is inherently *parametric*: you specify a model that depends upon a set of parameters, and the updating formula in Equation 1.10 defines how uncertainty about these parameters changes with observed data. This is in contrast to the ideas of *nonparametric* inference, where you quantify uncertainty on results of a given procedure without assuming the correctness of the models behind that procedure. There is a field of "nonparametric" Bayesian analysis, but this title is a misnomer.[11] The field is closer to what I'd call *semiparametrics*: it applies flexible models that can relax common assumptions (e.g., linearity) but still rely upon restrictive model structure to facilitate inference in high dimensions (see Chapter 9).

Bradley Efron[12] compares Bayesian inference to the parametric bootstrap, and this might help give you some intuition around the practical application of Bayesian inference. He shows that, under certain common priors, parametric bootstraps yield a sampling distribution that looks similar to the corresponding Bayesian posterior. Recall from earlier that the parametric bootstrap, like the nonparametric bootstrap, uses repeated model fits to quantify uncertainty. However, instead of resampling from the original data, the parametric bootstrap first *estimates* the model using the full sample and then *simulates* from this fitted model to generate data for each model fit. Thus, the parametric bootstrap is quantifying uncertainty by simulating from the assumed *parametric* model.

If this assumed model is incorrect, the parametric bootstrap results can have little connection to reality. In contrast, the nonparametric bootstrap, which we've covered in detail earlier, gives accurate uncertainty quantification for the estimation you've executed even if your estimators are based on silly assumptions. However, the *parametric* bootstrap requires much less data and will "work"—if your model is correct—in extremely high dimensions. It is a practical option where the more robust procedure is impossible. This same characterization applies to many Bayesian procedures.

Ideally, when making business decisions, everything is nonparametric: you always accumulate enough data so that prior beliefs are no longer relevant, and you work in a way that is not sensitive to model assumptions. Of course, the reality is that every decision involves uncertainty and will be based upon both instinct (prior) and data. But in our material on causal and structural inference—Chapters 5 and 6—we will indeed focus on robust inference that, while not always nonparametric, at least has some guarantees of being valid when our models are not quite correct. This is a nice property to have, and it is attainable in causal inference settings where the target of inference is low dimensional (typically univariate) and we have a large amount of sample data.

---

11. Called *npBayes* for short, this is the area of my Ph.D. dissertation. During the 2000s there was a great cross-discipline communication between ML and npBayes: both fields were working to build computationally feasible algorithms that gave reasonable inferential results in ultra-high-dimensional models. Many people in the current deep learning community have roots in or connections to the npBayes community.

12. Bradley Efron. Bayesian inference and the parametric bootstrap. *The Annals of Applied Statistics*, 6, 2012.

Unfortunately, model-free inference is possible only in such datarich settings—when you have many observations (large $n$) and a low-dimensional inference target (small $p$). Following from our earlier discussions of the nonparametric bootstrap, you will fail in nonparametrics if your *observed* data gives you a poor picture of the population distribution. Frequentist inference in general becomes difficult in high dimensions, as you have already seen from our discussion of multiple testing where the best you can hope for is to control some average false discover rate. You will see throughout this text that much of contemporary data science occurs in environments that are super-high-dimensional. In such settings, you don't have the luxury of being nonparametric. Instead, to get workable results, you need to make assumptions about the model and give some reasonable *prior* guesses about the parameters of those models. Bayes is the language that facilitates this process.

Throughout the rest of this book, you will be exposed to Bayesian ideas without them being referred to as explicitly Bayesian. For example, the penalties in Chapter 3 are interpretable as the effects of Bayesian priors, and the ensemble methods behind random forests in Chapter 9 are a version of Bayesian model averaging. In such cases, we generally won't discuss inference directly. Rather, the methods we work with will be engineered to produce point estimates that perform well in high-dimensional environments where there is a lot of uncertainty. That is the strength of Bayes and the reason why model builders tend to think as Bayesians. To build a learning algorithm that *works* when given only messy unstructured data, you need a framework that lets you bring prior experience to bear and that is transparent about how to combine data with beliefs.

# Regression

## 2

T he vast majority of problems in applied data science require regression model-ing. That is, you have a *response* variable (*y*) that you want to model or predict as a function of a vector of *inputs* or covariates (**x**). This chapter introduces the basic framework and language of regression. We will build on this material through-out the rest of the book.

## Linear Models

A basic but powerful regression strategy is to deal in *averages* and *lines*. We model the conditional mean for *y* given **x** as

$$\mathbb{E}[y \,|\, \boldsymbol{x}] = f(\boldsymbol{x}'\boldsymbol{\beta}). \tag{2.1}$$

Here, $\boldsymbol{x} = [1, x_1, x_2, \ldots x_p]$ is a vector of covariates and $\boldsymbol{\beta} = [\beta_0, \beta_1, \beta_2, \ldots \beta_p]$ are the corresponding coefficients. The *vector* notation, $\boldsymbol{x}'\boldsymbol{\beta}$, is shorthand for the sum of element-wise products:

$$\boldsymbol{x}'\boldsymbol{\beta} = \beta_0 + x_1\beta_1 + x_2\beta_2 + \ldots + x_p\beta_p. \tag{2.2}$$

Here, for convenience we have included $x_0 = 1$ for the intercept (alternatively, we sometimes write $\alpha = \beta_0$ for an explicit intercept). The symbol $\mathbb{E}$ denotes expectation, such that $\mathbb{E}[y \,|\, \boldsymbol{x}]$ is read as "the average for response *y* given inputs **x**." The function $f(\cdot)$ denotes any generic function; we'll consider different forms for this "link func-tion" *f* to account for different types of response *y*.

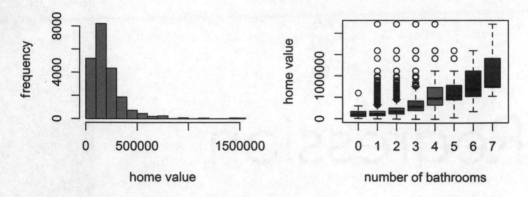

**FIGURE 2.1:** Illustration of marginal versus conditional distributions for home prices. On the left, all of the home prices are grouped together. On the right, home price distributions are broken out by the number of bathrooms.

Regression is all about understanding the *conditional* probability distribution for "$y$ given $x$," which we write as $p(y \mid x)$. Figure 2.1 illustrates the conditional distribution in contrast to a *marginal* distribution, which is so named because it corresponds to the unconditional distribution for a single margin (i.e., column) of a data matrix. While the *marginal* mean is a simple number, the *conditional* mean is a function (e.g., $x'\beta$). The data is distributed randomly around these means, and the assumptions you make about this distribution drive your estimation and prediction strategies.

The first model that we will work with is the basic linear regression model. This is a workhorse of data science. It is fast to fit (in terms of both analyst and computational time), it gives reasonable answers in a variety of settings (so long as you know how to ask the right questions), and it is easy to interpret and understand.

The model is as follows:

$$\mathbb{E}[y \mid x] = x'\beta = \beta_0 + x_1\beta_1 \ldots + x_p\beta_p. \tag{2.3}$$

This corresponds to using a link function $f(z) = z$ in the regression model of Equation 2.1. With just one input $x$, you can write the model as $\mathbb{E}[y \mid x] = \alpha + x\beta$ and plot it as in Figure 2.2. Here, $\mathbb{E}[y \mid x]$ increases by $\beta$ for every unit increase in $x$, and $\alpha$ is the *intercept*: $\alpha = \mathbb{E}[y \mid x = 0]$.

When estimating a regression model—i.e., when fitting the $\beta$ coefficients—you make some assumptions about the full conditional *distribution* beyond its center at $\mathbb{E}[y \mid x]$. Linear regression is usually fit for Gaussian conditional distributions:

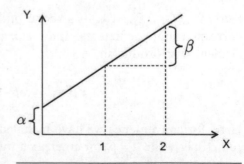

**FIGURE 2.2:** Simple linear regression.

$$y \mid x \sim \mathrm{N}\left(x'\beta, \sigma^2\right). \tag{2.4}$$

That is, the distribution for $y$ as a function of $x$ is distributed normally around $\mathbb{E}[y \mid x] = x'\beta$ with *variance* $\sigma^2$. The same model is often commonly written with an additive error term,

$$y = x'\beta + \varepsilon, \text{ with } \varepsilon \sim N(0, \sigma^2). \qquad (2.5)$$

Equations 2.4 and 2.5 describe the same model.

As a concrete example, consider sales data for orange juice (OJ) from Dominick's grocery stores. Dominick's was a Chicago-area chain. This data was collected in the 1990s and is publicly available from the Kilts center at the University of Chicago's Booth School of Business. The data include weekly prices and sales (in number of cartons "moved") for three OJ brands—Tropicana, Minute Maid, Dominick's—at 83 Chicagoland Stores, as well as an indicator, feat, showing whether each brand was advertised (in store or flyer) that week.

```
> oj <- read.csv("oj.csv")
> head(oj)
  sales  price      brand feat
1  8256   3.87  tropicana    0
2  6144   3.87  tropicana    0
3  3840   3.87  tropicana    0
4  8000   3.87  tropicana    0
5  8896   3.87  tropicana    0
6  7168   3.87  tropicana    0
> levels (oj$brand)
[1] "dominicks" "minute.maid" "tropicana"
```

Figure 2.3 shows the prices and sales broken out by brand. We see that each brand occupies a well-defined price range: Dominick's is the budget option, Tropicana is the luxury option, and Minute Maid lives between. In the right panel of Figure 2.3, we see that sales are clearly decreasing with price. This makes sense: demand is *downward* sloping, and if you charge more, you sell less. More specifically, it appears that *log* sales has a roughly linear relationship with *log* price. This is an important point. Whenever you are working with linear (i.e., additive) models, it is crucial that you try to work in the space where you expect to find linearity. For variables that change *multiplicatively* with other factors, this is usually the log scale.

Recall the logarithm definition,

$$\log(a) = b \Leftrightarrow a = e^b. \qquad (2.6)$$

Here, $e \approx 2.72$ is the natural base. We will always use natural logs. The base $e$ plays a central role in science and modeling of dynamic systems because $e^x$ is its own derivative: $de^x/dx = e^x$. In a linear model for logged response, $\beta$ is added to $\log(y)$ for each unit increase in $x$:

$$\log(y) = \alpha + \beta x. \qquad (2.7)$$

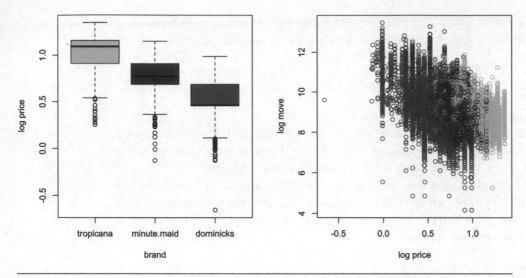

**FIGURE 2.3:** Dominick's OJ prices and sales (`move`) by brand. Note the use of log scale for both continuous variables.

The fact that we are working in log space makes this model *multiplicative* in $y$. Recall some basic facts about logs and exponents: $\log(ab) = \log(a) + \log(b)$, $\log(a^b) = b\log(a)$, and $e^{a+b} = e^a e^b$. Exponentiate both sides of Equation 2.7:

$$y = e^\alpha e^{\beta x}. \tag{2.8}$$

Considering $x^* = x + 1$, we see that

$$y^* = e^\alpha e^{\beta x^*} = e^\alpha e^{\beta x + \beta} = y e^\beta. \tag{2.9}$$

Therefore, each unit increase in $x$ leads $y$ to be *multiplied* by the factor $e^\beta$.

How will you know when variables should be modeled as changing multiplicatively? One indicator is everyday language. Be on the lookout for variables whose change is usually expressed in percentage rather than absolute terms. For example, these are both typically modeled in log space:

- Prices: "*Foreclosed homes sell at a 20% to 30% discount.*"

- Sales: "*Your y.o.y. sales are up 20% across models.*"

More generally, variables that are strictly non-negative (e.g., volatility, counts of errors or events, rainfall) are often treated as changing linearly on a log scale.

Another common scenario models against each other two variables that *both* move multiplicatively. For example, Figure 2.4 shows the national GDP versus imports for several countries. Fitting a line to the left panel would be silly; its slope will be entirely determined by small changes in the U.S. values. In contrast,

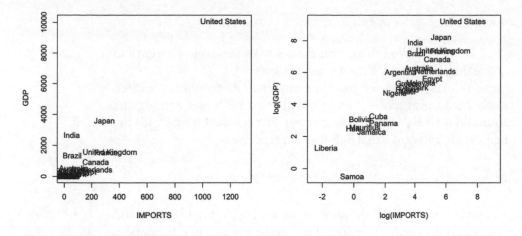

**FIGURE 2.4:** National GDP against imports, in original and log scale.

the right panel shows that in log space, the GDP and imports follow a neat linear relationship.

Returning to our OJ example, Figure 2.3 indicates that this *log-log* model might be appropriate for our OJ sales versus price analysis. One possible regression model is then

$$\log(\text{sales}) = \alpha + \beta \log(\text{price}) + \varepsilon. \qquad (2.10)$$

This says that, regardless of brand, log sales increase by $\beta$ for every unit increase in log price.

Conveniently, log-log models have a much more intuitive interpretation: sales increase by $\beta$% for every 1% increase in price. To see this, write $y = \exp\left[\alpha + \beta \log(x) + \varepsilon\right]$ and differentiate against $x$:

$$\frac{dy}{dx} = \frac{\beta}{x} e^{\alpha + \beta \log(x) + \varepsilon} \;\Rightarrow\; \beta = \frac{dy/y}{dx/x}. \qquad (2.11)$$

Here, $\beta$ is the proportional change in $y$ over the proportional change in $x$. In economics there is a special name for such $\beta$: *elasticity*. The concept of elasticity will play an important role in many of our analyses.

If you take a look at the right panel of Figure 2.3, it seems clear that the three brands have log-log sales-price distributions that are concentrated around three separate lines. If you suspect that each brand has the same $\beta$ elasticity but a different intercept $\alpha$ then you would use a slightly more complex model:

$$\log(\text{sales}) = \alpha_{\text{brand}} + \beta \log(\text{price}) + \varepsilon. \qquad (2.12)$$

Here, $\alpha_{\text{brand}}$ is shorthand for a separate indicator for each OJ brand, which we could write out more fully as

$$\alpha_{\text{brand}} = \alpha_d \mathbb{1}_{[\text{brand}=\text{dominicks}]} + \alpha_m \mathbb{1}_{[\text{brand}=\text{minutemaid}]} + \alpha_t \mathbb{1}_{[\text{brand}=\text{tropicana}]}.$$

Hence, Equation 2.12 says even through all brand sales have the same elasticity to price, at the same price they will have different expected sales.

To run this regression in R, we can use the glm command.[1] As mentioned earlier, glm stands for "generalized linear model," and we will use it for linear and logistic regression. The command is straightforward to use: you give it a data frame with the data argument and provide a formula that defines your regression.

```
> reg <- glm(y ~ var1 + ... + varP, data=mydata)
```

The fitted object reg is a list of useful things (type names(reg) to see them), and there are functions to access the results: summary(reg) prints a bunch of information, coef(reg) gives coefficients, and predict(reg, newdata=mynewdata) predicts.[2] We fit the regression in Equation 2.12 using glm and access the coefficients:

```
> reg <- glm(log(sales) ~ brand + log(price), data=oj)
> coef(reg) ## fitted coefficients
    (Intercept)  brandminute.maid  brandtropicana  log(price)
     10.8288216         0.8701747       1.5299428  -3.1386914
```

There are a few things to notice here. First, we see that $\hat{\beta} = -3.1$ for the log price effect: sales drop by about 3% for every 1% price hike. Second, notice that there are distinct model coefficients for Minute Maid and Tropicana but not for Dominick's. The first step of glm is to create a *model matrix* (also called a *design matrix*) that defines the numeric inputs $x$. It does this with a call to the model.matrix function, and you can pull that step out to see what it is doing:

```
> x <- model.matrix( ~ log(price) + brand, data=oj)
> x[c(100,200,300),]
    (Intercept) log(price) brandminute.maid brandtropicana
100           1  1.1600209                0              1
200           1  1.0260416                1              0
300           1  0.3293037                0              0
```

Since brand is not a number, model.matrix has expanded these categories into a couple of dummy variables. For example, brandtropicana is one for Tropicana rows and zero otherwise. For comparison, consider the same rows from the original data frame:

---

1. lm would also work for this example.
2. For prediction, mynewdata must be a data frame with the same format as mydata (same variable names, same factor levels).

```
> oj[c(100,200,300),]
    sales price        brand feat
100  4416  3.19    tropicana    0
200  5440  2.79  minute.maid    0
300 51264 1.39    dominicks    1
```

There is no `branddominicks` indicator because you need only three variables to represent three categories: when both `brandminute.maid` and `brandtropicana` are zero, the *intercept* gives the value for Dominick's log sales at a log price of zero. Each factor's reference level is absorbed by the intercept and the other coefficients are "change relative to reference" (here, Dominick's). To check the reference level of your factors,[3] type `levels(myfactor)`. The first level is reference. To change this, you can do `myfactor = relevel (myfactor, "myref")`.

The fitted values from the regression in Equation 2.12 are shown in Figure 2.5 alongside the original data. You see three lines shifted according to brand identity. *At the same price,* Tropicana sells more than Minute Maid, which in turn sells more than Dominick's. This makes sense: Tropicana is a luxury product that is preferable at the same price.

All of the lines in Figure 2.5 have the same slope. In economic terms, the model assumes that consumers of the three brands have the same price sensitivity. This seems unrealistic: money is less of an issue for Tropicana customers than it is for the average Dominick's consumer. You can build this information into your regression by having log price *interact* with brand.

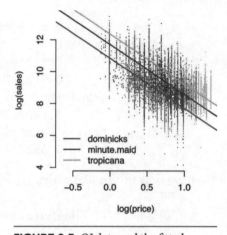

**FIGURE 2.5:** OJ data and the fitted means for each brand under the model in Equation 2.12.

An interaction term is the coefficient on the product of two inputs:

$$\mathbb{E}[y \,|\, x] = \ldots + \beta_k x_k + \beta_j x_j + x_j x_k \beta_{jk}. \tag{2.13}$$

In this equation, the effect of a unit increase in $x_j$ is $\beta_j + x_k \beta_{jk}$ such that it depends upon $x_k$. Interactions are central to scientific and business questions. For example:

- *Does gender change the effect of education on wages?*
- *Do patients recover faster when taking drug X?*
- *How does consumer price sensitivity change across brands?*

In each case here, you want to know whether one variable modulates the effect of another. You don't want to know whether women earn less than men (they do: just take a simple difference in averages). Rather, you want to know whether they are being

---

3. Once you start introducing penalization on the coefficients, you will no longer have a reference level, and all categories will have an explicit coefficient.

compensated unequally despite having the same levels of education and preparation. Similarly, in many medical situations the body will heal itself if given enough time; the question is then whether your treatment can accelerate recovery.

In our price sensitivity example, we want to include interaction between each of the brand indicator terms and the log price. We can do this in glm with the * term in the input formula:[4]

```
> reg_interact <- glm(log(sales) ~ log(price)*brand, data=oj)
> coef(reg_interact)
                (Intercept)                   log(price)
                10.95468173                  -3.37752963
           brandminute.maid              brandtropicana
                 0.88825363                   0.96238960
log(price): brandminute.maid  log(price):brandtropicana
                 0.05679476                   0.66576088
```

We have now fit a model with a separate intercept and slope for each brand, b:

$$\mathbb{E}[\log(y)\,|\,x] = \alpha_b + \beta_b \log(\texttt{price}). \tag{2.14}$$

As before, the reference category is dominicks; this brand is absorbed into both the intercept and the main slope term on log price. You find the elasticities for the other brands by adding the log(price):brand interaction terms to this main slope. The results are in Table 2.1. We see that Tropicana customers are less sensitive than the others: –2.7 versus around –3.3. The price sensitivity in model Equation 2.10, –3.1, was the result of averaging across these two distinct populations of consumers.

We conclude this introduction to linear models—and the study of orange juice—with a look at the role of advertising in the relationship between sales and prices. Recall that the OJ data include a feat dummy variable, indicating that a given brand was promoted with either an in-store display promo or a flier ad during the week that sales and prices were recorded. The ads can increase sales at all prices, they can change price sensitivity, and they can do both of these things in a brand-specific manner:

$$\mathbb{E}[\log(y)\,|\,x] = \alpha_{b,\texttt{feat}} + \beta_{b,\texttt{feat}} \log(\texttt{price}). \tag{2.15}$$

This encodes a three-way interaction between price, brand, and feat.

**TABLE 2.1:** Price elasticities fit under the model in Equation 2.14.

| Dominick's | Minute Maid | Tropicana |
|---|---|---|
| −3.4 | −3.3 | −2.7 |

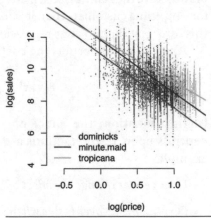

**FIGURE 2.6:** Fit for model Equation 2.14. Note that if you extrapolate too far, the linearity assumption implies Tropicana selling less than Minute Maid at the same price. This is a reminder that linear models are approximations and should be used with care away from the center of the observed data.

---

4.  Note * also adds the *main effects*—the terms from model Equation 2.12.

```
> ojreg <- glm(log(sales) ~ log(price)*brand*feat, data=oj)
> coef(ojreg)
                          (Intercept)                         log(price)
                          10.40657579                        -2.77415436
                     brandminute.maid                       brandtropicana
                           0.04720317                         0.70794089
                                 feat           log(price):brandminute.maid
                           1.09440665                         0.78293210
             log(price):brandtropicana                    log (price): feat
                           0.73579299                        -0.47055331
                 brandminute.maid: feat                 brandtropicana: feat
                           1.17294361                         0.78525237
     log(price): brandminute.maid: feat    log (price): brandtropicana: feat
                          -1.10922376                        -0.98614093
```

The brand and ad specific elasticities are compiled in Table 2.2.

**TABLE 2.2:** Brand- and ad-dependent elasticities. Test your understanding of the regression equations by recovering these numbers from the R output.

|              | Dominick's | Minute Maid | Tropicana |
|--------------|:----------:|:-----------:|:---------:|
| Not Featured |    −2.8    |    −2.0     |   −2.0    |
| Featured     |    −3.2    |    −3.6     |   −3.5    |

We see that being featured always leads to more price sensitivity. Minute Maid and Tropicana elasticities drop from −2 to below −3.5 with ads, while Dominick's drops from −2.8 to −3.2. Why does this happen? One possible explanation is that advertisement increases the population of consumers who are considering your brand. In particular, it can increase your market beyond brand loyalists, to include people who will be more price sensitive than those who reflexively buy your orange juice every week. Indeed, if you observe increased price sensitivity, it can be an indicator that your marketing efforts are expanding your consumer base. This why Marketing 101 dictates that ad campaigns should usually be accompanied by price cuts. There is also an alternative explanation. Since the featured products are often also discounted, it could be that the demand curve is nonlinear—at lower price points the average consumer is more price sensitive. The truth is probably a combination of these effects.

Finally, notice that in Table 2.1 Minute Maid had a price elasticity similar to that of Dominick's—it behaved like a budget product. However, in Table 2.2, we see that Minute Maid and Tropicana have nearly identical elasticities and that both are different from Dominick's. What happened?

The answer is that the overly simple model in Equation 2.14 led to a *confounding* between advertisement and brand effects. Figure 2.7 shows that Minute Maid was

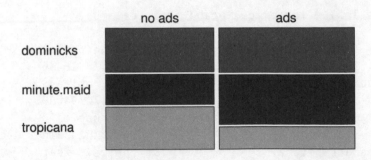

**FIGURE 2.7:** A mosaic plot of the amount of advertisement by brand.

featured more often than Tropicana. Since being featured leads to more price sensitivity, this leads Minute Maid to artificially appear more price sensitive when we don't account for the ad's effect. The model in Equation 2.15 corrects this by including `feat` in the regression. This phenomenon, where variable effects can get confounded if you don't *control* for them correctly, will play an important role in the later discussions of causal and structural inference.

## Logistic Regression

Linear regression is just one instance of the linear modeling framework. Another technique (perhaps even more common in practice) is *logistic* regression. This strategy is used for modeling *binary* response: a $y$ that is either 0 or 1 (true or false).

Binary responses arise from a number of prediction targets:

- Will this person pay their bills or default?
- Is this a thumbs-up or thumbs-down review?
- Will the Edmonton Oilers win or lose this game?
- Is the writer a Republican or Democrat?

Even when the response of interest is not binary (e.g., revenue), it will sometimes be that your decision-relevant information is binary (e.g., profit versus loss) and it is simplest to think in these terms.

Recall the general linear model specification: $\mathbb{E}[y \mid x] = f(x'\beta)$. When the response $y$ is 0 or 1, the conditional mean becomes

$$\mathbb{E}[y \mid x] = p(y = 1 \mid x) \times 1 + p(y = 0 \mid x) \times 0 = p(y = 1 \mid x).$$

Therefore, the expectation you're modeling is a *probability*. This implies that you need to choose the *link function* $f(x'\beta)$ to give values between zero and one:

$$p(y = 1 \mid \boldsymbol{x}) = f(\beta_0 + \beta_1 x_1 \ldots + \beta_p x_p).$$

Logistic regression uses a *logit* link function:

$$p(y = 1 \mid \boldsymbol{x}) = \frac{e^{x'\beta}}{1 + e^{x'\beta}} = \frac{\exp[\beta_0 + \beta_1 x_1 \ldots + \beta_p x_d]}{1 + \exp[\beta_0 + \beta_1 x_1 \ldots + \beta_p x_d]}. \qquad (2.16)$$

See Figure 2.8 for a picture of the logit function. To see how this link works, consider extreme values for $\boldsymbol{x'\beta}$. At large negative values, $f(-\infty) = 0/(1 + 0) = 0$ and $y = 1$ has zero probability. At large positive values, $f(\infty) = \infty/(\infty + 1) = 1$ and $y = 1$ is guaranteed. Thus, the logit link maps from the "real line" of numbers to the $[0, 1]$ space of probabilities.

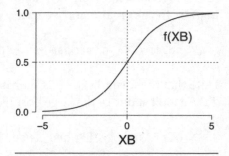

**FIGURE 2.8:** A logistic link function.

To interpret the $\beta$ coefficients, writing $p = p(y = 1 \mid \boldsymbol{x})$ and a little algebra shows that

$$\log\left[\frac{p}{1-p}\right] = \beta_0 + \beta_1 x_1 \ldots + \beta_p x_p.$$

Thus, logistic regression is a *linear model for log odds*. The odds of an event are the probability that it happens over the probability that it doesn't. For example, if an event has a 1/4 probability, then its odds are "one in three," or 1/3. You should get used to thinking about uncertainty in terms of odds—much of your modeling will occur on this scale. Following the same logic as we had for log linear models earlier, $e^{\beta_k}$ is then interpretable as the *multiplicative* effect[5] for a unit increase in $x_k$ on the *odds* for the event $y = 1$.

For our first logistic regression example, we'll build a filter for email "spam"—junk mail that can be ignored. Every time an email arrives, your inbox performs binary regression: Is this *spam* or *not spam*? We'll train our filter by fitting logistic regression to previous emails.

As training data, spam.csv has for 4600 emails (about 1800 spam) indicators for the presence of 54 keywords or characters (e.g., free or !), counts for capitalized letters (total number and longest continuous block length), and a spam variable for whether or not each email has been tagged as spam by a human reader.

```
> email[c(1,4000), c(16,56,58)]
     word_free capital_run_length_longest spam
1            1                         61    1
4000         0                         26    0
```

---

5. What happens if $\beta_k = 0$? Nothing!

Notice that email #1, which contained the word *free* and had a block of 61 capitalized letters, was tagged as spam. Email #4000, with its more modest sequence of 26 capital letters, is not spam.

Logistic regression is easy in R: you use the glm command as you would for linear regression, except that the response is now binary and you add the argument family='binomial'. The response variable can take a number of forms: numeric (0/1), logical (TRUE/FALSE), factor (e.g., win/lose), or even a two-column binary matrix. In the email data, we have $y = 1$ for spam and $y = 0$ for important emails.

```
> spammy <- glm(spam ~ ., data=email, family='binomial')
```

Note that the formula "y ~." is shorthand for "regress y on to all variables in the data." Take a look at one of the large positive coefficients in our fit:

```
> coef(spammy)["word_free"]
 word_free
  1.542706
> exp(1.542)
[1] 4.673929
```

Thus, the *odds* that an email is spam increase almost 5 times if that email contains the word free. On the other hand, we see next that if the email contains the word george, the odds of it being spam drop by a factor larger than 300.

```
> coef(spammy)["word_george"]
 word_george
   -5.779841
> 1/exp(-5.78)
[1] 323.7592
```

This is an old dataset collected from the inbox of a guy named George. Spammers were not very sophisticated in the 1990s, so emails containing your name were most likely not spam.

When you run the spam regression, R warns that fitted probabilities numerically 0 or 1 occurred. You need not worry: this just says that the regression is able to fit some data points *exactly*—for example, a spam email is modeled as having a 100% probability of being spam. This situation is called *perfect separation*; it can mess with your standard errors but is largely benign. It is a symptom of *overfit*, which is covered in Chapter 3.

As with linear regression, prediction for logistic regression is easy after you've fit the model with glm. We call the predict function on our fitted glm object and provide some newdata, with the same variable names as the training data, at the locations where we want to predict. The output will be $x'\hat{\beta}$ for each row $x$ of mynewdata.

```
> predict (spammy, newdata=email[c(1,4000),])
        1        4000
 2.029963   -1.726788
```

Of course, these are *not* probabilities. To get those, you need to transform through the logit link as $e^{x'\hat{\beta}}/(1 + e^{x'\hat{\beta}})$. R's predict function lets you add the type='response' argument to get predictions on the scale of the response (i.e., in [0, 1] probability space).

```
> predict(spammy, newdata=email[c(1,4000),], type='response')
        1        4000
 0.8839073   0.1509989
```

The first email (true spam) has an 88% chance of being spam, while email #4000 (not spam) has a 15% chance of being spam—in other words, an 85% chance of being important email that George wants to read.

Logistic regression is very similar to linear regression. You still use glm, and you just need to adjust your thinking to odds instead of means. In the next section, we introduce the important ideas of deviance and likelihood, which tie the estimation techniques behind linear and logistic regression together into a single framework. Gaining this unified view is essential for our later work on penalized models and machine learning.

## Deviance and Likelihood

When you call the summary function on a fitted glm object, you get back a lot of information about the estimated coefficients as well as some information about overall model fit (e.g., the fit illustrated visually in Figure 2.9). The model fit information

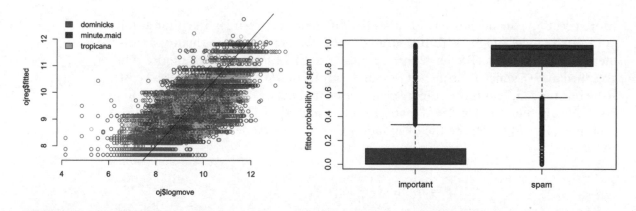

**FIGURE 2.9:** Fit plots, of $\hat{y}$ versus $y$, for both our OJ linear regression (left) and the spam logistic regression (right). Since the true $y$ is binary for spam, we give a boxplot rather than a scatterplot. In general, it is a good practice to plot $\hat{y}$ versus $y$ as a check for model misspecification and other problems. As a test of your intuition, imagine what a *perfect* fit (i.e., $\hat{y} = y$) would look like for each of these regressions.

at the bottom, which is the same for both linear and logistic regression, is especially useful. For example, here is our *linear* OJ regression:

```
summary(oj reg) ...
(Dispersion parameter for gaussian family taken to be 0.48)
    Null deviance: 30079 on 28946 degrees of freedom
Residual deviance: 13975 on 28935 degrees of freedom
AIC: 61094
```

And our spam regression:

```
summary(spammy) ...
(Dispersion parameter for binomial family taken to be 1)
    Null deviance: 6170.2 on 4600 degrees of freedom
Residual deviance: 1548.7 on 4543 degrees of freedom
AIC: 1664.7
```

What are these statistics? We need to introduce two complementary concepts:

- *Likelihood* is the probability of your data given parameters. You want to make it as big as possible.

- *Deviance* measures to the distance between data and fit. You want to make it as small as possible.

These two quantities are mirror images of each other, and they are tied together through a mathematical relationship:

$$\text{Deviance} = -2\log[\text{Likelihood}] + C. \tag{2.17}$$

More precisely, the deviance is –2 times the difference between log likelihoods for your fitted model and for a "fully saturated" model where you have as many parameters as observations. The term corresponding to this fully saturated model gets wrapped into $C$, which is a constant we can mostly ignore. We view deviance as a cost to be minimized. This is the guiding principle behind the way we estimate our models. Ignoring the complexities of model selection and regularization (next chapter), and using lhd($\beta$) to denote the likelihood function, our model coefficients are fit to achieve

$$\hat{\beta} = \operatorname{argmin}\left\{-\frac{2}{n}\log \operatorname{lhd}(\beta)\right\}. \tag{2.18}$$

Because of the relationship between deviance and likelihood, this deviance minimization strategy is commonly referred to as *maximum likelihood estimation* (MLE).

Let's work through an example with linear regression and Gaussian (normal) errors. The probability model is $y \sim N(x'\beta, \sigma^2)$, where the Gaussian probability density function is

$$N(x'\beta, \sigma^2) = \frac{1}{\sqrt{2\pi\sigma^2}} \exp\left[-\frac{(y - x'\beta)^2}{2\sigma^2}\right]. \tag{2.19}$$

Given *n* *independent* observations,[6] the likelihood (i.e., the probability of the data) is

$$\prod_{i=1}^{n} p(y_i \mid x_i) = \prod_{i=1}^{n} N(y_i; x_i'\beta, \sigma^2) = (2\pi\sigma^2)^{-\frac{n}{2}} \exp\left[-\frac{1}{2\sigma^2}\sum_{i=1}^{n}(y_i - x_i'\beta)^2\right]. \tag{2.20}$$

Using Equation 2.17, this leads to the following deviance:

$$\text{dev}(\beta) \propto \sum_{i=1}^{n}(y_i - x_i'\beta)^2. \tag{2.21}$$

Here, the $\propto$ symbol denotes "proportional to"—in other words, ignoring multiplicative and additive terms that do not depend upon $\beta$.[7]

Looking at Equation 2.21, we see that to minimize the deviance we need to minimize the *sum of squared errors*. The deviance minimizing estimates for $\beta$—the MLE—are exactly the *least-squares* estimates. Thus, "standard" or normal linear regression is a synonym for the common procedure of ordinary least-squares (OLS) regression.[8]

Given that deviance minimization for a linear regression is the same as least squares regression, why bother to introduce the extra concepts of likelihood and deviance? It's because these concepts apply also to alternative probability models—like the model behind logistic regression. For binary response with probabilities $p_i = p(y_i = 1)$, the likelihood is

$$\text{lhd} = \prod_{i=1}^{n} p(y_i \mid x_i) = \prod_{i=1}^{n} p_i^{y_i}(1 - p_i)^{1-y_i}. \tag{2.22}$$

Using our logistic regression equation for $p_i$, this becomes

$$\text{lhd}(\beta) = \prod_{i=1}^{n}\left(\frac{\exp[x_i'\beta]}{1 + \exp[x_i'\beta]}\right)^{y_i}\left(\frac{1}{1 + \exp[x_i'\beta]}\right)^{1-y_i}. \tag{2.23}$$

---

6. Recall that independent random variables have the property that $p(y_1, \ldots, y_n) = p(y_1) \times p(y_1) \times \ldots p(y_n)$. Thus, your likelihood is a *product* of the probabilities for each independent observation.

7. The negative log likelihood, which is also a function of $\sigma^2$, is proportional to $n\log(\sigma^2) + \sum_{i=1}^{n}\frac{1}{\sigma^2}(y_i - x_i'\beta)^2$.

8. Economists, in particular, prefer the OLS terminology. We will use both OLS and MLE terms.

Taking log and multiplying by –2 gives you the logistic regression deviance:

$$\text{dev}(\boldsymbol{\beta}) = -2 \sum_{i=1}^{n} \left( y_i \log(p_i) + (1 - y_i) \log(1 - p_i) \right)$$

$$\propto \sum_{i=1}^{n} \left[ \log\left(1 + e^{x_i'\beta}\right) - y_i x_i' \boldsymbol{\beta} \right]. \tag{2.24}$$

This is the function that `glm` minimizes for logistic regression.

The summary for `glm` outputs two types of deviance:

```
> summary(spammy)...
(Dispersion parameter for binomial family taken to be 1)
    Null deviance: 6170.2 on 4600 degrees of freedom
Residual deviance: 1548.7 on 4543 degrees of freedom
AIC: 1931.8
```

The *residual deviance*—say, $D = \text{dev}(\hat{\boldsymbol{\beta}})$—is the deviance for the fitted model as in Equation 2.21 or 2.24. It is what `glm` has fit $\hat{\boldsymbol{\beta}}$ to minimize. The *null deviance*—say, $D_0 = \text{dev}(\boldsymbol{\beta} = 0)$—is the deviance for a "null" or basic model,[9] where all of the $\beta_j = 0$. That is, the null deviance corresponds to the model where you don't use $x$ and instead just set $\hat{y}_i = \bar{y}$:

- $D_0 = \Sigma (y_i - \bar{y})^2$ in linear regression;

- $D_0 = -2 \Sigma [y_i \log(\bar{y}) + (1 - y_i) \log(1 - \bar{y})]$ in logistic regression.

The difference between $D$ and $D_0$ is due to information contained in the covariates. An important metric of how tightly your regression fits is the *proportion of deviance explained by* $x$, commonly labeled the $R^2$:

$$R^2 = \frac{D_0 - D}{D_0} = 1 - \frac{D}{D_0}. \tag{2.25}$$

This measures how much response variability you are able to model as a function of the regression inputs. In these two examples,

- Spammy: $R^2 = 1 - \dfrac{1549}{6170} = 0.75$ and

- ojreg: $R^2 = 1 - \dfrac{13975}{30079} = 0.54$,

so that our inputs are able to explain about ½ and ¾ of the variation in spam occurrence and OJ sales, respectively.

---

9. This language comes from the idea of a null hypothesis.

These $R^2$ formulas might look familiar. From Equation 2.21, the linear regression deviance is just the sum of squares. This means that the residual (or fit) deviance is the common sum-squared-errors statistic (SSE) and the null deviance is the sum-squared-total (SST). Thus, *for linear regression only,*

$$R^2 = 1 - \frac{\text{SSE}}{\text{SST}}, \tag{2.26}$$

as in the familiar $R^2$ formula from an introductory statistics class.[10] The advantage of re-expressing this $R^2$ in terms of deviance is that it is now a more general fit statistic that applies to *almost any machine learning model.* You can think of deviance as a useful generalization of squared-errors for more flexible modeling.

There are two additional statistics on the summary output for glm that we need to discuss. Look again at the glm summary:

```
> summary(ojreg)...
(Dispersion parameter for gaussian family taken to be 0.48)
Null deviance: 30079 on 28946 degrees of freedom
Residual deviance: 13975 on 28935 degrees of freedom
AIC: 61094
```

The *dispersion parameter* is a measure of variability around the fitted conditional means. Basically, all you need to know is that for the Gaussian family (i.e., for linear regression) the dispersion parameter is an estimate for $\sigma^2$, your error variance. Hence, in the OJ regression, R has estimated the dispersion parameter by taking the variance of your fitted residuals:

$$\hat{\sigma}^2 = \text{var}(\varepsilon_i) = \text{var}(y_i - \boldsymbol{x}'\hat{\boldsymbol{\beta}}) = 0.48. \tag{2.27}$$

In logistic regression, there is no corresponding "error term," so R just outputs Dispersion parameter for binomial family taken to be 1. If you don't see this, then you might have forgotten to put "type=binomial."

The last term in the R output that needs to be defined is the "degrees of freedom." This is a confusing term here because what R calls degrees of freedom in this output is more properly the "residual degrees of freedom," defined as the number of observations minus the number of parameters. Throughout the rest of the book we will use *degrees of freedom* (df) to refer to the "model degrees of freedom": *the number of parameters in the model.* Hence, R's residual degrees of freedom refers to $n - df$ in the notation of this book.

---

10. You might also recall that $R^2 = \text{cor}(y, \hat{y})^2$ in linear regression, where $\hat{y}$ denotes "fitted value" $\hat{y} = f(\boldsymbol{x}'\hat{\boldsymbol{\beta}}) = \boldsymbol{x}'\hat{\boldsymbol{\beta}}$. This property is unique to linear regression.

## ◆ Regression Uncertainty

We are interested not just in the point-estimates of the regression parameters but also in the *uncertainty* around these estimates. The usual way people quantify uncertainty about regression coefficients is to simply trust the standard errors output by the software. These "standard" standard errors are OK for many purposes, so long as your model is close to representing the true data-generating process. However, the standard errors reported by R (and virtually every other software package) are sensitive to misspecification. That is, they are constructed using a theory that is reliant on the specified regression model being true. For example, in the linear regression case, the usual standard errors will be wrong if there are heteroskedastic errors—in other words, if there is not a shared $\sigma^2$ variance for all $\varepsilon_i$. And in both linear and logistic regression, the standard errors will be incorrect if there is any dependence between observations.

To get more robust standard errors, you need to make use of *nonparametric* methods that account for the possibility that the stated model is not quite a perfect fit. As covered in Chapter 1, one useful tool for this is the bootstrap, a strategy in which you resample the data (with replacement) and use the uncertainty across samples as an estimate of actual sampling variance. You can use a bootstrap to *nonparametrically* quantify the uncertainty associated with regression coefficients. Figure 2.9, for example, compared parametric and nonparametric uncertainty estimates for the coefficient on an indicator for broadband access when predicting online spending.

In the special case of OLS regression—i.e., linear regression—there are also a number of theoretical tools you can use to obtain robust standard errors. One of the most important and useful is the class of so-called *sandwich* variance estimators. Consider a multivariate representation of our linear regression distribution:

$$y \sim N(X\beta, \Sigma). \tag{2.28}$$

Here, $X\beta$ is matrix-vector multiplication yielding a vector with elements $\hat{y}_i = x_i'\beta$, the conditional mean in linear regression.[11] In our usual *homoskedastic* linear regression setup, the conditional variance matrix is $\Sigma = \sigma^2 I$ (i.e., all zeros except for $\sigma^2$ along the diagonal), and every observation is assumed independent with the same error variance. Leaving $\Sigma$ unspecified in Equation 2.28 allows for *generalization* of our usual regression setup to scenarios with different error structures.

The *sandwich* variance estimators are built around the result that, for the model in Equation 2.28, the sampling variance of the regression coefficients can be written as

$$\mathrm{var}(\hat{\beta}) = (X'X)^{-1}X'\Sigma X(X'X)^{-1}. \tag{2.29}$$

---

11. Note that here $X$ includes the intercept.

This has the error variance, $\Sigma$, "sandwiched" by the projection $X(X'X)^{-1}$. To intuit where this comes from, expand the usual OLS formula for estimated coefficients:

$$\hat{\beta} = (X'X)^{-1} X' y = (X'X)^{-1} X'(\mathbb{E}[y] + \varepsilon) = \beta + (X'X)^{-1} X'\varepsilon. \tag{2.30}$$

Here, $\hat{\beta}$ is the vector of true coefficients plus an error term multiplied by this $X(X'X)^{-1}$ projection. Standard results then have that $\mathrm{var}(a'\varepsilon) = a'\mathrm{var}(\varepsilon)a$ for fixed vector $a$ and random $\varepsilon$, yielding Equation 2.29.

Consider the usual homoskedastic model, where $\Sigma = \sigma^2 I$. In that case, Equation 2.29 becomes $\sigma^2 (X'X)^{-1}(X'X) (X'X)^{-1} = \sigma^2(X'X)^{-1}$, the standard formula for OLS sampling variance (this is the formula R uses to get its standard errors). Moving to a more general model, you can use Equation 2.29 to quantify uncertainty in the common *heteroskedastic* scenario where each observation has a different error variance. That is, where $\Sigma = \mathrm{diag}(\sigma^2) = \mathrm{diag}([\sigma_1^2, \sigma_2^2, \ldots, \sigma_n^2])$ with a different diagonal entry for each observation. The *heteroskedastic consistent* [12] (HC) standard errors are constructed by replacing $\Sigma$ in Equation 2.29 with an estimate that allows for such heteroskedasticity:

$$\hat{\Sigma}_{\mathrm{HC}} = \begin{bmatrix} e_1^2 & 0 & & \\ 0 & e_2^2 & & \\ & & \ddots & 0 \\ & & 0 & e_n^2 \end{bmatrix}. \tag{2.31}$$

Here, $e_i = y_i - x_i' \hat{\beta}$ are your fitted regression residuals. The HC procedure uses these squared residuals as an estimate of observation-specific variance $\sigma_i^2$ to get standard errors that allow for such heteroskedasticity.

The AER package can be used to obtain HC standard errors with little effort. Consider a little example using data on air pollution in New York. The data include daily measurements on parts-per-billion (ppb) ozone from May 1 to September 30, 1973. For this example, we'll look at the effect of the wind (measured in miles per hour, or MPH) on ozone while controlling for temperature and solar radiation (amount of sunshine). Running a simple OLS regression, we find that an extra MPH of wind leads to a drop of three ppb ozone with a standard error of 0.65.

```
> data(airquality)
> fit <- glm(Ozone ~ ., data=airquality)
> summary(fit)$coef["Wind",]
    Estimate     Std. Error        t value        Pr(>|t|)
-3.318444e+00  6.445095e-01  -5.148789e+00   1.231276e-06
```

The vcovHC function in AER just takes the fitted glm (or lm) object as input and returns an estimate of $\mathrm{var}(\hat{\beta})$ that is robust to heteroskedasticity:

12.  Halbert White. A heteroskedasticity-consistent covariance matrix estimator and a direct test for heteroskedasticity. *Econometrica: Journal of the Econometric Society*, pages 817–838, 1980.

```
> library(AER)
> bvar <- vcovHC(fit)
> round (bvar, 1)
           (Intercept) Solar.R  Wind  Temp  Month   Day
(Intercept)      432.9     0.1 -13.3  -3.6   -3.2   0.3
Solar.R            0.1     0.0   0.0   0.0    0.0   0.0
Wind             -13.3     0.0   0.8   0.1   -0.2  -0.1
Temp              -3.6     0.0   0.1   0.1   -0.1   0.0
Month             -3.2     0.0  -0.2  -0.1    1.8   0.0
Day                0.3     0.0  -0.1   0.0    0.0   0.1
```

This is the sampling *covariance* matrix of the coefficients; variances are along the diagonal. To get the standard error, which is the sampling *standard deviation*, you need to take the square root of the diagonal variance estimate.

```
> sqrt(bvar["Wind","Wind"])
[1] 0.9128877
```

This is *much larger* (about 40% larger) than the standard error of 0.645 from the R output. The assumption of homoskedasticty yields an artificially small uncertainty estimate. To see why this happens, consider the fitted residuals shown in Figure 2.10: the heteroskedasticity is clear, with much larger residuals occurring on low-wind days.

The HC standard errors are useful, and you will use them often. There is also an interesting relationship between HC standard errors and the bootstrap. It turns out that, for OLS, the parameter variance estimates you get from the nonparametric bootstrap are actually *approximated* by the HC procedure.[13] That is, you can use the HC standard errors as a fast alternative to bootstrapping for OLS. This relationship also implies that the assumption of the normal distribution in Equation 2.28 is not especially important for the HC standard errors—they are robust to deviations from Gaussianity in the errors. To illustrate, we can run a quick bootstrap on the airquality data.

```
> B <- 10000
> beta <- vector (length=B)
> n <- nrow(airquality)
> for (b in 1:B) {
```

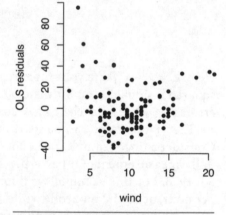

**FIGURE 2.10:** Fitted residuals from the airquality OLS regression.

13. Dale J Poirier. Bayesian interpretations of heteroskedastic consistent covariance estimators using the informed Bayesian bootstrap. *Econometric Reviews*, 30(4): 457–468, 2011.

```
+     bs = sample.int (n,n,replace=TRUE)
+     bsfit <- lm(Ozone ~., data=airquality, subset=bs)
+     beta[b] <- coef(bsfit) ["Wind"]}
> sd(beta)
[1] 0.8753398
```

To a first decimal place, the standard error matches that of the HC procedure. The sampling distributions are illustrated in Figure 2.11.

All of the uncertainty estimators discussed so far—all of those shown in Figure 2.11—assume independence between observations. The HC procedure, for example, keeps zeros on the off diagonals in $\hat{\Sigma}$. There are additional procedures and tools you can use in the case of *dependence* between observations. Sandwich estimators that allow for dependence, sometimes called *clustered standard errors*, will be discussed in Chapter 5; these techniques are commonly used when estimating treatment effects in randomized controlled trials. You can also deal with dependence by *modeling* it in your regression, making the dependence between observations explicit by including them in each other's mean functions. In the next section, we discuss how to model such dependence in the specific context of spatial and temporal processes.

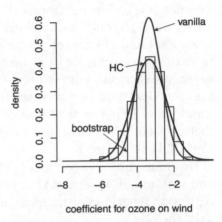

**FIGURE 2.11:** Estimated sampling distributions for the wind coefficient in our airquality regression. HC denotes the heteroskedastic consistent procedure, and *vanilla* refers to the usual results that rely upon homoskedasticity.

## Space and Time

Much of the material in this book is focused on *independent* observations. For example, independence was key in our development of deviance and likelihood in the previous section. However, many events that occur geographically near to each other, or one after the other, can be *dependent*. For example, maybe sales are always higher in spring/summer, or when one restaurant has a busy night, the neighboring restaurants also gain traffic from those who couldn't get a table. In this section we'll figure out how to deal with such information.

Fortunately, the main tricks for working with space-time dependence fit within a standard regression framework. You simply include the variables behind dependence in your set of inputs, controlling for trends in time (e.g., month) and space (e.g., regional location) and for auto-regression, which is dependence between neighboring outcomes.

Traditional statistics texts spend a large amount of time carefully hand-building these trend and autoregressive effects. Fortunately, the regularization and model selection material of later chapters lets us simply include a huge set of possible space/time variables and rely upon the data to tell us what works best. Thus, the remainder of this section will focus on helping you understand the universe of space-time effects rather than telling you how to choose among them.

As a simple example, consider the series of monthly total international airline passengers shown in Figure 2.12. We see an increasing monthly oscillation around an upward trend. If we want to do *linear* regression and it appears that noise is increasing over time, we likely need a transformation. Passenger numbers are like sales volume—they are always positive and are often discussed in percentage terms. This suggests that we should be working on the log scale. Indeed, Figure 2.13 shows that log passenger volume has a roughly constant oscillation and a plausibly linear trend.

Including time as a continuous variable $t$ (i.e., date $1, 2, 3, \ldots$) and with month $m_t$ denoting the calendar month at time $t$, a regression model that includes a *linear time trend* and *monthly fixed effects* is

$$\log(y_t) = \alpha + \beta_t t + \beta_{m_t} + \varepsilon_t.$$

We can use glm to fit this in R, after creating a time variable and factorizing the months:

```
month <- factor(airline$Month)
time <- (year-min(year))*12 + airline$Month
air <- glm(log(passengers) ~ time + month)
```

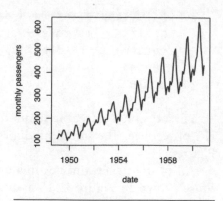

**FIGURE 2.12:** International air passengers.

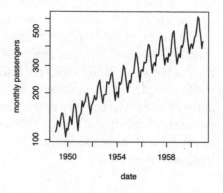

**FIGURE 2.13:** Same counts on log scale.

Figure 2.14 shows the fitted values for this regression. It seems that the linear trend and month effects do a nice job of summarizing the passenger traffic (on log scale).

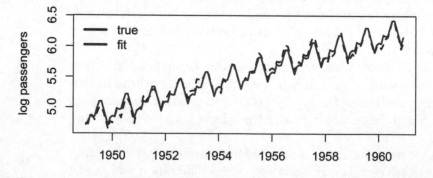

**FIGURE 2.14:** Airline passenger regression.

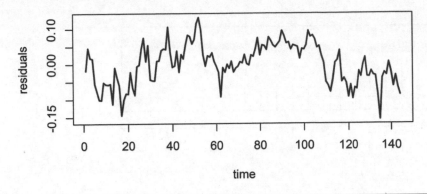

**FIGURE 2.15:** Log-count residuals from our passenger regression.

Now de-trending is easy. If your data include dates, then you should create indicator variables for, say, each year, month, and day. The most important thing to remember is to *proceed hierarchically*: if you are going to include an effect for may-1981, then you should also include broader effects for may and for 1981. This allows the model to use the latter effects as baselines, and the may-1981 effect will only summarize deviations from this base. In the language of Chapter 3, may-1981 will be "shrunk" toward baseline levels for may and 1981. The same logic applies for space: if you condition on counties, then you should also include broader state and region effects.

A more subtle issue is that of *autocorrelation*. Consider the residuals for the passenger regression shown in Figure 2.15. There appears to be stickiness in the series: when residuals are high in one month, they are often high the next month. The errors appear correlated in time, such that $\varepsilon_t$ is related to $\varepsilon_{t-1}$. That relationship violates our basic *independence* assumption, which holds that $\varepsilon_i \perp\!\!\!\perp \varepsilon_j$ for all $j \neq i$.

This phenomenon is called *autocorrelation*: correlation with yourself. Time-series data is simply a collection of observations gathered over time. For example, suppose $y_1 \ldots y_T$ are weekly sales, daily temperatures, or five-minute stock returns. In each case, you might expect what happens at time $t$ to be correlated with time $t - 1$. For example, suppose you measure temperatures daily for several years. Which would work better as an estimate for today's temperature:

- The average of the temperatures from the previous year?

- The temperature on the previous day?

In most cases, yesterday's temperature is most informative. That means you view the *local* dependence as more important than the broad annual pattern.

You can summarize dependence with an autocorrelation function (ACF) that tracks "lag-$l$" correlations:

$$\mathrm{acf}(l) = \mathrm{cor}(\varepsilon_t, \varepsilon_{t-l}). \tag{2.32}$$

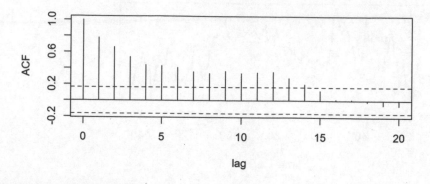

**FIGURE 2.16:** ACF for the residual time series shown in Figure 2.15. Note that acf(0) = 1 because this is the correlation between $y_t$ and itself. The dashed lines are heuristics for "big" correlations.

Figure 2.16 shows the ACF for our airline regression residuals. It confirms our visual inspection of the residual time series: there is significant dependence. The correlation between $y_t$ and $y_{t-1}$ is around 0.8, which is pretty huge.

How do you model this type of data? Consider a simple cumulative error process:

$$y_1 = \varepsilon_1,$$
$$y_2 = \varepsilon_1 + \varepsilon_2,$$
$$y_3 = \varepsilon_1 + \varepsilon_2 + \varepsilon_3 + \dots.$$

Each $y_t$ is a function of every previous observation all the way back to time zero. Fortunately,

$$y_t = \sum_{i=1}^{t} \varepsilon_i = y_{t-1} + \varepsilon_t,$$

so all you need to know to predict at $t$ is what happened at $t - 1$. More specifically, in this process we have $\mathbb{E}[y_t \,|\, y_{t-1}] = y_{t-1}$. This is called a *random walk* model for $y_t$: the expectation of what will happen is always what happened most recently.

Random walks are one version of a general *autoregressive* (AR) model. In an autoregressive model of order 1, the following holds:

$$AR(1): y_t = \beta_0 + \beta_1 y_{t-1} + \varepsilon_t. \qquad (2.33)$$

This is simply $y_t$ regressed onto lagged $y_{t-1}$. The random walk corresponds to $\beta_1 = 1$, and nonzero $\beta_0$ is then referred to as *drift*. To fit the AR(1) model, you need to create lagged versions of your response and then include them in the regressions. This usually requires removing the first observation from your training data. For example, we can rerun the airline regression including an AR(1) term:

```
> lag <- head(log(passengers), -1) # see help(head)
> passengers <- passengers [-1]
> month <- month [ - 1]
> time <- time [-1]
> summary(airAR <- glm(log(passengers) ~ time + month + lag))
...
lag            0.7930716  0.0548993  14.446  < 2e-16  ***
```

Figure 2.17 shows the resulting residuals and their ACF plot. Now, everything looks nice and linear. It appears the single lag term solved all of our autocorrelation problems.

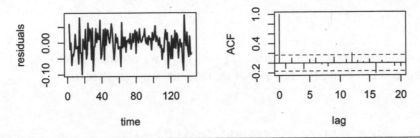

**FIGURE 2.17:** Airline residuals after including an AR(1) term.

The AR(1) model is simple but hugely powerful. If you have any suspicion of autocorrelation, it is a good move to include lagged response as a covariate. The coefficient on this lag gives you important information about the time-series properties:

- If $|\beta_1| = 1$, you have a random walk.
- If $|\beta_1| > 1$, the series explodes.
- If $|\beta_1| < 1$, the values are mean reverting.

In a random walk, the series just wanders around, and the autocorrelation stays high for a long time (see Figures 2.18 and 2.19). More precisely, the series is nonstationary: it has no average level that it wants to be near but rather diverges off into space. For example, consider the monthly Dow Jones Average (DJA) composite index from 2000 to 2007, shown in Figure 2.20. The DJA appears as though it is just wandering around. Sure enough, the regression fit looks like a random walk with $\beta_1 \approx 1$:

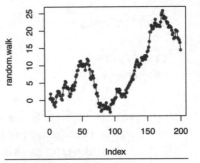

**FIGURE 2.18:** A random walk.

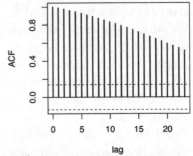

**FIGURE 2.19:** ACF for a random walk.

```
> summary(ARdj <- glm(dja[2:n] ~ dja[1: (n-1)]))
...
Coefficients:
                  Estimate  Std. Error  t value  Pr(>|t|)
(Intercept)       7.05419   4.00385     1.762    0.0782 .
dja[1: (n - 1)]   0.99764   0.00121     824.298  <2e - 16 ***
```

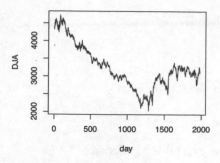
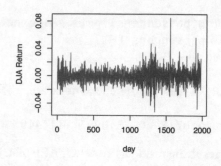

**FIGURE 2.20:** Dow Jones Average.

However, when we switch from prices to returns, $(y_t - y_{t-1})/y_{t-1}$, we get data that looks more like white noise. Rerunning the regression on returns, we find that the AR(1) term is not significant:

```
> returns <- (dja[2:n]-dja [1:(n-1)])/dja[1:(n-1)]
> summary( glm(returns[2:n] ~ returns[1: (n-1)]) )
....
Coefficients:
                   Estimate Std. Error t value Pr(>|t|)
(Intercept)      -0.0001138  0.0002363  -0.482    0.630
returns[1:(n - 1)] -0.0144411  0.0225321  -0.641    0.522
```

This property is implied by the series being a random walk: the *differences* between $y_t$ and $y_{t-1}$ are independent. If you have a random walk, you should perform this returns transformation to obtain something that is easier to model.

For AR(1) terms larger than one, life is more complicated. This case results in what is called an *exploding* series because the $y_t$ values move exponentially far from $y_1$. For example, Figure 2.21 shows how quickly the observations diverge even for $\beta_1 = 1.02$, very close to one. Since these series explode, they are useless for modeling and prediction. If you run a regression and find such an AR(1) term, you are likely missing a trend variable that needs to be included in your regression.

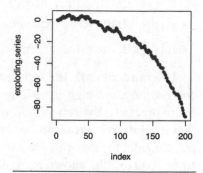

**FIGURE 2.21:** An exploding series with AR(1) coefficient $\beta_1 = 1.02$.

Finally, the most interesting series have AR(1) terms between −1 and 1. These series are called *stationary* because $y_t$ is always pulled back toward the mean. These are the most common, and most useful, type of AR series. The past matters in a stationary series, but with limited horizon and the autocorrelation drops off rapidly (see Figures 2.22, 2.23, and 2.24).

An important property of stationary series is mean reversion. Think about shifting both $y_t$ and $y_{t-1}$ by their mean $\mu$:

$$y_t - \mu = \beta_1 (y_{t-1} - \mu) + \varepsilon_t.$$

Since $|\beta_1| < 1$, $y_t$ is expected to be closer to $\mu$ than $y_{t-1}$. Mean reversion is common, and you can use it to predict future behavior.

It is also possible to expand the AR idea to higher lags:

$$AR(p) : Y_t = \beta_0 + \beta_1 Y_{t-1} + \ldots \beta_p Y_{t-p} + \varepsilon.$$

The drawback of considering high-order autoregression has always been that hypothesis testing breaks down as a method for selecting the appropriate lags to include (because of multicollinearity). However, the model selection methods of Chapter 3 make it straight-forward to let the data choose the appropriate lags. Using those tools, you can feel free to consider bigger $p$ in your $AR(p)$. The only problem is that the simple interpretations for $\beta_1$ no longer apply if you include higher lags. In addition, the need for higher lags sometimes indicates that you are missing a more persistent trend or periodicity in the data.

Finally, what about space? Space is just like time, but with another dimension. We've already discussed de-trending with geographic effects. To deal with spatial auto-dependence, you simply include $y_s$ for $s$ that is nearby your modeled location. For example, you can condition on the average for neighboring states in a map or the average of the neighboring pixels in an image. These models are referred to as spatial autoregressive (SAR) models, and as in temporal AR you can deal with most dependencies by including only the immediate neighbors. We won't cover this technique in detail, but you should explore SAR modeling using, for example, the California housing data that we work with in Chapter 9. Also in Chapter 9, we outline the Gaussian Process (GP) models that are commonly used for modeling spatially dependent data. To model SAR using a GP you simply add "space" (e.g., latitude and longitude) as an input to the GP regression function.

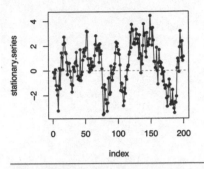

**FIGURE 2.22:** A stationary (i.e., mean-reverting) time series with $\beta_1 = 0.8$.

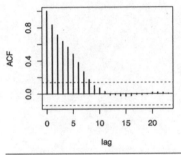

**FIGURE 2.23:** Stationary series ACF.

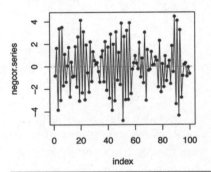

**FIGURE 2.24:** A stationary series with $\beta_1 = -0.8$. It is possible to have negatively correlated AR(1) series, but you will see these far less often in practice.

# Regularization

## 3

I n high-dimensional settings, where you have many possible signals that can be included in your model, you need to be careful to select the best model for predicting *future* data and avoid overfit. To do this, you first use recipes that provide a good array of candidate models. You then select among these candidates to minimize estimates for the error rate when predicting on new data. This chapter introduces the key tools for such high-dimensional modeling.

## Out-of-Sample Performance

In the previous chapter, we introduced *deviance* as a measure of how tightly your model fits the training data. When you apply your models for prediction and decision-making, you don't actually care about the *in-sample* deviance. All that matters is the *out-of-sample* (OOS) deviance; in other words, how easy does your model fit *new* data?

The only $R^2$ you ever really care about is out-of-sample $R^2$. The difference between *in-* and *out*-of-sample $R^2$ is what data is used to fit $\hat{\boldsymbol{\beta}}$ and what the deviances are calculated on. Suppose that you have data $[\boldsymbol{x}_1, y_1] \ldots [\boldsymbol{x}_n, y_n]$ and you use this data to fit $\hat{\boldsymbol{\beta}}$ in a linear regression. The in-sample deviance is then

$$\mathrm{dev}_{IS}(\hat{\boldsymbol{\beta}}) = \sum_{i=1}^{n}(y_i - \boldsymbol{x}_i'\hat{\boldsymbol{\beta}})^2. \tag{3.1}$$

For out-of-sample $R^2$, $\hat{\boldsymbol{\beta}}$ is the same (still fit with observations $1 \ldots n$), but the deviance is now calculated over new observations; for example:

$$\mathrm{dev}_{OOS}(\hat{\boldsymbol{\beta}}) = \sum_{i=n+1}^{n+m} (y_i - \boldsymbol{x}_i'\hat{\boldsymbol{\beta}})^2.$$

This distinction is massively important. When you have big data and many inputs, it is easy to *overfit* the training data so that your model is being driven by noise that will not be replicated in future observations. That adds errors to your predictions, and it is possible that the overfit model becomes worse than no model at all.

As an example, let's consider quality-control data from a semi-conductor manufacturing process. This industrial setting involves many complicated operations with little margin for error. There are hundreds of diagnostic sensors along the production line, measuring various inputs and outputs in the process. Our goal is to build a model that maps from this sensor data to a prediction for chip failure. Then chips at risk of failure can be flagged for further (expensive, human) inspection.

For training data we have 1500 observations of a length-200 vector $\boldsymbol{x}$ of diagnostic signals, along with binary data on whether the chip was a failure.[1]

The logistic regression model is then

$$p_i = \mathrm{p}(\mathtt{fail}_i | \boldsymbol{x}_i) = \frac{e^{\alpha + \boldsymbol{x}_i'\beta}}{(1 + e^{\alpha + \boldsymbol{x}_i'\beta})}. \tag{3.2}$$

We can fit this in R and calculate the *in-sample* deviance using `glm`.[2]

```
> full <- glm(FAIL ~ ., data=SC, family=binomial)
Warning message:
glm.fit: fitted probabilities numerically 0 or 1 occurred
> 1 - full$deviance/full$null.deviance
[1] 0.5621432
```

---

1. The $x_{ij}$ inputs here are actually orthogonal: they are the first 200 Principal Component directions from a bigger set (see Chapter 7 on factorization).
2. When you run this in R you will get the same perfect fit warning you had for spam regression. Recall that this is possibly symptomatic of overfit.

We see that this regression has an $R^2$ of 56%—more than half of the variation in failure versus success is explained by the 200 diagnostic signals. Note that, since this is logistic regression, this $R^2$ uses the binomial deviance from Equation 2.24.

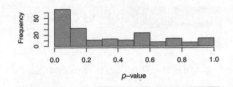

**FIGURE 3.1:** Histogram of $p$-values for the semiconductor regression coefficients.

Figure 3.1 shows the distribution of the 200 $p$-values for tests of null hypothesis $\beta_k = 0$ in our semiconductor regression. Recall from our FDR discussion in Chapter 1 that $p$-values from the null have a uniform distribution; in contrast, here we see a spike near zero (indicating useful diagnostic signals), while the remainder sprawl out toward one (most likely useless signals for failure prediction). You can use the Benjamini – Hochberg algorithm to obtain a smaller model with controlled false discovery rate (FDR; see Chapter 1). Figure 3.2 illustrates the procedure for an FDR of 10%. This yields an $\alpha = 0.0122$ $p$-value rejection cutoff and implies 25 significant regression coefficients (of which you expect 22 to 23 are true signals).

We can identify these 25 significant signals and rerun glm on only those variables, yielding a much more parsimonious model.

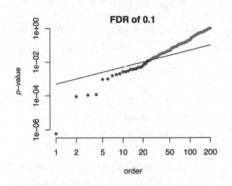

**FIGURE 3.2:** FDR for the semiconductor $p$-values. The points below the line are the 25 $\beta_k$ that are significant with an FDR of 10%.

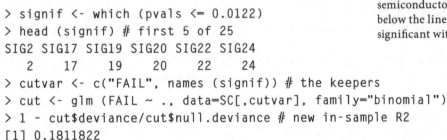

```
> signif <- which (pvals <= 0.0122)
> head (signif) # first 5 of 25
SIG2 SIG17 SIG19 SIG20 SIG22 SIG24
   2    17    19    20    22    24
> cutvar <- c("FAIL", names (signif)) # the keepers
> cut <- glm (FAIL ~ ., data=SC[,cutvar], family="binomial")
> 1 - cut$deviance/cut$null.deviance # new in-sample R2
[1] 0.1811822
```

Notice that the *cut* model, using only 25 signals, has $R^2_{cut} = 0.18$. This is much smaller than the *full* model's $R^2_{full} = 0.56$. In general, the *in-sample $R^2$ always increases with more covariates*. This in-sample $R^2$ is exactly what MLE $\hat{\beta}$ is fit to maximize, so if you give glm more knobs to turn (more $\hat{\beta}_k$'s), then it will be able to get you a tighter fit. This is exactly why we don't care about IS $R^2$—it can be made to look arbitrarily good just by adding junk variables to the design. The real question is, how well does each model predict *new* data?

Of course, you can't know about performance on unseen data because you don't have it. However, you can mimic the experience of predicting on unseen data by evaluating your models on data that was left out of the training sample. Algorithm 4 details the experiment.

---

| ALGORITHM 4 | *K*-Fold Out-of-Sample (OOS) Validation |

---

Given a dataset of $n$ observations, $\{[\boldsymbol{x}_i, y_i]\}_{i=1}^n$:

- Split the data into $K$ evenly sized random subsets (*folds*).

- For $k = 1 \ldots K$:

  - Fit the coefficients $\hat{\boldsymbol{\beta}}$ using all but the $k$th fold of data.

  - Record $R^2$ on the left-out $k$th fold.

This will yield a sample of $K$ OOS $R^2$ values. This sample is an *estimate* of the distribution of your model's predictive performance on new data.

---

For the semiconductor data, we can do OOS validation on both the *full* and *cut* regression models. To do this, we first need to define some functions to calculate deviance and $R^2$.

```
> ## pred must be probabilities (0<pred<1) for binomial
> deviance <- function (y, pred, family=c ("gaussian", "binomial")){
+     family <- match.arg (family)
+     if (family=="gaussian"){
+         return ( sum( (y-pred) ^2 ) )
+     }else{
+         if (is.factor(y)) y <- as.numeric (y)>1
+         return ( -2*sum( y*log(pred) + (1-y)*log(1-pred) ) )
+     }
+ }
>
> ## get null devaince too, and return R2
> R2 <- function(y, pred, family=c("gaussian","binomial")){
+     fam <- match.arg(family)
+     if (fam=="binomial"){
+         if (is.factor(y)){ y <- as.numeric(y)>1 }
+     }
+     dev <- deviance(y, pred, family=fam)
+     dev0 <- deviance(y, mean(y), family=fam)
+     return (1-dev/dev0)
+ }
```

These functions can be used for either linear or logistic regression. In later chapters you'll be using R package functions that have these deviance calculations as built-ins, but it is good to code them yourself once. Next, we split the data into folds.

```
> n <- nrow(SC) # the number of observations
> K <- 10 # the number of 'folds'
> # create a vector of fold memberships (random order)
> foldid <- rep(1:K,each=ceiling(n/K))[sample(1:n)]
> # create an empty dataframe of results
> OOS <- data.frame(full=rep(NA,K), cut=rep(NA,K))
```

Finally, we run the OOS experiment as a for loop.

```
> for(k in 1:K){
+       train <- which(foldid!=k) # train on all but fold 'k'
+
+       ## fit the two regressions
+       rfull <- glm(FAIL~., data=SC, subset=train, family=binomial)
+       rcut <- glm(FAIL~., data=SC[, cutvar], subset=train, family=binomial)
+
+       ## get predictions: type=response so we have probabilities
+       predfull <- predict(rfull, newdata=SC[-train,], type="response")
+       predcut <- predict(rcut, newdata=SC[-train,], type="response")
+
+       ## calculate and log R2
+       OOS$full[k] <- R2(y=SC$FAIL[-train], pred=predfull, family="binomial")
+       OOS$cut[k] <- R2(y=SC$FAIL[- train], pred=predcut, family="binomial")
+
+ ## print progress
+ cat(k, " ")
+ }
1  2  3  4  5  6  7  8  9  10
```

When we plot the resulting OOS $R^2$ samples, the results are striking. Figure 3.3 shows that the full model actually yields *negative $R^2$*! How can this happen? Look at the $R^2$ formula: $1 - \text{dev}(\hat{\beta})/\text{dev}(\beta = 0)$. The $R^2$ will be negative if your fitted model performs worse than the null model. That is, if your $\hat{y}$ estimates are further from the truth than the overall average, $\bar{y}$. In this application, you are better off simply throwing away every 15th chip instead of using some process based upon your overfit full model.

You may have never seen a negative $R^2$ before. If so, it is because you have been looking only at in-sample performance. Out-of-sample, negative $R^2$ are unfortunately more common

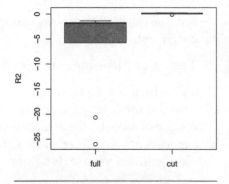

**FIGURE 3.3:** OOS $R^2$ for both full (200 signal) and cut (25 signal) semiconductor logistic regressions.

than you might expect. In this case, the average OOS $R^2$ are $-6.5$ for the full model (or $-650\%$) and a positive $0.09$ for the cut model. So, while the cut-model's performance is lower OOS than IS (about $1/2$), it still manages to do 9% better than the null.

This example is a dramatic demonstration of the basic principle: *all that matters is out-of-sample $R^2$*. You don't care about in-sample $R^2$, because you can get better numbers simply by adding junk variables and inducing overfit. Using OOS experiments to choose the best model is called *cross validation*. It will play a big role in this text, since using data in selection of "the best" model is at the core of all modern analytics. But before getting to selection, you first need strategies to build good sets of candidate models from which to choose.

> Note that **we've cheated here:** the full sample was used to choose the 25 variables that are in the cut model. A true OOS experiment would have done FDR control *inside* the `for` loop, such that the OOS results are a validation of the end-to-end selection procedure. As a general rule, for anything that you do to the data, do it without the left-out fold if you want to get an accurate assessment of OOS performance.

## Regularization Paths

How do you build sets of models? With any realistic input dimension, it is impossible to simply catalog all possible models. For example, if you have a regression setting with $p$ potential covariates, there are $2^p$ different models possible depending upon whether each covariate is included. With just 20 covariates, this implies already more than 1 million candidate models.

This section introduces the crucial idea of *regularization*: penalizing model complexity in such a way that you can enumerate a list of promising candidate models, ranging from simple to complex.

One common but crude approach to model selection is based upon $p$-values.

- Run the full MLE regression using `glm`, yielding $p$-values on each candidate input's coefficient.

- Then rerun `glm` using only those inputs whose $p$-values are below some $\alpha$ threshold.

Going further, one could use a sequence of $\alpha$ thresholds—perhaps corresponding to FDR rates as implied by the Benjamini–Hochberg FDR control algorithm—to generate a sequence of models. These models could then be compared in the sort of out-of-sample experiment you did earlier for semiconductors.

This common practice is a *bad* idea for a couple of reasons:

- When you have *multicollinearity*—correlation between inputs—the $p$-values for all of these variables will be large (they will look insignificant) even if any one of the variables provides a useful signal on the response. You will end up including none because you don't know which one of them should be included.

- The $p$-values are based on an overfit model. For example, in the semiconductor analysis, the $p$-values are estimated from a model that does far worse than $\bar{y}$ in prediction tasks. If you use these $p$-values, you will be building a set of candidate models on the foundation of a terrible regression fit. When $p > n$, there is no full model because glm will fail to converge.

This general approach—looking at a full model fit and then cutting it down to size—is sometimes called *backward stepwise regression*. You should avoid it.

A better solution is to proceed in the opposite direction, building from simplicity to complexity in a *forward stepwise regression*, as laid out in Algorithm 5.

---

**ALGORITHM 5** | **Forward Stepwise Regression**

---

- Fit all univariate models. Choose that with the highest in-sample $R^2$ and put that variable—say, $x_s$—in your model.

- Fit all bivariate models including $x_s$,

$$y \sim \beta_s x_s + \beta_j x_j \ \forall j \neq s,$$

and add $x_j$ from the one with highest $R^2$ to your model.

- Repeat: given current inclusion set of variables $S$, represented by the vector $\boldsymbol{x}_S$, fit all models,

$$y \sim \boldsymbol{\beta}_S' \boldsymbol{x}_S + \beta_j x_j \ \forall j \notin S,$$

and again add $j$ to $S$ for the $x_j$ that maximizes in-sample $R^2$.

You can either keep going until reaching a predetermined level of complexity or stop when some model selection rule (e.g., R uses the AIC that you will study later in this chapter) is lower for the current model than for any of the models that add one variable.

---

Algorithm 5 is our first example of a *greedy* search strategy. We proceed myopically, at each point adding the next iteration of complexity that seems most useful given the current search state. Despite not optimizing for *global* properties of the search path, greedy algorithms are fast and stable, and they play a prominent role in many ML strategies.

You will soon see that this specific forward stepwise procedure is a bit naive and that it can be improved upon dramatically via modern regularization ideas. But the general approach of proceeding forward in your search, from simplicity to complexity, is useful for a number of reasons. One big advantage is stability. A backward scheme is *unstable* because if you jitter the data slightly (or get a slightly different sample) the full complexity model can change dramatically (because it is overfit) and thus your entire search path of candidate models will change. In contrast, simple univariate or null models will remain roughly the same under data resampling, such that our *forward* search path is always starting in the same place.

R provides the step() function to execute this stepwise routine. You give a starting point, called the null model, and a biggest possible model, called the scope. Using our semiconductors for an example:

```
> null <- glm(FAIL~1, data=SC)
> # forward stepwise: it takes a long time!
> system.time (fwd <- step (null, scope=formula(full), dir="forward") )
...
Step:  AIC=92.59
FAIL ~ SIG2
...
    user   system elapsed
151.66    12.58   97.88
> length(coef(fwd))
[1] 69
```

This procedure enumerated 70 models, ranging from a univariate model including only SIG2 up to a model with 68 input signals (plus the intercept). The algorithm stopped at 68 because the AIC score for that model was lower (better) than any of the AIC scores for models with 69 inputs.[3] The greedy search procedure stopped when it thought it had found the best model, making the assumption that since the AIC is not getting any better when moving from 68 to 69 inputs it will not improve with 70+ inputs.

Notice that this step() procedure is *very* slow: on my laptop, it required 98 seconds to run for this small semiconductor dataset. This is true in general for any subset selection algorithm that enumerates candidate models by applying maximum likelihood estimation for subsets of coefficients (with the rest set to zero). Subset selection is slow because adding one variable to a regression can lead to large changes to the coefficients fit for all of the other variables. Thus, each model must be fit from scratch.

A related (but massively important) issue with subset selection is its *instability*. Since the fitted models are completely different across different candidate subsets, the

---

3. The AIC is an approximation for out-of-sample predictive performance. See the next section.

quality of out-of-sample performance will differ dramatically. You can easily make a small mistake in selection (say, including 69 rather than 68 covariates) that leads to a massive change in predictive ability. Moreover, if you jitter the data slightly and there is a small change in the path—for example, the fifth variable to be included changes— then the entire set of candidate models will be completely different. This instability is the enemy of reliable model selection; fortunately, we can stabilize the algorithms by introducing the concept of penalization.

**THE KEY TO MODERN STATISTICS IS REGULARIZATION**. This is the strategy of penalizing complexity so as to depart from optimality and stabilize a system. Recall that, for most classical statistics procedures, you are minimizing a deviance (equivalently, maximizing a likelihood): $\hat{\beta} = \text{argmin} \{-\frac{2}{n} \log \text{lhd}(\beta)\}$. A regularization strategy will instead involve minimizing a *penalized* deviance:

$$\hat{\beta} = \text{argmin} \left\{ -\frac{2}{n} \log \text{lhd}(\beta) + \lambda \sum_k c(\beta_k) \right\}. \tag{3.3}$$

Here, $c(\beta)$ is a cost on the size of the coefficient. In the case where $c(\beta) = |\beta|$—the absolute value cost—we get the common and useful *lasso* estimator. It will play a major role in your data science life.

Let's unpack Equation 3.3. We've simply added a penalty—the $\lambda \Sigma_k c(\beta_k)$ term—to the MLE deviance minimization of Equation 2.18. This penalty puts a *cost* on the size of each $\beta_k$. That penalizes *complexity,* because the $\beta_k$ coefficients are what allow your predicted $\hat{y}$ values to move around with different input $x$ values. If you force them to all be close to zero, your $\hat{y}$ values will be *shrunk* toward $\bar{y}$, and the entire system moves around less—it is stable.

Another way to think about Equation 3.3 is through the lens of decision theory—a framework built around the idea that choices have costs. If you consider the decision-making process in classical statistics—focused on a two-stage process of estimation and hypothesis testing—what are the costs?

- *Estimation cost:* Deviance! This is the cost of distance between data and the model, and it is what you minimize to obtain the MLE.

- *Testing cost:* There is a fixed price placed on $\hat{\beta}_j \neq 0$. This is implicit in the hypothesis testing procedure, where you set $\hat{\beta}_j = 0$ unless you have *significant evidence otherwise.* That is, the null is *safe,* and you need to pay to decide otherwise.

Thus, in classical statistics, the cost of $\hat{\beta}$ is the in-sample deviance plus a penalty for being away from zero. However, the cost of moving away from zero—the cost of instability—is hidden inside the hypothesis-testing scenario. Equation 3.3 makes both costs explicit.

What should the penalty function look like? First, $\lambda > 0$ is the penalty weight. It is a tuning parameter that needs to be selected in some data-dependent matter, and the final section of this chapter is focused on how to do this. For now let's consider it fixed. The rest of the penalty is determined by the shape of the cost function. In all cases, $c(\beta)$ will be lowest at $\beta = 0$, and you pay more for $|\beta| > 0$. This structure is implied by our preference for stability. Otherwise, the variety of options is wide; Figure 3.4 shows a few.

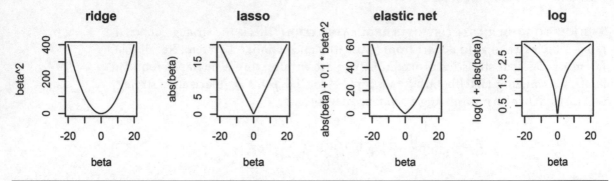

**FIGURE 3.4:** Common penalty functions: ridge $\beta^2$, lasso $|\beta|$, elastic net $\alpha\beta^2 + |\beta|$, and a "nonconvex" penalty $\log(1 + |\beta|)$.

Each of these encourages different sorts of model behavior. The ridge penalty, $\beta^2$, places little penalty on small values of $\beta$ but a rapidly increasing penalty on large values. This will be appropriate for scenarios where you believe each covariate has a small effect, with no big coefficients dominating the model. The lasso's absolute value penalty, $|\beta|$, places a constant penalty on deviations from zero. Moving $\beta$ from 1 to 2 costs the same as a move from 101 to 102. And the "elastic net" is an elaborate name for the simple combination of ridge and lasso.

Penalties like the log penalty on the far right are special because they have *diminishing bias*: they place extreme cost on the move from zero to small values of $\beta$, but for large values the rate of penalty change is small. These penalties encourage lots of zeros in your fit while allowing large signals to be estimated without any bias. Such nonconvex penalties are favored by theoretical statisticians, but they need to be treated with care in practice because they introduce many of the instability and computational issues that we observe with stepwise regression. Indeed, you can interpret stepwise regression as solving for a penalized deviance under $L_0$ costs, where $c(\beta) = \mathbb{1}_{[\beta \neq 0]}$. The problems of subset selection—needing to refit a completely different model every time you add a variable—are extreme versions of the problems associated with any nonconvex penalty scheme.

An advantage of the lasso is that it gives the least possible amount of bias on large signals while still retaining the stability of a convex penalty like the ridge. Another massive advantage of the lasso, and of all the three right "spiky" penalties in Equation 3.2, is that it will yield automatic variable screening. That is, some of the solved $\hat{\beta}_k$ values will be exactly equal to zero—not close to zero, but zero as in "they are not in the model, so you don't need to store or think about them." The reason that this happens is illustrated in Figure 3.5: the deviance is smooth while the absolute value function is pointy, and the minimum of their sum can be at zero if the penalty dominates. Any penalty that involves a $|\beta|$ term will do this—for example, all but ridge in Figure 3.4.

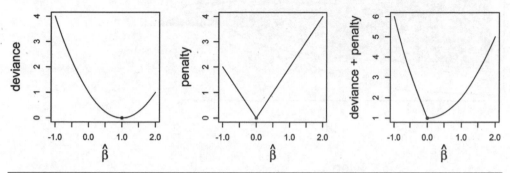

**FIGURE 3.5:** Illustration of penalized deviance minimization leading to $\hat{\beta} = 0$.

In summary, there are *many* penalty options. As you will see, the lasso is a fantastic default. You can think of it as a baseline and consider others only if you have a strong reason to do so.

**THE LASSO ALONE CANNOT DO MODEL SELECTION.** Rather, it provides a mechanism to *enumerate* a number of candidate models to choose among. A lasso regularization path minimizes, for a *sequence* of penalties $\lambda_1 > \lambda_2 \ldots > \lambda_T$, the penalized log likelihood:

$$-\frac{2}{n} \log \text{lhd}(\beta) + \lambda \sum_j |\beta_j|. \tag{3.4}$$

This provides a sequence of estimated regression models, with co-efficients $\hat{\beta}_1 \ldots \hat{\beta}_T$. Given this sequence, model selection tools are used to choose best $\hat{\lambda}$. For example, you can do an out-of-sample experiment to compare performance across the different penalties.

---

**ALGORITHM 6** | **Lasso Regularization Path**

Begin with $\lambda_1 = \min\{\lambda : \hat{\boldsymbol{\beta}}_\lambda = \mathbf{0}\}$.
For $t = 1 \ldots T$:

- Set $\lambda_t = \delta \lambda_{t-1}$ for $\delta \in (0, 1)$.

- Find $\hat{\boldsymbol{\beta}}_t$ to optimize Equation 3.4 under penalty $\lambda_t$.

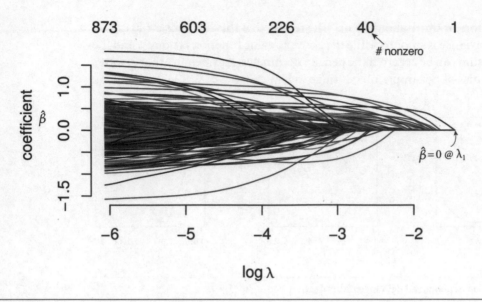

**FIGURE 3.6:** A lasso path plot for the browser data. The regularization path algorithm proceeds from right to left, with decreasing $\lambda_t$.

Algorithm 6 outlines this simple recipe. You start with $\lambda_1$ just big enough that $\hat{\boldsymbol{\beta}}_1 = \mathbf{0}$. This is always possible, via the formula

$$\lambda_1 = \max\left\{\left|\frac{\partial\left[-\frac{2}{n}\log \text{lhd}(\boldsymbol{\beta})\right]}{\partial\beta_k}\right|\right\}_{k=1}^{p}.$$

Most software will find this starting point automatically. You then iteratively shrink $\lambda$ while updating $\hat{\boldsymbol{\beta}}_\lambda$, where $\hat{\boldsymbol{\beta}}_\lambda$ denotes the solution to Equation 3.4 under penalty weight $\lambda$. A crucial detail here is that the coefficient updates are smooth in $\lambda$; that is,

$$\hat{\boldsymbol{\beta}}_t \approx \hat{\boldsymbol{\beta}}_{t-1} \text{ for } \lambda_t \approx \lambda_{t-1}.$$

This leads to both *speed* and *stability* for the lasso algorithm. The speed comes from the fact that each update $\hat{\boldsymbol{\beta}}_{t-1} \to \hat{\boldsymbol{\beta}}_t$ is small and hence fast. Stability is the mirror image of this property: even if the selected $\lambda$ changes across data samples, it will remain in a local neighborhood, and the selected $\hat{\boldsymbol{\beta}}$ will thus also stay in a small neighborhood. Unlike for subset selection, jitter to your data does not lead to big changes in the $\hat{y}$ prediction rules.

The whole enterprise is easiest to understand visually. For illustration, we introduce the `browser` dataset containing web browsing logs for 10,000 people. We've extracted a year's worth of browser logs for the 1000 most heavily trafficked websites. Each browser in the sample spent at least $1 online in the same year. As an example regression, we can treat total online spending as the response of interest and regress this onto the percent of time that users spend on various websites. That is, we seek to predict consumption from browser history. We will use a log-linear model,

$$\log(\text{spend}) = \alpha + \boldsymbol{\beta}'\boldsymbol{x} + \varepsilon. \tag{3.5}$$

Here, $\boldsymbol{x}$ is the vector of site-visit percentages. This model could, for example, be used to segment expected user budget as a function of browser history.

The *path plot* in Figure 3.6 illustrates Algorithm 6. The algorithm moves *right to left*, with decreasing values of $\lambda$. The $y$-axis here is $\hat{\boldsymbol{\beta}}$, with each colored line a different $\hat{\beta}_j$, as a function of $\lambda_t$. Each vertical slice of the plot represents a candidate model. As the path proceeds, the models become increasingly complex as the $\hat{\beta}_t$ include more and larger nonzero $\hat{\beta}_k$ values (the plot header marks the number of nonzero $\hat{\beta}_k$ at certain segments).

This picture and the underlying path estimation were executed using the gamlr package for R. You will use this package heavily; it provides fast and reliable lasso paths. There are other great options for lasso estimation in R, but since I wrote the gamlr software, it has the advantage of providing for special features covered in this book (e.g., corrected AIC and distributed multinomial regression).

> The glmnet package is also an excellent option for lasso estimation. Both gamlr and glmnet use similar syntax and use similar optimization routines (coordinate descent). The difference is in what they can do beyond the lasso: gamlr offers diminishing bias penalization, like the log penalty in Figure 3.4 (see also Figure 3.7), while glmnet provides for the elastic net of that same figure.

Running a lasso in gamlr is easy. The main difference from glm is that you need to create the numeric model-matrix yourself. But once you have this—say, xweb for the browser data—gamlr will by default run an entire path.

```
> spender <- gamlr(xweb, log(yspend))
> spender

gaussian gamlr with 1,000 inputs and 100 segments.
```

The path plot in Figure 3.6 is created by plot(spender). You can also do logistic lasso regression through the family argument.

```
gamlr(x=SC[, -1], y=SC$FAIL, family="binomial")
```

The default behavior of `gamlr` solves for a sequence of 100 $\lambda_T$, ranging down to $\lambda_T$, which is 1% of the starting point $\lambda_1$. There are a number of common arguments that you can change as needed:

- `verb=TRUE`: To get a progress printout.

- `nlambda`: $T$, the length of your $\lambda$ grid.

- `lambda.min.ratio` (or `lmr`): $\lambda_T/\lambda_1$, defines the path end.

Type `?gamlr` for abundant documentation and help.

The most difficult part of using `gamlr` (and it's not hard) is specification of the numeric model-matrix. You can use the `model.matrix` command, which is called by `glm`. However, `gamlr` (along with `glmnet` and many other ML R packages) is able to take advantage of the Matrix library representation for sparse matrices. A sparse matrix is one with many zero entries, which is a common scenario in modern data analysis. For example, many interacting categorical variables will—when represented as 0/1 indicator variables—lead to sparse designs. It is then efficient to ignore zero elements in the matrix whenever you can. Packages like `gamlr` are able to take advantage of sparse matrix structures for lower storage costs and faster computation. This will be essential for practical applications.

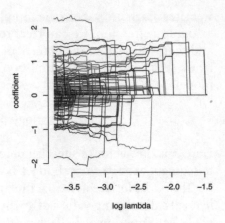

**FIGURE 3.7:** As an aside, `gamlr` can execute a forward-stepwise subset-selection procedure. Figure 3.8 shows the corresponding path plot for the browser data; notice how the jagged solution paths in this figure contrast with the smooth lasso paths of Figure 3.6. This *discontinuity* in the solution paths is the source of instability in subset selection.

One common sparse representation is a simple triplet matrix (STM) with three key elements: the row $i$, column $j$, and entry value $x$. Everything else in the matrix is assumed zero. Here's an example:

$$\begin{bmatrix} -4 & 0 \\ 0 & 10 \\ 5 & 0 \end{bmatrix} \text{ is stored as } \left\{ \begin{array}{l} i = 1, 3, 2 \\ j = 1, 1, 2 \\ x = -4, 5, 10 \end{array} \right\}.$$

The Matrix library provides tools for creating and working with sparse matrices. For example, the `sparseMatrix` function lets you create a matrix from these $i, j, x$ elements. This is how we built `xweb` for the browser regressions:

```
> ## The table has three colums: [machine] id, site [id], [# of] visits
> web <- read.csv("browser-domains.csv")
> ## Read in the actual website names and relabel site factor
> sitenames <- scan("browser-sites.txt", what="character")
Read 1000 items
> web$site <- factor(web$site, levels=1:length (sitenames), labels=sitenames)
> ## also factor machine id
```

```
> web$id <- factor(web$id, levels=1: length (unique(web$id)))
>
> ## get total visits per-machine and % of time on each site
> ## tapply (a,b,c) does c(a) for every level of factor b.
> machinetotals <- as.vector (tapply(web$visits,web$id,sum))
> visitpercent <- 100*web$visits/machinetotals[web$id]
>
> ## use this info in a sparse matrix
> ## this is something you'll be doing a lot; familiarize yourself.
> xweb <- sparseMatrix(
+     i=as.numeric(web$id), j=as.numeric(web$site), x=visitpercent,
+     dims=c(nlevels(web$id), nlevels(web$site)),
+     dimnames=list(id=levels (web$id), site=levels (web$site)))
>
> # what sites did browser 1 visit?
> head (xweb [1, xweb[1,]!=0])
        atdmt.com        yahoo.com              msn.com
        4.0520260       11.8559280            0.2501251
        google.com            aol.com questionmarket.com
        6.5282641        0.1500750            1.3506753
```

When your data come in triplet format (which is common for output from data-bases), the model matrix can be built using sparseMatrix. When the data come in a data frame, including categorical entries, you can use sparse.model.matrix—the sparse version of our familiar model matrix command. Recalling the OJ example from earlier, we can redo the indicator variables part of the design using this new tool.

```
> xbrand <- sparse.model.matrix( ~ brand, data=oj)
> xbrand[c (100,200,300),]
3 × 4 sparse Matrix of class "dgCMatrix"
    (Intercept) brandminute.maid brandtropicana
100           1                .              1
200           1                1              .
300           1                .              .
```

This creates the sparse version of the design used in Chapter 2. However, we need to be a bit more careful: this is not the right design for a lasso regression.

For MLE regressions, it didn't matter whether Dominick's or Tropicana was the reference level of the brand factor. Even though one of them will get subsumed into the intercept, you end up with the same predicted $\hat{y}$ values. But, under penalization, *factor reference levels now matter!* Since the penalty rewards $\hat{\beta}_k$ values closer to (or at) zero, you are shrinking every factor coefficient toward the intercept—toward the reference level. And it makes a difference whether you push Minute Maid toward Tropicana instead of Dominick's.

The solution is to simply get rid of the reference level. Once you add a penalty to the deviance, there is no reason to have only $K - 1$ coefficients for a $K$-level factor. If every category level is given its own dummy variable, then every factor level effect is shrunk toward a shared intercept. You are shrinking toward a shared mean, with only significantly distinct effects getting nonzero $\hat{\beta}_k$.

You can force R to create separate dummies for each level by creating an *extra* factor level.[4] In particular, the following utility functions make NA (R's code for "missing") the reference level.

```
> xnaref <- function(x){
+     if (is.factor(x))
+         if(!is.na(levels(x)[1]))
+             x <- factor(x, levels=c(NA, levels(x)), exclude=NULL)
+     return(x) }

> naref <- function(DF) {
+     if(is.null(dim(DF))) return(xnaref(DF))
+     if(!is.data.frame(DF))
+         stop ("You need to give me a data.frame or a factor")
+     DF <- lapply(DF, xnaref)
+     return(as.data.frame(DF)) }
```

We use this to create a new OJ design with entries for every brand.

```
> # with -1 to drop the intercept
> oj$brand <- naref(oj$brand)
> xbrand <- sparse.model.matrix( ~ brand, data=oj)
> xbrand [c(100,200,300),]
3 × 4 sparse Matrix of class "dgCMatrix"
    (Intercept) branddominicks brandminute.maid brandtropicana
100           1              .                .               1
200           1              .                1               .
300           1              1                .               .
> oj$brand[c(100,200,300)]
[1] tropicana minute.maid dominicks
Levels: <NA> dominicks minute.maid tropicana
```

---

4. This has the extra advantage of providing a framework for missing data. See the "Heterogeneous Treatment Effects" section of Chapter 6 for an example of missing data imputation.

The only other thing to recognize with lasso regression designs is that size (of the covariates) now matters. Since the $\beta_k$ values are all penalized by the same $\lambda$, you need to make sure they live on comparable scales. For example, $x\beta$ has the same effect as $(2x)\beta/2$, but $|\beta|$ is twice as much penalty cost as $|\beta/2|$. The common solution to this is to multiply $\beta_j$ by sd($x_j$), the standard deviation of $x_j$, in the cost function to standardize across scales. That is, instead of Equation 3.4, you minimize $-(2/n)\log \text{LHD}(\boldsymbol{\beta}) + \lambda\Sigma_j \text{sd}(x_j)|\beta_j|$. This implies that $\beta_j$'s penalty is now measured on the scale of 1 standard deviation change in $x_j$ and, for example, switching from meters to feet or Fahrenheit to Celsius won't change your model fit.

This standardization scaling is the default in `gamlr` (and in most other lasso implementations) via the argument `standardize=TRUE`. There are some occasions where you instead want `standardize=FALSE`. Most commonly, you might want `standardize=FALSE` if you have all indicator variables indicating category membership (such as brand or geographic region). In this case, the standardization would put *more* penalty on common categories (since sd($x_j$) will be higher) and less penalty on rare categories, which might be undesirable. However, unless you have strong reason to do otherwise, you should stick with the default `standardize=TRUE`.

## Model Selection

As mentioned many times, the lasso is used to obtain paths of promising candidate variables. The penalty weight $\lambda$ is a signal-to-noise filter. *It works like the squelch on a VHF radio.* If you turn it all the way up, you don't hear anything. If you turn it all the way down, you hear only static. The key to being able to communicate on a radio is finding the sweet spot in the middle where you hear the other person's voice and none of the background noise. It is the same for good statistical prediction: you need to find the $\lambda$ that gives you good signal with little noise.

Given a path of candidate models, you select the best one by asking, "Which model does best in predicting unseen data?" Of course, you can't know this in practice since unseen data is unseen. However, you can build a selection recipe around the out-of-sample experiments that we've already been using to estimate predictive performance. The procedure of using such experiments to do model selection is called *cross validation* (CV). It follows the basic recipe in Algorithm 7.

---

**ALGORITHM 7** | *K-Fold Cross Validation*

---

Split the data into $K$ random and roughly evenly sized subsets, called *folds*. Then, for $k = 1 \ldots K$:

- Use all data *except* the $k$th fold to train candidate models.
- Record the error rate for predictions from this fitted model on the left-out fold.

The end result will be a sample of OOS errors for each candidate model, and you can use these samples to estimated which is best.

---

Folding your data in this way guarantees that each observation is left out once for validation. Each data point is given a chance to *screw up* a prediction exercise. Doing this, rather than randomly sampling overlapping subsets, reduces the variance of CV model selection.

> Be careful to not cheat, for example, as we did in the semiconductors example at the beginning of this chapter when we selected our 25 cut variables using the full data. As a rule, if you do something to the data, do it *inside* the CV loop over folds.

We usually measure the "error rate" as the deviance. But for different applications, you might choose to focus on other OOS statistics, such as misclassification rates or error quantiles. As a general point, you want the CV scheme to mirror how you will actually be applying the model in practice. For example, if you are going to be predicting time-series data, then you might want to use only past training data to predict future leftout folds.

A common question is "How do I choose $K$?" The short answer is that more is better, but you shouldn't waste time, so just use whatever you need. After running CV, you will have a distribution of errors associated with each model—say, $\varepsilon_{t1} \dots \varepsilon_{tK}$ for model $t$. The estimated *average* error rate is then $\bar{\varepsilon}_t$ with standard error $\mathrm{sd}(\varepsilon_{tk})/\sqrt{K}$. If these standard errors are too large for you to tell which is really the smallest $\bar{\varepsilon}_t$—for example, if all of the $\bar{\varepsilon}_t \pm \mathrm{sd}(\varepsilon_{tk})/\sqrt{K}$ are overlapping—then you can increase $K$ to reduce sampling uncertainty. The default for gamlr is nfold=5, which is often enough, but you can increase if needed.

> There is a limit on the precision increase with extra folds. The extreme case of leave-one-out CV, with $K = n$, is nice because it has no Monte Carlo error. However, it will give bad results if there is even a tiny amount of dependence between your observations. Smaller values of $K$ lead to CV that is more robust to this type of misspecification.

CV for the lasso is especially straightforward because the full paths of candidate models are easy to estimate. Algorithm 8 outlines the procedure.

---

**ALGORITHM 8** | *K-Fold CV Lasso*

---

Begin by minimizing Equation 3.4 over the sequence of penalty weights $\lambda_1 > \lambda_2 \dots > \lambda_T$ to obtain a path of candidate models $\hat{\beta}_1 \dots \hat{\beta}_T$.
Then, for each of $k = 1 \dots K$ folds:

- Using this same $\lambda_t$ sequence, fit the lasso path $\hat{\beta}_1^k \dots \hat{\beta}_T^k$ on all data data *except* the $k$th fold, say, fold$_k$.

- For each $\hat{\beta}_t^k$, calculate the fitted deviance on *left-out* data,

$$e_t^k = -\frac{2}{n_k} \sum_{i \in \mathrm{fold}_k} \log \mathrm{p}(y_i \,|\, x_i'\hat{\beta}_T^k),$$

where $n_k$ is the number of observations in $\mathrm{fold}_k$.

Set $\bar{e}_t = \frac{1}{K} \sum_k e_t^k$ and $\mathrm{se}(\bar{e}_t) = \sqrt{\frac{1}{(K-1)} \sum_k (e_t^k - \bar{e}_t)^2}$ as your estimate and sampling error for the OOS deviance at each $\lambda_t$. Finally, use the results to choose the "best" $\hat{\lambda}_t$ and use the corresponding full-sample coefficient estimates, $\hat{\beta}_t$, for your modeling and predictions.

Once again, the procedure is easiest to understand visually. Fortunately, gamlr wraps all of Algorithm 8 together in cv.gamlr, which uses the same syntax as the standard gamlr function.

```
cv.spender <- cv.gamlr(xweb, log(yspend))
plot(cv.spender)
```

Note that there are two options for $\lambda$ selection shown in Figure 3.8. The obvious one, called the CV-min rule, simply selects the $\lambda_t$ corresponding to the minimum

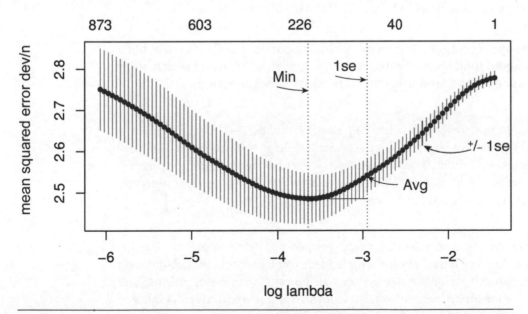

**FIGURE 3.8:** Cross-validated lasso for the browser data. The blue dots are mean OOS errors, and the error bars mark ± 1 standard error. CV-min and CV-1se rules are marked with vertical lines.

average OOS error. The second option, called the CV-1se rule, defines as best the biggest $\lambda_t$ with average OOS deviance no more than one SE (the $\text{se}(\bar{e}_t)$ from Algorithm 8) away from the minimum. In Figure 3.8, this corresponds to the rightmost dotted line.

For most applications, I recommend using the CV-min rule. This is the best choice if you are focused on OOS predictive performance. The CV-1se rule is more *conservative*: it hedges toward a simpler model in a reasonable but ad hoc fashion. This should be used if you are going to put a lot of weight on interpreting the nonzero $\hat{\beta}_k$, for example, as being special or representing some underlying truth. In high dimensions, such interpretation should be done with care anyway because multicollinearity can make it somewhat arbitrary which coefficients end up nonzero. Hence, I focus on predictive performance. However, the CV-1se rule is the default in gamlr because it is the default in glmnet and we don't want to rock the boat. You need to add the flag select="min" to get the CV-min selection.

When you call coef on a fitted cv.gamlr object, it automatically does the selection.

```
> betalse <- coef(cv.spender) ## 1se rule; see ?cv.gamlr
> betamin <- coef(cv.spender, select="min") ## min cv selection
> cbind (betalse, betamin) [c("tvguide.com", "americanexpress.com"),]
2 × 2 sparse Matrix of class "dgCMatrix"
                          seg36          seg49
tvguide.com               .          -0.0002379178
americanexpress.com 0.04230693   0.0488043737
```

We see that time spent on tvguide.com has no loading under the CV-1se rule, but a negative signal about total spending under the CV-min rule. Browsers with history on americanexpress.com tend to spend more under either selection rule.

> What is the difference between bootstrapping and cross validation? The difference is whether you are doing with- or without-replacement sampling. In the last section of this chapter, we discuss how the standard nonparametric bootstrap tends to underestimate predictive uncertainty, and we describe alternative algorithms that can provide uncertainty quantification for the lasso.

If the CV algorithms and selection rules seem complicated, it might be helpful to recall that they are based upon a simple idea: you use errors on left-out data to approximate what your predictive errors will be on future observations. The curve in Figure 3.8 is an *estimate* of what the out-of-sample predictive deviance—in this case, $(\hat{y}_f - y_f)^2$—will be for different values of $\lambda$. For example, you can simply read off the graph that, at the CV-min $\hat{\lambda} = \exp[-3.7]$, you can expect an out-of-sample $R^2$ of around $1 - 2.5/2.78 \approx 0.10$.[5] The 1 standard error intervals give a measure of frequentist uncertainty around each deviance estimate. If these error bounds are too large for you to decide which $\lambda$ is best, then you can simply increase the number of folds to increase your sample size of deviance estimates.

**INFORMATION CRITERIA (IC) PROVIDE AN ALTERNATIVE TO CROSS VALIDATION FOR MODEL SELECTION.** These IC are analytic approximations to the types of OOS errors that CV attempts to estimate through a computational experiment. You might want to use one of these IC if you don't have time for a CV experiment (if doing something once is expensive, you can't repeat it $K$ times) or if you don't like the Monte Carlo variation in CV selection (since the folds are random, if you run the algorithm multiple times, you will get slightly different answers).

There are many information criteria out there: AICc, AIC, BIC, and so on. All of these approximate the distance between a fitted model and "the truth" for different definitions of truth and using different analytic approximations. Since the IC measure a distance, you can apply them in model selection by choosing the model with minimum IC.

The most common is Akaike's criterion,

$$AIC = \text{deviance} + 2df, \tag{3.6}$$

where the deviance is calculated *in-sample* and the *df* are your *model* degrees of freedom.

For example, the `summary.glm` output reports the following:

```
Null deviance: 731.59 on 1476 degrees of freedom
Residual deviance: 599.04 on 1451 degrees of freedom
AIC: 651.04
```

Note again that the `degrees of freedom` in R output is "degrees of freedom left after fit": $n - df$ in our terminology. Many statistics books recommend the model with smallest AIC.

In an MLE fit, the *df* is simply the number of parameters in the model. More generally, it measures the correlation between $\hat{y}$ and $y$—how much flexibility you have to make the model fit look like the observed data. For deep theoretical reasons,[6] the lasso, like for MLE models, has *df* simply equal to the number of nonzero $\hat{\beta}_j$ at a given $\lambda$. This

---

5. The null model OOS deviance of approximately 2.78 is the rightmost dot, corresponding to your largest penalty $\lambda_1$, where all penalized coefficients are estimated equal to zero.
6. Hui Zou, Trevor Hastie, and Robert Tibshirani. On the degrees of freedom of the lasso. *The Annals of Statistics*, 35: 2173–2192, 2007.

is *not* true for any other penalization cost function and is yet another advantage of lasso regression (for example, with ridge regression all coefficients will be nonzero, but *df* will be less than the full model dimensions because the coefficients are shrunk toward zero). Hence, one can apply the AIC for lasso penalty selection by calculating the full-sample `gamlr` path and feeding the number of nonzero coefficients and the in-sample deviance into Equation 3.6. As usual, R has a function to do this.

```
> AIC(spender)
      seg1       seg2       seg3       seg4
10236.678  10221.410  10205.650  10191.269
...
     seg97      seg98      seg99     seg100
 9076.301   9083.091   9102.082   9109.330
```

However, AIC tends to lead to overfit in high dimensions. It's common to claim the AIC approximation is good for "big *n*," but in actual fact it is only good for big *n/df*. The 2*df* complexity cost is too small when *df* is large relative to *n*, and hence you get a more complex model than you would want for optimal prediction. To understand why, you need to dig a bit into what the AIC is attempting.

*The AIC is an estimate for OOS deviance.* It is targeting the same statistic that you are estimating in a CV experiment: what your deviance would be on another *independent* sample of size *n*. You know that the IS deviance is too small—since the model is tuned to this data, the IS errors are an underestimate of the OOS errors. Some more deep theory[7] shows that IS minus OOS deviance will be approximately equal to 2*df*, and this is the basis for Akaike's AIC. But if you dig a bit deeper, in the context of linear regression, the difference between IS and OOS deviance is actually equal to $2df\,\mathbb{E}[\sigma^2/\hat{\sigma}^2]$ where $\sigma$ is the true standard deviation of the additive errors and $\hat{\sigma}$ is its in-sample analog: the standard deviation of the fitted residuals. Akaike assumed that these will be roughly equal, which is true for low-dimensional models but will fail when the model is overfit (e.g., if $df \approx n$). Thus, an improved approximation to OOS deviance is

$$\text{AICc} = \text{deviance} + 2df\,\mathbb{E}\left[\frac{\sigma^2}{\hat{\sigma}^2}\right] = \text{deviance} + 2df\,\frac{n}{n-df-1}.$$

This is the *corrected AIC*.[8] It is a massively useful model selection tool. It works in linear or logistic regression or for any other generalized linear model (fit via MLE or with

---

7. H. Akaike. Information theory and the maximum likelihood principle. In B.N. Petrov and F. Csaki, editors, *2nd International Symposium on Information Theory*. Akademiai Kiado, 1973.
8. Clifford M Hurvich and Chih-Ling Tsai. Regression and time series model selection in small samples. *Biometrika*, 76: 297–307, 1989.

a lasso penalty). In the majority of examples, it will yield a model selection result that is near to the CV-min rule. Indeed, when AICc and CV-min disagree, I worry that something weird is going on and trust neither. Notice that for big $n/df$, AICc $\approx$ AIC. So, you should *always* use AICc instead of AIC: it works where the AIC doesn't and gives the same answer where it does.

The gamlr package uses AICc for selection by default. The AICc selected segment is marked on the path plot with a vertical line. If you are asking for coefficients from a fitted gamlr object, they will be the AICc minimizing choice.[9]

```
B <- coef(spender) [-1,]
B[c(which.min(B), which. max(B))]
     cursormania.com shopyourbargain.com
          -0.998143          1.294246
```

Beyond the AIC and its improved cousin, the AICc, there is one other commonly used option. The BIC, where $B$ stands for Bayes, is

$$BIC = deviance + \log(n) \times df. \tag{3.7}$$

This *looks* just like AIC but comes from a different place. The BIC is attempting to approximate the Bayesian posterior model probability—say, $p(\lambda_t | \text{data})$—which is roughly interpreted as the probability that $\lambda_t$ is a parameter in the true process that generated the data. This is done under a certain prior: your probability that a model is true *before* you saw any data.[10] Basically, while AIC and AICc are trying to optimize prediction, the BIC is attempting to get at a "true" model. This leads the BIC to be more conservative, and in small to medium-sized samples it behaves much like the CV-1se rule. However, in large samples we find that it tends to underfit for prediction purposes—it chooses $\lambda$ that are too big and models that are too simple.

Figure 3.9 shows all our OOS error estimates, and Figure 3.10 shows the corresponding model selection rules. We note that both AIC and AICc curves look like the CV curve; however, the AICc selection rule is nearly the same as the CV-min rule,

---

9. It will be hidden from you in the software, but for the deviance calculations going into the AICc, you need to use the full deviance that expands the constant C in Equation 2.17. This is because the AIC and AICc are actually defined for the negative log likelihood, which is the deviance plus the log likelihood for a "fully saturated" model. In the case of normal linear regression, this means you use $\text{dev}(\beta) = n \log(\tilde{\sigma}^2) + \sum_{i=1}^{n} (y_i - x_i' \beta)^2 / \tilde{\sigma}^2 = n(\log[\tilde{\sigma}^2] + 1)$ after replacing $\tilde{\sigma}^2 = \sum_i (y_i - x_i' \beta)^2 / n$.

10. BIC uses a "unit-info" prior: $N(\hat{\beta}, \frac{2}{n} \text{var}(\hat{\beta})^{-1})$.

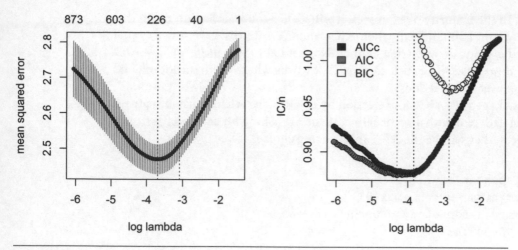

**FIGURE 3.9:** CV and IC estimates for the OOS performance.

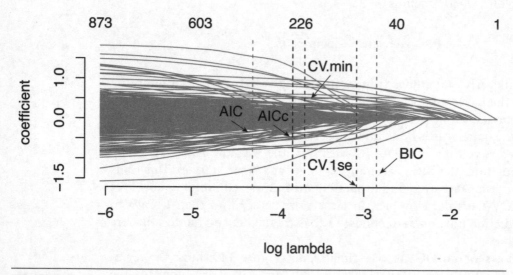

**FIGURE 3.10:** CV and IC selection rules along the lasso path.

while AIC chooses a smaller $\lambda$ (more complex model). In this case, the BIC and CV-1se rules give similar model choices. In larger samples, you will see these two diverge with BIC choosing much more simple models (and tending to underfit). With all of these selection rules, you get a range of answers. As a general rule, if you have time and the answer is important, do CV. But AICc is fast and stable, and I tend to use a combination of AICc and CV-min selection rules.

**TO TIE IT ALL TOGETHER, LET'S LOOK AT SOME HOCKEY DATA.** As part of the gamlr package, I've included a bunch of data on all of the goals in the 2002–2014 seasons of the National Hockey League (NHL). You can type ?hockey to get details and references to papers on this (obviously super-important) subject.[11]

The motivation here is to build an improved version of the player "plus-minus" (PM), a common hockey performance metric. The classic PM is a function of goals scored while that player is on the ice: the number of goals for his team minus the number against. The limits of this approach are obvious: there is no accounting for teammates or opponents. In hockey, where players tend to be grouped together on "lines" and coaches will "line match" against opponents, a player's PM can be artificially inflated or deflated by the play of his opponents and peers.

Can we build a better performance metric with regression? Consider constructing a binary response for every goal, equal to 1 for home-team goals and 0 for away-team goals.

```
> head (goal)
  homegoal season team.away team.home period differential playoffs
1        0 20022003      DAL      EDM      1           0         0
2        0 20022003      DAL      EDM      1          -1         0
3        1 20022003      DAL      EDM      2          -2         0
4        0 20022003      DAL      EDM      2          -1         0
5        1 20022003      DAL      EDM      3          -2         0
6        1 20022003      DAL      EDM      3          -1         0
```

We can then regress this onto dummy variables indicating who was on the ice, where home-team players get a value of +1 and away players get −1 (everyone off the ice is zero). This design is stored in R as the player sparse matrix.

```
> player [1:3, 2:7]
3 × 6 sparse Matrix of class "dgCMatrix"
    ERIC_BREWER ANSON_CARTER JASON_CHIMERA MIKE_COMRIE ULF_DAHLEN ROB_DIMAIO
[1,]          1            .             1           .          .         -1
[2,]          .            1             .           1         -1          .
[3,]          .            1             .           1          .         -1
>
```

Beyond controlling for the effect of who else is on the ice, we also want to control for things unrelated to player ability (crowd, coach, schedule, etc.). To this end, we add a "fixed effect" for each team season, $\alpha_{team,season}$. In addition, special-teams

11. Robert Gramacy, Matt Taddy, and Sen Tian. Hockey performance via regression. *Handbook of Statistical Methods for Design and Analysis in Sports*, 2015.

configurations (e.g., a five-on-four power play) are controlled for through $\alpha_{config}$ effects. The full logistic regression model is then

$$\log \frac{p(\texttt{home.goal})}{p(\texttt{away.goal})} = \alpha_0 + \alpha_{team,season} + \alpha_{config} + \sum_{\substack{home \\ players}} \beta_j - \sum_{\substack{away \\ players}} \beta_j.$$

We interpret $\beta_j$ as the $j$th player's partial effect: when a goal is scored and player $j$ is on ice, odds are multiplied by $e^{\beta_j}$ that his team scored. This is a regression-based improvement on the traditional PM score.

You can run the model and use CV selection with a call to cv.gamlr.

```
> x <- cBind(config, team, player) # cBind binds together two sparse matrices
> y <- goal$homegoal
> cv.nhlreg <- cv. gamlr(x, y, verb=TRUE, # verb prints progress
+       free=1: (ncol(config)+ncol(team)), # free denotes unpenalized columns
+       family="binomial", standardize=FALSE)
fold 1,2,3,4,5,done.
```

The cv.gamlr object stores a gamlr object (the full data path fit) as one of its entries, and you can plot both the regularization paths and the CV experiment as in Figure 3.11:

```
> par(mfrow=c(1,2))
> plot(cv.nhlreg)
> plot(cv.nhlreg$gamlr)
```

Both AICc and CV-min choose a $\lambda$ that is a bit smaller than $e^{-9}$. The CV-1se rule chooses a bigger lambda (more simple model) at around $e^{-8}$. The AIC chooses a $\lambda$ near the AICc choice; it is not overfit because $n/df$ is large: we have $n \approx 70,000$ goals and 2400 players.

```
> log(cv.nhlreg$gamlr$lambda) [which.min(AIC(cv.nhlreg$gamlr))]
    seg55
-9.165555
```

On the other hand, the BIC is conservative and selects the null model where $\hat{\beta} = 0$.

```
> which.min(BIC(cv.nhlreg$gamlr))
seg1
   1
```

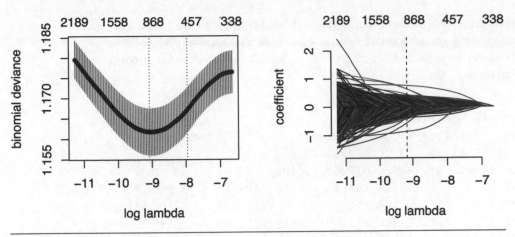

**FIGURE 3.11:** OOS error (left) and path (right) plots for the hockey regression.

The BIC is trying to find $\lambda$ with the highest probability of having the minimum OOS error, which is subtly different than finding the $\lambda$ corresponding to the lowest expected OOS error. For example, if there is more uncertainty about OOS error at the $\lambda$ with minimum expected error, then it could be that another value with higher expected error but lower uncertainty around this value will have a higher probability of being best. However, on a more practical level, the BIC simply tends to mechanically under-fit as $n$ gets large.

The null model here is not just an intercept but rather includes on-ice configuration info along with indicators for the team and season. So, the BIC is not saying that no players matter but rather that it cannot confidently tell them apart from their team's average level of play in a given season.

Taking a quick look at the regression, we see that the AICc selects 646 nonzero measurable player effects.

```
> Baicc <- coef(nhlreg) [colnames(player),]
> sum(Baicc!=0)
[1] 646
```

There are a few things to note here. First, we've introduced the free argument. This denotes columns of the design matrix that we *do not* want penalized. In this case, we're using it to keep the special-teams and team-season variables unpenalized —we know that we want them in the model, and so we let them enter without restriction.

Second, notice that we've used standardize=FALSE. This is one of the special cases where all of our penalized variables are on the same scale (player presence or absence). Without standardize=FALSE, we'd be multiplying the penalty for each coefficient (player effect) by that player's standard deviation in the player matrix. The players with big standard deviation are guys who play a lot. Players with small standard deviation are those who play little (almost all zeros). Hence, weighting penalty by standard deviations in this case is exactly what we don't want: a bigger penalty for people with many minutes on ice, a smaller penalty for those who seldom play. Indeed, running the regression without standardize=FALSE leads to a bunch of farm-team players coming up on top.

```
> nhlreg.std <- gamlr(x, y,
+      free=1: (ncol(config)+ncol(team)), family="binomial")
> Bstd <- coef(nhlreg.std) [colnames(player),]
> Bstd[order(Bstd, decreasing=TRUE) [1:10]]
        JEFF_TOMS        RYAN_KRAFT      COLE_JARRETT    TOMAS_POPPERLE
        1.7380706         1.4826419         1.2119318         1.1107806
    DAVID_LIFFITON  ALEXEY_MARCHENKO     ERIC_SELLECK       MIKE_MURPHY
        1.0974872         1.0297324         1.0060015         0.9600939
        DAVID_GOVE        TOMAS_KANA
        0.9264895         0.8792802
```

In contrast, the top players from the main analysis are almost all recognizable stars.

```
> # Here are the top 10 players
> Baicc[order(Baicc, decreasing=TRUE) [1:10]]
PETER_FORSBERG  TYLER_TOFFOLI    ONDREJ_PALAT   ZIGMUND_PALFFY   SIDNEY_CROSBY
    0.7548254       0.6292577       0.6284040        0.4426997       0.4131174
JOE_THORNTON    PAVEL_DATSYUK  LOGAN_COUTURE        ERIC_FEHR    MARTIN_GELINAS
    0.3837632       0.3761981       0.3682103        0.3677283       0.3577613
```

The bottom players from the main analysis are not those with little ice time, but rather those with much ice time who underperform.

```
> # Here are the bottom 10
> Baicc [order (Baicc)[1:10]]
    TIM_TAYLOR   JOHN_MCCARTHY   P. J._AXELSSON   NICLAS_HAVELID   THOMAS_POCK
    -0.8643214      -0.5651886       -0.4283811       -0.3854583    -0.3844128
MATHIEU_BIRON   CHRIS_DINGMAN    DARROLL_POWE    RAITIS_IVANANS   RYAN_HOLLWEG
    -0.3512101      -0.3342243       -0.3339906       -0.3129481    -0.2988769
```

Digging a little more, we see that whenever a goal is scored, Pittsburgh's odds of having scored (rather than having been scored on) increase by 51% if Sidney Crosby is on the ice.

```
> exp(Baicc["SIDNEY_CROSBY"])
SIDNEY_CROSBY
     1.511523
```

Meanwhile, the Blue Jackets (or Kings, before 2011–2012) odds of having scored drop by around 22% if Jack Johnson is on the ice.

```
> exp(Baicc ["JACK_JOHNSON"])
JACK_JOHNSON
   0.7813488
```

Finally, as a simple gut-check, we can look at the intercept for a *home-ice advantage*.

```
> exp(coef (nhlreg) [1])
[1] 1.084987
```

This says that, without conditioning on any of the other covariates, the home team is around 8% more likely to have scored any given goal. That is a big home-ice advantage!

 ## Uncertainty Quantification for the Lasso

At the beginning of Chapter 1, we discussed how there are two high-level approaches to dealing with uncertainty about model parameters. You can, as we did in that chapter, attempt to quantify the uncertainty around parameter estimates and use this uncertainty in your decision-making process. Alternatively, you can do as we have in this chapter and use regularization to *denoise* your estimates without doing an explicit accounting of uncertainty. That is, you use procedures that give reliable point estimates in the presence of uncertainty by shrinking toward the safe null hypothesis. Rather than the classical dichotomy between estimation and testing, your decision-making around whether a variable is zero or nonzero has been incorporated into a single optimization objective.

In this section, we introduce a hybrid scenario: you have used the lasso to perform high-dimensional analysis but then need to provide some measure of the uncertainty around the lasso estimates. This will be relevant, for example, if the analysis goals are more complex than basic prediction, if you have asymmetric losses for over- and underestimation, or if the audience expects to see something like a confidence interval around any results.

Uncertainty quantification for tools like the lasso is not easy. The presence of a penalty term wreaks havoc with the usual estimators for sampling distributions and standard errors. Moreover, it is impossible to accurately quantify uncertainty for very high-dimensional objects: you can build marginal intervals for a single $\beta_j$, not a joint interval for the full vector $\beta$. However, there are a couple of tools that you can use to get good approximations to frequentist uncertainty after lasso estimation. We will discuss two here: the parametric bootstrap and subsampling. Refer also to Chapter 6 for the method of sample splitting.

You need to look beyond the uncertainty quantification methods of Chapter 1 because these fail for the lasso. First, there are no good theoretical standard errors available for lasso estimates. The CLT-based results that we rely upon for MLE regression are invalid for estimation under penalization and in high dimensions. Second, the nonparametric bootstrap will not work well in scenarios where you are doing model selection. To see why this happens, imagine executing one fold of a cross-validation routine on a bootstrap sample. Since the observations have been resampled *with-replacement*, you are likely to have some of the same observations in both the training sample and in the left-out fold. This makes prediction seem easier than it would be in reality since the same (unpredictable) random noise is in both your training and validation fold. As a result, the bootstrapped CV routine will tend to select a smaller penalty than it would on the full sample. That is, the bootstrap samples will be overfit relative to the actual estimator, and thus they cannot be used to quantify uncertainty for this estimator.

However, the alternative *parametric* bootstrap algorithm can be made to work with the lasso. Recall that, instead of sampling from the data for each bootstrap sample, the parametric bootstrap generates *new* observations from an estimate of your assumed data-generating process. Because these are new unrepeated observations, the overfit described earlier will not occur.

For the parametric bootstrap, you might not want to sample from the full sample lasso fit. One way to think about your decision to use regularization is that you are trading variance for bias: you push the coefficients toward zero so that they are more stable and move around less with random noise. However, in an ideal world, the model generating simulated data in your parametric bootstrap should be an *unbiased* estimate of the true data generating process. In low dimensions, you can just simulate from the MLE fitted model (most theory on parametric bootstrapping assumes such a scenario). However, in high-dimensional problems the MLE can be a bad model estimate (or it may not even exist, in the case that you have more parameters than observations). In practice, I recommend simulating from a model that is fit with less bias than the full sample lasso but is not actually a zero bias estimate. There is no hard rule for how to do this, but a guideline that has worked for me in practice is to take the full sample AICc or CV-min selected penalty—say, $\hat{\lambda}$—and fit the model for data generation using a penalty that is around 25% its size, say, $\bar{\lambda} \approx \hat{\lambda}/4$. However, you should consider sensitivity to this choice in real applications and compare to, for example, the alternative subsampling procedure discussed in a moment.

Again, because the lasso is a biased estimator, you should target confidence intervals directly rather than via standard error estimates. This parallels the discussion of the CI bootstrap in Algorithm 2: you want to quantify how the bootstrap estimates differ from the original estimator and if they are biased high or low. The full procedure is detailed in Algorithm 9.

---

| **ALGORITHM 9** | **Parametric Bootstrap for Lasso Confidence Intervals** |

You have data $\{[x_i, y_i]\}_{i=1}^n$ and full sample lasso coefficient estimate $\hat{\beta}$ under penalty $\hat{\lambda}$ (selected via, e.g., AICc or CV-min rules).

Obtain low/no penalty estimates $\bar{\beta}$ via either likelihood maximization (for low dimensions) or lasso with a smaller penalty, $\bar{\lambda} \approx \hat{\lambda}/4$. Then, for $b = 1 \ldots B$:

- Generate $n$ response observations $\{y_i^b\}_{i=1}^n$ from the fitted regression model parameterized by $\bar{\beta}$ and with sample covariates, $\{x_i\}_{i=1}^n$. For example, in linear regression, generate

$$y_i^b \sim N(x_i'\bar{\beta}, \bar{\sigma}^2), \tag{3.8}$$

where $\bar{\sigma}^2$ is the variance of the residuals corresponding to the $\bar{\beta}$ fit.

- Obtain your bootstrap coefficient estimate, $\hat{\beta}_b$, on data $\{[x_i, y_i^b]\}_{i=1}^n$ with the same penalty selection algorithm as when estimating $\hat{\beta}$.

To get the $\alpha$% CI for a function of the coefficients—say, $f(\beta)$—you then calculate the $\alpha/2$ and $1 - \alpha/2$ percentiles of the errors $\{f(\hat{\beta}_b) - f(\hat{\beta})\}_{b=1}^B$—say, $t_{\alpha/2}$ and $t_{1-\alpha/2}$—and set your interval as follows:

$$[f(\hat{\beta}) - t_{1-\alpha/2}, f(\hat{\beta}) - t_{\alpha/2}]. \tag{3.9}$$

---

Recall our hockey example. From the right panel of Figure 3.11, you can see that the AICc selected penalty weight is $\hat{\lambda} \approx \exp[-9]$. We'll run a parametric bootstrap with simulation from the model fit for a smaller penalty on this same path, $\bar{\lambda} \approx \exp[-11.25]$. To generate from this fitted model, we first obtain the binomial probabilities corresponding to this $\bar{\beta}$.

```
> log(nhlreg$lambda[61])
> Qlowpen <- drop(predict(nhlreg, x, select=61, type=" response"))
```

We can then use the `rbinom` function to generate new 0/1 response values indicating whether each goal was scored by the away or home team in the bootstrap sample.

We'll run Algorithm 9 for a relatively small set of iterations, $B = 100$, due to the time cost in running each lasso fit.

```
> Bhat <- coef(nhlreg)
> Bparboot <- sparseMatrix(dims=c(nrow(Bhat),0),i={},j={})
> B <- 100
```

```
> for(b in 1:B){
+   yb <- rbinom(nrow(x), Qlowpen, size=1)
+   fitb <- gamlr(x, yb,
+     free=1:(ncol(config)+ncol(team)),
+     family="binomial", standardize=FALSE)
+   Bparboot <- cbind(Bparboot, coef(fitb)) }
```

The resulting matrix `Bparboot` is a $p \times B$ sample of $\hat{\beta}_b$ coefficient estimates (those obtained under AICc penalty selection). You can obtain a 90% interval for any specific coefficient here by applying the formula in Equation 3.9. For example, perhaps you want to know the 90% CI for the goal odds multiplier due to Sidney Crosby. Since this is logistic regression, the odds multiplier for player $j$ is $f(\boldsymbol{\beta}) = e^{\beta_j}$.

```
> # try other players too
> WHO <- "SIDNEY_CROSBY"
> fB <- exp(Bhat[WHO,])
> tval <- quantile(exp(Bparboot[WHO,]), c(.95,.05))
> 2*fB - tval
      95%        5%
1.383667 1.786985
```

We find that Crosby's presence on the ice increases the odds that the Penguins have scored by somewhere between 38% and 79%. We can also provide uncertainty bounds for the home-ice advantage calculated at the end of the previous subsection.

```
> fB <- exp(coef(nhlreg) [1,])
> tval <- quantile (exp(Bparboot[1,]), c(.95,.05))
> 2*fB - tval
      95%        5%
1.068819  1.096128
```

The probability that the home team scored is, all things equal, 6% to 10% higher than the probability that the away team scored.

The drawback of a parametric bootstrap is that it relies heavily upon the correctness of your assumed data generating process. For example, if you are working with a linear lasso, you will need to generate new errors from a Gaussian distribution, typically with a constant variance, and hence assuming that the model in Equation 3.8 from Algorithm 9 holds *exactly*. In practice, you will often use a linear lasso for regression estimation even if you don't believe that this model holds true. As is the case with OLS, linear modeling can give good estimates for $\beta$ even if, say, the errors are heteroskedastic and each observation has its own variance $\sigma_i^2$. However, if you apply the parametric bootstrap under such misspecification, it can give you radically inaccurate uncertainty estimates (typically, underestimates).

**SUBSAMPLING PROVIDES AN ALTERNATIVE TO BOOTSTRAPPING**. The nonparametric bootstrap doesn't work with model selection because the repeated observations in with-replacement samples make prediction seem artificially easy. In subsampling,[12] you instead re-estimate your target using $B$ *without-replacement* subsamples of size $m$, where $m$ is smaller than the full sample size $n$. Ideally, these subsamples have no overlap: you would split the data into something like $B = n/m$ folds and obtain parameters on each independent fold. However, you need simultaneously $B$ big enough to get a good picture of the sampling distribution and $m$ big enough to get estimator behavior that resembles the full sample result. For example, in lasso problems, $m$ can't be so small that all of the coefficients are set to zero in the subsample estimates. But perhaps that only happens for $m \geq n/5$, and you need more than $B = 5$ subsample estimates to get a reasonable confidence interval.

In practice, you should choose $B$ as big as you have computational time for,[13] and choose $m$ as small as possible where your estimation routine still gives reasonable-looking point estimates. This latter recommendation is subjective; I use $m \approx n/4$ as a rule of thumb, but you will want to move this number around to make sure your intervals are not overly sensitive to its value.

Similarly to the bootstrap algorithms, variability of your estimates across subsets can be used to model the sampling variability of your full-sample estimator. But, unlike for the nonparametric bootstrap, each subsample estimate is based on roughly independent data. And for this reason subsampling works in settings (such as lasso estimation and after model selection) where the bootstrap fails.

The problem with subsampling is that each of your estimates is based on a smaller sample than you actually have. For that reason, subsampling algorithms require you to assume a *learning rate* that allows you to adjust the size-$m$ sample uncertainty for your size-$n$ sample estimate. The learning rate defines how quickly your standard errors decrease with the sample size. For example, in the common mean-estimation setting you use the sample mean $\overline{x}_n = (1/n) \sum_i x_i$ as an estimator of the true mean $\mathbb{E}[x]$ (where the $n$ subscript denotes dependence on sample size), and this estimator has the standard error

$$\text{se}(\overline{x}_n) = \sqrt{\frac{\text{var}(x)}{n}}. \qquad (3.10)$$

Here, we would say that the learning rate is $\sqrt{n}$: since $\text{var}(x)$ is a constant quantity, the standard error is decreasing with the square root of the sample size. For example,

---

12. Subsampling is given detailed treatment in the book by Politis et al. [1999].
13. Remember that you can use parallel computing to speed up any subsampling or bootstrapping algorithm.

suppose you have $\bar{x}_m$, the mean of a smaller size-$m$ sample of $x_i$ values. You can relate uncertainty across the two different sample sizes as

$$se(\bar{x}_n) = \sqrt{\frac{m}{n}}\, se(\bar{x}_m).$$ (3.11)

It turns out that, for reasons related to the central limit theorem,[14] a $\sqrt{n}$ learning rate holds (at least approximately) for a wide variety of estimation algorithms. For example, MLEs all have $\sqrt{n}$ learning rates. The assumption of $\sqrt{n}$ learning becomes more difficult once you add model selection and penalization. However, it can be shown[15] that if your parameter dimension is not *too* large,[16] then the lasso estimates have a $\sqrt{n}$ learning rate. If you are willing to make this assumption, then you can make use of the subsampling procedure in Algorithm 10 to obtain nonparametric confidence intervals for functions of lasso estimates.

---

**ALGORITHM 10** | **Subsampling CI Under $\sqrt{n}$ Learning**

You have data $Z = \{z\}_{i=1}^{n}$ and some full sample estimate $\hat{\theta}$ that is calculated from this data to approximate the population target $\theta$.

Set a subsample size $m$, where $m$ is no larger than $n/2$. As a default value, use $m = n/4$. Then, for $b = 1 \ldots B$:

- Draw a without-replacement subsample $Z_b$ of $m$ observations from the full sample $Z$.

- Run your estimation on $Z_b$ to obtain $\hat{\theta}_b$, the subsample estimate for $\theta$.

- Calculate the *error*, $e_b = (\hat{\theta}_b - \hat{\theta})$.

Given $\{e_b\}_{b=1}^{B}$, you obtain the $\alpha\%$ CI for $\theta$ by first calculating the $\alpha/2$ and $1 - \alpha/2$ percentiles on this sample of errors—say, $t_{\alpha/2}$ and $t_{1-\alpha/2}$—and setting the interval as

$$\left[ \hat{\theta} - \frac{\sqrt{m}}{\sqrt{n}}\, t_{1-\alpha/2},\ \hat{\theta} - \frac{\sqrt{m}}{\sqrt{n}}\, t_{\alpha/2} \right].$$ (3.12)

---

14. For those who are mathematically inclined, the reason is that most estimators have sampling distributions whose second-order Taylor series expansion yields a variance that is proportional to $1/n$.

15. Keith Knight and Wenjiang Fu. Asymptotics for lasso-type estimators. *Annals of Statistics*, pages 1356–1378, 2000.

16. In detail, you need that the selected penalty $\hat{\lambda}$ can decrease as fast as $1/\sqrt{n}$ as you add data. This is possible only if you are not adding parameters as you add observations, and hence it excludes settings like bag-of-words modeling where the vocabulary grows as you observe more text.

Turning again to the hockey analysis, we draw $B = 100$ subsample estimates of size $m = 17,362 \approx n/4$.

```
> n <- nrow(x)
> B <- 100
> ( m <- round(n/4) )
[1] 17362
```

Since $n$ is not a factor of $B$, the resulting subsets are a mix of size $m_b = 3473$ and $m_b = 3472$. We can now run Algorithm 10. As discussed earlier, we will target statistics of the form $\theta = e^{\beta j}$, the odds multipliers.

```
> Esubs <- sparseMatrix(dims=c(nrow(Bhat),0),i={},j={})
> for(b in 1:B){
+       subs <- sample.int(n, m)
+       fitb <- gamlr(x [subs,], y[subs],
+           free=1: (ncol(config)+ncol (team)),
+           family="binomial", standardize=FALSE)
+       eb <- (exp(coef(fitb)) - exp(coef(nhlreg)))
+       Esubs <- cBind(Esubs, eb) }
```

Looking again at the home-ice advantage, subsampling finds a 95% CI that is close to the interval we obtained from the parametric bootstrap.

```
> thetahat <- exp(coef(nhlreg)[1,])
> tval <- quantile(Esubs[1,], c(.95,.05))
> thetahat - tval*sqrt(m)/sqrt(n)
      95%        5%
1.066916 1.095240
```

To the first percentage decimal place, this shows a 7% to 10% advantage in home versus away scoring probabilities.

Looking at the Sid Crosby effect, however, we get an interval that is noticeably different from the parametric bootstrap CI.

```
> WHO <- "SIDNEY_CROSBY"
> thetahat <- exp(coef(nhlreg)[WHO,])
> tval <- quantile(Esubs[WHO,], c(.95,.05))
> thetahat - tval*sqrt(m)/sqrt(n)
      95%        5%
1.453544 1.766025
```

Instead of the parametric bootstrap's interval of 38% to 79%, the subsampling 90% CI has Crosby's odds increase as between 45% and 77%. The subsampling interval is narrower and centered slightly higher (at 61% instead of 59%).

Which result should you believe? Unfortunately, there is no clear answer. Both the parametric bootstrap and subsampling rely on strong assumptions about the way the world works. In the case of the parametric bootstrap, you're assuming that the actual goal probabilities are independent draws from some true logistic regression model. In contrast, the subsampling procedure allows for dependence between observations (this will show up in the subsampled blocks), and it allows for the possibility that your logistic regression model is misspecified. However, subsampling relies *heavily* on the assumed $\sqrt{n}$ learning rate[17] (which is basically impossible to check). Moreover, the methods involve tuning parameters that you need to choose: the reduced penalty $\bar{\lambda}$ for parametric bootstrapping and the sample size $m$ for subsampling. In the end, both methods should be viewed as approximation tools and with a healthy dose of skepticism. Here, I'd choose the most conservative interval and conclude that the Crosby increase is between 38 and 79 percent.

Finally, note that both subsampling and parametric Bootstrap intervals for Crosby's effect are *not* centered on the full sample estimate of 51%. What is happening here? Recall that intervals such as Equation 3.12 in subsampling and Equation 3.9 in the parametric bootstrap (as well as Equation 1.6 in the nonparametric CI bootstrap) are designed to correct for *bias* in the full sample estimator. In this case, the subsampling and parametric bootstrap estimates are consistently smaller than the full-sample estimate. See Figure 3.12 for the distribution of $\{e_b\}_{b=1}^{B}$ for Crosby's effect in subsampling. This indicates that the full-sample estimate is likely also biased downward relative to what you would estimate on an unlimited amount of data—in other words, relative to the true population parameter. Hence, you've detected a *downward* bias, and the resulting 90% intervals correct for this bias by revising upward from your original estimate of Crosby's odds multiplier.

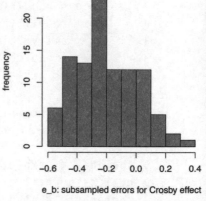

**FIGURE 3.12:** Histogram of the $B = 100$ subsampling errors $e_b$ for Sidney Crosby's multiplier on the odds that his team has scored, $\theta = \exp[\beta_{\text{crosby}}]$.

---

17. I doubt the assumption of $\sqrt{n}$ learning in this particular example. With more games you will have more players, so this is a scenario where the assumption of dimension not growing with sample size seems unrealistic.

# Classification

M any of the prediction questions that we face are classification questions. You might want to predict a website user's intent among several options, a speaker's political affiliation among a few parties, or the subject of an untagged image. These examples fit in our usual regression framework, where response $y$ is a function of inputs $x$. The difference is that $y$ now represents membership in a category: $y \in \{1, 2, \ldots, m\}$. The prediction question is, given a new $x$, what is our best guess at the response category, $\hat{y}$?

## Nearest Neighbors

We have already worked with two-category classification via logistic regression, where $y \in \{0, 1\}$ and $p(y = 1 \,|\, x)$ is modeled with a logit link. This *binary* logistic regression is a special case of general *multinomial* logistic regression for more than two classes. We'll return to that modeling approach later in this chapter, but first we cover a simple and intuitive classifier: the nearest neighbor algorithm.

The $K$ nearest neighbor ($K$-NN) algorithm predicts class $\hat{y}$ for $x$ by asking, "What is the most common class for observations around $x$?" Figure 4.1 illustrates the $K$-NN routine in Algorithm 11. The black point is $x_f$, where we'd like to predict the class label. For a $K = 3$ routine, the dashed lines indicate the nearest neighbors: two white and one dark gray. The modal neighbor is thus white and the 3-NN prediction is $\hat{y}_f = white$. The neighbors also provide a *crude* estimate of class probabilities, and here we could say $\hat{p}_f(white) = 2/3$.

Since distance is measured on the raw $x$ values, units matter. As we did for regularization, we will default to using units of *standard deviation* for $K$-NN distance calculations. R's `scale` function can be used to transform from $x_j$ to $\bar{x}_j = x_j / \operatorname{sd}(x_j)$, which can then be input to a $K$-NN algorithm.

| ALGORITHM 11 | *K* Nearest Neighbors |
| --- | --- |

Given input vector $x_f$ where you would like to predict the class label, find the $K$ nearest neighbors in the dataset of labeled observations, $\{[x_i, y_i]\}_{i=1}^{n}$, where nearness is measured in Euclidean distance:

$$d(x_i, x_f) = \sqrt{\sum_{j=1}^{p}(x_{ij} - x_{fj})^2} \; .$$

This yields a set of the $K$ nearest observations with labels:

$$[x_{i1}, y_{i1}] \ldots [x_{iK}, y_{iK}].$$

The predicted class for $x_f$ is the most common class in this set:

$$\hat{y}_f = \operatorname{mode}\{y_{i1} \ldots y_{iK}\}.$$

As a real example, let's turn to a dataset involving the properties of shards of glass. The *forensic glass* dataset is included as `fgl` in the MASS[1] library for R.

```
> library (MASS)
> data(fgl) ## loads the data into R
```

The data include, for each of 214 shards of glass, measurements on the refractive index (RI) and chemical composition in percentages by weight of oxide for elements Na, Mg, Al, Si, K, Ca, Ba, and Fe. This information is used as input for the task of predicting among six possible glass types:

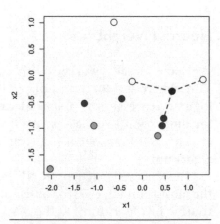

**FIGURE 4.1:** *K*-NN illustration. The black point is the $x$ location where you'd like to predict a class label, and the other points have class label denoted by color (dark gray, light gray, or white).

1. W.N. Venables and B.D. Ripley. *Modern Applied Statistics with S*, 4th edition. Springer, 2002.

- `WinF`: Float glass window[2]

- `WinNF`: Nonfloat glass window

- `Veh`: Vehicle window

- `Con`: Container (bottles)

- `Tabl`: Tableware

- `Head`: Vehicle headlamp

The data are plotted in Figure 4.2. We see that some of the inputs are clear *discriminators*. For example, `Ba` is almost always present only in trace amounts except for headlamps, where it is relatively abundant. `Mg` is common for windows of all types—house or vehicle. Other inputs are more subtle discriminators or may matter only in interaction.

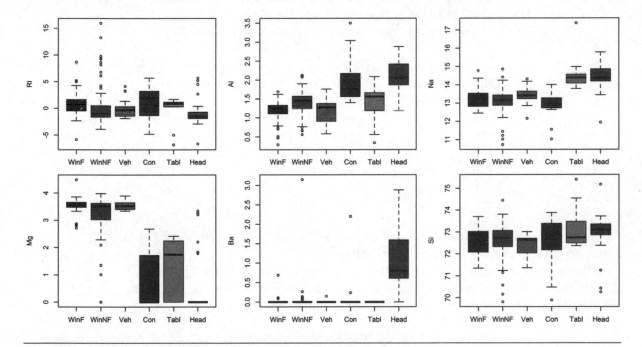

**FIGURE 4.2:** Distribution of the elemental composition of shards by glass type.

2.  Float glass is used in most modern windows, and it is created by floating molten glass on a bed of molten metal. Alternatives include the older process of cooling molten glass on a solid metal surface.

To run nearest neighbors in R, you can load the class package, which includes the function knn. You then need to create *numeric* matrices of training data *x* values, accompanied by labels *y*, and provide new test values where you would like to predict. Unlike glm, for knn you must supply test data: there is no model being fit, knn is simply counting neighbors for each observation in test.[3]

For our glass example, we first scale the data so that distances are in standard deviations.

```
> x <- scale(fgl[,1:9]) # column 10 is the class label
> apply (x,2,sd) # see ?apply
RI Na Mg Al Si  K Ca Ba Fe
 1  1  1  1  1  1  1  1  1
```

Now every variable has a standard deviation of 1. We can then run both 1-NN and 5-NN algorithms where a random sample of test observations are left out for prediction.

```
> test <- sample(1:214,10)
> nearest1 <- knn(train=x [- test,], test=x [test,], cl=fgl$type[- test], k=1)
> nearest5 <- knn(train=x[-test,], test=x[test,], cl=fgl$type[-test], k=5)
> data.frame(fgl$type[test], nearest1,nearest5)
   fgl.type.test. nearest1 nearest5
1            WinF     WinF     WinF
2            WinF     WinF     WinF
3            Tabl     Tabl     Tabl
4             Veh    WinNF    WinNF
5             Con      Con     Head
6           WinNF     WinF     WinF
7            Head     Head     Head
8            WinF     WinF     WinF
9            WinF     WinF     WinF
10          WinNF    WinNF    WinNF
```

In this case, 1-NN manages 80% accuracy, while 5-NN obtains 70%. However, if you rerun on random test sets, these numbers will move a lot.

There are a some major problems with practical application of KNN. First, we can deduce that *K*-NN predictions will be *unstable* as a function of *K*. For example, using the counts as probabilities, in Figure 4.1 we see the following:

$$K = 1 \Rightarrow \hat{p}_f(white) = 0,$$
$$K = 2 \Rightarrow \hat{p}_f(white) = 1/2,$$
$$K = 3 \Rightarrow \hat{p}_f(white) = 2/3,$$
$$K = 4 \Rightarrow \hat{p}_f(white) = 1/2.$$

---

3. This is a reason the *K*-NN is computationally impractical for large problems, although there do exist approximative nearest neighbor algorithms that are more efficient.

The predicted $\hat{y}_f$ also changes with each of these different $K$. As mentioned in Chapter 3, such instability of predictions makes it hard to choose the optimal $K$ and hence cross validation doesn't work well for KNN. Moreover, since prediction for each new $x_f$ requires a computationally intensive counting of the nearest neighbors, KNN is too expensive to be useful in most big data settings.

Thus, KNN is much like forward stepwise regression—a good idea, giving solid intuition about how you can approach the problem, but too crude to be useful in practice. The solution is to move to models for *probabilities* and use these as the basis for classification.

## Probability, Cost, and Classification

Before diving deeper into modeling, we need to discuss the relationship between probabilities and classification. To introduce the ideas, let's simplify back to binary problems where $y \in \{0, 1\}$. There are two ways to be wrong in a binary problem:

- False *positive*: predict $\hat{y} = 1$ when $y = 0$.
- False *negative*: predict $\hat{y} = 0$ when $y = 1$.

There can be different costs associated with each type of error. A doctor might place a lower cost on over-treatment than on a missed diagnosis, and the U.S. criminal justice system puts a higher cost on punishment of innocents than on letting the guilty walk free.

More generally, *decisions have costs*. To make optimal decisions, you need to estimate probabilities on possible outcomes. These probabilities are what allow you to assess the *expected loss* associated with different actions. Suppose that you know the probabilities of each outcome—say, $p_k$ for possible outcomes $k = 1 \ldots K$—and that each outcome $k$ has cost $c(a, k)$ under action $a$. Then the expected loss for action $a$ is

$$\mathbb{E}[loss(a)] = \sum_k p_k c(a, k). \tag{4.1}$$

Expected loss is often called *risk* by statisticians. We'll avoid this term because it is also commonly used to measure variance (and functions thereof) for losses in finance and economics.

For example, suppose that the action $a$ is that you decide to loan \$100 to someone under the agreement that they pay you back \$125 next week. If you decide that there is a 10% chance that they *do not* pay you back, then the expected loss is $100 \times 0.1 - 25 \times 0.9 = -12.5$ (the minus here is because profit is negative cost). You expect to *make* \$12.50 on such a loan and so would likely benefit from doing the deal. Once you know the probabilities of the various outcomes, then you can assess expected profits and losses and make optimal decisions.

Fortunately, we know how to estimate probabilities via logistic regression. To work through the steps of probability-based classification, we'll use a real dataset on loans and credit from a set of local lenders in Germany.[4] Credit scoring is a classic problem of classification, and it remains one of the big application domains for ML: use previous loan results (default versus payment) to train a model that can predict the performance of potential new loans.

After a bunch of data cleaning in `credit.R`, we have a data frame of borrower and loan characteristics alongside the binary `Default` outcome.

```
> head(credit)
  Default duration amount installment age  history      purpose foreign  rent
1       0        6   1169           4  67 terrible goods/repair foreign FALSE
2       1       48   5951           2  22     poor goods/repair foreign FALSE
3       0       12   2096           2  49 terrible          edu foreign FALSE
4       0       42   7882           2  45     poor goods/repair foreign FALSE
5       1       24   4870           3  53     poor       newcar foreign FALSE
6       0       36   9055           2  35     poor          edu foreign FALSE
> dim(credit)
[1] 1000    9
```

We'll be running logistic lasso regression for `Default` onto all of these inputs *interacted* with each other (i.e., we include all pairwise interactions). To get a design that includes all factor levels (without a reference level in the intercept), we use the `naref` function that was detailed in Chapter 3. We can call it on the data that is input to `gamlr`.

```
> library(gamlr)
> source("naref.R")
> credx <- sparse.model.matrix( Default ~ . ^ 2,
  data=naref(credit))
> default <- credit$Default
> credscore <- cv.gamlr(credx, default, family= "binomial")
```

Figure 4.3 shows the resulting regularization path and OOS prediction performance. We see that the AICc chooses a slightly more complex model than the CV-min procedure, although this can change if you repeat the (random) OOS experiment. For this set of random folds, we have 20 variables selected by CV-min. AIC and AICc both select 21 variables, and the BIC yields 19. The CV-1SE rule is more conservative, with only 12 variables selected. We'll work with the AICc selected model for the rest of this example.

---

4. Taken from the UC Irvine Machine Learning Repository.

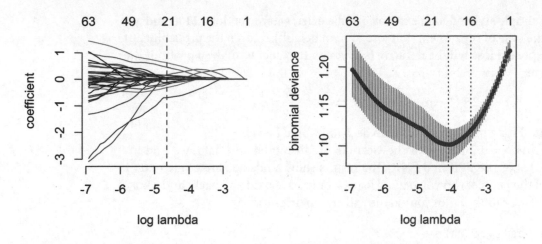

**FIGURE 4.3:** Regularization path and CV results for the German credit logistic lasso. AICc selection is marked on the path plot, and CV-min and CV-1se are on the other plot.

Given this fitted model, we can get probabilities of default using the `predict` function.

```
pred <- predict(credscore$gamlr, credx, type="response")
pred <- drop(pred) # remove the sparse Matrix formatting
```

Figure 4.4 shows the resulting *in-sample* fit. This is a tough noisy problem, and it appears that there is a lot of overlap between probabilities for the true defaults and the true nondefaults. This means that any classification rule we choose will induce a number of false negatives and false positives.

A classification rule, or cutoff, is the probability $p$ at which you predict $\hat{y}_f = 0$ for $p_f \leq p$ and $\hat{y}_f = 1$ for $p_f > p$. As mentioned at the outset, any such rule will have two types of errors associated with it: false positives, where $\hat{y} = 1$ but $y = 0$, and false negatives, where $\hat{y} = 0$ but $y = 1$. These can be converted into *rates*:

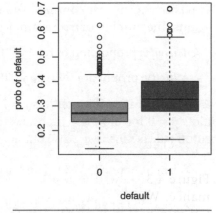

**FIGURE 4.4:** IS fit for the credit lasso.

$$\text{False Positive Rate} = \frac{\text{expected \# false positives}}{\text{\# classified positive}}$$

$$\text{False Negative Rate} = \frac{\text{expected \# false negatives}}{\text{\# classified negative}}$$

These are similar to the false discovery rates that we studied in the context of hypothesis testing.

Recall the simple stylized loan example from earlier, where you loan $100 and are paid $125 in the case of repayment (but lose $100 in default). With $p$ the probability of default, the expected loss will be negative (i.e., you will expect to make a profit) if the following is true:

$$-25\cdot(1-p)+100\cdot p<0 \iff p<\frac{25}{125}=\frac{1}{5}.$$

Hence, the cutoff for a no-loan versus loan decision would be at $p = 0.2$.[5]

Applying this $p = 0.2$ rule with the German credit model and data, we find in-sample estimates of the FPR and FNR. The results show a false positive rate of 0.61 (so that 61% of the people who you denied loans would have paid you back) and a false negative rate of 0.07 (only 7% of your loans will end in default).

```
## false positive rate
> sum( (pred<rule) [default==0] )/sum(pred>rule)
[1] 0.6059744
## false negative rate
> sum( (pred<rule) [default==1] )/sum(pred<rule)
[1] 0.07744108
```

For comparison, a $p = 0.5$ cutoff yields FPR=0.32, FNR=0.25. Our derived decision rule leads to far more false positives than negatives because you've put a higher cost on defaults.

In the case of FPR and FNR, your errors are normalized by the number of examples that you've classified a certain way (e.g., false positives over the number *classified* as positive). Another common summary for classification errors instead normalizes against the number of *true* examples in each class:

*sensitivity*: proportion of true $y = 1$ classified as such.

*specificity*: proportion of true $y = 0$ classified as such.

A rule is sensitive if it predicts $\hat{y} = 1$ for most $y = 1$ observations. It is specific if it predicts $\hat{y} = 0$ for most $y = 0$ observations. In the German credit example, our $p = 0.2$ cutoff rule is sensitive (92%) but not specific (only 39%).

```
> mean( (pred>1/5) [default==1] ) # sensitivity
[1] 0.9233333
> mean( (pred<1/5) [default==0] ) # specificity
[1] 0.3914286
```

Again, this occurs because of the asymmetric costs associated with defaults and loan repayments.

---

5. In general, for this simple setup where you get $100 + X$ in case of repayment, you expect to profit if $p < X/(100 + X)$. Hence, given the default probability $p$, you could set the total interest charge as $X > 100\cdot p/(1 - p)$, the loan amount times the odds of default.

A nice visual summary of potential classification rules is the ROC curve that plots sensitivity against 1-specificity. The name here comes from signal processing, with ROC denoting the receiver operating characteristic. A tight fit has the curve forced into the top-left corner, indicating that you are able to obtain high sensitivity while maintaining high specificity. As with any fit statistic or plot, we can obtain both in-sample and out-of-sample versions of the ROC plot (and the latter is always the more interesting).

Figure 4.5 shows ROC curves for the German credit example. The OOS plot corresponds to an AICc-selected lasso model that was fit on half the data and evaluated for specificity and sensitivity on the left-out half. Notice that the OOS curve is slightly flatter (closer to diagonal) than the IS curve: the sensitivity versus specificity trade-off for new predictions will be a bit worse than implied by in-sample fit.

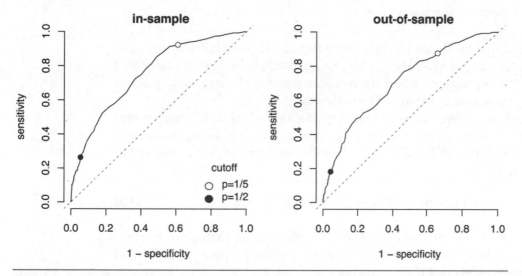

**FIGURE 4.5:** IS and OOS ROC curves for the German credit example, with both $p = 0.2$ and $p = 0.5$ rules marked.

This credit analysis raises an important caution about the use of retrospective analysis in future decision-making. Consider Figure 4.6, which shows the proportion of defaulters as a function of credit history. You can see that the default rate *decreases* with worsening credit history! What could be happening here?

The issue is that the context around loans being given out is not the same across different credit histories. Those with good history are able to get big loans for riskier projects, while those with terrible history are only able to get small loans in scenarios where it is nearly certain they can avoid default. Thus, the customers in different history groups have been *selected* into different types of loans. There is a correlation between history and default in the data that is the opposite of what we would expect as the causal relationship.

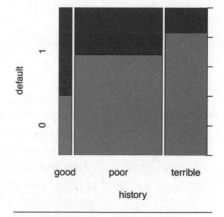

**FIGURE 4.6:** Mosaic plot for credit history against loan outcome.

Some of this issue can be fixed by conditioning on the right control variables. If you include loan size and scenario as covariates in a regression, that will perhaps account for this selection issue and yield the correct causal model. Doing this correctly is the subject of Chapter 5. In general, however, it is dangerous to make changes to future behavior based on a naive analysis of past data. In this case, I'd be confident using this data to analyze the expected default rate for a large set of loans that are "on the books" (since those loans are generated from the same loan-approval process that generated this training data). I'd be much more cautious about using this model as the basis for any sort of *robot banker* that automates future loan approvals.

## Multinomial Logistic Regression

We've established that good classification starts from good probability models. For binary classification, you can use a binary logistic regression to build your probability models. In *multiclass* problems, where the response is one of $K$ "categories," you can build a similar generalized linear model formulation.

First, we need to rewrite the multiclass response as the length-$K$ binary vector $y_i = [0, 1, \ldots, 0]$, where $y_{ik} = 1$ if response $i$ is class $k$. Then, following the generic linear model formulation of Equation 2.1, from way back in Chapter 2, we need to model the following:

$$\mathbb{E}[y_{ik} \,|\, \boldsymbol{x}_i] = p(y_{ik} = 1 \,|\, \boldsymbol{x}_i) = f(\boldsymbol{x}_i' \boldsymbol{B}) \text{ for } k = 1 \ldots K. \tag{4.2}$$

Here, $\boldsymbol{B} = [\boldsymbol{\beta}_1 \cdots \boldsymbol{\beta}_K]$ is a *matrix* with columns of coefficients for each outcome class. The extension of logistic regression that works nicely for this purpose is *multinomial logistic regression*, with probability modeled as

$$p(y_j = 1 \,|\, \boldsymbol{x}) = p_j(\boldsymbol{x}) = \frac{e^{\boldsymbol{x}' \boldsymbol{\beta}_j}}{\sum_{k=1}^{K} e^{\boldsymbol{x}' \boldsymbol{\beta}_k}}. \tag{4.3}$$

The link function here, $e^{z_j} / \sum_k e^{z_k}$, is the multinomial logit. In ML it is often called a *softmax* function, and it is the most common way to translate from real values (e.g., $\boldsymbol{x}_i' \boldsymbol{\beta}_k$) to probabilities. You might see it elsewhere specified with denominator $1 + \sum_k e^{\boldsymbol{x}' \boldsymbol{\beta}_k}$, which corresponds to setting a "reference" outcome class where $\boldsymbol{\beta}_j = \boldsymbol{0}$. As was the case for factor reference levels, this is an artifact of maximum likelihood estimation (you need to restrict the space of variables to get a welldefined maximum), and the issue disappears with regularization.

For multinomial distributions, the likelihood is simple. Given probabilities $p_{ik}$ for $y_{ik} = 1$, the probability of the observed data is proportional to

$$\prod_{i=1}^{n} \prod_{k=1}^{K} p_{ik}^{y_{ik}}, \tag{4.4}$$

where we recall that $a^0 = 1$ and $a^1 = a$.

As an exercise, you can compare this to Equation 2.22 and confirm that the binomial likelihood corresponds to Equation 4.4 in the case where $K = 2$ (noting that the definition of $y_i$ has changed from a scalar number to a binary vector of length 2).

Taking the log of Equation 4.4 and multiplying by $-2$ yields the multinomial deviance:

$$\text{dev} = -2 \sum_i \sum_k y_{ik} \log(p_{ik}).$$ (4.5)

Finally, applying the logit link of Equation 4.3 to get $p_{ik}$ as functions of the regression coefficients $\boldsymbol{B} = [\boldsymbol{\beta}_1 \ldots \boldsymbol{\beta}_K]$, we obtain

$$
\begin{aligned}
\text{dev}(\boldsymbol{B}) &= -2 \sum_{i=1}^{n} y_{ik} \log p_{ik}(\boldsymbol{x}_i' \boldsymbol{B}) \\
&= -2 \sum_{i=1}^{n} \left[ \sum_{k=1}^{K} y_{ik} \, \boldsymbol{x}_i' \boldsymbol{\beta}_k - m_i \log \left( \sum_{k=1}^{K} e^{\boldsymbol{x}_i' \boldsymbol{\beta}_k} \right) \right],
\end{aligned}
$$ (4.6)

where $m_i = \sum_k y_{ik}$ is the total number of "successes" for observation $i$. (It is a good math exercise to derive the second line from first line here.) In the current classification examples, $m_i = 1$ because only one outcome is possible. However, Equation 4.6 will be useful in other settings where $y_{ik}$ instances are counts and can be any positive integer. For example, in text analysis the $y_{ik}$ will be counts for words in a document.

As always, we will estimate our multinomial logistic regressions through penalized deviance minimization:

$$\hat{\boldsymbol{B}}_\lambda = \operatorname{argmin} \left\{ -\frac{2}{n} \sum_{i=1}^{n} y_{ik} \log p_{ik}(\boldsymbol{x}_i' \boldsymbol{B}) + \lambda \sum_k \sum_j |\beta_{kj}| \right\}.$$ (4.7)

Here, we have a single penalty $\lambda$ across all classes $k$; we'll relax this in later estimation strategies.

The `gamlr` package doesn't include the estimation routine in Equation 4.7. Instead, it feeds into an efficient parallel computing strategy called *distributed multinomial regression* (DMR) that is described in the next section. In the meantime, we can fit your multinomial logistic regressions using the `glmnet` package with the `family = "multinomial"` flag. Glmnet and `gamlr` use almost the exact syntax, but there are small differences. Both have detailed help documentation.

We'll illustrate on the forensic glass data from our investigation of $K$-NN algorithms. As for `gamlr`, `glmnet` works with sparse matrices. The design matrix includes all of the chemical composition variables interacting with the refractive index.

```
library(glmnet)
xfgl <- sparse.model.matrix(type~.*RI, data=fgl) [,-1]
```

We can then call `cv.gamlr` to minimize Equation 4.7 and run a CV experiment.

```
gtype <- fgl$type
glassfit <- cv.glmnet(xfgl, gtype, family="multinomial")
```

The `cv.glmnet` object is similar to the `cv.gamlr` object. You can plot the OOS deviance results across folds, as in Figure 4.7. We see that the lowest OOS deviance is around 2.0 and the null model deviance is around 3.0, implying a rough $R^2$ of around 1/3. Figure 4.8 shows the lasso paths. In Figure 4.8 we see that there is a separate path plot for each glass type—in other words, for each $\beta_k$. However, in the model specification there is a single $\lambda$ across all classes. From Figure 4.7, the CV-min rule selects path slices at $\log \lambda \approx -6$.

The `predict` function yields probabilities for the fitted model.

```
probfgl <- drop(predict(glassfit, xfgl, type="response"))
```

For classification, these probabilities can be combined with decision costs, as described in the previous section (things are a bit more complicated for multiclass problems, but the logic is unchanged). In the common setting where you have symmetric costs, you can just use a *maximum probability rule*: $\hat{k} = \text{argmax}_k \{\hat{p}_k : k = 1 \ldots K\}$. You get this in R with `apply(probs, 1, which.max)`, which gives the maximizing column index for each row of `probs`.

We can create a picture of the in-sample fit for multinomial distributions that is analogous to our fit plots for linear and logistic regression. Figure 4.9 shows box plots of $\hat{p}_{ik_i}$ for the in-sample observations, where $k_i$ denotes the true class (i.e., $y_{ik_i} = 1$). A tight fit has all of the boxes in this plot pushed up toward 1. We are well able to discriminate headlamp glass (from Figure 4.2, because of the Barium) but less confident about the others. Vehicle window, container, and tableware glass shards have low fitted probabilities, but they are also rare in this sample (box width is proportional to sample size).

To get the regression coefficients, we use the familiar `coef` function. As we did for `cv.gamlr`, we can add `select="min"` to apply CV-min selection. The raw output for `glmnet` is a list with an element for each outcome class, and we do some simple formatting[6] to change this into the $p \times K$ matrix $\hat{\mathbf{B}}$.

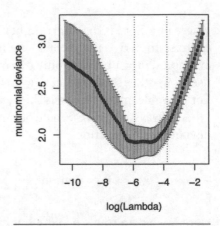

**FIGURE 4.7:** OOS deviance across CV folds for multinomial logistic lasso regression on the forensic glass data. The vertical lines again mark CV-min and CV-1se selection rules.

---

6. Since `glmnet` gives back predictions as an $n \times K \times 1$ array, use `drop()` to make it an $n \times K$ matrix.

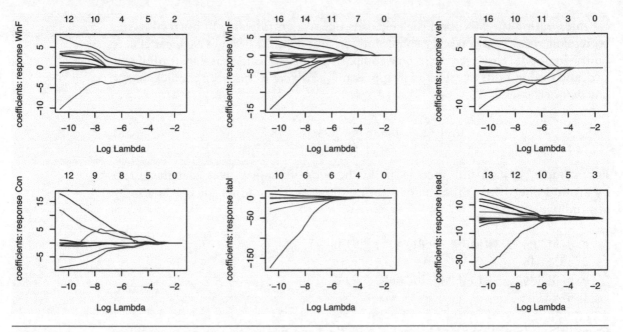

**FIGURE 4.8:** Lasso regularization paths for glmnet multinomial logistic lasso regression on the glass data.

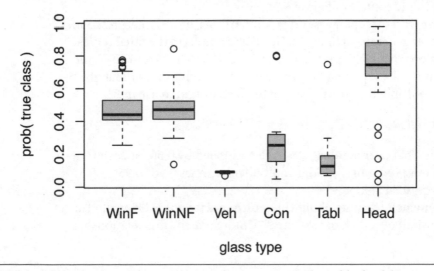

**FIGURE 4.9:** IS fit for the glass multinomial logistic lasso regression. The width of each box is proportional to the sample size for that class.

```
B <- coef(glassfit, select="min")
B # it's a list of coefficients, 1 matrix per glass type.
## combine into a matrix
B <- do.call(cBind, B)
## annoyingly, column names are dropped
colnames(B) <- levels(gtype) # add them back
```

Interpreting the MN logit coefficients is not straightforward. In binary logistic regression, recall that you had a simple interpretation for the $\beta$ values as linear effects on the log-odds. However, we're now comparing across $K$ categories, instead of just two, and the log-odds interpretation applies on the *difference* between coefficients for any *pair* of classes:

$$\log\left(\frac{p_a}{p_b}\right) = \log\left(\frac{e^{x'\beta_a}}{e^{x'\beta_b}}\right) = x'[\beta_a - \beta_b]. \tag{4.8}$$

For example, with a 1-unit increase in Mg, the odds of nonfloat over float glass drop by around one-third while the odds of nonfloat over container glass *increase* by around two-thirds:

```
exp(B["Mg", "WinNF" ]-B["Mg", "WinF"])
0.6633846
exp(B["Mg", "WinNF"] -B["Mg", "Con"])
1.675311
```

From this we infer that more Mg makes both float and nonfloat windows more likely but that the probability of float glass increases more than the probability for nonfloat glass. This makes sense in the context of Figure 4.2.

Once you get familiar with these pairwise odds comparisons, model interpretation is the same as for any other generalized linear model. For example, in the fitted regression, the RI:Mg interaction coefficient is estimated as $\hat{\beta}_{\text{winNF, RI:Mg}} = -0.05$ for WinNF and 0 for WinF. Thus, the multiplicative effect of a unit extra Mg on odds of nonfloat glass over float glass is itself multiplied by the following for each unit increase in RI:

$$\exp\left[\hat{\beta}_{\text{winNF, RI:Mg}} - \hat{\beta}_{\text{winF, RI: Mg}}\right] = e^{-0.05} \approx 0.95.$$

From earlier, the odds of float over nonfloat glass are multiplied by 0.66 for each unit increase in Mg *at a refractive index of zero*. This multiplier becomes $0.66 \cdot 0.95^5 \approx 0.51$ at RI $= 5$ and $0.66 \cdot 1.05^5 \approx 0.84$ at RI $= -5$.

A common question when learning about the multinomial logit is "How do the odds for one class against all others change with $x$?" Unfortunately, this relationship is *nonlinear*:

$$\log\left[\frac{p_k}{1-p_k}\right] = \log\left[\frac{p_k}{\sum_{j \neq k} p_j}\right] = x'\beta_k - \log\sum_{j \neq k} e^{x'\beta_j}. \tag{4.9}$$

There is no fixed relationship for, say, the effect of a unit change in one covariate. You need to calculate the probabilities at two different input locations and do an explicit comparison.

Once you work with logistic multinomial models a bit, you will get familiar with the idea of $e^{x'\beta_k}$ acting as an *intensity* for each class. Each of these intensities battle against each other to determine the probabilities across potential classes. This interpretation forms the basis for the algorithm that is covered in the next section.

## Distributed Multinomial Regression

If you went and ran the regressions in the previous section, or other multinomial logits, you might have noticed that multinomial regression can be slow. This is because, compared to the linear and logistic lassos, you now have $K$ times more coefficients since everything needs to be repeated $K$ times. A computational bottleneck occurs because the deviance for each $\hat{\beta}_k$ depends on all of the other category coefficients through the logit link: $p_k = e^{x'\beta_k} / \sum_j e^{x'\beta_j}$.

Through a well-known relationship between Poisson and multinomial distributions, it turns out that multinomial logistic regression coefficients will be—for all practical purposes—similar to those that we can get through *independent* estimation for each of the log-linear equations:

$$\mathbb{E}[y_{ik}|\boldsymbol{x}_i] = \exp(\boldsymbol{x}_i'\boldsymbol{\beta}_k). \tag{4.10}$$

The trick is that we need to estimate the coefficients in Equation 4.10 using a Poisson distribution likelihood, rather than the Gaussian distributions (squared error loss) that we've previously used with log linear models. That is, we will assume that

$$y_{ik} \sim \text{Poisson}\,(\exp[\boldsymbol{x}_i'\boldsymbol{\beta}_k]). \tag{4.11}$$

This leads to the Poisson deviance objective,

$$\text{dev}(\boldsymbol{\beta}_k) \propto \sum_{i=1}^{n} \exp(\boldsymbol{x}_i'\boldsymbol{\beta}_k) - y_i(\boldsymbol{x}_i'\boldsymbol{\beta}_k). \tag{4.12}$$

Adding lasso penalty regularization, we can then estimate regression coefficients by minimizing a penalized deviance:

$$\hat{\boldsymbol{\beta}}_k = \text{argmin}\left\{\sum_{i=1}^{n} \exp\,(\boldsymbol{x}_i'\boldsymbol{\beta}_k) - y_i(\boldsymbol{x}_i'\boldsymbol{\beta}_k) + \lambda_k \sum_j |\beta_{kj}|\right\}. \tag{4.13}$$

The Poisson distribution is used for *count* data: $y \in \{0, 1, 2, \dots\}$. When you *know* that $y_{ik} \in \{0, 1\}$, this is a misspecified (i.e., incorrect) model. However, research[7] has demonstrated that the two models are practically interchangeable, especially for prediction purposes. Use of Equation 4.13 to estimate multinomial logit parameters is what we refer to as *distributed multinomial regression* (DMR). This Poisson

---

7.  Matt Taddy. Distributed multinomial regression. *The Annals of Applied Statistics*, 9:1394–1414, 2015b.

approximation scheme can even lead to *improved* prediction in a lasso setting because it allows you to validate and select a different $\lambda_k$ for each outcome class.

The biggest advantage of using DMR is that you can now estimate each $\hat{\beta}_k$ in *parallel*. To "compute in parallel" is to do many calculations at the same time on different *processors*. Scientific supercomputers have long used parallelism for massive speed, but since the early 2000s it has become standard to have many processor "cores" on consumer machines. Even small mobile devices, like a phone, will have two to four cores. This parallelization is the key to modern computing, and you are likely already taking advantage of it. For example, you can run multiple applications at the same time on a laptop, and digital videos run on special graphical processing units (GPUs) that contain thousands of tiny cores for massive parallelization.[8]

R's `parallel` library makes it easy to take advantage of multiple cores. You can do `detectCores()` to see how many you have The `parallel` library works by organizing *clusters* of processors, which we can create with the `makeCluster` command.[9]

```
> library(parallel)
> detectCores()
[1] 4
> cl <- makeCluster(4)
> cl
socket cluster with 4 nodes on host 'localhost'
```

There is a large ecosystem of R functions that are designed to work with these clusters for parallel computing. For example, see the `parLapply` function for a parallel alternative to the usual `for` loops. As good practice, you can do `stopCluster(cl)` when you're done with your parallel computing to ensure that these processors are freed up for other tasks.

The `dmr` function in the `distrom` library implements our DMR parallel estimation strategy for multinomial logistic regression. You give `dmr` a `parallel` cluster object, and it will outsource `gamlr` runs for the Poisson lasso regressions of Equation 4.13 to each of the available cores. It is simply a faster way to fit multinomial logistic regression. Since `dmr` is based on `gamlr`, the syntax will be familiar. You just call `dmr(cl, covars, counts, ...)` where

- `cl` is a `parallel` cluster,
- `covars` is $x$,
- `counts` is $y$, and
- `...` are any additional arguments to `gamlr`.

You can also call `dmr` with the option `cv=TRUE`, in which case it runs `cv.gamlr` for each of the Poisson regressions. Note that we will be validating on Poisson rather than multinomial OOS deviance in this case.

---

8. These GPUs are the same hardware that is used for training deep neural networks.
9. This assumes that your computer is set up for parallelization. This *should* be true, but if not, you'll need to debug; doing an Internet search on the errors you are getting is usually a good place to start.

We can run `dmr` on the glass data, and the output will be a `list` of `gamlr` objects, one for each different glass type.

```
> glassdmr <- dmr(cl, xfgl, gtype, verb=TRUE)
fitting 214 observations on 6 categories, 17 covariates.
converting counts matrix to column list ...
distributed run.
socket cluster with 4 nodes on host 'localhost'
> names (glassdmr)
[1] "WinF" "WinNF" "Veh" "Con" "Tabl" "Head"
> glassdmr [ ["WinF"]]
poisson gamlr with 17 inputs and 100 segments.
```

Conveniently, each of these list elements is the same familiar `gamlr` object that we've been working with for linear and logistic lassos. It contains a path plot of $\hat{\beta}_k$ along a path of $\lambda_{kt}$ penalty weights. You can plot these paths or do anything else you might do with a standard `gamlr` object. See Figure 4.10 for the path plots.

Notice the AICc selection in Figure 4.10: it moves around across outcome classes since different penalties are best for different $\hat{\beta}_k$. We can call `coef` and `predict` directly on the `dmr` object to get AICc selected coefficients and predictions (or use the `select` argument to ask for any other model choice).

```
> Bdmr <- coef(glassdmr)
> round(Bdmr, 1)
18 × 6 sparse Matrix of class "dmrcoef"
             WinF  WinNF   Veh   Con   Tabl   Head
intercept  -28.4   13.4  169.4  118.2  -12.1  -22.2
RI            .      .      .      .      .      .
Na          -0.3   -0.2   -0.3   -2.5    0.6    0.6
Mg           0.8    .      2.3   -1.5    .     -0.3
Al          -1.1    0.4   -0.4    1.4    0.8    0.9
Si           0.4   -0.1   -2.8   -1.3    .      0.1
K            .      .     -3.1    .     -8.5    .
Ca           .     -0.5    3.3    0.3    0.2    .
Ba           .     -2.3    .      .     -6.2    0.7
Fe          -0.5    1.0   -2.3    5.1  -10.9    .
RI:Na        .      .      .      0.2    .      .
RI:Mg        0.0   -0.1    .     -0.1   -0.1    .
RI:Al        .     -0.1    .      .      .      .
RI:Si        .      0.0    .      .      .      .
RI:K         .      0.1    .      .      .      .
RI:Ca        .      .     -0.2   -0.2    0.0    .
RI:Ba        .      0.1    .     -0.6    .      .
RI:Fe       -0.4   -0.2    3.1   -1.9    .      .
```

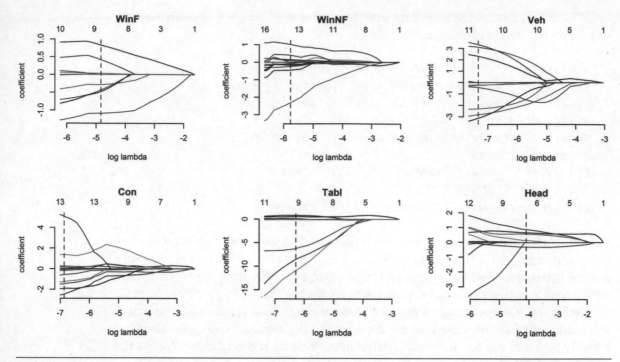

**FIGURE 4.10:** Lasso paths for the glass data multinomial regression via dmr. Dashed lines show AICc selection.

If you run and compare to the glmnet results, you will find differences across coefficients. The intercepts are wildly different; however, these differences wash away after normalization in the softmax function. The regression coefficients are also different—this is largely because of the different $\lambda_k$ penalties selected for each glass type, as opposed to the single shared $\lambda$ for glmnet (selected at $\hat{\lambda} \approx e^{-5}$ under the CV-min rule). When it comes to prediction, however, they give similar results. The 20-fold OOS experiment plotted in Figure 4.11 shows no change in OOS performance for dmr versus glmnet when measured in terms of multinomial deviance. In this small-data ($n = 214$) case, there are no real differences even when you consider different model selection criteria. In larger examples, we see dmr sometimes significantly outperform glment in such experiments, and you can attribute this to the use of class-specific $\lambda_k$ penalties.

In examples like the glass data classification, the parallelization strategy of dmr gives a useful efficiency boost: if you have four processors, you can compute all of the model estimates in about one-fourth the time. However, the real advantage for such methods comes when you are fitting multinomial logistic regressions for a *massive* number of outcome classes. In that case, parallelization can make the difference between feasibility and impossibility.

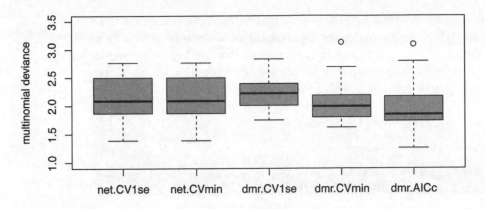

**FIGURE 4.11:** OOS performance for `dmr` and `glmnet` on a 20-fold experiment using the glass data. All model selection (including CV) is executed without the left-out test data for each fold.

The motivating example behind the development of DMR was in text analysis. As we detail in Chapter 7, it is often useful to summarize documents as counts of words. A *multinomial inverse regression* model looks to analyze these counts as a function of document attributes in a multinomial logistic regression where "word" is the outcome class. Using the approximate formulation in Equation 4.10, the task is then to estimate $\hat{\beta}_k$ for $\mathbb{E}[y_{ik} \mid x_i] = \exp(x_i'\beta_k)$ where $y_{ik}$ is the count for word $k$ in document $i$ and $x_i$ are document attributes (author, date, etc.). This requires you to fit as many sets of regression parameters as there are words. If you are dealing with a vocabulary of, say, 500,000 words, then such a task would be impossible without large amounts of parallelization.

We will detail these ideas in more detail in Chapter 7. But they raise the point that efficient data management and parallelization is an essential (not just convenient) part of modern analysis. It turns out the DMR is not just parallel but also *distributed*, and the difference between these terms is key to large-scale computing.

## Distribution and Big Data

An algorithm is *parallel* if it does many computations at once. When each of these calculations needs to see all of the same data, the algorithm is merely parallel. When each computation is able to work with a subset of the data, the algorithm is *distributed*. Parallel computing is good for intensive computation, but for true big data you need distributed algorithms. Indeed, the oldest use of the term *big data* referred to datasets that were too big to be stored on a single machine—thus distributed algorithms were necessary for any analysis.

The idea behind contemporary big data storage and analysis is to *shard* your data into many little pieces on many machines. You then take advantage of massive bandwidth to allow communication between these machines during analysis. Systems such as Hadoop HDFS, Amazon's S3 (see Figure 4.12), or Microsoft's Azure Blob Storage split your data into little pieces (e.g., 64KB of a file) that are kept wherever is convenient (to protect against data loss, pieces of data are often kept in more than one place). As the end user, you interact only with a map of where things are.

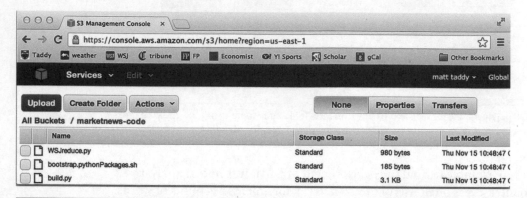

**FIGURE 4.12:** An Amazon S3 console, which looks like a standard file browser, but the file content is distributed across machines (or even across data centers).

This model was originally built around unstructured data, such as text and images, that benefited less from being stored locally in a structured database with columns and fixed entry sizes. But the distributed storage model is essential to cloud computing, and it now provides the underlying logic for a vast proportion of the world's data (especially business data). There are plenty of algorithms that have been developed to facilitate statistical analysis on these massive distributed datasets. Many fit within a framework known as *MapReduce* (MR), a simple but powerful recipe for algorithms that was popularized in 2004 by researchers at Google.[10] To use MapReduce, you need to be able to specify a *key* that indexes subgroups of data that can be analyzed in isolation.

---

**ALGORITHM 12** **MapReduce Framework**

Given a *key* indexing data to subgroups, you proceed to do the following:

- map: Calculate and sort relevant statistics by key.

- Partition and pipe the outcome of map so that outcomes with the same key end up on the same machine.

- reduce: Apply a summarization operation within the subgroup defined by each key.

---

10. Jeffrey Dean and Sanjay Ghemawat. MapReduce: Simplified data processing on large clusters. In *Proceedings of Operating Systems Design and Implementation*, pages 137–150, 2004.

As a simple example, imagine the task of tabulating word occurrence by date across a large database of documents (e.g., books, magazines, newspapers). The MapReduce routine is applied on the distributed corpus of documents:

- Apply a `map` operation for each document, extracting the date and counts for each word. The mapper outputs multiple lines containing `date|word count`. Here's an example if the document uses the word "tacos" five times on June 4, 2017:

$$2017/06/04|\texttt{tacos 5}$$

- The *key* in this example is `date|word`, for example, `2017/06/04|tacos`. The data is sorted and streamed so that each line with the same key ends up on the same reducer machine.

- `reduce` all lines with the same key using the `sum` operator, such that the output is a single line per key: `date|word total`. Here's an example if `tacos` was used 501 times across all documents on June 4, 2017:

$$2017/06/04|\texttt{tacos 501}$$

This simple example can be extended into a number of more complex schemes. For example, the DMR algorithm is distributed with respect to the response counts: each regression need only see $y_{ik}$ for its respective category $k$. In the case of text regression, $k$ refers to a word in a vocabulary. Consider the example where you are looking to understand how some time-dependent variables—for example, market data or political events—affect language choice. If this is a relatively small set of variables, the full design matrix will be small enough to pass among many machines. For example, you might have the following reported returns in the S&P 500 and VIX financial market indices on each date:

$$X = \begin{bmatrix} \texttt{date} & \texttt{SP500} & \texttt{VIX} \\ \texttt{2017/06/02} & \texttt{0.0037} & \texttt{-0.0142} \\ & \vdots & \end{bmatrix}. \tag{4.14}$$

The MapReduce version of DMR is then as follows:

- `map` and partition exactly as described earlier in the word-count MR so that all counts for the same `date|word` key go to the same machine.

- *Broadcast* your set of date-indexed covariates so that every reducer machine contains a copy of $X$.

- `reduce` using a Poisson regression for the word counts onto the corresponding S&P 500 and VIX returns for each day. The output is the length-2 vector of word-market $\beta_{kj}$ coefficients.

After collecting all of the coefficients, you've estimated a large text model. Such results can be used to understand how, for example, news drives change in market indices.

The implementation of basic MapReduce algorithms is straightforward. One common scheme acts exactly as described earlier, with the results of the mapper *streamed* line by line to the reducers. Suppose you've written a mapper script (e.g., `mapper.py` since Python is good at text parsing) that takes raw input and produces single lines of key tagged output and a reducer script (e.g., `reduce.R` since you want to run `gamlr` regressions in R) that takes these single lines as input. Then kicking off a big MapReduce job in the cloud is easy using, say, Amazon's EMR (elastic mapreduce) command tools.

```
EMR -input s3://indir -output s3://outdir
-mapper s3://map.py -reducer s3://reduce.R
```

More generally, the tools facilitating distributed computing are rapidly improving. One prominent system is `Spark`, a layer built on top of `Hadoop` that makes it easier to incorporate machine learning and statistical algorithms (especially iterative algorithms that need to touch the data repeatedly). `Spark` tries to organize the process so that results and data can stay "in memory" on each machine until you are done (instead of writing to hard disk, which is really slow). More recently, even friendlier layers are being built on top of `Spark`. For example, `SparkR` facilitates the use of R as a front end to a `Spark` cluster of distributed machines, and companies like Microsoft offer cloud computing platforms that will organize your data storage and allow you to interact with it through a web-based R server.

A full technical guide to `Spark` or `Hadoop` is beyond the scope of this text, but there is abundant training material available, and you need to be broadly aware of how data distribution works if you are going to interact with big data. The new mantra of scaling is always "build out, not up." In other words, focus on more machines, not just faster machines. Fortunately, all of this is getting closer to the nonengineering mainstream and easier to use every day. The best practices that you learn in this text—how to think about model building, prediction, causation, and validation—will keep you safe when modeling even if the data is distributed across the globe.

# Experiments

Every method we have discussed so far is able to detect patterns in past data. These patterns will be useful for predicting the future, *assuming that the future looks mostly like the past*. As the cliché goes, "Correlation is not causation." But correlation might be all that you need. If people who rent the movie *Frozen* also tend to like the movie *Sing*, then you can reliably use this information for future recommendations. Both preferences are likely caused by a third unseen signal—that these people have small children who like cartoon musicals—but that doesn't lessen the usefulness of the discovered pattern.

However, when you are analyzing business and economic systems, you need to dig deeper and get at causation. You need to be able to predict a future that will be different from the past because you are going to take actions that make it different. A decision that changes your product, marketing, or pricing creates a new data generating process that can break the correlation patterns that you've seen in the past. Suppose that you are a hotelier considering offering a discount to increase business. This price change is an action, and you need to know how sales will change *because* of that action.

In the past, hotel room prices have moved up or down according to projections of demand. For example, rooms are more expensive over holidays because you anticipate higher demand. This will lead to a correlational pattern where prices are high when sales are high—during holidays there are no vacancies, and the prices are very high. Of course, sales are not high *because* prices are high. Rather, the two are (like viewership of *Frozen* and *Sing*) codependent upon a third variable—in this case, the underlying demand for hotel rooms. If you act to change prices and break the past dependence structure, then this correlational pattern disappears.

Price optimization is a setting that requires *counterfactual* prediction.[1] You want to know what will happen to your sales if you charge price $p_1$ instead of price $p_0$. There might be a complex chain of causation between price and sales, but you don't really care. You just want to know the counterfactual sales numbers for $p_1$ vs $p_0$. The only way to really know this is to move prices independently of everything else and see what happens. Most commonly, one could set prices randomly to get an estimate of the consumer demand curve. This is the purest form of experimentation—a randomized trial—and it is the gold standard for estimating counterfactuals.

Counterfactual analysis is the focus of this and the next chapter. We start with experimentation, moving from simple randomized controlled trials through more complicated designs. Every setting in this chapter involves some amount of explicit randomization. In contrast, the next chapter deals with *observational studies* where you need to create settings that look like experiments by *controlling* for confounding influences (e.g., the holiday demand spike in the earlier pricing example). Between the two chapters, I hope to provide a primer on the state-of-the-art for counterfactal (or causal) analysis.[2] This type of analysis plays a huge role in how data is used in economics and business. The material in these two chapters is essential knowledge for anyone hoping to use data to have an impact on strategic decisions.

## Randomized Controlled Trials

The gold standard for measuring the effect of an action is an experiment. "Try it and see what happens" was at the core of the scientific revolution during the seventeenth century. It was given the formalism of frequentist statistics in the beginning of the twentieth century by Sir Ronald Fisher and his peers. And the Internet era has made Fisher's randomized controlled trials (RCTs)—under the new label *AB testing*—an essential part of business optimization.

The language that we use to discuss counterfactual inference is rooted in experimentation. We refer to estimation of a *treatment effect* (TE) even in cases where we do not have control of treatment assignment. A "treatment" variable—say, $d$—is a special input to your prediction models. It is special because it can be changed *independently* from all other upstream influences on the response of interest. The notion of independence is the key statistical property of treatments in a causal analysis: we want to know what will happen if we *act* to change the treatment variable(s).[3]

Treatment variables can be discrete or continuous. For example, the variable in a pharmaceutical trial could be $d_i = 1$ for subjects $i$ who are given a new drug and $d_i = 0$ for those receiving a placebo or control dose. Price is a common continuous treatment

---

1. See the text by Morgan and Winship [2015] for discussion on the relationship between causal modeling and counterfactual analysis. In the context of business decision-making, you can usually focus on counterfactual "what if?" questions without getting lost in deeper philosophical issues of causation.
2. This and the next chapter provide a relatively brief primer on counterfactual analysis. See Imbens and Rubin [2015] for a much more comprehensive overview of these topics by two of the leading thinkers in the area.
3. This idea is formalized in the do-calculus of Pearl [2009].

variable: as a business you decide to "treat" your potential customers to price $d_t$ at time $t$, and they will choose to buy or not buy your product at this price. You can also have multiple treatments of all different sorts; for example, television marketing campaigns for consumer goods are often accompanied by price promotions so that you have a discrete marketing treatment (show or don't show ad) and a continuous price treatment (discount size). We will focus our introductory discussion on discrete treatments, but the ideas translate to continuous settings and we will cover examples for a variety of scenarios.

Experiments can be discussed in terms of their *design*: the scheme through which treatment is assigned. Many readers will be familiar with the notion of an *AB* trial, which is Silicon Valley's label for a *completely randomized design* wherein the experiment subjects are randomly assigned to treatment status. For example, you might randomize your website users into groups *A* and *B*; those in *A*, the control group, see the current website, and those in *B* see a new layout.

On large-scale online platforms, it is difficult to make sure that treatment is truly randomly designed. For example, in a website experiment, it could be that one of the many entry points to your site leads users only to the control (version *A*) landing page. To check that this is not happening, *AB* platforms typically run "*AA*" tests that show the same website in groups *A* and *B*. If you see a significant difference between groups in an *AA* trial, then something is likely wrong in your randomization.

The massive advantage of an *AB* trial is that since treatment is completely randomized, it is easy to estimate the *average treatment effect* (ATE) on the response *y*. Suppose that the treatment variable is $d_i = 0$ for users $i$ in group *A* and $d_i = 1$ for those in group *B*. Then the ATE is the mean difference in response, averaged over all other influences on *y* in your distribution of users, for option *B* instead of *A*:

$$\text{ATE} = \mathbb{E}[y \mid d = 1] - \mathbb{E}[y \mid d = 0]. \tag{5.1}$$

Crucially, for Equation 5.1 to have a causal interpretation, we require that *d* is *independent* of all other factors that could influence *y*. In an *AB* trial, this independence is achieved through randomization. See the end of this section for a more flexible formulation of the ATE that makes use of the concept of *potential outcomes*.

When treatment has been randomized, you know that differences between the two treatment groups have been caused by their difference in treatment status. Thus, estimation for the ATE becomes simply estimation for the difference in means between two groups. This is material you learn in your first statistics class. Suppose $\bar{y}_0 = \frac{1}{n_0}\sum_{d_i=0} y_i$ and $\bar{y}_1 = \frac{1}{n_1}\sum_{d_i=1} y_i$ are the sample means for the $n_0$ and $n_1$ users in groups *A* and *B*, respectively. Then your ATE point estimate is

$$\widehat{\text{ATE}} = \bar{y}_1 - \bar{y}_0. \tag{5.2}$$

Assuming that the users are all *independent* from each other, the standard error on this ATE is available through the standard formula:

$$\text{se}(\bar{y}_1 - \bar{y}_0) = \sqrt{\frac{1}{n_0}\widehat{\text{var}}(y_i \mid d_i = 0) + \frac{1}{n_1}\widehat{\text{var}}(y_i \mid d_i = 1)}$$

$$= \sqrt{\frac{\sum_{d_i=0}(y_i - \bar{y}_0)^2}{n_0(n_0 - 1)} + \frac{\sum_{di=1}(y_i - \bar{y}_1)^2}{n_1(n_1 - 1)}} \ .$$

(5.3)

Usual central limit theorem arguments imply that the sample means are normally distributed for large samples and a 90% confidence interval for the ATE is $\bar{y}_1 - \bar{y}_0 \pm 2\text{se}(\bar{y}_1 - \bar{y}_0)$.

As an example, let's look beyond web experiments to a large-scale policy experiment. In 2008, the state of Oregon gained funding to expand its coverage for Medicaid—the U.S. social program that provides health insurance to people who cannot afford private insurance. Since demand was (correctly) expected to outstrip supply, the state worked with researchers[4] to design a lottery that randomly allocated eligibility for Medicaid enrollment among the state's low-income population. This led to the Oregon Health Insurance Experiment (OHIE), a randomized controlled AB trial for measuring the treatment effect of Medicaid eligibility.

There are many outcomes of interest here. Since the people in each treatment group were tracked for only 12 months, we don't get to observe long-term differences between the two groups and it is difficult to draw conclusions about the effect of insurance on public health. However, we can observe how Medicaid changes the use of health services. This is important both for estimating the cost of expanded public insurance and for modeling the downstream public health improvements. For example, researchers found a small increase in hospitalization for those selected in the Medicaid lottery (hereafter the *treated* or *selected* group) but no increase in usage for emergency room (ER) services (indeed, the point estimate shows slightly *decreased* ER usage). This helps put an upper bound on cost projections.

Data from OHIE is available at `nber.org/oregon/4.data.html`, and the analysis code is on this book's website. The `doc_any_12m` variable is based upon a 12-month follow-up survey results from 23,000 of the total 75,000 people in the full sample. Finkelstein et al. argue convincingly that survey targeting and nonresponse was balanced across treatment groups so that you can treat these results as representative of the population. However, nonresponse and other tracking problems (e.g., missing users because of cookie clearing in web experiments) are common sources of bias in survey results.

---

4. Amy Finkelstein, Sarah Taubman, Bill Wright, Mira Bernstein, Jonathan Gruber, Joseph P. Newhouse, Heidi Allen, Katherine Baicker, and Oregon Health Study Group. The Oregon health insurance experiment: Evidence from the first year. *The Quarterly Journal of Economics*, 127(3):1057–1106, 2012.

We'll focus on the treatment effect on *primary care usage*. The response variable doc_any_12m is coded as $y_i = 1$ for patients who saw a primary care physician (PCP; i.e., a "family doctor") in the 12 months of the study, and $y_i = 0$ for those who did not visit a PCP. Primary care usage is generally viewed as a *good thing*: PCP visits are a relatively low-cost form of healthcare and they can prevent the need for expensive acute care from hospitalization or via the ER. After some basic data cleaning, we have available this outcome for each patient along with information about their treatment status.

```
> head(P)
  person_id household_id doc_any_12m selected medicaid numhh
1         1       100001           0        1        0     1
2         2       100002           0        1        1     1
5         5       100005           0        1        0     1
6         6       100006           1        1        0     1
8         8       102094           0        0        0     2
9         9       100009           1        0        0     1
> nrow(P)
[1] 23107
```

Each of these 23,107 individuals was enrolled into the *lottery* for the chance to apply for Medicaid. The treatment of interest is (for now) the selected variable, which is 1 for the approximately 50% of people who were randomly selected in the lottery to be able to apply for Medicaid.

```
> table(P$selected)

    0     1
11629 11478
```

The additional medicaid variable is 1 if these selected people then actually enrolled for Medicaid. Not all those who were selected ended up actually enrolled; they might not have bothered applying, or they could have been found ineligible for a variety of reasons (e.g., if their income was higher than the state expected). Later in this chapter we introduce the concept of *instrumental variables* and use this to measure the direct effect of medicaid. The other variables shown here are household_id—some people in the study shared a household—and numhh, the number of people from each household that applied for Medicaid.

The standard ATE estimate is available via two lines of R code:

```
> ybar <- tapply(P$doc_any_12m, P$selected, mean)
> ( ATE <- ybar['1'] - ybar['0'] )
         1
0.05746606
```

We've estimated that being selected in the Medicaid application lottery leads to a 6 percentage point increase in the probability that you visit a PCP in the following year ($y$ is binary so its expectation is a probability). This is statistically significant: we have 90% confidence of a 4.5- to 7-point increase in PCP visit rates due to lottery selection.

```
> nsel <- table(P[,c("selected")])
> yvar <- tapply(P$doc_any_12m, P$selected, var)
> ( seATE <- sqrt(sum(yvar/nsel)) )
[1] 0.006428387
> ATE + c(-2,2)*seATE
[1] 0.04460929   0.07032284
```

Oregon can plan for this range of increased PCP usage when it expands Medicaid eligibility to a wider population, and models that condition on PCP access when predicting public health can use this information to project the societal benefits of increased access to health insurance.

The OHIE data also contain weights that can be used to map from the sample of individuals in the experiment to the future treatment population. For example, perhaps young people are harder to reach for a phone survey and they are under-represented in the sample (in both treatment and control groups—this is a different issue than covariate imbalance). We need to worry about such differences because individual subjects do not all respond the same way to treatment. In this scenario, the *weighted* means will be more representative of the treatment effect for the average eligible Oregonian than $\bar{y}_1 - \bar{y}_0$. This is a basic form of the heterogeneous treatment effect modeling that is covered in later sections. Here, the adjustment makes little difference—only 2/10 of a percentage point change in estimated ATE:

```
> nsel_w <- tapply(weights, P$selected, sum)
> ybar_w <- tapply(weights*P$doc_any_12m, P$selected, sum)/nsel_w
> ( ATEweighted <- ybar_w['1'] - ybar_w['0'] )
        1
0.05539111
```

This sort of reweighting, to map from the sample to the population of interest, is a standard step in many statistical analyses. For example, political pollsters are always battling to figure out how their sample of potential voters maps to the characteristics of the future voting population. An interesting contemporary overview of this area by Andrew Gelman and coauthors[5] tackles the problem of using abundant survey through nontraditional venues—e.g., via the Microsoft Xbox gaming platform—for

---

5.  Wei Wang, David Rothschild, Sharad Goel, and Andrew Gelman. High-frequency polling with nonrepresentative data. In *Political Communication in Real Time*, Routledge, 2016.

insight about voting intentions of the wider population. As pollsters' recent lack of success demonstrates (e.g., Trump, Brexit), the sample-to-population mapping problem is a tricky one.

For many business settings, this is less of an issue because you are able to sample representatively from your customers. In such a setting, it is tough to find a treatment effect estimator for randomized designs that will perform better than $\bar{y}_1 - \bar{y}_0$. However, there are alternatives. Most prominently, *regression adjustment* is sometimes advocated as offering a reduced-variance version of the $\widehat{\text{ATE}}$ from Equation 5.2. With observable covariates $x_i$ for each individual (e.g., gender, race, online activity), a regression adjustment first fits a linear model for each treatment group:

$$\mathbb{E}[y \mid x, d] = \alpha_d + x'\beta_d. \tag{5.4}$$

Given *pooled* covariate average (across treatment groups) $\bar{x}$, the regression adjusted ATE estimator is then

$$\widehat{\text{ATE}} = \alpha_1 - \alpha_0 + \bar{x}'(\beta_1 - \beta_0). \tag{5.5}$$

When the covariates encode a mapping into mutually exclusive subgroups (e.g., $x_{ij} = 1$ if person $i$ is in group $j$), then this procedure is sometimes referred to as *post-stratification*.

The idea behind Equation 5.5 is that adjusting for differences due to covariates can reduce the variance in the ATE estimate because of random imbalances across groups (e.g., having slightly more men in $A$ than $B$). However, we tend to advise against these adjustments unless you have small sample sizes and know of a few factors that have a large influence on the response (in which case you should consider the sort of blocked design mentioned at the end of this section). David Freedman[6] argued that the regression adjustments can introduce strange biases, and we[7] find that any reduction in variance due to adjustment is vanishingly small in large samples. The extra complexity of regression adjustment usually is not worth the effort. For a large $AB$ experiment with a perfectly randomized design, you can stick with $\widehat{\text{ATE}} = \bar{y}_1 - \bar{y}_0$.

◆ **UNFORTUNATELY, PERFECT EXPERIMENTS ARE RARE.** Only in the classic website $AB$ trial, where the treatment is a small change and the experiment runs over a short one- to two-week period, do you commonly see something like an ideal randomization scheme. Even in that setting there are problems; for example, when you randomize across devices visiting your website, this exposes people with multiple devices to multiple treatment states. Or, when using browser cookies to track people,

---

6.  David A Freedman. On regression adjustments in experiments with several treatments. *The Annals of Applied Statistics*, 2:176–196, 2008.
7.  Matt Taddy, Matt Gardner, Liyun Chen, and David Draper. Nonparametric Bayesian analysis of heterogeneous treatment effects in digital experimentation. *Journal of Business and Economic Statistics*, 2016a.

you will lose some portion of users as they clear their browsers. Unless your website experience is completely locked behind a sign-in wall, then you will have difficulties in randomizing the user-level experience.

These issues usually lead to small, assumed ignorable, imperfections in website trials. But with more complex treatments and in longer studies the treatment groups can differ in systematic ways that will influence your results. As mentioned earlier, online platforms use *AA* tests—with identical treatments across groups—to audit their randomization schemes (although these won't catch all problems, especially those due to differential non-response). Fortunately, so long as you know the factors that are causing a lack of balance between treatment groups, you can use basic regression techniques to *control* for these factors and recover solid ATE estimates.

Consider the Oregon health insurance experiment. The previous analysis ignored two problems in the experiment design, both of which are common in randomized trials.

1. *Imperfect randomization*: Each person selected in the lottery could apply for Medicaid for all of their family members so that these people are then also selected. This leads to an over-representation of large families in the selected group.

2. *Dependence between units*: The sample includes members of the same household whose behavior—for example, the decision to visit a PCP—will be correlated. This violates the usual assumption of independence between observations.[8]

You will repeatedly encounter both of these issues in the analysis of experiments, and we'll consider corrections for each in turn.

For the first issue, we know the mechanism through which covariate imbalance is introduced: people are able to apply for Medicaid for their entire household so that people in larger households have a higher chance of being selected. This shows up clearly in the data (recall that there are around 11,500 people in each treatment group):

```
> table(P[,c("selected","numhh")])
        numhh
selected    1     2    3+
       0 8684  2939    6
       1 7525  3902   51
```

If healthcare consumption changes for individuals depending upon family size, then one possible model is

$$\mathbb{E}[y \mid d, \text{numhh}] = \alpha_{\text{numhh}} + d\gamma. \tag{5.6}$$

---

8. The notion of independence between observations plays an important role in causal inference, and it is formalized as SUTVA: the stable unit treatment value assumption. See Imbens and Rubin [2015] for detail on this topic.

Here, $y$ is the `doc_any_12m` variable and $d$ is `selected` so that $\gamma$ is the expected treatment effect—the ATE. By adding the household-size-specific intercept $\alpha_{numhh}$, we are controlling for the change in $y$ across treatment groups that is due to household size. We can use `glm` to fit this model with least-squares in R.

```
> lin <- glm(doc_any_12m ~ selected + numhh, data=P)
> summary(lin)

Coefficients:
            Estimate Std. Error t value Pr(>|t|)
(Intercept)  0.590184   0.004863 121.366 < 2e-16 ***
selected     0.063882   0.006452   9.901 < 2e-16 ***
numhh2      -0.065738   0.007065  -9.305 < 2e-16 ***
numhh3+     -0.173657   0.064772  -2.681 0.00734 **
```

The ATE estimate is higher than before we controlled for `numhh`: it has increased from 0.055 to 0.64. This correction is due to the inferred negative effect on PCP visit probability for the larger households (which, again, were more common in the `selected` group).

The moment you lose perfect randomization, you are forced to start making modeling assumptions. Now that we have started down this road, it makes sense to see whether the model in Equation 5.6 can be improved upon and make sure that the ATE estimate is not overly sensitive to model assumptions. In particular, it seems plausible that the treatment effect of lottery selection is itself changing with the household size. This implies the following model, which is a version of the full interaction model of Equation 5.4 used in regression adjustment:

$$\mathbb{E}[y \mid d, \text{numhh}] = \alpha_{numhh} + d\gamma_{numhh}. \tag{5.7}$$

The easiest way to calculate the adjusted ATE is to first shift the covariates so that $\bar{x} = 0$ and Equation 5.5 simplifies as $\alpha_1 - \alpha_0$.

```
> x <- scale( model.matrix( ~ numhh, data=P) [,-1], scale=FALSE)
> colMeans(x)
         numhh2         numhh3+
 -3.723165e-17  -3.149334e-20
```

We then use interaction terms to fit $\mathbb{E}[y \mid d, x] = \alpha + d\gamma + x'\beta_d$, so that the coefficient on $d$ (i.e., on `selected`) is the ATE estimate.

```
> linadj <- glm(doc_any_12m ~ selected*x, data=P)
> summary(linadj)
```

```
Coefficients:
                   Estimate Std. Error t value Pr(>|t|)
(Intercept)        0.570410   0.004562 125.040  < 2e-16 ***
selected           0.064230   0.006460   9.943  < 2e-16 ***
xnumhh2           -0.051951   0.010407  -4.992 6.02e-07 ***
xnumhh3+          -0.420160   0.199162  -2.110   0.0349 *
selected:xnumhh2  -0.025518   0.014173  -1.801   0.0718 .
selected:xnumhh3+  0.272023   0.210619   1.292   0.1965
```

The new ATE estimate is 0.064, practically unchanged from the model that controlled for main effects of numhh but did not have the effect of selected change with numhh. As a general rule, when you have systematic covariate imbalance, I favor using this later "full-interaction" regression adjustment to the more simple control for confounders in Equation 5.6. Practitioners often use the simpler no-interaction model, but the full interaction model is more robust to heterogeneous (covariate-dependent) treatment effects. When there is a covariate that has a large effect on $y$, there is good reason to suspect that it also moderates the effect of $d$ on $y$.

The second problem with our earlier OHIE analysis is the possibility of dependence between observations due to the inclusion of multiple people from the same household in the study. Like covariate imbalance, this is a common issue in experiments. It turns out that linear (i.e., OLS) regression is *robust* to this type of misspecification: the regression parameter estimates, and the estimate for the ATE, will approach the truth even if you have dependent errors. However, the out-of-the-box standard error calculations will be wrong (and hence your confidence intervals will be wrong).

One way to correct this is to estimate effects on the household rather than person level. This is easy here because the treatment (selected) and covariates (numhh) are always constant across a household—we can just average the response and collapse across covariates to get a single household level ATE.[9] The model is then

$$\mathbb{E}[\bar{y} \mid d, x] = \alpha + d\gamma + x'\beta. \tag{5.8}$$

Here, $\bar{y}$ is the household-level rate of PCP visits, while $x$ and $d$ encode the household's numhh and selected variables, respectively. We fit the model after doing the household level collapsing manually:

```
> # build the household effects
> yhh <- tapply(P$doc_any_12m, P$household_id, mean)
> zebra <- match(names(yhh), P$household_id)
> selectedhh <- P$selected[zebra]
> xhh <- x[zebra,]
> summary(glm(yhh ~ selectedhh*xhh))
```

---

9. If you have within household variation in covariates and collapse those via averaging, you end up with a version of the instrumental variables setup that we discuss in a later section.

```
Coefficients:
                       Estimate Std. Error t value Pr(>|t|)
(Intercept)            0.572661   0.004889 117.133  < 2e-16 ***
selectedhh             0.063291   0.006838   9.255  < 2e-16 ***
xhhnumhh2             -0.043883   0.012183  -3.602 0.000317 ***
xhhnumhh3+            -0.475715   0.273384  -1.740 0.081856 .
selectedhh:xhhnumhh2 -0.029237   0.016467  -1.775 0.075835 .
selectedhh:xhhnumhh3+ 0.337775   0.289368   1.167 0.243109
```

Both the estimate and standard error for $\gamma$ change slightly from our corresponding person level model shown earlier. However, the differences are small and the 90% confidence intervals are practically identical:

```
> ## person-level estimate
> 0.064230 + c(-2,2)*0.006460
[1] 0.05131 0.07715
> ## household-level estimate
> 0.063291 + c(-2,2)*0.006838
[1] 0.049615 0.076967
```

The group-level and individual-level models are similar here because there are a large number of groups—most households in the sample contain only a single person (there are 20,476 households and 23,107 individuals). In an example with more clustering (i.e., a smaller number of total groups), the differences will be much more pronounced.

You can also obtain *nonparametric* standard errors through the use of a bootstrap. When you have dependence between observations, you need to use a *blocked* bootstrap that resamples on the group rather than individual level. In this case, we resample *households* with-replacement while fitting the person-level model for each bootstrap sample. The boot package can be used to implement this after we use split to create a map from households to individuals:

```
> library(boot)
> n <- nrow(P)
> hhwho <- split(1:n, P$household_id) # rows grouped by HH
> bootfit <- function(hhlist, boothh) {
+     bootsamp <- unlist(hhwho[boothh])   # map from HH sample to rows
+     coef(glm(doc_any_12m ~ selected*x, data = P, subset=bootsamp)) [2]
+ }
> bs <- boot(names(hhwho), bootfit, 99)
```

The standard error and confidence intervals are similar to those we found earlier:

```
> sd(bs$t)
[1] 0.006586946
> quantile(bs$t, c(.05,.95))
       5%         95%
0.05365116 0.07514728
```

As a last note on correlated errors, economists often address this issue by using *clustered standard errors*. The procedure uses an extension of the Huber–White heteroskedastic consistent (HC) variance from Chapter 2. Recall that a nonparametric estimate for the variance of regression coefficients with regression design matrix $X$ (now including the intercept and all inputs) is

$$(X'X)^{-1}X'\Sigma X(X'X)^{-1}. \tag{5.9}$$

Here, $\Sigma$ is a good estimate of the variance matrix for the vector of errors across observations, $\varepsilon$. In the HC estimator, independence between observations is assumed, and you use for $\Sigma$ a diagonal matrix with entries $\hat{e}_i^2$, the squared regression residuals. Now, since independence within groups is no longer assumed, you have nonzero off-diagonal entries of $\hat{e}_i \hat{e}_k$ if observations $i$ and $k$ are from the same group (cross-group entries are still zero since those errors are assumed independent). This clustering is implemented in the vcovCL function of the AER package. We can apply it to the interaction-adjusted regression:

```
> library(AER)
> sqrt(vcovCL(linadj, cluster = P$household_id) [2,2])
[1] 0.006589621
```

Note that this is, to the 5th decimal place, the same as the bootstrap standard error estimate. The two procedures—clustered SEs and blocked bootstrapping—are both attempting to approximate the same target and hence will tend to give similar results.

As a final thought on regression adjustment, why are we using linear regression here? There is no great reason for this. Indeed, the response is binary, and from earlier chapters, we know that logistic regression is the preferred model in such a setting. Linear regression (i.e., OLS) is often used for ATEs because the treatment effect is thought of as additive and because steps like regression adjustment are easiest in linear models. Moreover, OLS will give a robust estimate for the ATE even if the truth is nonlinear and the errors are non-Gaussian. However, it often makes more sense to talk about multiplicative effects and, especially if you have covariates, a logistic regression might do a better job in real data examples at recovering the true conditional mean function.

Here, we can add `family="binomial"` to our existing regressions to get the logit results:

```
> lgt <- glm(doc_any_12m ~ selected*numhh, data=P, family="binomial")
```

The regression adjustment makes calculating the ATE a bit tricky because the mean prediction is no longer the model prediction at mean covariates (i.e., you can't just feed in $\bar{x}$). So, we need to actually predict over the covariate space for each treatment status, take the difference in probabilities as our treatment effect, and then average. We can do this by calculating the difference in predicted PCP visit probabilities at each numhh value and then summing these differences with weights equal to the proportion of observations at each numhh level:

```
> predlocs <- data.frame(selected=c(1,1,1,0,0,0),
+       numhh=c('1','2','3+','1','2','3+'))
> predy <- predict(lgt, newdata=predlocs, type='response')
> ( pdiff <- predy[1:3] - predy[4:6] )
          1          2          3
0.07111385 0.04559574 0.34313725
>
> ( mu_numhh <- table(P$numhh)/nrow(P) )
          1          2         3+
0.701475743 0.296057472 0.002466785
> pdiff%*%mu_numhh
            [,1]
[1,] 0.06423005
```

The resulting ATE estimate, 0.064, is close to our OLS-estimated ATE. You can apply the bootstrap, again with household blocks, to get the standard errors for this estimate—it will be close to that from OLS, but there is no reason that it will be the same (different models, different errors). In my bootstrap, I find that the logit standard error is about 15% smaller than that from OLS.

**THERE IS A HUGE WORLD OF EXPERIMENTAL DESIGN.** This section only scratches the surface, and there are a number of strategies other than complete randomization. For example, when you know in advance that external factors have an influence both on the response and on the treatment effectiveness, you can reduce the variance of the ATE estimates by randomizing within *blocks* of experimental subjects that share similar properties.

As a famous application, Fisher's agricultural experiments of the 1920s had the problem that variation in growing conditions across fields could be large relative to his treatment effects of interest, such as the effect of a fertilizer. The solution is a *blocked randomized design*: split the growing area into fields of relative homogeneity and apply each treatment level within subregions of each field. The blocked ATE estimate is then the average *difference* between outcomes for the treated subregions. That is, if $y_{kd}$ is some measure of crop yield in field $k$ of $K$ under treatment $d$, then the estimated ATE is

$$\widehat{\text{ATE}} = \frac{1}{K} \sum_{k=1}^{K} (y_{k1} - y_{k0}). \tag{5.10}$$

This estimator will tend to have lower variance than the ATE in Equation 5.2 for a completely randomized design that just allocated each field to a single treatment status.

A related strategy is *matched pairs*, common in medical trials, where two similar patients are paired and each given a different treatment. The difficulty in this later setting is that, unlike the agricultural example where a single field is split in two, the matched pair contains two distinct people who will inevitably differ on many observable and unobservable characteristics. ATE estimators based on human pairs are thus sensitive to the matching procedure and don't always offer reliable variance reduction.

Other useful strategies include factorial designs, where combinations of treatments are organized in a manner that forces independence from confounding factors and allows one to understand interaction effects, and sequential designs that use information from early trials to inform later trials in a dynamic experiment. Many of these more complex setups are best understood through a *potential outcomes*[10] framework wherein each subject is modeled as having its own treatment effect:

$$y_i(1) - y_i(0). \tag{5.11}$$

Here, $y_i(1)$ is the response for individual $i$ if they are treated, and $y_i(0)$ is their response in an alternative untreated world. Of course, in most settings, you only ever get to see $y_i(d_i)$ for $d_i = 1$ or 0, and thus Equation 5.11 is partially unobservable. But the concept of potential outcomes turns out to be a useful formalism for the analysis of real-world experimental settings. For example, this allows for a concise definition of the average treatment effect:

$$\text{ATE} = \mathbb{E}[y(1) - y(0)]. \tag{5.12}$$

This removes the need for the extra conditions listed after our earlier ATE definition in Equation 5.1.

Potential outcomes is not the only way to think about causation, but it is a framework that works nicely for practical applications. We will make use of it in the coming sections and in future chapters.

---

10. See Imbens and Rubin [2015] for a detailed treatment of potential outcomes modeling by two of the leading thinkers in this area.

## Near-Experimental Designs

There are several common scenarios where a randomized $AB$ trial is impossible but you can nonetheless recover causal treatment effect estimates under a small set of additional assumptions.[11] Maybe you introduce a new product/treatment to only a portion of the markets—for example, the United States but not Canada. These are different places, but if you can model the pretreatment differences between them, there is a hope to build a causal interpretation around post-treatment changes. Or, perhaps only individuals with income less than a fixed threshold receive some form of social assistance. This is a nonrandom sample, but you might assume that those people who barely miss out on the social program (i.e., they made slightly too much money) are otherwise comparable to those who barely qualified and use these two groups as treatment and control samples.

The first example mentioned allows for a *difference-in-difference* (diff-in-diff) analysis, and the latter is a setting for *regression discontinuity* (RD) estimation. There are many other near-experimental setups, but variations on these two cover a large proportion of business applications. We'll look at two applications from Internet marketing to illustrate each framework.

A DIFF-IN-DIFF ANALYSIS applies when you have two groups whose pretreatment differences can be isolated and modeled so that post-treatment differences are the basis for causal estimates of the treatment effect. The framework consists of nothing more than some basic regression modeling along with strong assumptions about treatment independence. The canonical example has two markets, say, Canada and the United States, with only one receiving some sort of sales promotion, say, free shipping in the United States. You can model the trend in sales in both countries before and after treatment—free shipping—is rolled out in the United States. If sales grow in the United States relative to Canada after treatment, then you have a positive treatment effect *if you assume that this difference is not because of external shocks that hit only one of the two countries*. This last assumption is the Achilles heel of diff-in-diff analysis, and there is no way to get around it. For this reason, diff-in-diff results are only as reliable as the two groups are truly comparable.

Our diff-in-diff example is taken from the paper by Blake et al. [2014],[12] researchers from eBay who studied the effect of search engine marketing (SEM). *Sponsored* or *paid* search refers to the advertisements and links that you see around web search results on, for example, Google. Figure 5.1 shows an example web page returned after search, dominated by paid search results. The research question is simple: "What is the effect of paid search advertising?" Or, to turn it around, what would happen to sales revenue if eBay stopped paying for SEM? Since a big website like eBay will show up anyway in the

---

11. We're making a somewhat arbitrary distinction here between "near-experimental" and the conditional ignorability (CI) setting of the next chapter. CI is usually applied when treatment was completely out of control of the researcher, but all of these topics have conceptual overlap.
12. Tom Blake, Chris Nosko, and Steve Tadelis. Effectiveness of paid search. *Econometrica*, 2014.

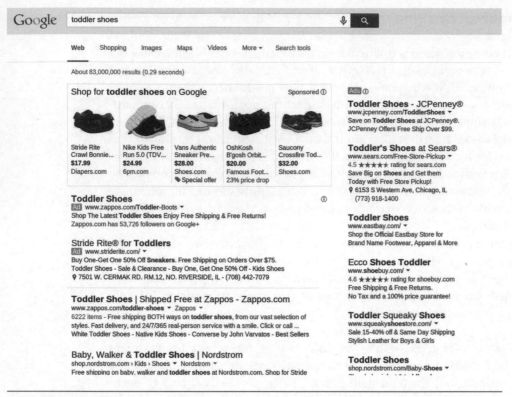

**FIGURE 5.1:** SEM around search results on Google. Almost everything in the screenshot is "sponsored"— it has been paid for and has not risen *organically* through Google's relevance metrics. The only organic results are the bottom two listings in the main column, first for Zappos and second for Nordstrom.

organic results (e.g., see Zappos in both organic and paid results in Figure 5.1), do they get any benefit from also appearing in sponsored slots? And how big is the benefit? Is it worth the cost?

Questions about marketing ROI are generally tough to answer. The sponsored results get clicked and lead to conversions, but you have no idea if these users would have followed the organic result if there was no sponsored option. And you can't compare the pages where eBay ads don't appear to those where they do: the ads appear with the searches that eBay and Google think are most likely to lead to clicks. That is, the pages where ads don't appear will expect to see fewer clicks on eBay links for search-relevance reasons independent of the presence or absence of sponsored results.

Blake et al. managed to convince the powers at eBay to run a large-scale experiment where SEM was turned off for a portion of users. This created a unique opportunity to measure the treatment effect of paid search (for a single company), something that had never before been reliably measured. In particular, eBay stopped bidding on any AdWords (the marketplace through which Google SEM is sold) for 65 of the 210 "designated market areas" (DMA) in the United States for the eight weeks following May 22, 2012. These DMAs are viewed as roughly independent markets around metropolitan centers ranging from Boston to Los Angeles. Google guesses the DMA on a browser and eBay can track users by their shipping address, allowing for DMA-specific treatment assignment and response tracking.

The data are shown in Figure 5.2.[13] The top line corresponds to those DMAs that are never treated (SEM is always on), and the bottom line is for those where SEM was turned off on May 22 (marked with the dashed vertical). *This was not a fully randomized trial.* That is immediately clear from the difference between treatment and control DMAs *before* May 22. It turns out that not all DMAs were eligible for treatment (e.g., the largest markets were excluded) and that there was an attempt to "match" DMAs across treatment and control that didn't result in balanced revenues. Clearly, you can't just look at $\bar{y}_B - \bar{y}_A$ to estimate the ATE: there is a big difference even before group $B$ is treated.

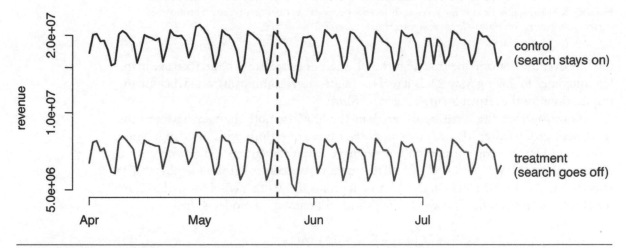

**FIGURE 5.2:** Average "revenue" for treatment and control DMAs. The dashed line is May 22, when SEM (bidding on AdWords) was turned off for the treatment group.

However, this is a great setting for a diff-in-diff analysis. We have no reason to think that there was anything other than the SEM turnoff that would cause the relative difference between treatment and control group DMAs to change after May 22. Thus, if SEM works, the revenue difference between treatment and control groups should be larger after May 22. This pre-post comparison across groups is the logic underlying a diff-in-diff analysis.

Here we will focus on differences in log revenue because we anticipate that the treatment and control groups are related on percentage scale. The treatment DMAs have about 38% of the revenue of the control DMAs when SEM is on for both. Figure 5.3 shows the log difference between average revenues in each group (this is the log of the ratio of the

---

13. Note that we are not analyzing the real data; we're looking at a scaled and shifted version that obscures real revenue numbers.

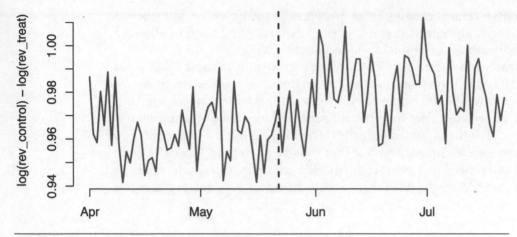

**FIGURE 5.3:** The log-scale average revenue difference between treatment and control groups: *log (average control revenue) – log (average treatment revenue).*

top line over the bottom line from Figure 5.2). There does appear to be an increase in the log difference following May 22. Is it real (i.e., statistically significant), and what are the implications for the return on investment for SEM?

Assuming that the nothing other than the SEM-turnoff changes between the treatment groups after May 22, we can answer these questions with basic regression modeling. Introducing some notation, we have DMA $i$ at time $t \in 0, 1$ where $t = 0$ denotes before May 22 and $t = 1$ after. Treatment versus control group membership is encoded as $d_i = 1$ if DMA $i$ is in the treatment group, $d_i = 0$ otherwise; thus, SEM is *on* for DMA $i$ at time $t$ *unless* $t \times d_i = 1$. The diff-in-diff regression model is then

$$\mathbb{E}[y_{it}] = \alpha + \beta_d d_i + \beta_t t + \gamma d_i t. \tag{5.13}$$

The treatment effect of interest is $\gamma$: the coefficient on the *interaction* between $d_i$ and $t$.

After some initial data wrangling, we have a simple dataset consisting of a row for each DMA in each of $t = 0$ and $t = 1$:

```
> head (semavg)
  dma t d        y
1 500 0 1 11.22800
2 501 0 0 14.58000
3 502 0 0 10.38516
4 503 0 0 10.48166
5 504 0 0 13.39498
6 505 0 1 12.81640
```

This format makes it easy to run the regression of Equation 5.13. However, note that these rows of data do not satisfy the standard independence assumption: each two observations on the same DMA will be correlated. For example, if one DMA corresponds to a larger city, then its log revenue ($y$) will tend to be larger than average for both the $t = 0$ and $t = 1$ observations. As we did in the previous section for dependence within households, we can use the *clustered* standard error estimator from the sandwich package.

```
> semreg <- glm(y ~ d*t, data=semavg)
> coef(semreg)
 (Intercept)            d            t          d:t
10.948646049   0.014080564 -0.039399629  -0.006586852
> sqrt(vcovCL(semreg, cluster=semavg$dma)['d:t','d:t'])
[1] 0.005534297
```

Recalling that the treatment effect in this model is $\gamma$, the *interaction coefficient* on $d_i \times t$, the 90% confidence interval for the ATE is

$$\gamma \in -0.00659 \pm 2 \times 0.00553 = [-0.177, 0.0045].$$

This says that the treatment—turning off paid search ads—has a small but not statistically significant negative effect on log revenue (0.66 percentage point drop with a standard error of 0.55 points). Even if the result was statistically significant, it is doubtful that paid search would have a positive ROI once the *cost* of the marketing is accounted for. A caution, however: This result is for a specific company and for situations where eBay results often occur in the organic search results. There will be a positive ROI for digital marketing in other cases, especially when the advertiser is not well known or would not occur in the organic results.

If the clustered standard errors are unintuitive, note that you can get a similar[14] result by *controlling* for the DMA-specific revenue levels in the regression mean equation itself. That is, you replace Equation 5.13 with a model including DMA-specific intercepts (i.e., what economists would call "DMA fixed effects"):

$$\mathbb{E}[y_{it}] = \alpha_i + d_i\beta_d + t\beta_t + \gamma d_i t. \tag{5.14}$$

Since we're now assuming independence conditional upon the DMA-specific levels, the usual regression standard errors apply.

```
> dmareg <- glm(y ~ dma + d*t, data=semavg)
> summary(dmareg)$coef["d:t",]
    Estimate    Std. Error      t value      Pr(>|t|)
-0.006586852   0.005571899  -1.182155571   0.238493640
```

---

14. Adding fixed effects is not the same as clustering standard errors, however both are approaches to accounting for dependence within a DMA. One approach is not obviously superior to the other, and each has different advantages. For example, the approach of adding fixed affects is easily extensible to more complex dependence structures.

The estimates for $\gamma$ and its standard errors are practically unchanged from our earlier regression analysis using clustered standard errors.

Our derivation and analysis here should convince you that the diff-in-diff procedure is just an example of applied regression modeling. However, the estimator is often presented in an alternative formulation that takes advantage of the *pairing* between pre- and post-treatment observations. In this form, you would first calculate the sample of pre-post *differences* for each DMA:

$$r_i = y_{i1} - y_{i0}. \tag{5.15}$$

You then collect the average difference for the treated and control groups, say $\bar{r}_1$ and $\bar{r}_0$, and use the difference between these averages as the ATE estimate, as shown here:

$$\hat{\gamma} = \bar{r}_1 - \bar{r}_0. \tag{5.16}$$

This routine is the source of the "difference in differences" name. Independence between DMAs implies independence for each $r_i$, and you can apply the usual formula to get the standard error for a difference in means: $\mathrm{se}(\hat{\gamma}) = \mathrm{se}(\bar{r}_1) + \mathrm{se}(\bar{r}_0)$.

```
> r <- tapply(semavg$y, semavg$dma, function(y) y[2]-y[1])
> d <- semavg[match(names(r), semavg$dma), "d"]
> rbar <- tapply(r,d,mean)
> rbarvar <- tapply(r, d, function(r) var(r)/length(r))
> rbar[2] - rbar[1]
            1
-0.006586852
> sqrt(sum(rbarvar))
[1] 0.005555082
```

The results are unchanged from our previous regression analyses.

**REGRESSION DISCONTINUITY ESTIMATORS** take advantage of another common near-experimental design: treatment allocation is determined by a threshold on some "forcing variable," and subjects that are close to the threshold, on either side, are comparable for causal estimation purposes. For example, Hahn et al. [1999] evaluate the causal effect of a discrimination law that applies only to firms with more than 15 employees. Here, the number of employees is the forcing variable and the authors compare firms on either side of the 15-employee threshold. Similar situations arise all over the place: grade thresholds determine access to education programs, income thresholds influence availability of social programs, and my kids had free entry at the museum until they turned 4. We'll consider a common digital marketing setting where the rules for ad display depend upon whether the highest (or second highest) ad auction "score" passes a reserve threshold.

The nice thing about a regression discontinuity (RD) design is that you know the only confounding variable that you need to control for: the forcing variable. Recall our earlier discussion of imperfect experimental designs. You need to control for (i.e., include in the regression) any variable that is correlated with both treatment allocation and the response. In a strict RD, the treatment is *fully determined* by the forcing variable so you just need to control for that variable. In the examples just given, you'd need to control for each firm's number of employees or each advertiser's score in the ad auction.

> There are also "fuzzy" RD designs where the threshold changes the probabilities for different treatments, but allocation is not deterministic; these are versions of the IV setup that we discuss in the next section. See Imbens and Lemieux [2008] for more detail.

An RD analysis requires an assumption about how the response varies with the forcing variable near the treatment threshold. You must assume that if the threshold were to move slightly, subjects switching treatment groups will behave similarly to those near them in their *new* treatment group. This is a *continuity* assumption. It means that you can look at the relationship between the forcing variable and the response on one side of the threshold and extrapolate to the other side.

Figure 5.4 shows observed (solid) and unobserved (dashed) expected response functions for each of two treatment groups. The RD continuity assumption implies the behavior that we see around the treatment threshold (where the solid line jumps). Even though there is a discontinuity (i.e., a jump) in the observed mean response, the underlying treatment group functions are each continuous around this point (i.e., each group mean response is smooth over the transition from solid to dashed). This allows you to compare the counterfactual response across the two treatment groups.

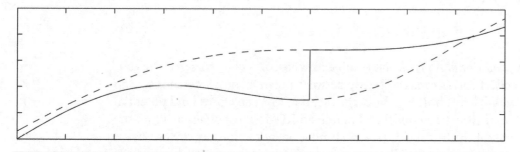

**FIGURE 5.4:** Illustration of the RD continuity assumption, taken from Imbens and Lemieux [2008]. Solid lines are the observed mean response (y-axis) given the forcing variable (x-axis), and dashed lines show the unobserved mean response for each group.

We can make this all more precise using the potential outcomes notation. Recall that $y_i(d)$ is the potential outcome for user $i$ under treatment $d$, and $d_i$ is their treatment group so that $y_i(d_i)$ is their observed response. For RD designs, we add the forcing variable $r_i$: the location of $r_i$ relative to your treatment threshold determines the treatment status. *For simplicity, we will assume that this threshold of interest is always zero.* You can just subtract a nonzero threshold from the forcing variable to make this true. Limiting ourselves to binary treatments, the treatment allocation with forcing variable $r_i$ is then

$$d_i = \mathbb{1}_{[r_i > 0]}. \tag{5.17}$$

This is a near experimental design because you need to control only for the forcing variable—treatment allocation is independent of the response given $r_i$:

$$[y_i(0), y_i(1)] \perp\!\!\!\perp d_i \mid r_i. \tag{5.18}$$

Finally, the important continuity assumption can be written (recalling that your treatment threshold is at $r_i = 0$) as follows for small $\varepsilon$:

$$\mathbb{E}[y_i(d) \mid r = -\varepsilon] \approx \mathbb{E}[y_i(d) \mid r = 0] \approx \mathbb{E}[y_i(d) \mid r = \varepsilon]. \tag{5.19}$$

   With all of these pieces in place, you can estimate the causal effect of treatment by fitting regression models on either side of the threshold and comparing their predictions at $r = 0$. For example, we will usually estimate separate linear regressions within some distance $\delta$ of the threshold:

$$\mathbb{E}[y_i \mid r_i, -\delta < r_i < 0] = \alpha_0 + \beta_0 r_i,$$
$$\mathbb{E}[y_i \mid r_i, 0 < r_i < \delta] = \alpha_1 + \beta_1 r_i. \tag{5.20}$$

Here, the first regression will have $d_i = 0$ and the second $d_i = 1$. The treatment effect estimate at $r_i = 0$ is then

$$\mathbb{E}[y_i(1) - y_i(0) \mid r_i = 0] = \alpha_1 - \alpha_0. \tag{5.21}$$

This gives you a *conditional* ATE for those subjects whose $r_i$ is close to zero. The estimated treatment effect corresponds to the gap between potential outcomes at the jump in Figure 5.4. You will learn nothing about the fact that this gap closes (and potential outcomes even cross) away from this threshold; in an RD design, you learn about the treatment effect only at the threshold. This is a limitation, but so long as you are aware that you are getting a conditional ATE, the results are often useful nonetheless.

   Treatment assignment for our digital marketing example is illustrated in Figure 5.5. The data correspond to sponsored search, as in the previous SEM diff-in-diff example, but here we have details on the process through which ads are assigned to positions on the search page. In an ad auction, the advertiser bids a certain amount for their ad to be shown. These bids are then combined with information from the ad platform (i.e., the search engine provider) about the likelihood that each ad will be clicked by the user (the platform gets paid only if the ad is clicked). There are a number of formulas for combining bids with click-probabilities—regardless of details,[15] the end result is a *rank score* that determines the order of ad priority in the auction. The ad with the highest rank score is shown first.

The response variable $y$ is a version of *ad revenue*—whether or not the ad was actually clicked, multiplied by the cost-per-click (CPC). You can imagine the CPC as the second highest bid in the auction (this data is simulated, so it is nobody's real revenue). The treatment that you're considering is the specific *position* effect of an ad showing up in the "mainline" ($d = 1$)—above the main search results—instead of on a sidebar ($d = 0$). The search platform has a reserve price for mainline ads: if the highest rank score *is not* above this reserve, then no ads are in the mainline and this ad is shown on the sidebar. If the rank score *is* above this reserve, then it is shown in the mainline. Thus the reserve price acts as a treatment allocation threshold for mainline positioning. We define the forcing variable as the rank score minus reserve price, such that the treatment threshold occurs at $r = 0$. This is the process plotted in Figure 5.5.

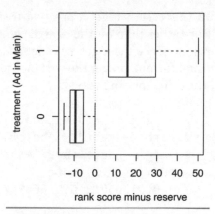

**FIGURE 5.5:** Forcing variable (rank score minus reserve) and treatment status (whether or not the ad is shown in the mainline, instead of the sidebar) in the digital marketing RD example. Notice that all and only ads with rank score greater than reserve are shown in the main line ($d = 1$).

Assuming that conditional expected revenue is smooth around this threshold, we can take advantage of the regression discontinuity to try to model the treatment effect of position on revenue. A simple approach is to just compare the mean revenue $y$ on either side of the $r = 0$ threshold. We first need to choose a window above and below the threshold. For illustration, we'll consider three rank score units on either side of the reserve price:

```
> w <- 3
> above <- which (D$score > 0 & D$score <w)
> below <- which (D$score < 0 & D$score >-w)
```

Then take the mean response for each window, and the difference is the estimated treatment effect:

```
> # constant model
> mua <- mean (D$y [above])
> mub <- mean (D$y[below])
> (te <- mua - mub)
[1] 0.01484979
```

15. Hal R. Varian. Online ad auctions. *The American Economic Review*, 99:430–434, 2009.

In this case, we get a positive treatment effect on "revenue"—being in the mainline rather than on the side of the search results leads to higher click rates at higher prices. Since these are all independent observations (by assumption), we can use the usual formula to get the variance for each window mean and for the treatment effect (the difference in means).

```
> vara <- var(D$y [above])
> varb <- var(D$y [below])
> sdte <- sqrt(vara/length (above) + varb/length(below))
> te + c(-2,2)*sdte
[1] 0.01305012 0.01664947
```

The resulting 95% confidence interval is entirely positive. Under this analysis we are almost certain that the mainline position has a positive effect on revenue (this seems pretty obvious when you think about it, at least in the short term).

This "difference in means" analysis is implicitly assuming a model where the response is constant within the window on either side of the threshold. This seems unlikely. Since the rank score increases with both advertiser bid and the expected click rate, it is reasonable to expect that higher $r_i$ (the rank score) will tend to lead to higher $y_i$—click rate times CPC. Indeed, this difference-in-means method of treatment effect estimation is generally seen as a *bad idea* for RD designs. It is typical that the response changes with the forcing variable independent of treatment—think about all of the RD examples cited earlier—and you thus need to control for this effect on either side of the threshold.

A better approach is to use localized linear regression. That is, you fit an ordinary least squares line in a window of $\pm\delta$ on either side of the threshold. This is exactly the procedure we previewed earlier in Equation 5.20. With use of interaction terms, we can write this system of two regressions as a single model:

$$\mathbb{E}[y_i] = \alpha + \gamma \mathbb{1}_{[r_i>0]} + r_i \left(\beta_0 + \beta_1 \mathbb{1}_{[r_i>0]}\right)$$
$$= \alpha + \gamma d_i + r_i \left(\beta_0 + \beta_1 d_i\right). \tag{5.22}$$

The treatment effect in Equation 5.22 is $\gamma$, equivalent to $\alpha_1 - \alpha_0$ in the formulation of Equation 5.20. Note again that this assumes specification such that the threshold—hence discontinuity—occurs at $r_i = 0$.

Also common in the literature is *weighted least-squares* regression on either side of the threshold with weights on observations that are decreasing with distance from the threshold. This can make the inferences less sensitive to the choice of window size; however, it introduces new parameters to tune (e.g., the decay rate in weights), and in practice we don't see a big advantage to the more complicated approach. The Loess smoother in Figure 5.6 is an example of a weighted least-squares fit.

We'll fit a localized linear regression estimator for the digital marketing example, again using a $\delta = 3$ unit window. This can be executed using interaction terms in R:

```
> h <- 3
> window <- which(D$score > -h & D$score < h)
> summary(linfit <- lm(y ~ treat*score, data=D, subset=window))

Coefficients:
              Estimate Std. Error t value Pr(>|t|)
(Intercept) 0.0820048  0.0011768  69.682  < 2e-16 ***
treat       0.0119216  0.0017396   6.853  7.3e-12 ***
score       0.0006188  0.0006627   0.934     0.35
treat:score 0.0007242  0.0010020   0.723     0.47
```

The estimated treatment effect is now 0.012. To get uncertainty around this estimate, we should use the heteroskedastic robust standard errors (since we have no reason to believe constant error structure on either side of the threshold).

```
> seate <- sqrt(vcovHC(linfit)["treat", "treat"])
> coef(linfit)["treat"] + c(-2,2)*seate
[1] 0.00834634 0.01549686
```

Note that this confidence interval, while still all greater than zero, is mostly lower than the interval from the earlier difference-in-means analysis.

The analysis is illustrated in Figure 5.6. The gap between the ends of the linear regression lines at the $r = 0$ threshold corresponds to the $\hat{\gamma} = 0.012$ from the above R output. The lighter gray line shows a loess smoothed estimate of the conditional mean (think of this as a moving average). The constant mean fits, mua and mub from earlier, are also shown; you can see that a difference-in-means analysis will lead to a biased-large treatment effect estimate whenever $y$ is increasing with $r$ on either side of the threshold.

Finally, any RD analysis is sensitive to the size of the local analysis window. We chose $\delta = 3$ here because the moving average (loess) mean estimates on the right of Figure 5.6 appear to be mostly linear in this window, but that is just a rough eye-ball decision. Moreover, looking at the left of Figure 5.6, there is no clear signal from the data that we can use to judge linearity (or anything else: until you take a moving average, the noise in this data overwhelms any apparent discontinuity).

The best practice is to calculate the RD treatment effect estimate for a range of windows. Figure 5.7 shows results for this example, and it is typical of what you see in other applications. After an initial high-variance region, where the window size is too small for you to estimate a reliable linear regression, the results settle down around $\hat{\gamma} = 0.012$. Moving to a wider window leads to lower uncertainty around the estimate, but this is at the expense of more restrictive linearity assumptions (you are assuming

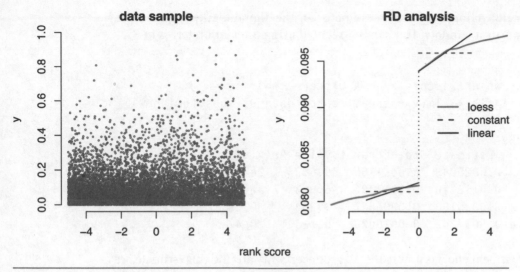

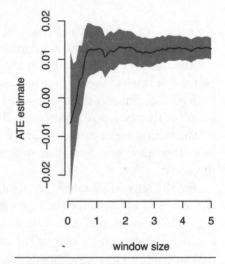

**FIGURE 5.6:** Illustration of the digital marketing RD analysis. On the left you can see a sample of the response $y$ values on either side of the treatment threshold at zero. On the right we show a zoomed-in view, with the conditional means for $y$ estimated using both the loess linear smoother in R (with degree = 1) and linear regression on scores ±3 units on either side of zero. The difference-in-means analysis is also shown, with a dashed line.

that the function is nearly linear for longer away from the threshold). In practice, this window-length selection is more art than science, and you should make sure that results are stable within a range of plausible values.

RD analysis is a common and useful tool in data analysis, and our coverage of the topic has been relatively brief. For more detail, you can look to Imbens and Lemieux [2008] and references therein. One particular situation is important to flag: it is possible to use similar tools for analysis when the treatment threshold is not strict (as we had here) but rather *fuzzy*: $r_i > 0$ changes the *probability* of treatment, but treatment allocation is not deterministic on either side of the threshold. These fuzzy RD designs turn out to be a special case of the instrumental variables design that we cover in the next section.

**FIGURE 5.7:** RD inference for the ATE—mean and 90% CI—as a function of the window size $\delta = 3$ in our digital advertising example.

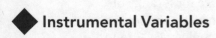  **Instrumental Variables**

In business and economic systems, you have a large set of inputs that combine to generate your outcome of interest. As we've highlighted throughout this chapter, understanding causation in such systems requires randomization—you need to have events that *look like* experiments. Thus far, we've considered analysis around the treatment effect of policies that have been themselves randomized. But it is common that you want to know the treatment effect for a policy that has not been *directly* randomized but rather has been *indirectly* randomized through experiments on variables that influence policy selection. These indirect randomizers, or upstream sources of randomization, are called *instrumental variables* (IVs). They form the basis for much of applied econometrics.

One intuitive IV example is the "intent-to-treat" setup. Consider a pharmaceutical trial that gives some drug to a random sample of patients. This is a completely randomized experiment, but the problem is that not every "treated" patient will take the drug. It might be that the drug is painful or inconvenient, and often people simply forget to take their medication. Thus, you have an experiment that randomizes *access* to the drug but is one step removed from actual drug treatment. Moreover, people may treat themselves differentially for reasons that are correlated with the response: sicker patients might find the drug more painful, or perhaps less sick patients are less willing to deal with an inconvenient treatment protocol. Thus, treatment is correlated with potentially *unobserved* factors that also influence the response, such that you can't easily control for the relevant differences between drug-takers and nontakers.

Fortunately, IVs provide a way to take this intent-to-treat problem and infer the drug's treatment effect. In this example, the single IV is the randomized group assignment (whether or not a subject has access to the drug). You are able to take advantage of this randomization by tracking how it changes the *probability* that a user takes the drug. If they are not assigned drug access, then the probability they take the drug is zero or small (it is possible they obtain the drug through alternative means). If they are assigned to the drug access group, then the probability they take the drug is much higher. An IV analysis models how this *change in probabilities* affects the patient outcomes (e.g., survival or other health metrics). By connecting the response to portion of treatment that is directly controlled by randomization (i.e., the treatment probabilities dictated by the IV), you can recover how the response changes that randomized component of treatment status. This allows you to model counterfactuals dependent upon whether the patient actually takes the drug.

We'll use some math to make this more precise. First, we need to explain the general problem of *endogeneity*. In the general IV model, you have some treatment variable $p$ and a response-of-interest $y$. You may or may not have observable covariates $x$ that directly influence the response, and you always have the *instrument $z$* which affects the response *only* through its influence on the treatment. In addition, there are *unobserved* factors or errors, say $e$, that have influence over both the treatment and response. The graph of this model is shown on the left of Figure 5.8. This graph makes clear the two crucial features of the instrument $z$: it acts on $y$ only through $p$, and it is completely independent from the unobserved error $e$.

The right side of Figure 5.8 connects these variables to the example of an intent-to-treat pharmaceutical trial. The response of interest is time-to-recovery and for

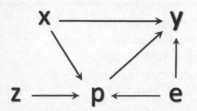 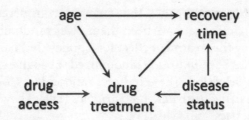

**FIGURE 5.8:** Diagram of a simple instrumental variables model. In each, the arrows are read as "*start* has a causal impact on *end*." On the left, $z$ is the IV, $p$ is the policy (treatment) variable, $x$ is an observed covariate, $y$ is the response, and $e$ is an unobserved variable that affects both treatment and response. On the right, you have these variables realized as components of the story about an intent-to-treat drug trial.

simplicity you can imagine a single unobserved variable called *disease status* that is correlated both with the patients propensity to take the drug and with their time to recovery (e.g., suppose patients with more advanced disease status take longer to heal and are less likely to take the drug). The instrument is randomized drug access (i.e., the patient's group assignment in the randomized controlled trial) and this randomization affects the response only by changing the likelihood of the patient taking the drug. Finally, you have the patient's age as an observable covariate—you can use this to model age-dependence in the drug's treatment effect.

We can write a version of this causal model as a regression:

$$y = g(x, p) + e, \quad \text{cov}(e, p) \neq 0. \tag{5.23}$$

Here, $g(x, p)$ is a *structural* function. We are imagining that this represents how $p$ acts causally on $y$ (perhaps also as a function of $x$; if it is easier for now, just ignore $x$ everywhere). The important distinction between Equation 5.23 and the usual regression model is the statement that the error and policy are correlated: $\text{cov}(e, p) \neq 0$. This implies that, in contrast to the usual statistician's regression, the error term is *not expected to be zero* given the treatment variable: $\mathbb{E}[e \mid p] \neq 0$. That is because the "error" influences policy selection, and hence policy realization gives you information about the error term.

In this setup we refer to the policy variable as *endogenous* to the response. It is jointly determined with the response as a function of unobserved factors or errors. In contrast, with *exogenous* errors you have $\text{cov}(e, p) = 0$, and the usual statistical regression models apply without any further thought. In the setting of Equation 5.23, however, applying off-the-shelf regression or ML when learning $g(p, x)$ will cause problems. Consider use of regression to estimate the noncausal conditional expectation for $y$:

$$\mathbb{E}[y \mid x, p] = \mathbb{E}[g(x, p) + e \mid x, p] = g(x, p) + \mathbb{E}[e \mid p]. \tag{5.24}$$

We're assuming for purposes of illustration that $x$ has no influence on $e$ so that $\mathbb{E}[e\,|\,x, p] = \mathbb{E}[e\,|\,p]$. This is not necessary for any of the methods we'll discuss, but it makes notation and intuition easier.

Thus, standard regression techniques here will recover the true structural relationship, $g(x, p)$, *plus a bias term*: $\mathbb{E}[e\,|\,p]$. This issue is referred to by economists as "omitted variable bias," and it haunts them whenever they need to work with nonexperimental data.

Equation 5.24 gets to the heart of what differentiates causal inference from common statistical or "predictive" inference. To the machine learner, in a setting where you want to predict a future that looks mostly like the past, $\mathbb{E}[e\,|\,p]$ is not a bias. Any patterns that help you predict $e$ given $p$ can be used to refine future predictions. But in a policy setting you are planning to *change p*—you are going to change prices or treat with a new drug. This means that, in the future, you will have *broken* the relationship between $p$ and $e$. The pattern for $\mathbb{E}[e\,|\,p]$ observed in past data will no longer exist, and any inference that confuses this term with $g$ is rightly considered a bias. That is, when comparing counterfactual policies $p_1$ and $p_0$, you want to know $g(p_1, x) - g(p_0, x)$ and adding to this $\mathbb{E}[e\,|\,p_1] - \mathbb{E}[e\,|\,p_0]$ will lead to incorrect conclusions and poor policy choices.

A CLASSIC EXAMPLE OF THIS "ENDOGENEITY" PROBLEM OCCURS IN DEMAND ANALYSIS. Consider air travel. During holidays and periods of peak demand, two things are true: flights are booked, and prices are high. Of course, it is not true that flights are booked *because* prices are high. Rather, both prices and sales are responding to changes in the underlying consumer demand. Airlines are good at tracking this demand and changing ticket prices to maximize profits.

In the previous example, if you regress sales on prices, you will find a *positive* relationship: sales increase with higher prices. This is the economist's dreaded "upward sloping demand curve." Such results are garbage: they don't describe any real economic system. But it is easy to see how this happens. Consider a simple linear demand system where demand shocks $e$ and prices $p$ increase and decrease sales, $y$:

```
> yfun <- function(e,p){
+     y = 2 + 10*e-3*p + rnorm(length(e),0,.1)
+     y[y<0] <- 0
+     return(y) }
```

For this illustration, the demand shocks will be random and independent.

```
> e <- rgamma(100,1,1)
```

We will draw two separate price sets. In the first "observed" case, imagine that you have past data from a price setter who was able to execute targeted price discrimination—they charged prices that were positively correlated with the demand shocks (they are equal to $e$ up to a random error $z$):

```
> z <- rgamma(100,1,1)
> p_observed <- e + z
```

In the second case, imagine that you were able to run an experiment where prices are completely randomized:

```
> pind <- rgamma(100,2,1)
```

Finally, you feed the demand shocks and both of these sets of prices through the sales function:

```
y_observed <- yfun(e, p_observed)
y_counterfactual <- yfun(e, p_counterfactural)
```

The results are shown in Figure 5.9. On the left, we see that the endogenously determined prices lead to a positive correlation between prices and sales. The OLS line fit to observed price data erroneously predicts an upward-sloping demand curve. On the right, random price variation allows OLS to pick up the correct (downward-sloping) demand relationship. The additional "2SLS" line is a fit that was able to recover the correct price/sales relationship from observational data. The analysis behind this line took advantage of the available instruments $z$, the random variation in prices.

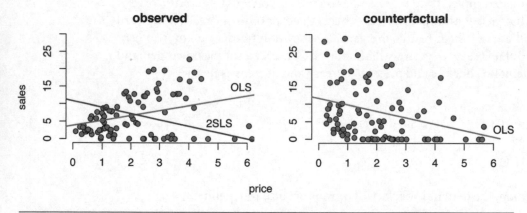

**FIGURE 5.9:** Illustration of the cartoon demand system. On the left, prices were determined endogenously (jointly) with the unobserved demand shocks. On the right, prices are determined randomly independent of demand. The two lines labeled OLS are OLS fit to each dataset. On the left you also see the 2SLS fit line, which matches up closely to the counterfactual OLS fit on the right.

TWO-STAGE LEAST SQUARES (2SLS) is a simple procedure for recovering causal effects from IV variation. Recall the regression equation in Equation 5.23, and take expectation of both sides of this equation after conditioning upon the instrument $z$. For now, we'll ignore the covariates $x$ so that $y = g(p) + e$. Taking the conditional expectation yields

$$\mathbb{E}[y\,|\,z] = \mathbb{E}[g(p)\,|\,z] + \mathbb{E}[e\,|\,z] = \mathbb{E}[g(p)\,|\,z]. \qquad (5.25)$$

This is because $e$ is independent of $z$ (a key feature of an IV) and so $\mathbb{E}[e\,|\,z] = \mathbb{E}[e] = 0$ under the standard assumption of zero-mean errors. Thus, given $z$, $y$ has conditional distribution with mean equal to the average of $g(p)$ given $z$. Note that $p$ is a random variable in this equation. For example, with binary treatment, you have

$$\mathbb{E}[g(p)\,|\,z] = g(0)\mathrm{p}(p = 0\,|\,z) + g(1)\mathrm{p}(p = 1\,|\,z). \qquad (5.26)$$

Making life even simpler, consider the usual linear treatment model where $g(p) = \gamma p$ and Equation 5.23 becomes

$$y = \gamma p + e. \qquad (5.27)$$

Combining this with Equation 5.25 yields the key equation for 2SLS:

$$\mathbb{E}[y\,|\,z] = \gamma\,\mathbb{E}[p\,|\,z]. \qquad (5.28)$$

Thus, you can estimate $\gamma$ with a two-step algorithm (and any covariates $x$ are just added to the conditioning set).

---

**ALGORITHM 13**  **Two-Stage Least Squares (2SLS)**

---

- Fit the first-stage expectation $\mathbb{E}[p\,|\,x,z] = \alpha_p + z_i\tau + x_i'\beta_p$ using OLS for $p$ on $x$ and $z$. For each observed $(p_i, x_i, z_i, y_i)$ tuple, this provides the *predicted* policy $\hat{p}_i = \hat{\alpha}_p + z_i\hat{\tau} + x_i'\hat{\beta}_p$.

- Run a second-stage regression for your response onto the predicted policy and the covariates, using OLS to estimate:

$$\mathbb{E}[y\,|\,\hat{p}_i, x_i] = \alpha_y + \hat{p}_i\,\gamma + x_i'\beta_y. \qquad (5.29)$$

You can then interpret the resulting $\hat{\gamma}$ estimate as the *causal* effect of $p$ on $y$.

---

In our earlier simulated pricing example, this algorithm proceeds in two simple steps. Recall that the observed prices were set as the sum of demand shocks and an independent random error: p_observed = e + z. Treating the z term as an observable instrument, we can run 2SLS:

```
> preg <- lm(p_observed ~ z)
> phat <- predict(preg, data.frame(z=z))
> lin2SLS <- lm(y_observed ~ phat)
> summary(lin2SLS)

Coefficients:
            Estimate Std. Error t value Pr(>|t|)
(Intercept)  11.9030     1.7697   6.726 1.17e-09 ***
phat         -2.2023     0.8168  -2.696  0.00825 **
```

The procedure recovers an estimate of $\gamma$ within one standard deviation of the true value (−3):

```
> summary(lm(y_observed ~ p_observed))

Coefficients:
            Estimate Std. Error t value Pr(>|t|)
(Intercept)   1.3751     1.0701   1.285    0.202
p_observed    3.0502     0.4503   6.774 9.37e-10 ***
```

This succeeds despite the fact that naive regression of sales on prices yielded a completely different (wrong) model.

**THE OREGON INSURANCE EXPERIMENT,** which we looked at to start this chapter, is actually an intent-to-treat setup. Although *access* to Medicaid insurance was randomized through the state's lottery, not all of those who became eligible for Medicaid took advantage of this and enrolled. For some people the enrollment process was just too inconvenient, and others likely had alternative insurance available. Thus, the earlier results describe not the treatment effect of enrolling in Medicaid but rather the indirect effect of expanded access. We can refine these results through an IV analysis.

As in our earlier analysis of the OHIE, the response of interest is $y_i = 1$ if the subject visited a primary care physician (PCP) and $y_i = 0$ otherwise. The treatment of interest was access to Medicaid health insurance. Now, this access to insurance will be the instrument $z = 1$ for those selected for enrollment and $z = 0$ otherwise. Our new treatment, $p$, is whether the patient actually *enrolls* in Medicaid. Since the $z$ is randomized (assigned in a lottery) and it only affects PCP visits through its influence on

Medicaid enrollment, this satisfies the definition of an instrumental variable. We can look at how the change in enrollment $p$ changes with the lottery access $z$ and infer the treatment effect of enrollment on PCP visitation.

In the simulated IV analysis shown earlier, $z$ was perfectly randomized. But in the OHIE analysis, we need to control for the household size, numhh, since people from larger households were more likely to obtain eligibility (any household member selected in the lottery makes all members eligible). As shown in Algorithm 13, this just means we need to include numhh in both the first- and second-stage regressions. We can run everything via calls to lm (or, equivalently, glm):

```
> stage1 <- lm( medicaid ~ selected + numhh, data=P)
> phat <- predict(stage1, newdata=P)
> stage2 <- lm(doc_any_12m ~ phat + numhh, data=P, x=TRUE)
> coef(stage2)
(Intercept)        phat       numhh2       numhh3+
 0.55883837  0.21259703  -0.05302372  -0.14483052
```

The estimated treatment effect, $\hat{\gamma}$, is the coefficient on phat: 0.21. This implies that enrollment in Medicaid makes the probability that you see a PCP 21 percentage points higher than if you don't enroll in Medicaid. Compare this to the earlier analysis, which found that being *eligible* for Medicaid enrollment raised the probability of PCP visitation by only five to six points. The earlier analysis gave an attenuated version of the IV results because eligibility is one step removed from actual enrollment and because those who are unlikely to enroll even if eligible are also less likely to visit a PCP.

**STANDARD ERRORS FOR IV ESTIMATES** require a bit of care. We intuitively want to use the "sandwich" HC variance estimator, but for subtle reasons[16] the "meat" of the sandwich needs to be residuals from the second-stage regression using the true treatment inputs (as opposed to using the $\hat{p}$ inputs that we actually used to fit this second stage regression). It makes for a fairly complicated sandwich construction:

```
> resids <- P$doc_any_12m - predict( stage2,
+ newdata=data.frame(numhh=P$numhh, phat=P$medicaid))
> meat <- Diagonal(x=resids^2)
> bread <- stage2$x%*%solve(t(stage2$x)%*%stage2$x)
> sandwich <- t(bread)%*%meat%*%bread
> print( segam <- sqrt(sandwich[2,2]) )
[1] 0.02112
```

16. Joshua D. Angrist and Jörn-Steffen Pischke. *Mostly Harmless Econometrics*. Princeton University Press, 2009.

We get a standard error of 0.021, which implies a 90% CI for the treatment effect of Medicaid on increased PCP visitation probability of between 17 and 25 percentage points:

```
> coef(stage2)["phat"] + c(-2,2)*segam
[1] 0.1703514 0.2548427
```

We have now done a step-by-step execution of Algorithm 13 and construction of the standard errors. Fortunately, in the future you can also just call functions that will go through all of the IV analysis steps for you and provide the correct standard errors. The same AER package that we've used for robust and clustered standard errors provides an ivreg function for IV analysis. The syntax is basically the same as for glm and lm, except that you use a pipe, |, to separate the first and second stage inputs.

```
> library(AER)
> aeriv <- ivreg(doc_any_12m ~ medicaid + numhh | selected + numhh, data=P)
```

In the previous example, the policy/treatment $p$ is the medicaid indicator. It is listed before the pipe, along with the numhh covariates, as the input of primary interest. After the pipe, you list all of your instruments (we have only one, $z$, the selected flag) and again the covariates that you need to control for because they are connected with imperfect randomization.[17] The summary results correspond to an IV analysis for the effect of Medicaid on PCP visitation:

```
> summary(aeriv)

Coefficients:
            Estimate Std. Error t value Pr(>|t|)
(Intercept)  0.558838   0.007147  78.191  < 2e-16 ***
medicaid     0.212597   0.021153  10.050  < 2e-16 ***
numhh2      -0.053024   0.006952  -7.627 2.49e-14 ***
numhh3+     -0.144831   0.063747  -2.272   0.0231 *
```

The point estimate of $\hat{\gamma} = 0.212597$ is unchanged from earlier. The standard error is also similar but slightly different at the fifth decimal place: 0.02115 versus 0.02112. This happens because, like for glm, the default standard errors from summary assume constant error variance in the second-stage regression (i.e., homoskedasticity). Applying the HC covariance function on the IV fit yields a result closer to the sandwich estimator shown earlier:

```
> sqrt(vcovHC(aeriv)[2,2])
[1] 0.02112588
```

---

17. The function automatically detects numhh in both sets of inputs and thus knows it should be treated as a covariate rather than an instrument.

These differences are tiny, but in other examples the heteroskedasticity can make a bigger difference. Finally, recall that in the original OHIE analysis we wanted to obtain standard errors that allowed for *clustering* at the household level (since individuals in the same house cannot be assumed independent). Again, we can just apply the AER library functions on the fitted IV object to get the appropriately clustered standard error:

```
> (seclust <- sqrt(vcovCL(aeriv, cluster = P$household_id)[2,2]) )
[1] 0.02163934
```

This standard error is a bit larger than those shown earlier, and it slightly widens the 90% CI for the treatment effect. We now get a 17- to 26-point increase in visitation probability if we round at the nearest percentage point.

```
> coef(aeriv)["medicaid"] + c(-2,2)*seclust
[1] 0.1693183 0.2558757
```

Instrumental variable analysis is a big topic. Models of this type are dominant in applied econometrics. The "mostly harmless" text of Angrist and Pischke [2009] is a great reference that goes deeper into these analysis frameworks. For example, they carefully detail the theory on how to interpret $\hat{\gamma}$ in the common scenario where the regressions of Algorithm 13 are only approximations to the true relationships between $z$, $p$, and $y$.[18] Those looking for a deeper understanding of IV analysis can start with that text and also the texts by Imbens and Rubin [2015] and Morgan and Winship [2015].

Instrumental Variables methodology originated in the 1930s and 1940s, with work by Jan Tinbergen and Trygve Haavelmo (and others) on measurement of the parameters of economic *systems*. At the same time as statisticians such as Fisher were developing the rules of randomized experimentation, these economists were trying to understand how to do social science in settings where randomization is impossible (e.g., they could not randomize the income of individuals in an economy). Due to this heritage, econometric theory is often focused on IV setups where the instruments, $z$, are not explicitly randomized. The exclusion structure in Figure 5.8 can hold without randomized instruments—you just need the instrument to be *independent* of the response conditional on the treatment. In demand analysis, analysts sometimes claim that factors affecting the supplier's *cost* of goods is an instrument for the sales *price*. For example, weather conditions in the North Atlantic (making it easier or harder to fish) have been proposed as instruments for

---

18. In general, even if the regressions in Algorithm 13 are misspecified, you can interpret $\hat{\gamma}$ as a *local average treatment effect*: the average treatment effect among individuals who are switched between treatment groups because of their instrument's realization (i.e., those who do or do not enroll in Medicaid because of the lottery outcomes). See, for example, Joshua D. Angrist, Guido W. Imbens, and Donald B. Rubin, Identification of causal effects using instrumental variables, *Journal of the American Statistical Association*, 91:444–455, 1996.

the price of fish in New York City.[19] IV analysis with weather instruments can be used to infer the treatment effect of price on sales.

These non-randomized-instrument examples are open to questions around the validity of the instrument. Is it really that the weather at sea is far enough removed from the weather in NYC to not directly affect fish sales? The answer in this case is probably yes, so long as you condition on the right things, and the cited Angrist et al. paper is a nice example of demand analysis. But this criticism has led practicioners to view IV analysis with skepticism (and rightly so: some IV analyses are bonkers). This skepticism is misplaced in cases where the instrument has been explicitly randomized, as in the intent-to-treat exercise. When the instruments are explicity randomized, you have a clear view of all of the dependencies involved and can be much more confident that the IV model and exclusion structure hold true. IV analysis in such settings is essentially as robust and interpretable as the results from a partially randomized experiment.

As a final point on the importance of IV models and analysis, note that when you are on the *inside* of a firm—especially on the inside of a modern technology firm—*explicitly randomized instruments are everywhere*. As discussed at the beginning of this chapter, the algorithms and processes used by firms are constantly being randomized. This is the pervasive strategy of *AB* experimentation. But it is often the case that decision-makers want to understand the effects of policies that are not themselves randomized but are rather downstream of the things being *AB* tested. For example, suppose an algorithm is used to predict the credit-worthiness of potential borrowers and assign loans. Even if the process of loan assignment is never itself randomized, if the parameters in the machine learning algorithms used to score credit are *AB* tested, then those experiments can be used as instruments for the loan assignment treatment. Such "upstream randomization" is extremely common, and IV analysis is your key tool for doing causal inference in that setting.

19.  Joshua D. Angrist, Kathryn Graddy, and Guido W Imbens. The interpretation of instrumental variables estimators in simultaneous equations models with an application to the demand for fish. *The Review of Economic Studies*, 67:499–527, 2000.

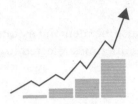

# Controls

## 6

L ife is easy if you have an experiment. Be it a completely randomized *AB* trial, a near experimental design, or an instrumental variables scenario: explicit randomization allows you to model the effect of moving the treatment variable *independently* from the other covariates. This is the key to counterfactual modeling: since you will be acting to apply treatment, you need to know how the response changes with *independent* movement in this variable.

Unfortunately, life doesn't always give you experiments. In business, it is typical that you will be asked to make a decision about future actions based upon historical data without the benefit of explicit randomization. Analysis of such data is referred to as an *observational study*. Instead of running an experiment where you get to set the treatment, you are stuck *observing* what happened. In such settings, counterfactual estimation depends upon the assumption of *conditional ignorability*: that you have tracked and can control for all confounding co-influences on treatment *d* and response *y*.

The process of choosing controls is subjective and labor intensive. Applied economics discussions are dominated by debates over whether all of the important factors have been controlled. Some of this subjectivity and debate is unavoidable: causal inference without experiments is hard. But there are basic recipes and best principles that will help you stay within the bounds of believability. There are also ways that you can use tools from machine learning to help with parts of the process; this will be increasingly important as you look to automate and accelerate business decision-making.

This chapter deals with all of the various approaches to counterfactual analysis under an assumption of conditional ignorability (CI). In the next section, we detail the CI assumption and explain how it works with familiar low-dimensional regression models. We then introduce a specific "partial linear" treatment effects model and show how ML tools can be used to *orthogonalize* against high-dimensional controls. This technique will be extended for modeling of heterogeneous treatment effects, an idea we illustrate in the context of consumer demand estimation. Finally, we describe the method of synthetic controls, sometimes referred to as *nowcasting* in the technology industry.

## Conditional Ignorability and Linear Treatment Effects

Conditional ignorability (CI) implies that you observe all of the variables that influence *both* the treatment and the response. Whenever you hear a causal statement that includes "after controlling for other factors," there is an implicit assumption of conditional ignorability. For example, the following is from *The Economist* on December 23, 2017:

> *A study of 240,000 children in 29 African countries found that, after controlling for other factors, those in polygamous families were more likely to die young.*

Unfortunately, conditional ignorability typically requires a leap of faith. In most settings, it is unrealistic that you have managed to observe *all* factors influencing both the treatment and the response (both polygamy and child health). Instead, you hope that you have controlled for enough of the main factors so that your results are *believable*.

To make things precise, the CI assumption is often introduced via potential outcomes notation. Recall that each individual $i$ has a *potential outcome*, $y_i(d)$, corresponding to each treatment status, say, $d = 0$ or $d = 1$. You don't observe $y_i(d)$ for all $d$, only for $d_i$: the *observed* treatment status for observation $i$. Conditional ignorability is expressed as

$$\{y_i(d)\,\forall d\} \perp\!\!\!\perp d_i \mid x_i. \tag{6.1}$$

This says that all of the potential outcomes $y_i(d)$ are independent from $d_i$ given the *controls* $x_i$. That is, after conditioning on all of the information in $x$, the potential outcomes across all treatment levels are unrelated to the treatment status you have actually been assigned.[1] After assuming the CI condition in Equation 6.1, you can *control* for the factors in $x$ simply by including them in your regression model. Life gets more difficult when $x$ has very high dimension or if you don't know the form of its influence on $d$ and $y$, but in later sections we will show how tools from ML can be used to help.

Consider the orange juice data used in Chapter 2. We regressed OJ unit sales onto prices and other information (brand and advertisement) to understand consumer price sensitivities. For purposes of illustration, we'll revisit this example while neglecting modeling of the brand or ad dependence in price elasticities (i.e., using a more

---

1. In the special case of binary treatments, Equation 6.1 takes a familiar form, $\{y_i(1), y_i(0)\} \perp\!\!\!\perp d_i \mid x_i$, such that the treatment effect $y_i(1) - y_i(0)$ is independent of treatment status.

basic model than we had in Chapter 2). A simple log-log regression yields an estimated −1.6 elasticity, such that sales drop by 1.6% for every 1% increase in prices.

```
> basefit <- lm(log(sales) ~ log(price), data=oj)
> coef(basefit)
(Intercept)  log(price)
  10.423422   -1.601307
```

For this elasticity to be interpreted *causally* under conditional ignorability, we need to assume that there are no other factors that jointly influence both price and sales. That's clearly false. As a start, we *know* that there are different brands of OJ here and some are more valuable than others. For example, we expect Tropicana to sell more volume than Dominick's would at the same price point, and the brands have been priced according to this expectation. When we *control* for brand effect, the elasticity estimate nearly doubles to −3.14.

```
> brandfit <- lm(log(sales) ~ brand + log(price), data=oj)
> coef (brandfit)
(Intercept)  brandminute.maid   brandtropicana    log(price)
  10.8288216         0.8701747        1.5299428    -3.1386914
```

What happened here? The premium brands, Minute Maid and Tropicana, had equivalent sales to Dominick's at higher price points. So if we don't control for brand, it looks as though prices can rise without affecting sales for those observations. This dampens the observable relationship between prices and sales and results in the (artificially) low elasticity estimate of −1.6. When we include brand in the regression, we see positive sales effects for both Minute Maid and Tropicana. The model attributes the higher sales to these brand effects, and we recover the more realistic −3.14 elasticity.

More mechanically, *how* does this happen in regression? OLS regression coefficients represent the *partial* effect for each input after its correlation with the other inputs has been removed. To see this, consider an alternative stagewise control algorithm that first regresses log(price) onto brand and then uses the *residuals* as inputs to predict log(sales).

```
> pricereg <- lm(log(price) ~ brand, data=oj)
> phat <- predict(pricereg, newdata=oj)
> presid <- log (oj$price) -phat
> coef(residfit <- lm(log(sales) ~ presid, data=oj))
(Intercept)      presid
   9.167864   -3.138691
```

The coefficient on presid, the residuals from regression of log price on brand, is exactly the same as what you get on log(price) in the multiple linear regression for log sales onto this and brand. This is one way that you can understand what OLS is doing: it is finding the coefficients on the part of each input that is *independent* from the other inputs.

The previous demonstration suggests a common *structural* model for conditional ignorability, the *linear treatment effects* (LTE) model:

$$y = d\gamma + x'\beta + \varepsilon, \quad \varepsilon \mid d, x = 0,$$
$$d = x'\tau + v, \quad v \mid x = 0. \tag{6.2}$$

Here, $d$ is a treatment status variable, $y$ is the response of interest, and $x$ is all of the variables that can influence both $d$ and $y$—in other words, our potential confounders. The conditions after the commas, $\varepsilon \mid d, x = 0$ and $v \mid x = 0$, encode the conditional ignorability assumption. They give you a roadmap for using ML tools to solve this class of causal inference problems.

We will use this LTE model as the basis for most of the methods in this chapter. It is a reasonable approximation to reality in many business scenarios. It is also well studied as a reduced-form model, and you should feel confident in its use under misspecification. The model can be extended in a number of ways, for example by having $\gamma$ change with $x$ in a heterogeneous treatment effect specification or replacing $x'\beta$ and $x'\tau$ with flexible functions $l(x)$ and $m(x)$ in a "partially linear" treatment effects model.

The first line of the system in Equation 6.2 looks like a generic linear regression—a reduced-form model where $\beta_j$ represents average change in $y$ with $x_j$ but without any worry about causation. The difference—what makes Equation 105 structural— is that the relationships between $\varepsilon$ and $x$ and $d$ are fully specified. The second line of Equation 6.2 states that $x$ contains all of the variables that influence both $d$ and $y$, such that the conditional ignorability assumption holds and $\gamma$ can be interpreted *causally*. That is, $\gamma$ represents change in $y$ when $d$ moves *independent* of all other influences.

When $x$ is simple and low dimensional—say, with dimension $p \ll n$—you don't need to worry about estimating the second line of Equation 6.2. Under conditional ignorability, a large $n$ and small $p$ implies that standard OLS regression estimates for $\mathbb{E}[y \mid d, x] = d\gamma + x'\beta$ will recover the correct causally interpretable $\hat{\gamma}$. Looking at our earlier explanation of the mechanics of regression controls, in OLS this happens because we are "identifying" $\gamma$ as the effect of $v$ on $y$. That is the reason for this common practical advice: "If you need to adjust for confounders, just include them in the regression." The vast majority of observational studies—in economics, medicine, business, or elsewhere—make do with such standard regression techniques. Logistic regression doesn't have the same mechanical "regression on residuals" interpretation as OLS, but it works in roughly the same way: if you want to control for a confounder, you just add it as an input.

Problems start arising only when you have so many variables to control for that the assumption of $n \gg p$ no longer applies. In that setting, you need to be much more careful about how you go about estimation. Unfortunately, it is almost always the case that you have many confounders! There are a vast number of possible external influences in almost any observational study. The *only* reason that analysts are able to use low-dimensional OLS techniques is because they have *selected*—through the basis of intuition, experience, and a variety of subjective tools—a smaller dimensional $x$ that contains the "important" confounders.

In practice, you have no way to know whether this is the right set of confounders. Hand-picking of controls is massively time-consuming, unstable, and hard to replicate. Results will always be subject to skepticism around the analyst's choices and motivations. Thus, almost all treatment effect estimation problems are high-dimensional problems when viewed from a high level, and we already know that standard OLS regression techniques are an imperfect tool for high-dimensional problems. You will need to adapt the ML tools, like lasso and CV, for causal inference under the conditional ignorability model.

## High-Dimensional Confounder Adjustment

Before diving into specific LTE estimation strategies, we will work through an example. In a study that was popularized in the book *Freakonomics*,[2] Donohue and Levitt argue a controversial thesis: that easier access to abortion *causes* decreased crime.[3] They have a variety of mechanisms proposed, the most commonly cited being that with access to abortion births are postponed until the mother is more ready. That is, they posit a causal chain where abortion leads to increased family stability, which leads to better upbringings, which leads to fewer criminals. Levitt and Donohue produce data analyses to support their claim. They fit regression models and find that abortion rates have a negative coefficient for prediction of, for example, the per capita murder rate.

There's obviously no experiment here. How are the Freakonomists coming up with these causal conclusions? The answer is that Levitt and Donohue have made an assumption of conditional ignorability after controlling for a basket of confounders. You can replicate their analysis by looking at publicly available data.[4] They study a number of criminal outcome variables, but we'll focus on the murder rate since it is not subject to changes in reporting over time or across states. Suppose $y_{st}$ is the logged murder rate in state $s$ in year $t$. The treatment variable $d_{st}$ is an effective abortion rate, measured in terms of the number of legal abortions per ten live births. The $d_{st}$ variable is constructed to aggregate past abortion rates according to their relevance to current criminals.

2.  S.D. Levitt and S.J. Dubner. *Freakonomics*. William Morrow, 2005.
3.  John J. Donohue and Steven D. Levitt. The impact of legalized abortion on crime. *The Quarterly Journal of Economics*, 116:379–420, 2001.
4.  The specific data we use matches that in the re-analysis of Belloni et al. [2014]; it excludes Alaska and Hawaii but is otherwise the same as the data from Donohue and Levitt [2001]. The abortion treatment variable $d_{st}$ is a weighted average of abortion rates where weights are determined by the fraction of murders committed by various age groups. For example, if 60% of murders were committed by 18-year-olds and 40% were committed by 19-year-olds in state $s$, the abortion rate for violent crime at year $t$ in state $s$ would be constructed as 0.6 times the abortion rate in state $s$ at year $t - 18$ plus 0.4 times the abortion rate at year $t - 19$.

The list of confounders, encoded as $x_{st}$, includes the following:

- `prison`: Log number of prisoners per capita
- `police`: Log number of police per capita
- `ur`: Current unemployment rate
- `inc`: Current per capita income
- `pov`: Current poverty rate
- `AFDC`: A measure of charitable generosity at year $t - 15$
- `gun`: A dummy for existence of a concealed weapons law
- `beer`: The current beer consumption per capita

This seems like a decent list of things to worry might pollute your causal estimates. Are there any others? Sure, but this is what we've got available, so we'll go ahead and do the analysis with this list. In addition, we include fixed state effects $\alpha_s$ and a linear time trend $t\delta_t$. These are useful for controlling for omitted confounders; for example, state effects control for variables that shift both murder and abortion rates for a single state.

The full regression model is then

$$\mathbb{E}\left[y_{st}\right] = \alpha_s + t\delta_t + d_{st}\gamma + x'_{st}\beta. \tag{6.3}$$

We fit it using OLS:

```
> summary(orig <- glm(y ~ d + t + s +., data=controls))$coef['d',]
     Estimate    Std. Error        t value      Pr.(>|t|)
-2.085088e-01  4.086665e-02  -5.102173e+00  4.592426e-07
```

The result says that abortion has a significant negative effect on the murder rate. Since our response is the logged murder rate, the estimated $\hat{\gamma}$ implies that one more abortion per ten live births (the units of $d$) leads to a 19% reduction in the per capita murder rate.

```
> 1 - exp(-2.085088e-01)
[1] 0.1882061
```

The effect is statistically significant, with a $p$-value below 0.005.

Donohue and Levitt [2001] use fixed-year effects $\alpha_t$ instead of the linear trend $t\beta_t$. This yields a lower $\hat{\gamma} = -0.12$ on this data. These controls and others are added in our later analysis.

Are you skeptical? You probably should be. Consider an alternative story about cell phones and murder. I can argue that cell phone use has caused lower murder rates. There are a number of mechanisms through with this occurs. For example, cell phones lead to faster response by paramedics (it's easier to call 911) so that fewer people die. Or perhaps cell phone usage is a surrogate for the move from manual labor to more gentle desk-and-phone jobs (making us weaker and more docile). Or maybe cell phones allow difficult conversations to be remote rather than in-person (where disagreements can get violent).

Regardless of the mechanism you prefer, I have the data to back up my thesis.[5] I've collected cell phone subscription rates by year and can use this variable instead of the abortion treatment. My new treatment variable phone is created as the number of cell phone subscribers in each year, measured in terms of phones per five people so that it lives in the same range as the abortion variable. Figure 6.1 shows both treatments.

Swapping the phone variable for abortion rates in a regression that otherwise matches the one from earlier, we do indeed find that cell phones lead to fewer murders:

```
> tech <- glm(y ~ phone + t + s + ., data=controls)
> summary (tech) $coef['phone',]
     Estimate        Std. Error          t value         Pr (>|t|)
-3.729846e-01     6.927458e-02     -5.384148e+00     1.068929e-07
```

Adding one cell phone per every five Americans results in a 31% drop in the murder rate.

```
> 1 - exp(-3.729846e-01)
[1] 0.3113242
```

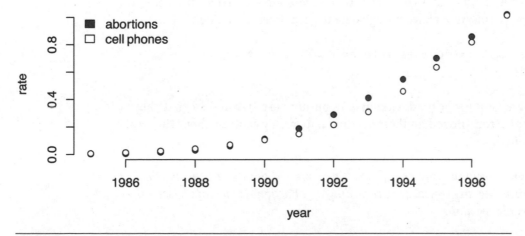

**FIGURE 6.1:** U.S. abortion and cell phone rates (per ten births and five people, respectively) during the sample.

---

5. For the record, I don't actually think that cell phones lowered the murder rate.

The effect is similar in magnitude and more statistically significant than the estimated abortion effect.

What is happening here? Figure 6.1 makes it clear that both cell phone and abortion rates move together, and moreover they have been increasing *quadratically* over the sample frame. That is, they are increasing with $t^2$. Murder rates have decreased quadratically over time (i.e., they follow a downward curve). In the original regression, we didn't include any other variable (other than abortion) that changed in this way, and for this reason any variable with the shape of change in Figure 6.1 shows up as having a significant effect on murder.

To control for such variables, you need control for more flexible time trends; you can do this by including different effects for each year, $\alpha_t$. It is also good practice to allow confounder effects to interact with each other (e.g., so that there is a different gun effect for high beer). Finally, we'll control for my cell phone story by including phone as an input and allowing it to interact with state (since we have only aggregate U.S. phone rates, we need to allow different effects for each state depending upon their individual level of cell phone adoption).[6] We can again fit this using OLS in R:

```
> t <- factor (t)
> interact <- glm(y ~ d + t + phone*s + .^2, data=controls)
> summary (interact)$coef["d",]
   Estimate   Std. Error   t value    Pr(>|t|)
  0.2764410   0.1779091   1.5538330   0.1208959
```

Significance disappears! The direction of the effect also changes—now abortion causes *more* murders—but really what is going on is that we've added so many variables to the model that $n \approx p$. We just don't have enough data to get a decent estimate.

```
> dim(model.matrix(formula(interact), data=controls))
[1] 624 154
```

The point here is not that the *Freakonomics* authors are "wrong" or that they've made a statistical error. Indeed, in their original paper they caution about the weakness we've exploited:

> *That abortion is only one factor influencing crime . . . points out the caution required in drawing any conclusions regarding an abortion–crime link based on time-series evidence alone.*

---

6. Note that allowing state-dependent cell phone effects is the step that really removes any significant abortion effect. More generally, as detailed by Belloni et al. [2014] and others, allowing for any smooth state-dependent trend leads to large standard errors and a lack of significance for the abortion effect. That is, the abortion effect disappears if you control for wiggly functions for each state.

Rather, this example illustrates that whenever your analysis is premised on conditional ignorability, you are always susceptible to others introducing additional controls until the model is nearly saturated and you can't measure anything. This is the weakness of using OLS—a low-dimensional method—as your regression tool.

**YOU CAN BETTER CONTROL FOR CONFOUNDERS BY MODELING THE TREATMENT ASSIGNMENT PROCESS.** That is, you need to take seriously and estimate the second "treatment regression" line of the LTE system in Equation 6.2. You can do this using ML tools such as the lasso and cross validation. The process involves many of the same ideas from how we used regularization to improve predictions in the face of many potential inputs. However, the fact that we are now estimating a *causal* treatment effect means that we need to completely rework our model-building recipes around this goal. A naive application of ML tools for causal inference can lead to a mess of incorrect results.

Going back to Chapter 3, we've followed a simple model-building recipe: use a path of penalties to create a set of *candidate* models and then use predictive performance—measured either via cross validation or an information criterion—as the metric for choosing the best model among this set. A key characteristic here is the focus on unstructured prediction as the basis for model evaluation: you are seeking to do the best job forecasting $y$ at new $x$ *drawn from the same distribution as the inputs in the training sample*. That is, you are choosing models to do well in predicting new data drawn from $p(x, y)$, the same *joint* data generating process (DGP) that provided the training data (think about the CV algorithm to convince yourself of this). However, you now have a special input $d$, the treatment, and you want to know the treatment effect on $y$ when $d$ moves *independent* of all other influences. That is, you no longer want to do a good job predicting $\hat{y}$ under the existing DGP but rather under the DGPs that arise when you change $d$ yourself.

The idea behind structural or counterfactual prediction is to remove from the treatment effect estimate, $\hat{\gamma}$, the effect of other influences that are correlated with $d$. As in the earlier discussions, these outside influences are called *controls* or *confounders*, and they can *pollute* your treatment effect estimate if their effect is confused with that of $d$. Again, this is simple when you have a low-dimensional set of potential confounders—you just include them in your regression. But when you have a large set of potential confounders, you need to do more modeling work.

Look back to the LTE system in Equation 6.2. The key to counterfactual estimation is to model the second line, the treatment allocation equation for $\mathbb{E}[d \mid x]$, in addition to modeling the response equation. In particular, we will proceed sequentially by first modeling the treatment allocation and then using the fitted values as controls in the second-stage regression.

See Algorithm 14. In this algorithm, by estimating $\hat{d}$ and including it in Equation 6.4, we've isolated where $d$ differs *randomly* from what is expected given the confounders. These random surprises are like experiments in $d$, and in the second step we estimate the effect of these surprise movements on $y$. That is, we are using the first "treatment regression" step to construct a near-experimental design.

---

**ALGORITHM 14** **LTE Lasso Regression**

i. Use a CV or AICc lasso to estimate $\mathbb{E}[d \,|\, x] = x'\tau$ and collect the fitted values $\hat{d}_i = x_i'\hat{\tau}$.

ii. Use a CV or AICc lasso to estimate

$$\mathbb{E}[y \,|\, x, d] = \hat{d}\vartheta + d\gamma + x'\beta \tag{6.4}$$

with *no penalty on* $\vartheta$ (i.e., you've included $\hat{d}$ unpenalized).

Then $\hat{\gamma}$ is your estimate for the treatment effect of $d$ on $y$.

---

To understand how this works, note that a theoretically equivalent (for big $n$) algorithm fits step i and then regresses $y$ onto $x$ and the fitted residuals, $\hat{v} = d - \hat{d}$. The coefficient on $\hat{v}$ then provides $\hat{\gamma}$, your treatment effect estimate. To see why the effect of $v$ is the same as the treatment effect of $d$, consider combining the information from the LTE system of Equation 6.2 into a single response equation:

$$\begin{aligned} \mathbb{E}[y \,|\, x, d] &= d\gamma + x'\beta \\ &= (x'\tau + v)\gamma + x'\beta \\ &= v\gamma + x'(\gamma\tau + \beta). \end{aligned}$$

The last line is the *structural* version of the reduced-form regression,

$$\mathbb{E}[y \,|\, x, d] = \hat{v}\gamma + x'\dot{\beta}, \tag{6.5}$$

where, $\dot{\beta} = \gamma\tau + \beta$. Thus $\gamma$ is the same across both models—the effect of $v$ on $y$ is the same as the structural effect of $d$ on $y$. Controlling for $\hat{d}$ unpenalized in Equation 6.4 is essentially the same as estimating the treatment effect of residuals $\hat{v}$. In both cases, $\hat{\gamma}$ is based on variation in $d$ that is orthogonal to $\hat{d}$ (i.e., independent from $\hat{d}$ in the sample).

Recall the *Freakonomics* abortion example from earlier. Where we left off, we had built a large set of controls $x$ consisting of the original Levitt and Donahue variables (interacted), state-specific cell phone effects, and time. If we run a straight "naive" lasso onto $d$ and $x$, AICc selects a negative abortion effect.

```
> x <- sparse.model.matrix (~ t + phone*s + .^2, data=controls)[,-1]
> dim(x)
[1] 624 154
> ## naive lasso regression
> naive <- cv.gamlr(cBind(d,x),y)
> coef(naive) ["d",] # effect is CV selected <0
[1] -0.1149923
```

But if we follow Algorithm 14 and fit the treatment effect regression, the AICc lasso selects $d$ as highly predictable given $x$.

```
> treat <-cv.gamlr(x, d, lmr=1e-4)
> dhat <-drop(predict(treat, x,type= "response"))
> cor(d, dhat) ^2
[1] 0.9871682
```

The in-sample $R^2$ is around 99% (see also Figure 6.2) so that there's almost no *independent* movement of abortion rates to measure as effecting crime. There is little pseudo-experimental variation. Sure enough, after including dhat without penalty in the murder lasso regression, the AICc selects zero residual effect for $d$.

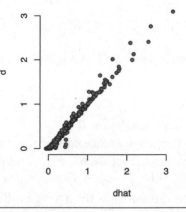

**FIGURE 6.2:** Predicted versus true abortion rate treatments in the *Freakonomics* example.

```
## free=2 here leaves dhat unpenalized
> causal <- gamlr(cBind(d, dhat,x), y, free=2, lmr=1e-3)
> coef (causal) ["d",]
[1] 0
```

Thus, the LTE lasso procedure finds no evidence for effect of abortion on murder.

**PROPENSITY MODELS ARE AN ADAPTATION OF THE LTE FRAMEWORK FOR BINARY TREATMENTS.** In this setting, the second line of the LTE system in Equation 6.2 is replaced with a binomial distribution on the treatment equation:

$$y = d\gamma + x'\beta + \varepsilon, \ \varepsilon \mid d, x = 0,$$

$$d \sim \text{Bernoulli}\,(q(x)), \quad q(x) = \frac{e^{x'\tau}}{1 + e^{x'\tau}}. \tag{6.6}$$

Thus, $d$ is modeled as having been drawn from a Bernoulli distribution (i.e., a coin toss) and the probability that $d = 1$ is a function of $x$ through our familiar logistic regression model (there are alternative formulations, but the logit link is most common).

The treatment probability $q$ is called the *propensity score*. Given an estimate of this score—say, $\hat{q}(x)$—there are a variety of treatment effect estimation options. Propensity score adjustment fits the linear regression $\mathbb{E}[y\,|\,d, \hat{q}(\boldsymbol{x})] = \alpha + d\gamma + \hat{q}(\boldsymbol{x})\varphi$, while propensity score weighting estimates $\mathbb{E}[y\,/\,\hat{q}(\boldsymbol{x})\,|\,d] = \alpha + d\gamma$. See Imbens and Rubin [2015] for more detail, but both of these will work for estimating true $\gamma$ so long as the model in Equation 6.6 is correctly specified. So-called doubly robust methods follow either approach but also include $\boldsymbol{x}$ in these second-stage regressions. I tend to favor a doubly robust procedure that closely resembles the LTE lasso of Algorithm 14: First fit a lasso logistic regression to estimate

$$\mathbb{E}[d\,|\,\boldsymbol{x}] = q(\boldsymbol{x}) = \frac{e^{\boldsymbol{x}'\tau}}{1 + e^{\boldsymbol{x}'\tau}}. \tag{6.7}$$

Then follow step 2 of Algorithm 14 and fit a lasso to estimate

$$\mathbb{E}[y\,|\,\boldsymbol{x}, d] = \hat{q}(\boldsymbol{x})\vartheta + d\gamma + \boldsymbol{x}'\boldsymbol{\beta} \tag{6.8}$$

with no penalty on $\vartheta$.

Propensity score *matching* is a related approach, common in medicine, where $\hat{q}(\boldsymbol{x}_i)$ is estimated for each subject and you run a matching algorithm to find pairs of individuals $(i^0, i^1)$ where $\hat{q}(\boldsymbol{x}_{i^0}) \approx \hat{q}(\boldsymbol{x}_{i^1})$ but $d_{i^1} = 1$ while $d_{i^0} = 0$. The treatment effect is then estimated as the average difference across $n$ matched pairs, $\hat{\gamma} = \frac{1}{n}\sum_i (y_{i^1} - y_{i^0})$. Matching is a pain to implement because the matching algorithms are computationally expensive for large $n$, and it is unstable because results are highly sensitive to how you choose the matching criterion (i.e., how close is close enough for a match). However, it has the advantage that it is an easy procedure to explain for nonstatisticians: "You have two patients who look identical, one gets treatment and the other gets the control … ." You should feel free to use such explanations to help build intuition around your results (I do this all the time) even if you are actually making use of the regression techniques we advocate in this section.

 ## Sample-Splitting and Orthogonal Machine Learning

The LTE lasso and related approaches can give you point estimates of the treatment effects, but they don't come with the nice *inferential* properties (i.e., standard errors) that you get from OLS. In Chapter 3, we introduced the parametric bootstrap and subsampling as methods for uncertainty quantification after model selection, and it is possible to adapt versions of those algorithms for use in treatment effect estimation. However, in the context of the LTE model, there is a nice alternative algorithm for inference: sample splitting.

In a sample splitting algorithm, you split the sample into, say, two pieces. You do model selection on one piece and then, conditional upon that selected model, do standard inference on the second piece. For example, with a linear lasso you could apply OLS (i.e., fit the MLE) in the second stage using only those covariates that had a nonzero selected coefficient in the first-stage lasso regression.

Recall the hockey example from Chapter 3. For every goal, coded as $y = 1$ for home-team goals and $y = 0$ for away-team goals, we regressed $y$ onto indicators for the teams, for the game scenarios (e.g., power plays), and for which players were present on the ice. These indicators were signed according to home versus away teams so that, for example, a home player on the ice for goal $i$ has $x_{ij} = 1$ and an away team player on the ice has $x_{ij} = -1$ (and those off the ice are all zeros). We then built a big lasso regression that predicted, given who is on the ice, which team scored every goal.

> Unlike the original analysis of Chapter 3, here we will penalize everything (including team and on-ice scenario coefficients). This is just to keep the example simple; you could also use sample splitting with the former specification.

To do inference via sample splitting, we first fit a regression model to half of the data:

```
> library(gamlr)
> data(hockey) # load the data
> x <- cBind(config, team, player)
> y <- goal$homegoal
> fold <- sample.int(2, nrow(x), replace=TRUE)
> nhlprereg <- gamlr(x[fold==1,], y[fold==1],
+   family= "binomial", standardize=FALSE)
```

We then figure out which columns of $x$ have a nonzero coefficient in this `nhlprereg` and fit an *unpenalized* (i.e., MLE) logistic regression on only those variables using the second half of the data.

```
> # the -1 to remove the intercept
> selected <- which(coef(nhlprereg)[-1,] != 0)
> xnotzero <- as.data.frame(as.matrix(x[,selected]))
> nhlmle <- glm(y ~ ., data=xnotzero,
+             subset=which (fold==2), family=binomial)
```

Now, suppose that you want to predict the probability that the home team scored for a given goal. For example, look at the first goal in the dataset, from a 2002 game between the Dallas Stars and the Edmonton Oilers played in Edmonton, Alberta:

```
> x[1,x[1,]!=0]
    DAL.20022003   EDM.20022003    ERIC_BREWER     JASON_CHIMERA      ROB_DIMAIO
              -1              1              1               1              -1
 DERIAN_HATCHER  NIKO_KAPANEN  JERE_LEHTINEN  JUSSI_MARKKANEN  JANNE_NIINIMAA
             -1            -1             -1               1               1
     RYAN_SMYTH  BRIAN_SWANSON   MARTY_TURCO    SERGEI_ZUBOV
              1              1             -1              -1
```

To get the home-team score probability and the appropriate standard errors, we apply the standard prediction routine for glm. Since the input design xnotzero was selected using different data from that used to fit nhlmle, the standard theory applies out of the box.

```
> predict(nhlmle, xnotzero[1,,drop=FALSE], type="response", se.fit=TRUE)$fit

        1
0.5241451

$se.fit
          1
0.002970447
>
> 0.5241451 + c(-2,2)*0.002970447
[1] 0.5182042 0.5300860
```

The 90% CI for the probability that Edmonton scored is 52% to 53%.

In this example, we were able to use sample splitting to get a confidence interval for a *predicted* value, $\hat{y} = e^{\tilde{x}'\beta} / (1 + e^{\tilde{x}'\beta})$, where the vector of covariates $\tilde{x}$ includes only the preselected *subset* of variables from the full input space, $x$. In the first stage we select a set of useful covariates, and in the second stage we quantify uncertainty for regression conditional on use of these specific covariates. As Economist Guido Imbens says in this context,[7] we have "moved the goal posts." This is justified because the model selection outcome (determining which coefficients are zero or nonzero) is not the primary object of interest—it is a *nuisance* that we can treat as given when we deploy the fitted prediction model. Sample splitting is *not* appropriate for quantifying uncertainty about individual coefficients that are subject to model selection. For example, if some $\beta_j$ coefficient on $x_{ij}$ is set to zero in the presample lasso, then sample splitting doesn't give you any way to quantify the uncertainty about this decision.

Sample splitting is a great method for dealing with high-dimensional controls because the effects of these controls are *nuisance functions*. They are not the primary object of interest; you just want to remove them from estimates of the treatment effect in a conditional ignorability model. The *Orthogonal ML*[8] framework of Chernozhukov et al. [2017a] provides a general recipe for use of sample splitting with high-dimensional controls. Their approach is easy to apply in the context of the LTE model in Equation 6.2: the nuisance functions are the expectations for treatment and response given controls, $\mathbb{E}[d|x]$ and $\mathbb{E}[y|x]$, and after estimating each of these on an auxiliary sample, you can use out-of-sample residuals as the basis for the treatment effect estimation. They also provide a clever *cross-fitting* algorithm that allows you to use all of your data in the

---

7. Crump, R. K., Hotz, V. J., Imbens, G. W., & Mitnik, O. A. (2009). Dealing with limited overlap in estimation of average treatment effects. *Biometrika*, 96(1), 187–199.
8. Also referred to as "double ML" by the authors, since the original algorithm involved running two ML routines. We use the "orthogonal" label because it emphasizes the importance of making your estimating equations orthogonal to—in other words, independent of—the nuisance control functions.

final treatment effect estimation (instead of throwing half away, like we did in the sample splitting earlier). The full algorithm, which is a sort of cross validation adapted for estimation rather than prediction goals, is outlined in Algorithm 15.

---

**ALGORITHM 15**  **Orthogonal ML for LTE**

Split the data into $K$ random and roughly equally sized folds.

  i. *Nuisance estimation*: For $k = 1 \ldots K$:

   - Use your ML tools of choice to fit the prediction functions,

$$\hat{\mathbb{E}}_k[d \,|\, x] \text{ and } \hat{\mathbb{E}}_k[y \,|\, x], \qquad (6.9)$$

   using all data *except* for the $k$th fold.

   - Calculate out-of-sample residuals for these fitted prediction functions on the $k$th fold:

$$\tilde{d}_i = d_i - \hat{\mathbb{E}}_k[d_i \,|\, x] \text{ and } \tilde{y}_i = y_i - \hat{\mathbb{E}}_k[y_i \,|\, x] \text{ for } i \text{ in fold } k. \qquad (6.10)$$

 ii. *Treatment effect inference*: Collect all of the OOS residuals from the nuisance stage, and use OLS to fit the regression:

$$\mathbb{E}[\tilde{y} \,|\, \tilde{d}] = \alpha + \tilde{d}\gamma. \qquad (6.11)$$

The resulting $\hat{\gamma}$ estimate can be paired with heteroskedastic consistent standard errors (via vcovHC) to obtain a confidence interval for the treatment effect.

---

A function to execute Algorithm 15 takes in two arbitrary regression models, for fitting each of $\hat{\mathbb{E}}_k[d \,|\, x]$ and $\hat{\mathbb{E}}_k[y \,|\, x]$, and outputs the results of the final residuals-on-residuals regression:

```
> orthoLTE <- function(x, d, y, dreg, yreg, nfold=2)
+ {
+     # randomly split data into folds
+     nobs <- nrow(x)
+     foldid <- rep.int(1:nfold,
+         times = ceiling(nobs/nfold))[sample.int(nobs)]
+     I <- split(1:nobs, foldid)
+     # create residualized objects to fill
```

```
+   ytil <- dtil <- rep(NA, nobs)
+   # run the OOS orthogonalizations
+   cat("fold:")
+   for(b in 1:length(I)){
+       dfit <- dreg (x[- I[[b]],], d[-I[[b]]])
+       yfit <- yreg(x[ - I[[b]],], y[-I[[b]]])
+       dhat <- predict (dfit, x[I[[b]], ], type="response")
+       yhat <- predict(yfit, x[I[[b]], ], type="response")
+       dtil[I[[b]]] <- drop(d[I[[b]]] - dhat)
+       ytil[I[[b]]] <- drop(y[I[[b]]] - yhat)
+       cat(b, " ")
+   }
+   rfit <- lm(ytil ~ dtil)
+   gam <- coef(rfit)[2]
+   se <- sqrt(vcovHC(rfit)[2,2])
+   cat(sprintf("\ngamma (se) = %g (%g)\n", gam, se))
+
+   return( list(gam=gam, se=se, dtil=dtil, ytil=ytil))
+   }
```

We can apply this algorithm to the *Freakonomics* abortion and crime analysis. For each of the treatment and response nuisance regressions, we apply a CV lasso via cv.gamlr. These functions are given as arguments dreg and yreg to orthoLTE, which implements the orthogonal ML procedure of Algorithm 15:

```
> dreg <- function (x,d){ cv.gamlr(x, d, lmr=1e-5) }
>
> yreg <- function (x,y){ cv.gamlr(x, y, lmr=1e-5) }
> resids <- orthoLTE( x=x, d=d, y=y,
+                 dreg=dreg, yreg=yreg, nfold=5)
fold: 1    2    3    4    5
gamma (se) = 0.0517967 (0.130621)
> 2*pnorm (-0.0517967/0.130621)
[1] 0.6917053
```

Consistent with our earlier analysis, the result is a small and statistically insignificant positive treatment effect estimate ($p$-value $\approx$ 0.7).[9]

We can also use Algorithm 15 to re-evaluate the hockey player performance study. Recall that in our original analysis we wanted to estimate player effects that were not polluted by different on-ice scenarios and team strength. A small set of variables was included without penalty (e.g., team indicators), and thus influence from those variables

---

9. Our use of vanilla cross validation is suspect here due to autocorrelation in murder and abortion rates. A better approach would use a CV routine developed for time series in which you use the past to predict the OOS future.

is completely removed from the player effects. The individual player effects, however, are of too high dimension to be included in the regression without penalty. We fit the model with a lasso penalty on all of those player coefficients. This is essentially the "naive" treatment effect lasso mentioned earlier, and thus each player's effect estimate has not *fully* controlled for the influence of their line-mates and common opponents.

Consider Sidney Crosby, the star captain of the Pittsburgh Penguins. The earlier lasso regression estimated that his presence on the ice increases by around 50% the odds that a goal has been scored by his team (rather than by his opponents).

```
> exp(coef(nhlreg)["SIDNEY_CROSBY",])
[1] 1.511523
```

Algorithm 15 can be applied to re-estimate the Sid Crosby treatment effect using orthogonal ML. Note that this implies a change in the assumed regression model: whereas the original logistic regression models a *multiplicative* effect on the odds that Sid's team (the Penguins) has scored, the LTE specification of Equation 6.2 models an *additive* effect on the probability that his team has scored.

We'll use an AICc linear lasso for the treatment (Sid's –1, 0, or 1 value in the design matrix) and an AICc logistic lasso for the binary response (you could use a linear lasso here too; the point is to just use whatever tool you think will predict best). Again, these functions are input to the orthoLTE function to execute orthogonal ML:

```
> sid <- grep("SIDNEY_CROSBY", colnames(x))
> dreg <- function(x,d) {
+     gamlr(x, d, standardize=FALSE, lmr=1e-5)}
>
> yreg <- function(x, d){
+     gamlr(x, d, family="binomial", standardize=FALSE, lmr=1e-5)}
>
> resids <- orthoLTE(x=x[,-sid], d=x[, sid], y=y,
+              dreg=dreg, yreg=yreg, nfold=5)
fold: 1 2 3 4 5
gamma(se) = 0.247739 (0.0211225)
> 0.247739 + c(-2,2) *0.0211225
[1] 0.205494 0.289984
```

This finds an *additive* effect between 0.21 and 0.29 on Pittsburgh's goal-scored probability due to Crosby being on the ice. To translate this to something comparable to the earlier logistic regression results, we can consider a baseline probability of around 1/2 that any given goal was scored by Pittsburgh rather than their opponents. Sid being on the ice moves the *odds* that any given goal was scored by Pittsburgh from 0.5/0.5 = 1 to between 0.71/0.29 = 2.45 and 0.79/0.21 = 3.76.

These Sid-caused increases in Pittsburgh's scoring odds, between 145% and 276%, are much larger than the 50% odds increase found in the earlier logistic lasso analysis.

In this sense, the original results were wrong. Why didn't the nhlreg lasso just "work" for treatment effect estimation? Because Sid is the best player on his team, when you don't fully control for the players he tends to play with and against, you will underestimate his effectiveness. This pattern repeats itself across players: the earlier lasso regression provides attenuated estimates of their player effects because their play is being conflated with that of their line-mates. The full right tail of star players is exposed only through proper causal analysis.

## Heterogeneous Treatment Effects

Thus far, we have ignored a glaringly obvious feature of treatment effects: they will be different for different subjects. This phenomenon, where the influence of the treatment (i.e., a policy variable that you control) varies as a function of who or what is being treated, is referred to as *heterogeneous treatment effects* (HTEs). Modern ML tools are making it easier to model HTEs, instead of just looking at the ATE average, and these higher-fidelity views into treatment effects are having a big impact on business decision-making.

As a first point to make clear, *heterogeneous treatment effects exist*. You will occasionally see a misguided academic testing for heterogeneity, but almost any practitioner would agree that their treatment—medicine, advertisement, web service—has a different effect on different individuals. For example, people shopping for clothing on eBay are more likely to buy when pictures are bigger, while those shopping for car parts prefer more items per page with smaller pictures. You don't need to know *why* this happens for it to be useful in website design. Your task is the same as in prediction: you seek to discover patterns that are indexed by observable covariates, say, $x$.

For randomized treatments—for example, in an AB trial—modeling HTEs is as easy as running a regression that interacts the treatment variable with sources of heterogeneity. For example, if $d$ has been randomized across subjects, you can fit the basic interaction model

$$\mathbb{E}[y_i \mid x_i, d_i] = \alpha + x_i'\beta + d_i\gamma_0 + (d_i \times x_i)'\gamma. \tag{6.12}$$

Here, $(d_i \times x_i)'$ is the vector of treatment-covariate interactions $[d_i x_{i1} \ldots d_i x_{ip}]$, and $\gamma' = [\gamma_1 \ldots \gamma_p]$ are the corresponding regression coefficients. The HTE for treatment $d_A$ versus $d_B$ for any individual subject is then

$$\mathrm{HTE}_i = \mathbb{E}[y_i \mid x_i, d_B] - \mathbb{E}[y_i \mid x_i, d_A] = (\gamma_0 + x_i'\gamma) \times (d_B - d_A). \tag{6.13}$$

Since $d_i$ is randomized, you don't actually need the $x_i'\beta$ term here. However, it is good practice to include a main-effect adjustment for the sources of treatment effect heterogeneity.

Again, if the $d_i$ values are randomized such that they are roughly independent from the $x_i$ values, then you can use your usual regression tools for fitting Equation 6.12. For example, with high-dimensional $x_i$ you can deploy lasso methods.

Recall the Oregon Health Insurance Experiment (OHIE) from the previous chapter, where we were interested in observing the treatment effect of randomly selected eligibility for Medicaid on the probability that someone visits a primary-care physician (PCP) at least once a year. The treatment variable is selected, indicating whether a person's household was selected for eligibility, and the response variable is binary doc_any_12m. Enrollment eligibility was imperfectly randomized because once anyone from a household was selected, the whole household became eligible. We fix this by controlling for numhh, the size of the household, when estimating the average treatment effect:

```
> lin <- glm(doc_any_12m ~ selected + numhh, data=P)
> round(summary(lin)$coef["selected",],4)
  Estimate Std.  Error  t value  Pr(>|t|)
    0.0639     0.0065   9.9006    0.0000
```

The resulting ATE is an increase in PCP usage between 6% and 7%.

As sources of heterogeneity, we have available a set of 27 covariates from a survey on subject demographics carried out 12 months after the Medicaid lottery. Many of these are categorical; for example, edu_12m is education-level categorization. We can use gamlr to run a linear lasso regression for the model in Equation 6.12, with the coefficient for the main effect of numhh unpenalized to make sure that we have controlled for this source of imperfect randomization. However, before finishing this example we need to digress on the nasty (but surmountable) problem of missing data.

**WE NEED TO DEAL WITH MISSING DATA IN THE SURVEY RESPONSES.** We have incomplete observations for some subjects. This is is an issue that will occur repeatedly in practice. The problem is not specific to HTEs or counterfactual modeling—missing data is a problem in any large-scale survey analysis (and in plenty of other settings). There are many different ways to deal with this problem. We will cover here some basic approaches for each of categorical (factor) and numeric (numeric or integer) variables.

For *categorical variables*, you simply treat the "missing" observations as a separate category. As described in Chapter 3 when introducing sparse model matrices, adding a category for NA observations is good practice when creating model matrices for the lasso. It forces R to have a separate coefficient for each observed category in each variable. You can do this for each factor variable with the naref function provided in that chapter:

```
> levels(X$edu_12m)
[1] "less than hs"               "hs diploma or GED"
[3] "vocational or 2-year degree" "4-year degree"
```

```
> levels(naref(X$edu_12m))
[1] NA                              "less than hs"
[3] "hs diploma or GED"            "vocational or 2-year degree"
[5] "4-year degree"
> X <- naref(X)
```

The last line of code here makes NA the reference level for all of the categorical variables in X.

You can take a similar approach with *numeric variables*: every missing dimension of an observation is flagged with an additional dummy indicator specific to the missing variable. But you need also to *impute* the missing numeric value so that it is not empty in the data matrix (which would cause problems for the optimization routines in the estimation procedure). There are a bunch of different ways that you can choose to impute the missing entries—missing data imputation, or guessing what the missing values *would* have been, is an interesting regression problem in its own right. Two simple approaches that work well for most problems are *zero* and *mean* imputation. In the former, which I recommend for sparse variables (those that are mostly zero), you replace missing values with zero. In the latter, you replace the missing values with the mean of the nonmissing entries.[10]

Looking at the OHIE covariates, there are only four numeric variables. The first (smk_avg_mod_12m) is sparse, and the others are dense.

```
> xnum <- X[, sapply(X, class)%in%c("numeric","integer")]
> xnum[66:70,]
   smk_avg_mod_12m birthyear_12m hhinc_pctfpl_12m hhsize_12m
66               0          1974               NA         NA
67              15          1963        150.04617          1
68              NA          1962        150.04617          1
69              20          1964         61.44183          3
70              10            NA         14.71825         10
> colSums(is.na(xnum))/nrow(xnum)
smk_avg_mod_12m  birthyear_12m  hhinc_pctfpl_12m  hhsize_12m
     0.14523737     0.02241745        0.09750292  0.05085039
```

The proportion of missing values (NAs) ranges from around 2% to 15% of the observations. To address this, we first create a matrix of indicators for missingness in each of these observations.

---

10. Mean imputation has better theoretical properties, but if you have sparse data, you don't want to lose that computationally convenient sparsity by imputing a bunch of close-but-not-quite-zero values (when the data is mostly zeros, the mean will be near zero).

```
> xnumna <- apply(is.na(xnum), 2, as.numeric)
> xnumna[66:70,]
smk_avg_mod_12m birthyear_12m hhinc_pctfpl_12m hhsize_12m
[1,]              0             0                1          1
[2,]              0             0                0          0
[3,]              1             0                0          0
[4,]              0             0                0          0
[5,]              0             1                0          0
```

We then replace the missing values with either the means of the nonmissing values or zero, depending upon the sparsity of the variable (see the function mzimpute that does the imputation).

```
> mzimpute <- function(v){
+     if(mean(v==0,na.rm=TRUE) > 0.5) impt <- 0
+     else impt <- mean(v, na.rm=TRUE)
+     v[is.na(v)] <- impt
+     return(v) }
> xnum <- apply(xnum, 2, mzimpute)
> xnum[66:70,]
      smk_avg_mod_12m birthyear_12m hhinc_pctfpl_12m hhsize_12m
[1, ]               0      1974.000         77.20707   2.987188
[2, ]              15      1963.000        150.04617   1.000000
[3, ]               0      1962.000        150.04617   1.000000
[4, ]              20      1964.000         61.44183   3.000000
[5, ]              10      1965.777         14.71825  10.000000
> # replace/add the variables in original data frame
> for(v in colnames(xnum)){
+     X[,v] <- xnum[,v]
+     X[,paste(v, "NA", sep=".")] <- xnumna[,v]}
```

After this code has been executed, the numeric variables in X have had their missing values imputed with variable means, and we've added indicators for the missingness pattern in each variable.

We can now put everything together in a sparse model matrix. We add to this matrix the numhh household variables that we need to control for because of imperfect randomization.

```
> xhte <- sparse.model.matrix(~., data=cbind(numhh=P$numhh, X))
    [,-1]
> xhte[1:2, 1:4]
2 x 4 sparse Matrix of class "dgCMatrix"
   numhh2  numhh3+ smk_ever_12mNo smk_ever_12mYes
```

```
1       .       .               .               1
2       .       .               1               .
> dim(xhte)
[1] 23107    91
```

We now have a matrix of rows $x_i$, where each $x_i$ is a length-91 vector of potential sources of heterogeneity.

**TURNING BACK THE HTE MODELING,** we will use an AICc lasso to fit the regression model in Equation 6.12.

```
> dxhte <- P$selected*xhte
> colnames (dxhte) <- paste("d", colnames (xhte), sep=".")
> htedesign <- cBind(xhte, d=P$selected, dxhte)
> # include the numhh controls and baseline treatment without penalty
> htefit <- gamlr (x=htedesign, y=P$doc_any_12m, free=c
  ("numhh2","numhh3+", "d"))
> gam <- coef (htefit) [-(1:(ncol(xhte)+1)), ]
> round(sort(gam) [1:6], 4)
               d.race_asian_12mYes d.employ_hrs_12mwork 20-29 hrs/week
                           -0.0446                           -0.0433
     d.hhinc_cat_12m$32501-$35000     d.hhinc_cat_12m$27501-$30000
                           -0.0293                           -0.0232
     d.hhinc_cat_12m$15001-$17500               d.race_hisp_12mYes
                           -0.0195                           -0.0173
> round(sort(gam, decreasing=TRUE) [1:6],4)
                         d        d.race_pacific_12mYes
                    0.0927                       0.0404
d.hhinc_cat_12m$2501-$5000   d.hhinc_cat_12m$5001-$7500
                    0.0221                       0.0137
d.live_other_12mYes               d.race_black_12mYes
                    0.0116                       0.0067
```

The baseline treatment effect is now a 9% increase in PCP visit rates.[11] But there are large sources of heterogeneity around this value. For example, people of Pacific Islander descent have 13% increase as their treatment effect, while for Asians the treatment effect is only a 5% increase. And as we will confirm in the causal tree reanalysis in Chapter 9, income plays a significant role in the size of the treatment effect.

---

11. Note that this is not an ATE since the means of the coefficients are not zero. The ATE is $\hat{\gamma}_0 + \bar{x}'\hat{\gamma} = 0.056$, which is in range of the previous estimates.

**CONSUMER DEMAND ESTIMATION IS A PROMINENT USE-CASE FOR HTE MODELING.**
It is also an area where controlling for confounders is super important. Understanding
of a full-demand system, including consumer learning and channel switching, requires
subtle economic modeling. However, in many settings you can aim to recover the *local*
effects of price changes (i.e., the short-term effects of small changes) using fairly basic
statistical modeling. In the final example of this section, we will combine the orthogonal ML methods with HTE modeling to study short-term price elasticities for some
consumer goods in grocery stores.

Price elasticity of demand—say, $\gamma$—is defined as the percentage change in quantity
sold over percentage change in price when viewing quantity sold as a function of price.
The famous equation is

$$\gamma = \frac{\Delta q}{q} \bigg/ \frac{\Delta p}{p} = \frac{p}{q} \frac{\Delta q}{\Delta p}, \tag{6.14}$$

with $\Delta$ denoting a fixed amount of change. For continuous functions, elasticity at a
point is the derivative of quantity with respect to price times price over quantity. This
elasticity is the key parameter in many demand systems and price optimization tasks.
For example, with constant elasticity and fixed firm cost-per-unit $c$, a heuristic rule of
thumb for optimal price $p^*$ is

$$p^* = \frac{\gamma}{1+\gamma} c \tag{6.15}$$

so that $\gamma/(1 + \gamma)$ dictates gross margin.[12]

Estimating the treatment effect of price on sales is an age-old economic problem.
Understanding consumer price sensitivity is essential for setting prices and understanding markets. It is also a problem where naive ML methods tend to fall short
(although that doesn't seem to stop people from using them and getting silly results).
Both prices and sales respond to a shared, unobserved, factor: consumer demand. For
example, consider hotel rooms during spring break: the rooms are all sold out (sales
are high) *and* the prices are super high. It is not the case that sales are high *because*
prices are high; rather, both prices and sales are functions of the underlying increase
in holiday demand. But a naive ML approach that regresses sales on prices can result
in "upward-sloping demand curves"—unrealistic models where higher prices cause
higher sales.[13]

Most analysts are aware that they can't naively rely upon observational studies
to determine consumer price sensitivity. Whenever possible, it is highly advisable to

12. Equation 6.15 applies only for $\gamma < -1$; goods with elasticity above –1, which means that sales drop less than 1%
per 1% price increase, are considered inelastic. In practice, this usually means the good is currently far too cheap
(from the firm's perspective), and at higher prices the elasticity will drop below –1 (constant elasticity is a heuristic
that is seldom true in the wild). Or, more commonly, it just means you've not managed to get a good estimate of the
true elasticity.
13. A rare place where upward-sloping demand might exist is for luxury goods with price signaling prestige or
quality. I've observed this in sales data for wine.

introduce random price variation to help estimation for the causal price effect (e.g., see studies involving Dominick's grocery stores done at the University of Chicago in the 1990s[14]). But there are many settings where experimentation can't happen or has not happened in the past. In that case, the common last-resort solution is a so-called conjoint analysis: asking focus-group members to make choices amongst product options using pretend money. However, as you might expect, focus groups and funny money are a poor approximation of reality.

Fortunately, you might be able to use the methods of this chapter to do your demand analysis. Consider the LTE model setting: for conditional ignorability to hold, you need to have available as controls $x$ the universe of variables that can potentially affect both prices and sales. Ignoring supply-side issues like stock-outs (which should be controlled for if they occur), this $x$ is going to consist of information relevant to consumer. But, more specifically, only those *demand signals* that are known to the price-setter need to be controlled for. It doesn't matter if consumer Joe hears a country song on the radio that makes him think of pick-up trucks, causing him to head to his local dealership looking for a truck at any price. So long as *the dealership* doesn't know that Joe's demand has increased and jacked prices, that country song effect is part of an error term on sales that is independent of price changes. In more basic terms, conditional ignorability in this setting assumes that you know all of the demand signals that determine price. If you work for the store that is setting the prices, you should be able to collect all of these signals.

There are a variety of standard structural demand models,[15] and you'll need to use economic modeling if you want to account for all of the complexities of demand (e.g., allowing for product competition or elasticities that change with overall wealth). But a basic log-log LTE model provides a surprisingly useful platform for analysis. Suppose that $q_{it}$ is some measure of quantity and $p_{it}$ is price for product $i$ in "transaction" $t$ (where $t$ can index aggregate sales at a specific time and store, across multiple stores, or a single consumer transaction). Our LTE demand model is

$$
\begin{aligned}
\log q_{it} &= \log p_{it}\gamma + x'_{it}\beta + \varepsilon_{it}, \\
\log p_{it} &= x'_{it}\tau + v_{it},
\end{aligned}
\tag{6.16}
$$

with $\varepsilon_{it}\,|\,p_{it}, x_{it} = 0$ and $v_{it}\,|\,x_{it} = 0$ as in Equation 6.2. Here, $x_{it}$ is the set of demand signals that were known to the price-setter. This model is nice because, recalling from Chapter 2, in a log-log model $\gamma$ is directly interpretable as the percentage change in $q$ per 1% change in $p$—that is, $\gamma$ is directly interpretable as the price elasticity of demand (hence the choice of notation in Equation 6.14). Moreover, as mentioned earlier, it is plausible for firm-side analysts to know all of the demand signals, $x_{it}$. The consequence

14. Stephen J. Hoch, Byung-Do Kim, Alan L. Montgomery, and Peter E. Rossi. Determinants of store-level price elasticity. *Journal of Marketing Research*, pages 17–29, 1995.

15. Two prominent econometric models are in Angus Deaton and John Muellbauer, An almost ideal demand system, *The American Economic Review*, 70:312–326, 1980; and Steven Berry, James Levinsohn, and Ariel Pakes, Automobile prices in market equilibrium, *Econometrica*, pages 841–890, 1995.

of this is that $\varepsilon \perp\!\!\!\perp v$, as required for conditional ignorability. The model defined in Equation 6.16 is then an instance of the LTE system from Equation 6.2, and it can be analyzed using the methods of this chapter.

As an example, we will consider data on sales of beer between 1989 and 1994 at Dominick's stores in the Chicagoland area.[16] For each beer unique product code (UPC), we have weekly total unit sales (MOVE) and average prices across 63 different stores.

```
> load ("dominicks-beer.rda")
> head(wber)
  STORE        UPC WEEK PRICE MOVE
1     8 1820000008   91  1.59    5
2     8 1820000008   92  1.59    7
3     8 1820000008   93  1.59    9
4     8 1820000008   94  1.59    4
5     8 1820000008   95  1.59    2
6     8 1820000008   96  1.59   10
```

For the UPCs, we have available their size in beer volume (OZ, for fluid ounces) and a short text description.

```
> head(upc)
                           DESCRIP OZ
1820000008  BUDWEISER BEER N.R.B 32OZ 32
1820000016        BUDWEISER BEER 6pk 72
1820000051           BUSCH BEER 6pk 72
1820000106  BUDWEISER LIGHT BEER 6pk 72
1820000117 BUDWEISER LIGHT BEER 32OZ 32
1820000157  O'DOUL'S NON-ALCH CA 6pk 72
> dim(upc)
[1]  287    2
```

There are 287 different UPCs in the data. They differ by a variety of characteristics, including brand, package size, and beer type. All of these differences, in addition to week and store trends, need to be incorporated into the set of demand signal controls.

The full sample of data includes more than 1.6 million UPC-store-week observations. To illustrate the strengths and weaknesses of various elasticity estimation techniques, we'll perform an analysis on a small subsample of 5000 transactions and use the full dataset for validation (or pseudovalidation, because we don't have an experiment that randomized prices).

16. This data is from the Kilts Center for Marketing at the University of Chicago Booth School of Business. See the book website for the code that wrangles the dataset here from the original files. The data also contain demographic information for each store; as an exercise, you might want to redo the analysis here to include store demographics as sources of heterogeneity.

```
> nrow(wber)
[1] 1600572
> ss <- sample.int(nrow(wber), 5e3)
```

In addition, to standardize the treatment variable, we calculate and work with the *log price per 12 ounces*.

```
wber$lp <- log(12*wber$PRICE/upc[wber$UPC, "OZ"])
```

Before turning to HTE modeling, let's first try to estimate a single elasticity (the ATE for log price) across beers. We find that fitting a regression without controls yields a suspiciously small elasticity:

```
> coef( margfit <- lm(log (MOVE) ~ lp, data=wber[ss,]))
(Intercept)          lp
 1.0124931   -0.7194031
```

This says that sales drop by only 0.7% per every 1% increase. As discussed earlier, elasticities greater than −1 indicate a good that is practically *inelastic*: increased prices are straight profit. This happens when you have goods that are massively underpriced, which is unrealistic for *all* beer in a supermarket, or when you have done a poor job of estimating elasticities. The latter is almost certainly the case here: we have not controlled for any product characteristics or time dynamics.

We can do better. To construct our set of controls $x$, we first create dummy indicator variables for the beer type (UPC), week, and store.

```
> # numeric matrices for week, store, item
> wber$s <- factor(wber$STORE)
> wber$u <- factor(wber$UPC)
> wber$w <- factor(wber$WEEK)
> xs <- sparse.model.matrix( ~ s-1, data=wber)
> xu <- sparse.model.matrix( ~ u-1, data=wber)
> xw <- sparse.model.matrix( ~ w-1, data=wber)
```

This allows for both sales and price to vary as functions of beer type, transaction week, and store.

However, having completely separate models for every type of beer is poor practice (especially in the small $n = 5000$ subsample). If a Bud Light 6-pack of cans is modeled as having demand that is completely independent from a Bud Light 12-pack of bottles, then we will have little data for modeling each individual beer type. Instead, as always with regularization, we should create a regression design that allows our models to find a *hierarchy* in the data. If we have a dummy variable for "Bud," another for "Light," and yet another for "Bud Light," then the model is able to shrink across brands and beer style. The individual beer UPC indicators are available to fill in the lowest levels of the hierarchy—for example, if "Bud Light 18-pack cans American Flag special edition" behaves differently than every other Bud Light product—but for the most part the beers will be modeled as similar to their hierarchical siblings.

All of this hierarchical information is available in retailer databases. But to save coding effort—and as an example of how ML with unstructured data can replace complicated human taxonomies—we'll just use the beer descriptions as our source of information. In a preview of Chapter 8, we use a *bag-of-words* representation and tokenize the descriptions into dummy indicators for the presence of each word in the beer-description vocabulary.

```
> library(tm)
Loading required package: NLP
> descr <- Corpus(VectorSource(as.character(upc$DESCRIP)))
> descr <- DocumentTermMatrix(descr)
> descr <- sparseMatrix(i=descr$i,j=descr$j, x=as.numeric(descr$v>0),
+              dims=dim(descr), dimnames=list(rownames(upc),colnames(descr)))
> dim(descr)
[1] 287 180
```

Each beer is now represented as a binary vector encoding presence and absence of the 180 possible vocabulary terms.

```
> descr[1:5,1:6]
5 × 6 sparse Matrix of class "dgCMatrix"
           32oz beer budweiser 6pk busch light
1820000008    1    1         1   .     .     .
1820000016    .    1         1   1     .     .
1820000051    .    1         .   1     1     .
1820000106    .    1         1   1     .     1
1820000117    1    1         1   .     .     1
> descr[287,descr[287,]!=0]
   6pk    red    ale  honey  oregon
     1      1      1      1       1
```

These terms encode a natural hierarchy. For example, many beers will be sold in 6-packs, but few will be from Oregon brewing, and even fewer will be red honey ales. This information, combined with week, store, and product indicators, forms our set of controls.

```
> controls <- cBind(xs, xu, xw, descr[wber$UPC,])
> dim(controls)
[1] 1600572     837
```

Running on the subsample, a naive lasso regression[17] for log sales onto log price and $x$ yields an average elasticity around –2.

```
> naivefit <- gamlr(x=cBind(lp=wber$lp,controls) [ss,],
+                   y=log(wber$MOVE) [ss],
+                   free=1, standardize=FALSE)
> print( coef(naivefit) ["lp",] )
[1] -2.132603
```

This is more realistic than the uncontrolled –0.7 elasticity found earlier, but it is still lower than what we find when running orthogonal ML for unbiased estimation of the treatment effect.

```
> source("orthoML.R")
> dreg <- function(x,d){
+     gamlr(x, d, standardize=FALSE, lmr=1e-5) }
>
> yreg <- function (x,y) {
+     gamlr(x, y, standardize=FALSE, lmr=1e-5) }
>
> resids <- orthoPLTE( x=controls[ss, ], d=wber$lp[ss], y=log(wber$MOVE) [ss], d$
fold: 1  2  3  4  5
gamma (se) = -3.39466   (0.167152)
```

The orthogonal ML procedure finds an average elasticity of between –3.1 and –3.7, which is in the range of values we would expect for beer (or, e.g., soft drinks as in Hoch et al. [1995]).

For comparison, we have the full sample of 1.6 million observations. This is enough data that we can reliably estimate all of the necessary week/store/UPC control effects using unbiased MLE estimation,[18] and hence we can use this as a gold-standard elasticity estimate in this example.

```
> fullfit <- gamlr(x=cBind(lp=wber$lp, controls),
+                   y=log(wber$MOVE), lambda.start=0)
> print( coef(fullfit) ["lp", ] )
[1] -3.567488
```

17. We use standardize=FALSE because the controls are all 0/1 values and we don't want to put extra penalty on more common brands or terms in descr.
18. Because the full data is too large to store in memory in dense format, we use gamlr with no penalty to calculate the MLE fit.

The full sample value is inside of the 90% interval provided by orthogonal ML on the small subsample.

Turning to HTE modeling, we will consider the bag-of-words representation of the UPC description text as a source of heterogeneity.[19] Recall that if you have run an experiment and have randomized treatments HTE modeling is as easy as running the regression in Equation 6.12. We don't have an experiment here, but we learned earlier that orthogonal ML yields treatment residuals, $\tilde{d}$, that are essentially random under the conditional ignorability assumption. The response residuals, $\tilde{y}$, have also had the effect of the controls removed. Hence, after running Algorithm 15, we can obtain HTE estimates for covariates $x$ by running the regression

$$\mathbb{E}[\tilde{y}_i \mid \tilde{d}_i, x_i] = \alpha + \tilde{d}_i \gamma_0 + (\tilde{d}_i \times x_i)' \gamma \qquad (6.17)$$

and calculating the HTEs for each observation as in Equation 6.13.[20]

Note that, despite our reuse of $x$ notation, the sources of heterogeneity don't need to be the same as the full set of controls. Indeed, it is typical to use only a subset of the full controls as potential sources for heterogeneity.[21]

To fit the regression in Equation 6.17, we create a design matrix that includes the bag-of-words matrix plus an intercept for $\gamma_0$.

```
> xhte <- cBind(BASELINE=1, descr[wber$UPC,])
```

We then use `gamlr` to fit an AICc lasso for the regression in Equation 120.

```
> dmlhte <- gamlr(x=xhte[ss,]*resids$dtil,
+                 y=resids$ytil,
+                 free=1, standardize=FALSE)
```

All we've done here is replace the OLS step from the end of Algorithm 15 with a lasso regression that interacts residuals with covariates. The resulting elasticities are plotted in Figure 6.3, and we can print some of the largest sources of heterogeneity.

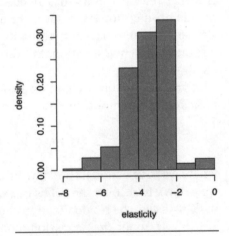

**FIGURE 6.3:** Beer-specific elasticities obtained by lasso regression on the orthogonal ML residuals.

---

19. You can also add UPC/week/store indicators if you want to extend the analysis, although it is hard to find much signal for these variables on the 5000-observation subsample.

20. Victor Chernozhukov, Matt Goldman, Vira Semenova, and Matt Taddy. Orthogonal machine learning for demand estimation: High dimensional causal inference in dynamic panels. *arXiv:1712.09988*, 2017b.

21. There is no scientific reason for this; however, in many applications you will just want to find the main movers of heterogeneity rather than build a detailed subject-specific treatment effect model. If you *do* want subject-specific effects, then you should look for heterogeneity from all of the variables you have available.

```
> B <- coef(dmlhte)[ -(1:2),]
> B <- B[B!=0]
> head(sort(round(B,2)))
   draft   lite  export  miller   girl  guinness
   -1.55  -1.22  -1.18   -1.16  -1.14   -1.08
> head(sort(round(B,2), decreasing=TRUE))
   sharp   ale  amstel heineken  strohs    btl
   3.58   2.50   2.05   1.24    0.79    0.70
```

We find that consumers (or potential consumers) of beers labeled "Draft," as well as of "Guinness" or "Miller," tend to be more price sensitive than the baseline (at least in the usual range of prices for these beers). This indicates that these are products that many consumers buy only when they are on sale. The most elastic products are 24-packs of Miller Lite.

```
> upc[names(sort(gamdml)[1:3]), ]
                              DESCRIP    OZ
3410057306     MILLER LITE BEER 24pk   288
3410064306     MILLER LITE "ICE" 24pk  288
```

A Miller Lite "two-four" has an elasticity of −7, meaning that the store sells 7% more of this product for every 1% price decrease. On the other side, we notice that bottles (btl) tend to have less elasticity than cans. The large positive effect for sharp is curious. Upon investigation, this term indicates a single product, Miller Sharp's non-alcoholic beer.

For comparison, we can also consider direct estimation of the HTEs using the basic regression model in Equation 6.12, rephrased here as

$$\mathbb{E}[y_i \mid x_i, z_i, d_i] = \alpha + z_i'\beta + d_i\gamma_0 + (d_i \times x_i)'\gamma, \tag{6.18}$$

where we have denoted the controls, $z$, as distinct from the HTE covariates, $x$. That is, we will try to recover the HTEs in a single regression (including the controls) without making use of the residualization and sample splitting of Orthogonal ML. First, we fit an AICc lasso for the regression model including the full set of controls and interacting log price with the text data.

```
> d <- xhte*wber$lp
> colnames (d) <- paste ("lp", colnames (d), sep=":")
> naivehte <- gamlr (x=cBind (d, controls) [ss,],
+                    y=log (wber$MOVE) [ss],
+                    free=1, standardize=FALSE)
```

Second, the dimension of the design is small enough here (1018 variables) that we can *attempt* to use MLE methods (i.e., OLS) to estimate the same model.

```
> mlehte <- gamlr(x=cBind(d,controls) [ss,],
+       y=log(wber$MOVE) [ss], lambda.start=0)
```

Figures 6.4 and 6.5 show the resulting elasticity estimates. The naive lasso estimates (i.e., without the benefit of orthogonalization) are highly peaked around values between −2 and −1.5. The MLE elasticities are all over the place, ranging from massively negative to massively positive values as high as 20, indicating a 20% *increase* in sales for each 1% price increase. (We have omitted from this plot two extreme negative values of −500 and −1300). The MLE results are completely unrealistic. There is little random price variation for each individual beer brand, so our estimates are data-starved and overfit. That this occurs despite that $n = 5000$ is a good bit larger than $p = 1018$ is a caution against the common economist's refrain that "the MLE is unbiased so it can't be too bad."

Finally, recall that all of this has been estimated on a subsample of the full dataset. For validation, we can refit the MLE for the regression of Equation 6.18 on all 1.6 million observations. Unlike in the subsample, this should be plenty of data to get precise MLE HTE estimates.

```
> fullhte <- gamlr(x=cBind(d,controls),
+             y=log(wber$MOVE), lambda.start=0)
```

Although the full sample MLE elasticities are not the "truth," they are pretty darn close under the assumption of conditional ignorability.[22] Figure 6.6 plots these full sample MLEs against the subsample estimates from Figures 6.3–6.5. The orthogonal ML estimates are (by far) closest; they appear roughly unbiased and, in an simple linear regression, explain more than 40% of the variation in the gold-standard estimates. In contrast, the naive lasso and MLE estimates of model Equation 6.18 explain only 15% and 1% of this variation. The naive lasso results are severely biased, and the MLE estimates are mostly noise.

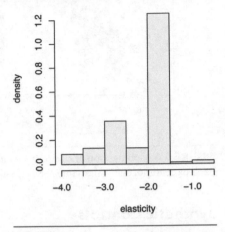

**FIGURE 6.4:** Beer-specific elasticities obtained by a (naive) lasso fit of a regression that includes all controls and log price interacted with the text data.

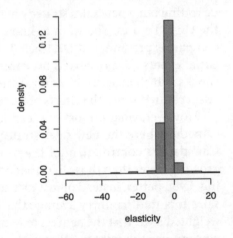

**FIGURE 6.5:** Beer-specific elasticities obtained by an MLE fit of the same regression used in Equation 5.9.

---

22. The full sample MLEs include some elasticities close to, or even above (this is again Miller Sharp's), zero. This indicates that, for at least a small set of beers, we have not controlled for all confounders that are correlated with both price and sales. I suspect that there are beer-specific temporal dynamics (e.g., discounts for seasonal items) that we need to model. You could start to do this by interacting the text with week indicators (or smoother temporal functions).

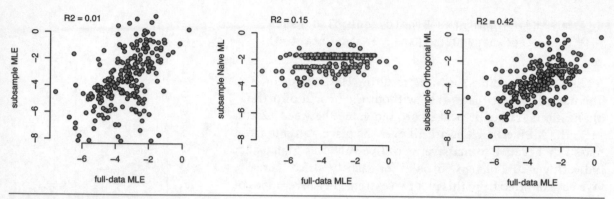

**FIGURE 6.6:** Comparison of elasticity estimates on the $n = 5000$ subsets to MLE results on the full 1.6 million observations. Each panel reports $R^2$ values for OLS regression of subsample estimates on full values.

## Synthetic Controls

To conclude this chapter on controls, we will introduce a simple strategy for causal inference that is commonly used to evaluate large-scale business policy decisions. In this setting, you have a set of *units* of aggregation—for example, geographic regions or product classes—and only one or two of these units are treated. For example, you might be rolling out a new sales strategy but do so only in a single geographic region such as the United States. You want to know the causal effect of this new strategy but simply comparing pre-and post-treatment U.S. sales could give you biased results. Other influential events have occurred over this same time period, including macro-economic shocks and changes in the natural sales cycle. You don't want to conflate the treatment effect estimate with the effects of these other contemporaneous changes.

However, what if most of these other events also affect sales across the border in Canada (where the new sales strategy has not yet been tried)? You can use sales in Canada as a control: if, after the new strategy rollout, sales in the United States are growing faster than those in Canada, you have evidence that the new strategy is working. Even better, instead of just focusing on Canada, you can compare post-treatment sales to a multicountry average that tracks with U.S. sales. Each country would be weighted such that the aggregate is, historically, a good estimate of U.S. sales. That is, you can use the sales in other, untreated, countries to predict what sales would have been in the United States if you had not introduced the new strategy.[23]

This is the method of *synthetic controls*.[24] Using potential outcomes notation, you have a time series of interest, say, the response (sales) on unit (country) $j$ at each time $t$, $y_{jt}(1)$ for the treated outcome and $y_{jt}(0)$ for the untreated. You get to observe only one of these

23. You might notice a similarity between how we describe synthetic controls and the diff-in-diff of Chapter 5. Indeed, synthetic controls can be understood as an aggregation of diff-in-diff analyses. For recent innovations in this space that take advantage of this relationship, see Dmitry Arkhangelsky, Susan Athey, David A. Hirshberg, Guido W. Imbens, and Stefan Wager, Synthetic difference in differences, 2018, arXiv:1812.09970.

24. Alberto Abadie, Alexis Diamond, and Jens Hainmueller. Synthetic control methods for comparative case studies: Estimating the effect of California's tobacco control program. *Journal of the American Statistical Association*, 105(490): 493–505, 2010.

outcomes at each time point, say, $y_{jt}$. For notational simplicity, let's say that $j = 1$. Unlike the usual conditional ignorability setting, you don't have the necessary full set of controls, $x_t$. However, you *do* have the response values for a bunch of related time series—the untreated units $y_{kt}(0)$ for $k \neq 1$. Under the (strong) assumption that these untreated series depend upon the same set of underlying unobserved controls as the treated series, you can use these other series to predict the untreated counterfactual, $y_{1t}(0)$.

Suppose that you introduce the treatment at time $T$. Then, for times $t = 1 \ldots T$, all of the series are untreated. That is, you observe $y_{jt} = y_{jt}(0)$ for all units $j = 1 \ldots J$. After time $T$, you observe $y_{kt} = y_{kt}(0)$ for all $k \neq 1$, and, for the treated series, you observe only $y_{1t} = y_{1t}(1)$. The treatment effects of interest are

$$\gamma_{1t} = y_{1t}(1) - y_{1t}(0), \text{ for } t > T + 1. \tag{6.19}$$

Since you observe $y_{1t} = y_{1t}(1)$ for $t > T$, to obtain the treatment effect, you need "only" estimate the untreated $y_{1t}(0)$. Fortunately, you observe a large number of untreated time series. At one time period after $T$, you have a mostly complete $J \times (T + 1)$ matrix of untreated values,

$$\boldsymbol{Y}^{T+1}(0) = \begin{bmatrix} y_{11}(0) & y_{12}(0) & \cdots & y_{1T}(0) & ? \\ y_{21}(0) & y_{22}(0) & \cdots & y_{2T}(0) & y_{2T+1}(0) \\ \vdots & & \vdots & & \vdots \\ y_{J1}(0) & y_{J2}(0) & \cdots & y_{JT}(0) & y_{JT+1}(0) \end{bmatrix}, \tag{6.20}$$

and if you look forward to future time points you will continue to miss only the first entry for each column.

Given this available data, a synthetic controls analysis first builds a model to predict $y_{1t}(0)$ from $\boldsymbol{y}_{-1t}(0) = [y_{2t}(0) \ldots y_{Jt}(0)]'$. This model is estimated using the fully observed data from periods $t \leq T$ and is then used to predict the unobserved control values $y_{1T+1}(0)$, $y_{1T+2}(0)$, etc. The original synthetic controls work of Abadie and Gardeazabal [2003] uses positive weights summing to one to combine the control series when predicting the treatment series. However, you should feel free to use whatever regression model works best for prediction in your application. Since there are typically many control series ($J$) relative to the number of time periods ($T$), it will often make sense to use a regularized regression like the AICc lasso.

---

**ALGORITHM 16**  **Synthetic Controls**

---

- Build a regression model for $\mathbb{E}[y_{1t}(0) \mid \boldsymbol{y}_{-1t}(0)]$, and estimate this regression using data from time periods $t = 1 \ldots T$.

- Use this regression to predict $\hat{y}_{1T+1}(0)$, $\hat{y}_{1T+2}(0)$, etc., and estimate the treatment effect at each time point as follows:

$$\hat{\gamma}_{1T+s} = y_{1T+s}(1) - \hat{y}_{1T+s}(0).$$

---

To illustrate the approach, we will revisit the data example from Abadie and Gardeazabal [2003] concerning the economic costs of terrorism in the Basque region of Spain. Beginning with a single killing in the summer of 1968, the terrorist group ETA began a campaign of killing and kidnapping that continued, with periodic cease fires, until 2010. The violence was high from the late 1970s through the early 1990s, with a peak of 92 people killed and 13 kidnapped in 1980. Almost 70% of the deaths occurred *in* the Basque country, and Basque business owners were common kidnapping targets.

Abadie and Gardeazabal ask the question: "How much did the ETA campaign harm the economy of the Basque country?" In addition to the obvious and tragic human cost of terrorism, the threat of violence will also deter investment and lower productivity. To answer this question, we can look at how the Basque region performed in comparison to the other regions in Spain (which experienced significantly less violence). For data, we have the GDP per capita (measured in 1986 $1000 USD) from 1955 through 1990 for each of the 17 regions in Spain. This data was obtained from the Synth package for R, which also implements the original estimators from Abadie and Gardeazabal. After some wrangling, it yields a matrix of the form in Equation 6.20 with the treated, Basque, region in the first row and the 16 "control" region series below. We print a portion of the matrix here:

```
> round(y[1:5,11:19],2)
                              1965 1966 1967 1968 1969 1970 1971 1972 1973
Basque Country (Pais Vasco)   5.47 5.55 5.61 5.85 6.08 6.17 6.28 6.56 6.81
Andalucia                     2.58 2.69 2.80 2.99 3.18 3.35 3.52 3.76 3.99
Aragon                        3.75 3.88 4.02 4.24 4.48 4.60 4.72 5.00 5.28
Principado De Asturias        3.74 3.91 4.07 4.31 4.55 4.63 4.70 5.02 5.35
Baleares (Islas)              5.18 5.47 5.74 6.16 6.58 6.89 7.17 7.57 7.96
```

Since the terrorism campaign started midway through 1968, we will assume that the first treated year is 1969 (i.e., $T = 1968$; results don't change much if $T = 1967$). We then create a simple function called synthc to execute Algorithm 16 using a gamlr AICc lasso for regression:

```
> synthc <- function(j, tyear=1968, . . .){
+ y0t <- t(y[,1:(tyear-1954)])
+ fit <- gamlr( y0t[,-j], y0t[,j], . . .)
+ y0hat <- predict(fit, t(y[-j,])) [,1]
+ return(list(w=coef(fit)[,1], y0hat=y0hat ))
+ }
```

Running synthc for $j = 1$, we find that the selected model for predicting untreated per capita GDP in the Basque region has nonzero positive weights on Castilla y León, the largest region bordering the Basque country, as well as on the Mediterranean region of Murcia and on the capital, Madrid. There are negative loadings on Valencia and the Balearic Islands, indicating that *after* controlling for León, Madrid, and Murcia, an *extra* increase in, say, Valencia's GDP tends to correspond to a decrease in GDP for the Basque country.

```
> sc <- synthc(1, lmr=1e-4)
> sc$w [sc$w!=0]
        intercept      Baleares   Castilla y Leon      Valencia
        0.8324923    -0.1436622         0.5159924    -0.3581780
           Madrid        Murcia
        0.4263979     0.8928448
```

These coefficients can then be used to predict what GDP per capita *would* have been in the Basque country if the ETA had not existed. This happens inside synthc with the creation of y0hat:

```
+ y0hat <- predict(fit, t(y[-j,]))
```

Note that we are predicting the synthetic control $\hat{y}_{1t}(0)$ for all $t$, not just for $t$ after 1968. Figure 6.7 shows the synthetic control series, $\hat{y}_{1t}(0)$, against the observed series, $y_{1t}$. The observed series is untreated until 1968, so $y_{1t} = y_{1t}(0)$, and treated afterward, so $y_{1t} = y_{1t}(1)$. The left panel of Figure 6.7 shows a clear break between the two series after 1968, and the results indicate a cost of terrorism ($\hat{\alpha}_{1t}$) as high as $1000 per capita in 1980.

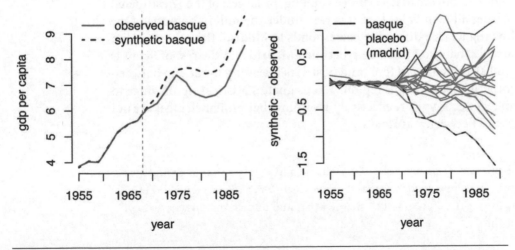

**FIGURE 6.7:** Synthetic controls analysis of the economic effects of Basque (ETA) terrorism. Per capita GDP values are in 1986 $1000 USD units. On the left, you can see the synthetic (no terrorism) GDP against the observed GDP. The right shows the difference between these counterfactuals against the available *placebos*: the difference between synthetic and realized GDP series for the 16 other regions in Spain.

How significant are these differences? For uncertainty quantification with synthetic controls, we can use *permutation testing* to create a sample from the null distribution. Under this method, you compare the estimated treatment effects to results obtained using the same methods on *placebo* units: regions where you know that no treatment has been applied. In this case, the placebo units are the 16 non-Basque regions of Spain. We can use synthc to replicate the synthetic control estimation across the series for these regions and then compare $\hat{y}_{jt}(0)$ to the observed $y_{jt}(0)$. We do this using a parSapply from the parallel library, which allows multiple regions to be predicted simultaneously.

```
> # permutation test
> library(parallel)
> cl <- makeCluster (detectCores())
> clusterExport (cl, c("y", "gamlr", "synthc"))
>
> gety0 <- function(j) { synthc(j, lmr=1e-4)$y0hat }
> Ysynth <- parSapply(cl, 1:nrow(y), gety0)
> diff <- Ysynth - t(y)
```

The resulting difference matrix, diff, contains the difference between synthetic and observed series, $\hat{y}_{jt}(0) - y_{tj}$, for every region in Spain. Only the first column of diff contains actual treatment effect estimates (for years after 1968). The other columns are full of placebo effect estimates: draws from the null distribution of what the method would predict as the treatment effect in the case where no treatment was actually applied.

The right panel of Figure 6.7 shows all of these differences. The Basque (treatment) series is highlighted. You can see that it is indeed among the largest of the 17 estimated differences, indicating a low *p*-value (i.e., it is rare under the null hypothesis). One placebo series showing a large difference corresponds to Madrid, the capital region of Spain. It is plausible that the relationship between Madrid and the rest of Spain is different before and after treatment (pre- and post-1968), leading to the gap between observed and synthetic series for this region. To designate statistical significance to the Basque treatment effects, you are effectively assuming that similar changes are not causing the difference between $\hat{y}_{1t}(0)$ and $y_{1t}$.

Permutation, or placebo, tests are generally a nice intuitive way to build confidence around your results in complicated inference scenarios. See, for example, Gentzkow et al. [2016], where we use a permutation test to quantify bias and uncertainty in measures of political partisanship.

The Madrid case illustrates the limitations of synthetic controls. The method relies upon there being *stationary* structural relationships between series—the model relating control to treated series cannot change before and after treatment. At a high level, such stationarity seems unlikely. For example, there was an attempted military coup in 1981, and Spain joined the European Commission in 1986. Both of these events, and many others, likely changed the structure of the economy in Spain and the relationships between its regions. The synthetic control method also requires independence between units (regions), which is again unlikely here (terrorism was not limited to the Basque region, and all of the regions trade with each other).

However, despite these limitations, synthetic controls provide a way to get decent estimates of causal treatment effects in cases where you don't have confidence that you've observed the full set of actual controls. You can also combine synthetic and observed controls; the covariates $x_t$ just enter as extra covariates in the regression model of Algorithm 16. And there are a variety of other useful extensions of Algorithm 16 in the literature. Researchers from Google[25] created the `causalInference` package for R that implements synthetic control methods using Bayesian time-series tools. More recently, Athey et al. [2017a] make the connection between synthetic control methods and the common ML problem of "matrix completion"—in other words, filling in the "?" in Equation 6.20. They show that off-the-shelf ML tools can be used to efficiently build synthetic thetic $\hat{y}_{jt}(0)$ series across large numbers of $j$. This is useful if you have many treated units.

All of the methods in this chapter, from basic low-dimensional OLS to synthetic controls, are best used in conjunction with available experimental evidence. Experimentation offers *unbiased* evidence of causal effects that can be complemented with observational studies on larger datasets. And any causal inference will likely be of little use without some domain structure. You should always try to ask yourself through what mechanisms the treatment can be acting on the response and use this information to guide your design of experiments, selection of controls, and modeling of heterogeneity. The ML and statistics tools of this and the previous chapter should be useful in your career as a business analyst, but you can't use them on autopilot without thinking about the structure of the problem at hand.

25. Kay H. Brodersen, Fabian Gallusser, Jim Koehler, Nicolas Remy, Steven L. Scott, et al. Inferring causal impact using Bayesian structural time-series models. *The Annals of Applied Statistics*, 9: 247–274, 2015.

# Factorization

## 7

One way to think about almost everything we do in data science is as *dimension reduction*. We are trying to *learn* from high-dimensional $x$ some low-dimensional summaries that contain the information necessary to make good decisions.

Dimension reduction can be supervised or unsupervised. In *supervised learning*, an outside "response" variable $y$ dictates the direction of dimension reduction. In regression, a high-dimensional $x$ is projected through coefficients $\beta$ to create the low-dimensional (univariate) summary $\hat{y}$. Chapters 2–4 were all about supervised learning.

In contrast, for *unsupervised learning* there is no response or outcome. You have a high-dimensional $x$, and you try to model it as having been generated from a small number of components. You are attempting to simplify $x$ for its own sake. Why? As one example, you might have partially observed values and want to predict the unknown entries from those you get to see; this is one way to think about "recommender engines." For example, suppose that $x$ is a vector where each element $x_j$ represents the score on 1 to 10 for how much a user liked "movie" $j$. Netflix tries to predict $x_j$ for movies that users haven't seen from those they have watched and scored.

Another common setting is that you really want to predict $y$ from $x$, but you have many observations of $x$ without $y$. For example, you might want to predict the sentiment of people from the words in their tweets; you will have a massive bank of all tweets (many $x$ observations) but for only a small percentage will you know whether they are expressing positive or negative sentiment (e.g., by hand-labeling the tweets using human readers). An unsupervised analysis will use all of the tweets to break the content into *topics*, and then you can easily sort these topics by sentiment on the subset of labeled tweets.

In this chapter, we'll explore different methods of *factorization*—tools that break the expectation for each $x$ into the sum of a small number of factors. We'll start with unsupervised factorization and finish by adding $y$ and considering supervised factor modeling. As always, we set up the problem with the goal of minimizing an out-of-sample deviance.

## Clustering

Cluster analysis is used to collect similar observations into groups. For example:

- To break a corpus of documents into topics

- To segment shoppers by preferences or price sensitivity

- To group voters according to the issues that drive their votes

- To find music listeners who tend to like the same genres or bands

Clustering works by representing data as the output of a *mixture distribution*. You assume that each observed $x_i$ is drawn from one of $K$ different *mixture components*, the probability distributions $p_k(x)$ for $k = 1 \dots K$. The properties of these component distributions, especially their means, define the clusters.

Even if the individual components are simple, their mixture can yield all sorts of complicated distributions. If you don't know the generating component $k$, then the *unconditional* (i.e., marginal) distribution for $x$ is

$$p(x) = \pi_1 p_1(x) + \dots \pi_K p_K(x). \qquad (7.1)$$

Here, $\pi_k$ is the probability for component $k$ in the population. This mixture distribution can have multiple modes, as in Figure 7.1, for each of the underlying components.

The data in Figure 7.1 correspond to the estimated speeds of galaxies in space. Astronomers are interested in this type of data as it gives them information about the

**probability density function**

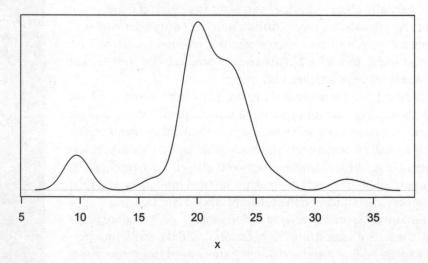

**FIGURE 7.1:** The unconditional distribution for galaxy speeds.

history of the universe. The underlying galaxy clusters can be used to help the mapping of space. However, all we have here is Figure 7.1—we don't know the underlying cluster memberships. How can they be estimated?

Suppose you have $K$ possible means for each observed $x_i$,

$$\mathbb{E}[x_i|k_i] = \mu_{k_i}, \; k_i \in \{1 \ldots K\}. \tag{7.2}$$

For example, if $k_i = 1$, then $\mathbb{E}[x_{i1}] = \mu_{11}$, $\mathbb{E}[x_{i2}] = \mu_{12}$, etc. This is not yet a mixture model; it is just the specification for the means. As in regression, you need to complete this specification with probability distributions so that you have a deviance to minimize.

The $K$-means *normal* mixture model is by far the most common foundation for clustering:

$$p_k(x) = N(x; \mu_k, \Sigma_k). \tag{7.3}$$

Here, $N(\cdot)$ denotes the *multivariate normal* distribution. Even more commonly, this is simplified to assume that each element of $x$ is *independent* from each other and has the same variance, such that the covariance matrix is written as

$$\Sigma_k = \text{diag}(\sigma_k^2) = \begin{bmatrix} \sigma_k^2 & 0 & & & \\ 0 & \sigma_k^2 & & \ddots & \\ & & \ddots & & \\ & \ddots & & \sigma_k^2 & 0 \\ & & & 0 & \sigma_k^2 \end{bmatrix}. \tag{7.4}$$

The probability distribution in Equation 7.3 then becomes the product of univariate normal distributions on each dimension, and the full mixture model is

$$p(x_i|k_i) = p_{k_i}(x_i) = \prod_j N(x_{ij}; \mu_{k_i j}, \sigma_k^2). \tag{7.5}$$

Estimation for this model leads to the $K$-Means method in Algorithm 17, which involves repeated steps of squared error minimization.

The $K$-means algorithm is a common way to estimate cluster memberships across $K$ components. It seeks to maximize the likelihood implied by Equation 7.5 by alternatively estimating component means $\hat{\mu}_k$ and updating memberships $k_i$ so that $x_i$ is close to $\hat{\mu}_{k_i}$. The least-squares step in Algorithm 17 minimizes the (conditional) deviance corresponding to the independent normal mixture model in Equation 7.5.[1] If you feed $K$-means a set of $x_i$ values, it will return the allocations $k_i$ and the *centers* $\hat{\mu}_k$.

---

1. *K*-means is only one way to fit mixture models. One big improvement can come by accounting for uncertainty about each $k_i$ when updating the $\hat{\mu}_k$ centers; this leads to the EM (expectation-maximization) algorithm.

Figure 7.2 shows an example state of convergence for 3-means clustering of two-dimensional $x$, and Figure 7.3 shows the 4-means clustering of the galaxy data from Figure 7.1.

---

**ALGORITHM 17**   *K*-Means

---

To cluster observations $\{x_i\}_{i=1}^n$ into $K$ groups, initialize by *randomly* drawing $k_i \in \{1 \ldots K\}$ for each $i$. Then, until convergence:

- Estimate the cluster centers

$$\hat{\mu}_k = \bar{x}_k = \frac{1}{n_k} \sum_{i:k_i = k} x_i,$$

where $\{i : k_i = k\}$ are the $n_k$ observations with $k_i = k$.

- For each $i$, update $k_i$ to the component with center $\hat{\mu}_k$ closest to $x_i$:

$$k_i = \operatorname{argmin}_k \sum_j (x_{ij} - \hat{\mu}_{kj})^2.$$

---

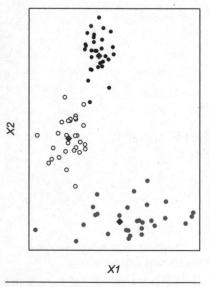

**FIGURE 7.2:** Convergence for 3-means.

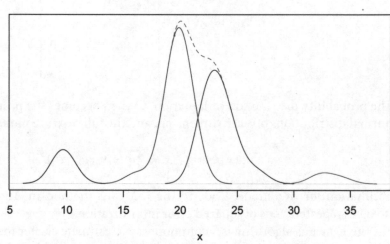

**FIGURE 7.3:** 4-means clustering for the galaxy-speed data. Each peak plotted is a density fit to a set of observations sharing the same fitted allocation, $k_i$.

There is one annoying difference between *K*-means and the other deviance minimization algorithms that we have seen thus far: if you run *K*-means multiple times, you can get different answers. This happens because of the random $k_i$ initialization, combined with the fact that the minimization objective is *nonconvex*. Nonconvexity says that the deviance surface is not a simple cup (e.g., like $x^2$) that has one single minimum; rather, it is a lumpy surface that can have multiple "solutions" where the $k_i$ can converge during Algorithm 17. For this reason, it is often recommended that you run $K$-means multiple times from different random starts and use the solution that gives the lowest deviance (lowest sum-squared error around the $\hat{\mu}_k$ centers).

More generally, this sort of indeterminacy should cause you pause: how much can the clusters represent some "true" state of the world if your estimates change every time you run the algorithm? Indeed, this lack of identification is a reason that we tend to caution against interpreting the results of clustering as anything more than useful exploratory or predictive summaries.

To illustrate the procedure, let's look at clustering various (former) European countries by food. We have data on protein consumption by country, in grams per person per day for 25 countries:

```
> food <- read.csv("protein.csv", row.names=1) # 1st column is country
> head (food)
               RedMeat WhiteMeat Eggs Milk Fish Cereals Starch Nuts Fr.Veg
Albania           10.1       1.4  0.5  8.9  0.2    42.3    0.6  5.5    1.7
Austria            8.9      14.0  4.3 19.9  2.1    28.0    3.6  1.3    4.3
Belgium           13.5       9.3  4.1 17.5  4.5    26.6    5.7  2.1    4.0
Bulgaria           7.8       6.0  1.6  8.3  1.2    56.7    1.1  3.7    4.2
Czechoslovakia     9.7      11.4  2.8 12.5  2.0    34.3    5.0  1.1    4.0
Denmark           10.6      10.8  3.7 25.0  9.9    21.9    4.8  0.7    2.4
```

To fit $K$-means in R, we need to first transform the data into a numeric matrix x (i.e., you need to expand any factors into dummy variables). In the case of this protein data, everything is numeric to start. However, we still need to think about *scaling*. As is always the case when you are minimizing squared errors across dimensions of x (e.g., as in $K$ nearest neighbors[2]), the *units* used for these dimensions will influence the result. We will convert to the units of *standard deviation* and cluster on the transformed $\tilde{x}_j = (x_{ij} - \bar{x}_j)/\text{sd}(x_j)$. These new units are also shifted to have mean of zero and are thus interpretable as units of *standard deviations from the pooled average*.

```
> xfood <- scale(food)
> round(head(xfood),1)
               RedMeat WhiteMeat Eggs Milk Fish Cereals Starch Nuts Fr.Veg
Albania            0.1      -1.8 -2.2 -1.2 -1.2     0.9   -2.2  1.2   -1.4
Austria           -0.3       1.7  1.2  0.4 -0.6    -0.4   -0.4 -0.9    0.1
Belgium            1.1       0.4  1.0  0.1  0.1    -0.5    0.9 -0.5   -0.1
Bulgaria          -0.6      -0.5 -1.2 -1.2 -0.9     2.2   -1.9  0.3    0.0
Czechoslovakia     0.0       0.9 -0.1 -0.6 -0.7     0.2    0.4 -1.0   -0.1
Denmark            0.2       0.8  0.7  1.1  1.7    -0.9    0.3 -1.2   -1.0
```

---

2. Even though $K$ nearest neighbors and $K$-means have similar names, they have almost nothing to do with each other beyond the fact that both require careful scaling of inputs.

The kmeans function takes argument centers to define *K* and nstart to determine the number of repeats of the algorithm (each corresponding to a different random start, as described earlier). The minimum deviance found across nstart runs is reported to the user. We fit a simple 3-mean model to the protein data:

```
> (grpMeat <- kmeans(xfood, centers=3, nstart=10))
K-means clustering with 3 clusters of sizes 6, 15, 4

Cluster means:
  RedMeat WhiteMeat Eggs Milk Fish Cereals Starch Nuts Fr.Veg
1    -0.8      -0.5 -1.2 -0.9 -1.0     1.4   -0.8  0.9   -0.5
2     0.5       0.5  0.6  0.6  0.1    -0.6    0.4 -0.7   -0.2
3    -0.5      -1.1 -0.4 -0.8  1.0     0.1   -0.2  1.3    1.6

Clustering vector:
     Albania     Austria     Belgium    Bulgaria   Czechoslovakia
           1           2           2           1                2
...
```

The grp$cluster object holds cluster assignments for each observation, and we've used them to plot the 3-means clustering in the red-meat versus white-meat plane in Figure 7.4. The results show one large group, with a smaller cluster created for the USSR and some neighboring satellites and another for a Western European Mediterranean block.

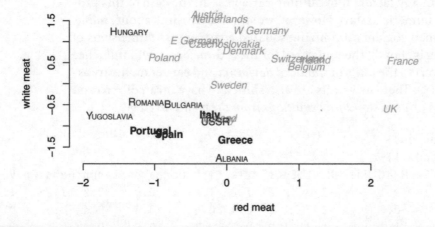

**FIGURE 7.4:** 3-means clustering of countries by protein consumption, shown in the red-meat versus white-meat plane (but fit on all protein categories).

For comparison, Figure 7.5 shows a 7-means clustering. Again, we are clustering on all nine protein categories but plotting in the red-meat versus white-meat plane. The shades and fonts indicate membership, and we see many familiar cultural and geographic groupings represented in the clustering learned through only protein consumption.

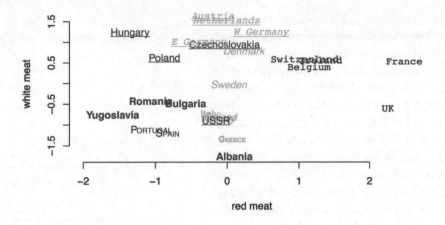

**FIGURE 7.5:** 7-means clustering of countries by protein consumption, shown in the red-meat versus white-meat plane.

**THE CHOICE OF K IS HIGHLY SUBJECTIVE.** There is little information in the data on how many clusters there are in reality, and algorithms that automatically select $K$ will be sensitive to assumptions about the component probability models. The exception to this is if you are using the cluster memberships *downstream* in some sort of prediction task, e.g., as inputs to a regression model. In that case, you can use the usual CV routines as a referee on the number of clusters. But otherwise, everything is descriptive—you are just trying to break the data into relatively homogeneous groups. It is wise to try a few $K$ and use the one leading to clusters that make sense to you.

If you choose to ignore this advice, it *is* possible to use data-based model building here. As always, the procedure follows a recipe of model enumeration followed by selection:

1. Enumerate models for $K_1 < K_2 \ldots K_T$ clusters.

2. Use a selection tool to choose the best model for *new x*.

The newness of $x$ is key: as always, you want the model to have low out-of-sample deviance. In-sample deviance is useless, as you could always get a deviance of zero by setting $K = n$.

A CV routine is possible here: for each $K$, fit the mixture on part of the data and evaluate the deviance on the left-out sample for the fitted *unconditional* likelihood in Equation 7.1.[3] It will be necessary to use a deviance built from the unconditional likelihood because you don't know $k_f$ for left-out $x_f$.

However, since $K$-means is computationally expensive, it is usually impractical to run a full CV experiment. It is more common to use an information criterion for selecting the number of clusters. The full in-sample deviance for $K$-means—for the model in

---

3. You can use $\hat{\pi}_k = n_k/n$ to estimate the mixture component weights.

Equation 7.5—is the sum of squares, $\sum_i \sum_j (x_{ij} - \hat{\mu}_{k_i j})^2$. The number of degrees of freedom is equal to the number of parameters in the cluster centers: $K \times p$. With these two facts, the usual AIC/AICc and BIC formulas apply. For example, Figure 7.6 shows the BIC surface for the protein data country clustering—it selects $K = 2$.

However, you should beware: all of these tools—from CV to BIC—are less reliable here than in regression. The CV routine will have trouble with the instability of the model fit as a function of $K$ (this is like forward stepwise regression, where CV does poorly) while the AIC/AICc/BIC rely upon theoretical approximations that are less valid here for mixtures than they are for the regression models. If you are going to use anything, there is some evidence that the BIC works well for mixtures,[4] and I'd trust it before the others. But I still don't trust it much at all. For example, Figure 7.6 shows the BIC selecting fewer clusters than intuition would suggest for our European protein example.

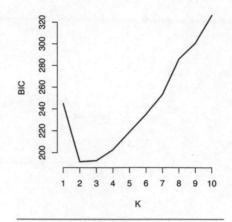

**FIGURE 7.6:** BIC for $K$ in the protein-consumption clustering example.

## Factor Models and PCA

Clustering and mixture modeling are special cases of a more general framework for unsupervised dimension reduction: factorization. Given a matrix of high-dimensional data $x$, you'd like to reduce this to a function of a few "important" factors. You do this by building a linear model for $x$ as a function of these unknown factors and then estimating both factors and model at the same time. A factor model has

$$\mathbb{E}[x_i] = \varphi_1 v_{i1} + \ldots \varphi_K v_{iK}, \tag{7.6}$$

where $x_i$ and $\varphi_k$ are all length-$p$ vectors, while the $v_{ik}$ are univariate scores indicating how observation $i$ loads on factor $k$.

When you use a $K$ that is much smaller than $p$, factor models provide a parsimonious representation for $x$. Each observation $x_i$ is mapped to $K$ factors $v_{i1} \ldots v_{ik}$, and these factors are a low dimensional summary of $x$. Consider the nifty example in Figure 7.7. This shows the fitted mapping from vectors of genetic SNP information (a high-dimensional $x$) to a 2D factor space. After shading by each person's country of origin, a pattern emerges: the factor representation resembles a (tilted) map of Europe. This means that the best two-dimensional summary of genetic material

---

4. K. Roeder and L. Wasserman. Practical Bayesian density estimation using mixtures of normals. *Journal of the American Statistical Association*, 92: 894-902, 1997.

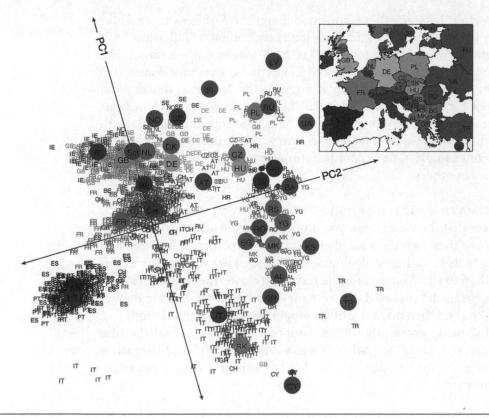

**FIGURE 7.7:** A two-factor representation of genetic sequences taken from Novembre et al. [2008]. Each point is an individual's genetic sequence, shaded by country of origin and located in the two-factor reduced dimension space.

simply corresponds to the latitude and longitude—in other words, knowing where you are from provides information about your genes.[5]

We can expand the model of Equation 7.6 for each individual dimension of $x$, writing

$$\mathbb{E}[x_{ij}] = \varphi_{j1}v_{i1} + \dots \varphi_{jK}v_{iK}, \ j = 1 \dots p. \tag{7.7}$$

Equations 7.6 and 7.7 describe the same model. The $v_{ik}$ values are attached to each observation; they are like the $x_{ij}$ inputs in regression, except that they are now unknown *latent* factors that need to be estimated. The $\varphi_{jk}$ coefficients are called *loadings* or *rotations*—these are properties of the model and are shared across all observations. They are coefficients for regression of $x_{ij}$ onto $v_i$.

---

5. The geographic pattern in Figure 7.7 is striking, but these first two factors only explain 0.45% of the original genetic variation. Don't be misled into overemphasizing the importance of geography on genes.

Note the connection between this factor model and the $K$-means representation in Algorithm 17. The mixture mean equation is equivalent to Equation 7.6 if you set $\boldsymbol{\mu}_k = \boldsymbol{\varphi}_k$ with $v_{ik_i} = 1$ and $v_{ij} = 0$ for $j \neq k_i$. The $K$-means representation is a factor model where the factor scores are forced to be a binary vector. That is, it is a factor model where you can load on only a single factor. In contrast, a general factor model allows for *mixed membership*. In the protein consumption example, $K$-means forced every country in a cluster to have the same expected diet. In contrast, a full factor model would have each country consuming a mix of shared underlying diets. For example, Greece could be similar to Italy in some dimensions and closer to Turkey in others.

**HOW DO YOU ESTIMATE A FACTOR MODEL?** You need to regress $x$ onto $v$, which would be easy except that the $v$ are latent: you don't know them and they need to be estimated. It turns out that there are a number of fast ways to estimate the model in Equation 7.6 using tools from linear algebra; indeed, it is easier to estimate a general factor model than to run $K$-means for the restricted clustering model. Without getting into the algebraic details, we'll describe a few heuristics for thinking about factor estimation. You can then make use of R's capable factorization functions.

Consider the following *greedy* algorithm. Suppose you want to find the first dimension of factors, $v^1 = [v_{11} \ldots v_{n1}]$, where we use superscript "1" to differentiate this from $v_1$, all factors for the first observation. We can write a system of equations for this single factor model,

$$\mathbb{E}[x_{i1} | v_{i1}] = \varphi_{11}v_{i1}$$
$$\vdots$$
$$\mathbb{E}[x_{ip} | v_{i1}] = \varphi_{1p}v_{i1},$$

for $i = 1 \ldots n$. Now, the problem is to find $v^1$ and $\boldsymbol{\varphi}_1$ that minimize the average sum squared error across all dimensions. Conveniently, this problem has a simple closed-form solution.[6] And, after solving for $v^1$ and $\boldsymbol{\varphi}_1$, you can proceed iteratively: calculate residuals $x_{ij} - \varphi_{1j}v_{i1}$ and then find $v^2$ to minimize a similar sum squared error criterion for these residuals. The process repeats until the residuals are all zero, which will happen after $\min(p, n)$ steps (i.e., when you have as many factors as either dimensions or observations, whichever comes first).

This procedure is called *principal component analysis* (PCA). The result of PCA is a set of *rotations* $\boldsymbol{\Phi} = [\boldsymbol{\varphi}_1 \cdots \boldsymbol{\varphi}_K]$. These can be used to obtain the factor scores $v_i$ for any observed $x_i$. The specific greedy algorithm shown previously is not actually used in practice—there are more efficient procedures—but the intuition is solid. We're

---

6. If you are familiar with linear algebra, $\boldsymbol{\varphi}_1$ is solvable as the first *eigenvector* of the covariance matrix $X'X$. Since arbitrary shifts and scales of $v_{i1}$ will give the same $R^2$ after adjustment to $\varphi_{ij}$, we add the restriction $\sum_j^p \varphi_{kj}^2 = 1$ to nail down scale.

repeatedly fitting both $\boldsymbol{\varphi}_k$ and latent $\boldsymbol{v}^k$ to *minimize deviance* across dimensions $j = 1 \dots p$ and observations $i = 1 \dots n$, for the model

$$\tilde{x}_{ij}^k \sim \mathrm{N}(v_{ik}\varphi_{kj}, \sigma_k^2), \tag{7.8}$$

where

$$\tilde{x}_{ij}^k = \tilde{x}_{ij}^{k-1} - v_{ik-1}\,\varphi_{k-1j}$$

is the residual after fitting $k - 1$ factors, starting from $\widetilde{X}^1 = X$. You can think about PCA as repeatedly fitting regression onto the best possible factors to explain current residuals.

Another way to build intuition around PCA is to understand what it is doing visually in low dimensions. Consider the two-dimensional data plotted in Figure 7.8. The line is the OLS fit for $x_2$ on $x_1$ (or vice versa; it's the same line). This line has a *length* spanning the range of observed data, and each data point can be mapped to a location on the line that is closest to its location in $[x_1, x_2]$ coordinates. The slope of the line is defined by loadings $\varphi_1$, and each point's mapped location on the line is its factor score, $v_{1i}$.

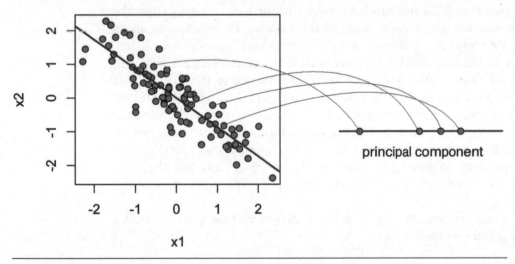

**FIGURE 7.8:** Illustration of PCA for two-dimensional data. PCA is equivalent to finding the line that fits through $x_1$ and $x_2$ and seeing where each observation is closest to on the line.

In finding this first PCA *direction*, we've projected from 2D onto a 1D axis. The next step of the algorithm would iterate, taking the residuals in $x_1$ and $x_2$ with respect to this line and repeating the projection procedure. If you take those residuals and regress one dimension on the other, you get the new line (PC2) in Figure 7.9. Since we have only two dimensions, this is where the algorithm stops. There is a 1:1 mapping from $[x_1, x_2]$ to the new factor space $[v_1, v_2]$—every point can be perfectly re-created from its PC1 and PC2 factor scores.

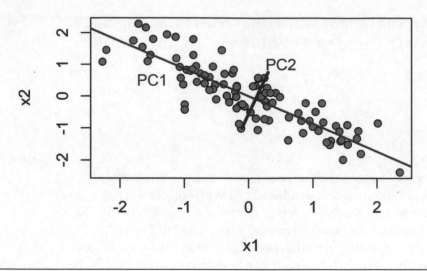

**FIGURE 7.9:** Two-factor PCA representation of the data from Figure 7.8.

Figure 7.9 shows that PCA has *rotated* the axes of the data, moving from the original coordinates to a space where most of the data variation is spread along the first coordinate and there is little spread along the second coordinate. Indeed, this is the point of PCA: it looks for projections from multivariate $x$ that will have *high variance*. The resulting $v_{ik}$ will be spread out along the longest line possible—for example, along the first PC1 direction in Figures 7.8 and 7.9. The resulting principal components will be ordered by the variance of the fitted projection so that $\text{var}(v_{1i}) > \text{var}(v_{2i}) \dots \text{var}(v_{pi})$. You can summarize most of the variation in the data by keeping track of only the first $K \ll p$ components. That is, you fit enough components to perfectly re-create the original data but then use only the first several—enough to explain the dominant directions of variation in $x_i$.

After you've fit your rotations $\Phi = [\varphi_1 \cdots \varphi_K]$, the $k$th principal component score for observation $i$ is fast and easy to obtain as

$$v_{ki} = x_i'\varphi_k = \sum_{j=1}^{p} \varphi_{kj}x_{ij}. \tag{7.9}$$

Typical practice is to keep $\Phi$ and use Equation 7.10 to recover the PC scores for any $x_i$ as needed.[7] Combining this equation with the previous discussion of factor

---

7. If you work through the details, this definition for $v_{ki}$ will be a shifted and rescaled version of the PC scores implied by the algorithms we've described elsewhere. Since the $v$'s are latent and have no inherent units, these definitions are all essentially equivalent.

variance, we can summarize the PC scores as a series of variance maximizations as in Algorithm 18.

---

| **ALGORITHM 18** | **Principal Components Analysis** |

Set $\tilde{X}^1 = X$, your $n \times p$ data matrix. Then, for $k = 1 \ldots \min(n, p)$,

- Find

$$\boldsymbol{\varphi}_k = \mathrm{argmax}_{\boldsymbol{\varphi}_k}\left[\mathrm{var}(\tilde{X}^k \boldsymbol{\varphi}_k) = \mathrm{var}\{v_{k1}, \ldots, v_{kn}\}\right], \tag{7.10}$$

where $v_{ki} = \boldsymbol{\varphi}_k' \boldsymbol{x}_i = \sum_{j=1}^{p} x_{ij} \varphi_{kj}$ and $\sum_{j=1}^{p} \varphi_{kj}^2 = 1$.

- Update rows of $\tilde{X}^k$ via $\tilde{\boldsymbol{x}}_i^{k+1} = \tilde{\boldsymbol{x}}_i^k - v_{ki} \times \boldsymbol{\varphi}_k$.

---

There are many ways to run PCA in R. After trying many different versions with my MBA classes, the most robust seems to be prcomp(x, scale=TRUE). The scale=TRUE argument here is important: since you're working with fitting the $x_{ij}$ directly, as in $K$-means and $K$ nearest neighbor, it is good to scale the data so that you are working in terms of standard deviations of $x_j$ rather than in some other arbitrary units. To illustrate, we'll apply this to the protein consumption data:

```
> pcfood <- prcomp(food, scale=TRUE)
> round(pcfood$rotation, 1)
            PC1  PC2  PC3  PC4  PC5  PC6  PC7  PC8  PC9
RedMeat    -0.3 -0.1 -0.3 -0.6  0.3 -0.5  0.2  0.0  0.2
WhiteMeat  -0.3 -0.2  0.6  0.0 -0.3 -0.1  0.0  0.0  0.6
Eggs       -0.4  0.0  0.2 -0.3  0.1  0.4 -0.4 -0.5 -0.3
Milk       -0.4 -0.2 -0.4  0.0 -0.2  0.6  0.5  0.1  0.2
Fish       -0.1  0.6 -0.3  0.2 -0.3 -0.1 -0.1 -0.4  0.3
Cereals     0.4 -0.2  0.1  0.0  0.2  0.1  0.4 -0.7  0.2
Starch     -0.3  0.4  0.2  0.3  0.7  0.1  0.2  0.1  0.1
Nuts        0.4  0.1 -0.1 -0.3  0.2  0.4 -0.4  0.2  0.5
Fr.Veg      0.1  0.5  0.4 -0.5 -0.2  0.1  0.4  0.1 -0.2
```

The "rotation" matrix here is $\boldsymbol{\Phi}$. Each column is $\boldsymbol{\varphi}_k = [\varphi_{k1} \ldots \varphi_{kp}]'$, the coefficients that translate from the $k$th PC direction to each dimension of $\boldsymbol{x}$ (here, protein types). If you want to get the PC scores—the $\boldsymbol{v}_i$ values—you apply predict to the fitted prcomp object. You can either provide a new $\boldsymbol{x}$ that you want mapped to $\boldsymbol{v}$ or call predict without providing any newdata and it will return the matrix of PC scores for **X**, the sample data used to fit the PC rotations.

```
> predict(pcfood, newdata=food["France",])
            PC1  PC2 PC3   PC4  PC5   PC6  PC7   PC8  PC9
France  -1.49 0.79   0 -1.96 0.25  -0.9 0.95 -0.02 0.54
> head( zfood <- predict(pcfood) )
                PC1  PC2  PC3  PC4  PC5  PC6  PC7  PC8  PC9
Albania         3.5 -1.6 -1.8 -0.2  0.0 -1.0 -0.5  0.8 -0.1
Austria        -1.4 -1.0  1.3 -0.2 -0.9  0.2 -0.2 -0.3 -0.2
Belgium        -1.6  0.2  0.2 -0.5  0.8 -0.3 -0.2 -0.2  0.0
Bulgaria        3.1 -1.3  0.2 -0.2 -0.5 -0.7  0.5 -0.8 -0.3
Czechoslovakia -0.4 -0.6  1.2  0.5  0.3 -0.8  0.3  0.0 -0.1
Denmark        -2.4  0.3 -0.8  1.0 -0.8 -0.2 -0.2 -0.6  0.5
```

Interpretation of the PC directions is a tricky game—as much art as science. Absent any outside context, these factors are defined only in terms of the repeated variance maximizations in Algorithm 18. They are scores in the directions that explain the most amount of variance possible. But it is often desirable to build a *story* around the factors. Indeed, the potential of interpretable low-dimensional factor structure is a driving motivation behind the use of PCA in many social science applications. If you are going to get into this story-building business, then there are two routes: bottom up and top down.

For a bottoms-up interpretation, you can look at big individual $\varphi_{kj}$ rotations to decipher the main drivers in the map between $v_{ki}$ and $x_{ij}$. In the protein consumption PCA, each country's factor score in the $k$th PC direction is

$$v_{ki} = \varphi_{k,\text{redmeat}} x_{i,\text{redmeat}} + \varphi_{k,\text{whitemeat}} x_{i,\text{whitemeat}} + \dots \varphi_{k,\text{nuts}} x_{i,\text{nuts}}.$$

This factor score represents a diet—a latent pattern representing one identifiable style of protein consumption. Since the $x_{ij}$ are scaled to units of standard deviation, each $\varphi_{kj}$ tells you the amount that a country will score in the direction of diet $k$ per one SD extra consumption of protein $j$. Consider rotations for the first two PCs:

```
> t(round(pcfood$rotation[,1:2],2))
     R.Meat  W.Meat Eggs  Milk  Fish  Cereal Starch Nuts Fr.Veg
PC1  -0.30  -0.31 -0.43 -0.38 -0.14    0.44  -0.30 0.42   0.11
PC2  -0.06  -0.24 -0.04 -0.18  0.65   -0.23   0.35 0.14   0.54
```

We see that you score high in PC1 if you consume a lot of cereals and nuts; conversely, you score low in PC1 if you consume expensive proteins such as meat, eggs, and milk.

The second PC is a Mediterranean diet: consumption of lots of fish and olives (a source of fruit and vegetable protein) pushes a higher $v_{2i}$ score.

For a top-down interpretation, you look at the fitted $v_{ik}$ and use domain knowledge about observation $i$ to build a narrative. Figure 7.10 shows PC scores plotted against each other for the first four directions in the protein consumption PCA. We see that PC1 provides a mostly western versus eastern (or perhaps wealthy versus poor) axis of countries, while PC2 represents an Iberian diet, identified by high scores for Spain and Portugal.

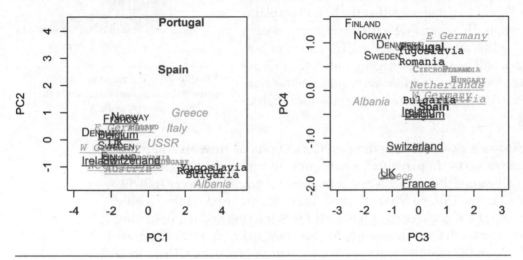

**FIGURE 7.10:** Protein consumption PC scores $v_{ki}$ for the first four PC directions. The countries are differentiated according to the $K$-means clustering of Figure 7.5.

Once you've fit all the PC directions, the next question is, how many do you need? As it was for the number of clusters in $K$-means, this is not a question that is easily answered unless you are using the factors in a downstream prediction problem (in which case the usual CV or IC tools apply). As a rough heuristic, it is common to look at the variance of each $v^k$ and see how quickly it is decreasing with $k$. If there is a big drop-off in the variance after a certain $k$, then perhaps you only need to keep PC1 through PC$k$. When you summarize the fitted `prcomp` object, it prints the running tally of variance across factors:

```
> summary(pcfood)
Importance of components:
                          PC1     PC2     PC3     PC4      PC5
Standard deviation     2.0016  1.2787  1.0620  0.9771  0.68106
Proportion of Variance 0.4452  0.1817  0.1253  0.1061  0.05154
Cumulative Proportion  0.4452  0.6268  0.7521  0.8582  0.90976
```

Since the sum of variances will be equal to the total variance across all $x_{ij}$, the summary also reports the *proportion* of variance explained by each PC direction. Each PC's contribution to this total variance is decreasing with $k$. You can also plot the `prcomp` object to get the *screeplot*, a visual representation of the variance for each PC direction.

You might make judgments about how many PCs are influential based upon these summaries, but it is never clear how small the variance needs to be before a PC is not worth tracking. For example, in Figure 7.11, it appears that the first PC explains most of the variation. However, PC2 has a clear interpretation in terms of the Mediterranean/Iberian diet. The choice of how many PCs to track will be subjective (again, unless the PCs are used as inputs to a prediction task). As recommended for clustering, use the PCs that make sense for your exploratory analysis and storytelling.

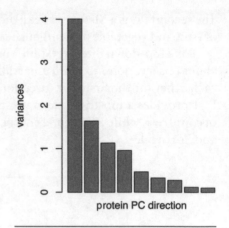

**FIGURE 7.11:** The variance for each principal component direction in the protein consumption PCA.

AS A MORE COMPLEX EXAMPLE, CONSIDER A PC ANALYSIS OF HOW MEMBERS OF THE U.S. CONGRESS VOTE. In particular, we are going to look at the Congressional Record for *roll-call votes*—those votes where attendance is taken and every individual's vote is added to the Congressional Record. These are archived on the website `voteview.com`, and the R package `pscl` has tools for extracting and manipulating this data. The set of votes that we are going to look at come from the 111th Congress covering 2009 to 2010, the first two years of Barack Obama's presidency. There were 445 voting members in the U.S. House of Representatives for this Congress, and we have recorded their votes on 1647 questions as −1 for nea, +1 for yea, and 0 for those who abstained or were absent. This leads to a large 445 × 1647 matrix with rows $x_i$ representing the voting record for politician $i$.

> You might ask why you would use least-squares to fit models for $\{-1, 0, 1\}$ data, as implied by the Gaussian interpretation of PCA in Equation 7.8. Good question! In the next chapter, we discuss multinomial factor models. However, PCA works fine in many non-Gaussian settings since it can also be interpreted as simply maximizing factor variances, as in Algorithm 18.

There is intuitive support for a low-dimensional factor structure in this setting. Although each of the votes are on different issues, the individual voters are aligned upon partisan and ideological axes—e.g., Republican versus Democrat or liberal versus conservative. If you believe that all votes are *in expectation* partisan, then the vote for member $i$ on issue $j$ could be predicted as

$$\mathbb{E}[x_{ij}] = \varphi_{1j} v_{i1},$$

where, $v_{i1}$ is the member's score along, say, a traditional left–right axis. This is precisely the sort of model that PCA can estimate.

After loading the vote data into R, we can run PCA using `prcomp`:

```
> head(votes[,1:6])
                    Vote.1 Vote.2 Vote.3 Vote.4 Vote.5 Vote.6
BONNER (R AL-1)         -1      1     -1      0      0      1
BRIGHT (D AL-2)          1     -1      1      1      1      1
ROGERS (R AL-3)         -1      1     -1     -1     -1      1
ADERHOLT (R AL-4)       -1      1     -1     -1      1      1
GRIFFITH (D/R AL-5)      1     -1      1      1      1     -1
BACHUS (R AL-6)         -1      1     -1      1      1      1
> pcavote <- prcomp(votes, scale=TRUE)
```

Figure 7.12 shows the screeplot for the resulting variances attributed to each PC direction. Notice that there are huge drops in variance from 1st to 2nd and 2nd to 3rd PCs. The political science literature[8] finds that a single component is able to explain the vast majority of variation in how politicians vote. A second dimension has been useful to understand voting at a few specific points in time, for example, during the civil war 1860s or during the civil rights battle 1960s when a north versus south (or racist versus less-racist) divide arises across party lines. We can ask the question of our data: "Is there an interpretable second dimension to the political space of 2009 to 2010?"

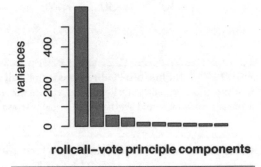

**FIGURE 7.12:** PC direction variances for the roll-call vote data.

The first two PC directions are plotted in Figure 7.13. These are the $v_i = [v_{i1}, v_{i2}]$ for each individual politician $i$. With the Republicans in black and Democrats in white (and independent in grey), we see a clear partisan divide on the first principal component. Our intuition is supported by data: most voting behavior is driven by a single-partisan factor. The second direction is orthogonal to party (which is necessary if PC1 aligns with party). This dimension matters little for most politicians, but a small group of politicians have large negative $v_{i2}$. What does it mean?

Let's start with a top-down interpretation exercise. Looking at factor scores for individual politicians, we find that the extremes of PC1 correspond to ideological extremes. That is, the PC1 direction doesn't just capture party membership but also represents the spectrum of liberal–conservative beliefs within each party. For example,

8.  Keith T. Poole. *Spatial Models of Parliamentary Voting*. Cambridge University Press, New York, 2005.

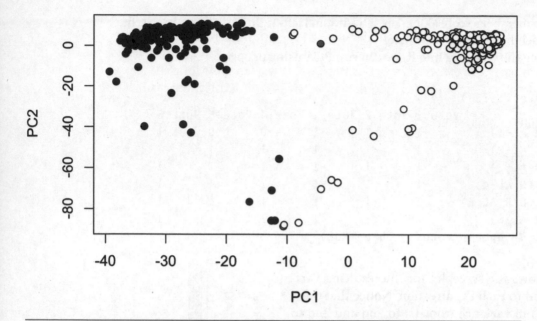

**FIGURE 7.13:** The first two PC directions for roll-call voting, with Republicans in black and Democrats in white. Inconveniently, the Republicans are on the left, and Democrats are on the right—PC signs are arbitrary, and you would get the same fit quality if you multiplied each $v_{il}$ by –1.

the most negative $v_{il}$ correspond to far-right (very conservative) Republicans, and the largest positive values are all liberal democrats.

```
> # Far right (very conservative)
> sort(votepc[,1])
    BROUN (R GA-10)      FLAKE (R AZ-6)   HENSARLIN (R TX-5)
       -39.3739409          -38.2506713           -37.5870597

# Far left (very liberal)
> sort(votepc[,1], decreasing=TRUE)
   EDWARDS (D MD-4)   PRICE (D NC-4)   MATSUI (D CA-5)
       25.2915083        25.1591151        25.1248117
```

In contrast, looking at the individuals with large (negative) scores for PC2, there is no obvious pattern. Indeed, it is not clear whether this group of people would ever be able to agree on any issue of political substance!

```
> sort(votepc[,2])
    SOLIS (D CA-32)    GILLIBRAND (D NY-20)    PELOSI (D CA-8)
       -88.31350926            -87.58871687        -86.53585568
  STUTZMAN (R IN-3)        REED (R NY-29)       GRAVES (R GA-9)
       -85.59217310            -85.53636319        -76.49658108
```

Moving to a bottoms-up interpretation, Figure 7.14 plots the distribution of PC1 loadings across specific votes. Looking in detail at votes with large positive or negative loadings, we find they correspond to bills that were extreme enough to cause members of each party to vote with the opposition. For example, a vote for a specific set of Republican amendments to the Affordable Health Care for America Act indicates a negative (more conservative) PC1. This bill included cuts in care that made many in the GOP uncomfortable; only the most fiscally conservative or libertarian members voted "yea." On the other end, a vote for the Targeted Asset Relief Program (TARP)—the controversial bail-out for financial institutions—is a push in the direction a positive (more progressive) PC1. This all confirms our interpretation of PC1 as representing the traditional liberal-conservative ideological axis.

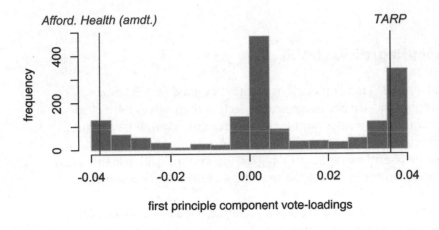

**FIGURE 7.14:** PC1 loadings $\varphi_{1j}$ for votes.

For PC2, we can investigate the large $|\varphi_{2j}|$ values to discern a pattern.

```
> loadings[order(abs(loadings[,2]), decreasing=TRUE)[1:5],2]
  Vote.1146    Vote.658   Vote.1090   Vote.1104   Vote.1149
0.05605862  0.05461947  0.05300806  0.05168382  0.05155729
```

After looking them up, we find that these votes all correspond to near-unanimous symbolic action. For example, 429 legislators voted "yea" for resolution 1146:

*Supporting the goals and ideals of a Cold War Veterans Day.*

If you didn't vote for this, you are not a politician. And indeed, that solves the mystery: the members who get pushed toward negative PC2 were *absent* for these votes. They voted 0 when all others voted +1 (which will lead to negative scores for the absent voters when you fit the PCA with `scale=TRUE`). Thus, PC2 represents attendance: those politicians with big negative scores in PC2 have terrible attendance records. Some because they have perhaps more important things to do, and others because they were elected only in by-elections midway through the congressional session.

```
> # members with the highest number of absences
> sort(rowSums(votes==0), decreasing=TRUE)
    SOLIS (D CA-32) GILLIBRAND (D NY-20)   REED (R NY-29)
           1628                 1619             1562
 STUTZMAN (R IN-3)     PELOSI (D CA-8)  GRAVES (R GA-9)
           1557                 1541             1340
```

We can conclude that in the 111th Congress there was only a single dominant ideological factor driving votes. The next biggest influence was whether you show up to vote regularly.

## Principal Component Regression (PCR)

Now that you've learned how to fit factor models, what are they good for? In some settings, as in the previous political science example, the factors themselves have clear meaning and can be useful in their own right for understanding complex systems. More commonly, unfortunately, the factors are of dubious origin or interpretation. However, they can still be useful as *inputs* to a regression system. Indeed, this is the primary practical function for PCA—as the first stage of principal components regression (PCR).

The concept of PCR is simple: instead of regressing $y$ onto $x$, use a lower-dimension set of principal components as covariates. This is a fruitful strategy for a few reasons:

- PCA reduces dimension, which is usually good.

- The PCs are independent, so you have no multicollinearity and the final regression is easy to fit.

- You might have far more unlabeled $x_i$ than labeled $[x_i, y_i]$ pairs.

This last point is especially powerful. You can use *unsupervised* learning (PCA) on a massive bank of unlabeled data and use the results to reduce dimension and facilitate *supervised* learning on a smaller set of labeled observations.

The disadvantage of PCR is that PCA will be driven by the *dominant* sources of variation in $x$. If the response is connected to these dominant sources of variation, PCR works well. If it is more of a "needle in the haystack response," driven by a small number of inputs, then PCR will not work well. For example, in finance it is commonly thought that equity returns are driven by a small number of factors (see our CAPM discussion in the Introduction). If you want to be able to trade on what the rest of the market *doesn't* know, then you will be looking for signal that is *not* summarized by these dominant factors. In such cases, PCR will not work well.

In practice, you do not know what scenario you are in until you try both PCR and, say, a lasso regression on the raw $x$ inputs.[9]

The two-stage PCR algorithm is straightforward: you run PCA and then run a regression procedure.

```
mypca = prcomp(X, scale=TRUE)
v = predict(mypca) [,1:K]
reg = glm(y~., data=as.data.frame(v))
```

Classically, the number of PCs to include in the regression can be selected using a version of subset selection where you build, say, $p$ different models using PCs 1 through $K$ for $K = 1 \ldots p$. The optimal choice for $K$ is then selected based on an information criterion or out-of-sample experimentation. Because the PCs are ordered (by their variance) and independent, this works better than subset selection on the raw dimensions of $x_i$ (which we've previously warned against).

This PC selection procedure is fine, but in my experience it is both easier and better to simply run a lasso regression on the full set of PCs. You can then use the usual selection procedures to choose the $\lambda$ regularization weight. This procedure makes it easy to incorporate other information in addition to the PCs. For example, one tactic that works well in practice is to put both $v$ and $x$—both the PCs and the raw inputs—into the lasso model matrix. This then allows the regression to make use of the underlying factor structure in $x$ *and* still pick up individual $x_{ij}$ signals that are related to $y$. This hybrid strategy is a solution to the disadvantage of PCR mentioned earlier—that it will only pick up dominant sources of variation in $x$.

---

**ALGORITHM 19**   **Principal Components (Lasso) Regression**

Given a sample of regression input observations $\{x_i\}_{i=1}^n$, accompanied by output labels $y_i$ for some subset of these observations:

1. Fit PCA on the full set of $x_i$ inputs to obtain $v_i$ of length $\min(n, p)$.

2. For the labeled subset, run a lasso regression for $y_i$ on $v_i$ (including selection for penalty $\lambda$ via either CV or AICc).

   (a) Alternatively, regress $y_i$ on $x_i$ and $v_i$ to allow simultaneous selection between PCs and raw inputs.

To predict for a new $x_f$, use the rotations from step 1 to get $v_f = \Phi x_f$ and then feed these scores into the regression fit from step 2.

---

9. In social science, PCR is sometimes preferred when the PCA factors have clear interpretation (e.g., as in the roll-call votes example). In these cases, PCR will lead to results that are easier to communicate than those from a raw lasso regression. However, be careful: social scientists are great at interpreting factors where they don't exist.

In Algorithm 19, we are breaking one of the rules of model selection: we are manipulating the data outside of the CV loop when we fit PCA in step 1 on the full sample. However, it is fine to use the full $x$ sample if you do not use the labels $y$ outside of the OOS loop. So long as the random errors in your test $y$ sample are not allowed to influence the model fit, then the result of your trained model on left-out data remains a good estimate of OOS performance. Indeed, the primary rule of CV is that you want an OOS experiment that mimics how the models will be fit and used on true future data. It is potentially the case that you will know the $x$ values for future observations and can include them in the PCA fitting even if you don't yet know their labels.

TO ILLUSTRATE PCR, LET'S CONSIDER TELEVISION DATA that include survey responses for focus groups on TV show pilots (first episodes of a new series) as well as the first year of ratings results (how many people ended up watching the show). The hope is that we can build a rule for predicting viewer interest from pilot surveys, thus helping the studios to make better programming decisions.

The survey data include 6241 views and 20 questions for 40 shows. There are two types of questions in the survey. Both ask you the degree to which you agree with a statement. For Q1, this statement takes the form of "This show makes me feelfeel . . . ." For Q2, the statement is "I find this showfeel . . . ."

We have a couple of interesting outcome variables. Classic measures of broadcast marketability are *ratings*. Specifically, *gross ratings points* (GRP) provide an estimated count of total viewership. In this data we also track the *projected engagement* (PE) as a more subtle measure of audience attention. After watching a show, viewers are contacted and quizzed on order and detail for events in the show. This measures their engagement with the show (and, perhaps more importantly, the ads shown). PE is reported on a 0 to 100 scale, with 100 being fully engaged and 0 meaning they didn't pay attention at all. Engagement matters on its own, as a driver of TRP and GRP, and also as an adjustment factor—for example, normalizing GRP/PE to get *adjusted GRP*.

We have these GRP and PE results for all 40 shows over their first year. The comparison is shown in Figure 7.15, with the programs differentiated by their genre—*reality, comedy,* or *drama/adventure* scripted series. Notice that higher engagement does tend to correspond to higher ratings but that comedies can have high engagement with lower ratings (i.e., they look better by adjusted GRP—GRP/PE—than by raw GRP). Reality shows tend to have lower engagements and lower ratings (but they are cheap to produce).

It might seem like there is a lot of data here—6241 pilot viewings—but there are only 40 shows and 20 survey questions. That is, there are only two observed $y$ values for each input dimension, such that it is a small dataset with big data dimensionality problems. To relate survey results to show performance, we need to first calculate the average survey question response by show. This leads to a $40 \times 20$ design matrix $X$, and we can fit PCA on this design.

```
> PCApilot['rotation'] [,1:3]
              PC1   PC2   PC3
Q1_Excited    -0.3   0.1  -0.1
Q1_Happy      -0.1   0.2  -0.5
Q1_Engaged    -0.3   0.0   0.0
Q1_Annoyed     0.2   0.3   0.1
Q1_Indifferent 0.2   0.4   0.1
Q2_Funny       0.1   0.2  -0.5
Q2_Confusing  -0.1   0.3   0.2
Q2_Predictable 0.2   0.3   0.0
Q2_Entertaining -0.3 -0.1  -0.3
Q2_Original   -0.3   0.1  -0.2
Q2_Boring      0.2   0.4   0.1
Q2_Dramatic   -0.2   0.0   0.4
Q2_Suspenseful -0.3   0.0   0.3
```

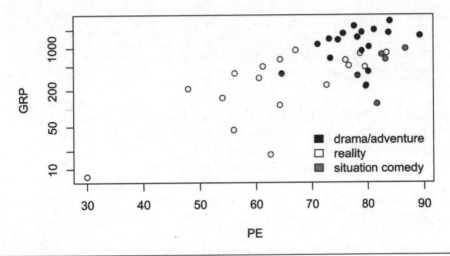

**FIGURE 7.15:** Ratings (GRP) and engagement (PE) for the 40 NBC shows.

Looking at the PC rotation output shown, PC1 seems to have simple interpretation as the "how much you dislike the show" factor (i.e., negative PC1 is a likability factor). A show scores low on PC1 if it made viewers feel excited and engaged and if the material was original, entertaining, and suspenseful. A show scores high on PC1 if people found it annoying and boring. PC2 is less clearly interpretable: you score high on PC2 if you find the show boring, confusing, and predictable, but also if you find it funny.

Figure 7.16 provides some insight. We see that the reality TV shows score high on both PC1 and PC2—they are both unlikable and can be annoying while funny—and the scripted dramas score low on both.

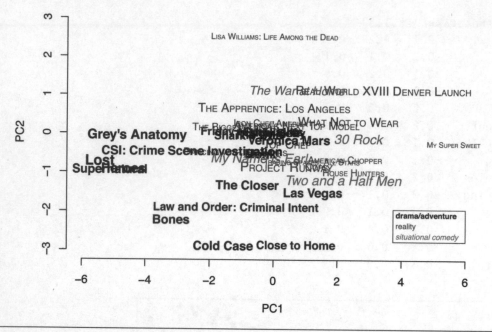

**FIGURE 7.16:** The first two PCs for average survey results on the 40 shows. The shows are differentiated by genre, as in Figure 7.15, and sized by their engagement score.

We'll regress engagement onto the PCs. Figure 7.17 shows the AICc surfaces across $K$ and $\lambda$ for both a classical PC subset-selection procedure and for the lasso PCR of Algorithm 19. The subset-selection procedure choose a model using PCs 1 through 7, while AICc selection for the lasso PCR chooses six PCs (not the first six).[10]

```
> LassoPCR <- gamlr (V, PE)
> B <- coef (LassoPCR) [-1,]
> B [B!=0]
    PC1     PC2     PC3     PC7    PC11    PC16
-2.1218 -0.8704 -1.2472 -4.2555 -0.5929 13.0778
```

Comparing this output to the left panel of Figure 7.17, we see that selected PCs 7, 11, and 16 all correspond to jumps in the subset-selection AICc surface. These PCs are judged useful by both procedures, but only the lasso is able to use that information effectively.

As a round-up on PCR, we contrast it to the lasso regression techniques from Chapter 3. Lasso on raw $x$ finds a *sparse* model (many $\hat{\beta}_j = 0$), whereas PCR assumes a *dense* model where all the $x_{ij}$ values matter but only through the information they

___
10. Both AICc curves are unstable here and bounce around across $K$ or $\lambda$ values. This will happen with small data samples, even when using generally stable techniques like the lasso.

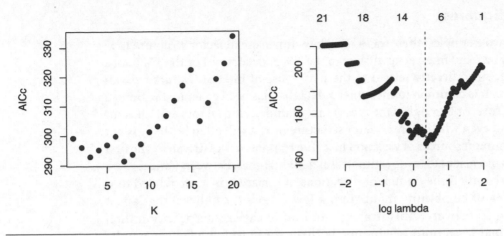

**FIGURE 7.17:** AICc selection results (left) across $K$ for glm of PE onto PCs $1 - K$ and (right) across $\lambda$ for a gamlr lasso onto all 20 fitted PCs.

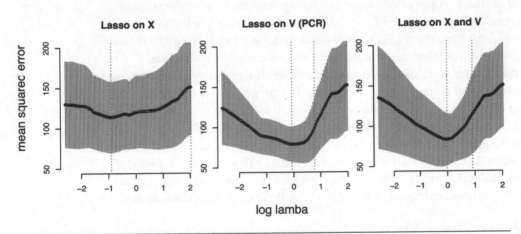

**FIGURE 7.18:** 20-fold OOS experiment results for three regressions attempting to predict projected engagement.

provide on a few simple factors. Both strategies rely upon dimension reduction; which is best will depend upon the application. Figure 7.18 shows results of a 20-fold (i.e., leave-out two shows each time) OOS prediction experiment for three regressions—a standard lasso for $y$ on $x$, a PCR lasso for $y$ on $v$, and a hybrid lasso onto both $x$ and $v$. In this example, the PCR regression outperforms the lasso onto $x$. The hybrid regression does roughly as well as the PCR lasso, but with some added variance across folds (wider uncertainty bars). It appears that, for this application, the individual survey responses provide little value beyond what they tell you about underlying factors. This is common with survey data: many of the questions are asking for versions of the same answer.

## Partial Least Squares

In the previous two examples, there was a clear low-dimensional factor structure in $x$: ideology in Congress and like-versus-dislike in the TV pilot survey. For the TV pilots, these factors were also directly related to the $y$ response of interest. *Nature will not always be this nice*. It is common to encounter $x$ data that has been generated without a clear factor structure, or through some messy mix of underlying factors and idiosyncratic shocks. And even when there is factor structure in $x$, it will often be that $y$ is not related to the dominant sources of variation in $x$. The response is not driven by the first few PCs, and it is inefficient to try to estimate $v$ as a middle-man between $y$ and $x$.

PCR will work only if the dominant directions of variation in $x$ are related to $y$. However, the idea of combining inputs into a few factors (or indices) that affect $y$ is an appealing framework. This strategy can lead to easier interpretation than a high-dimensional lasso onto raw inputs. Is there a way to force factors $v$ to be relevant to both $x$ and $y$? The answer is yes; this is referred to as *supervised factor modeling*, and it is a useful big data technique.

There is a big world of supervised factor modeling, and there are several algorithms for supervised adaptations of PCA.[11] We'll consider the simple but powerful method of *partial least squares* (PLS), a supervised factorization strategy that has its roots in 1970s chemometrics[12] but has been re-invented many times since.

To understand PLS, we start with the more basic algorithm of *marginal regression* (MR). In this scheme, you simply regress $y$ on to each dimension of $x$ *independently* and then use the resulting regression coefficients to map from $x$ to a univariate factor $v$. This factor aggregates the *first-order* effect of each input variable on $y$. It will be dominated by $x_j$ dimensions that both (1) have a big effect on $y$ and (2) move consistently in the same direction with each other (since their influence on the factor is additive). That is, marginal regression constructs a single factor that is connected both to $y$ and to a dominant direction of variation in $x$. It yields a supervised factor.

---

**ALGORITHM 20**   **Marginal Regression**

To build a model for prediction of $y$ from $x$:

- Calculate $\varphi = [\varphi_1 \ldots \varphi_p]$ where $\varphi_j = \mathrm{cor}(x_j, y)/\mathrm{sd}(x_j)$ is the OLS coefficient in a simple univariate regression for $y$ on $x_j$.

- Set $v_i = x_i'\varphi = \sum_j x_{ij} \varphi_j$ for each observation $i$.

- Fit the "forward" univariate linear regression $y_i = \alpha + \beta v_i + \varepsilon_i$.

Given new $x_f$, you can then predict $\hat{y}_f = \alpha + \beta \times (x_f'\varphi)$.

---

11. Eric Bair, Trevor Hastie, Paul Debashis, and Robert Tibshirani. Prediction by supervised principal components. *Journal of the American Statistical Association*, 101:119–137, 2006.

12. H. Wold. Soft modeling by latent variables: The nonlinear iterative partial least squares approach. In *Perspectives in Probability and Statistics, Papers in Honour of MS Bartlett*. Academic Press, 1975.

One big advantage of MR is computational efficiency. The rise of distributed computing has led to a rediscovery of MR because it is easy to code in the MapReduce framework. In the Map step, you produce $[x_{ij}, y_i]$ pairs that are indexed by the dimension key $j$; the Reduce step then runs univariate OLS for $y$ on $x_j$ and returns $\varphi_j$. A second quick MapReduce algorithm is used to calculate $v_i = x_i'\varphi$ and run the forward regression for $y$ on $v$. Another advantage of MR (over, say, OLS) is that it works in arbitrarily high dimensions, even if $p \gg n$. MR is a strategy for supervised learning in ultra-high dimensions.

As an example, let's look at the problem of mapping from chemical properties of gasoline to its octane rating—a key measure of quality that determines pricing at the pump. In traditional practice, this octane is measured by running the fuel in a test engine under different compression magnitudes. The compression ratio where the fuel ignites determines its octane.

Lower-cost octane testing could be possible through use of near-infrared (NIR) spectroscopy, which measures reflectance for light at wavelengths (around 400 here) that are longer than visible light. The path of the NIR measurements across wavelengths provides a signature of the underlying chemical properties. The goal in this example is to build a regression map between the NIR values $x$ and the octane $y$. We have 60 gas samples and 401 wavelengths, so this is a case where $p \gg n$. Figure 7.19 shows the $x$ NIR reflectance measurements over the range of wavelengths. There is a clear structure in the NIR $x$—the measurements move as a smooth function across wavelengths. Marginal regression will aggregate differences across these curves in a way that helps determine the octane level.

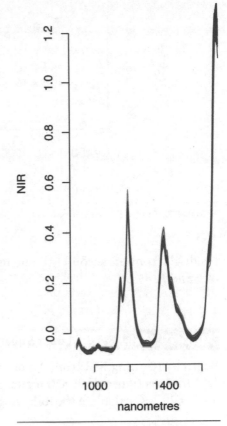

**FIGURE 7.19:** Gas samples plotted according to their near infrared (NIR) spectroscopy values across wavelengths.

We can translate Algorithm 20 into three lines of R code:

```
### marginal regression
> phi <- cor(nir, octane)/apply(nir,2,sd)
> v <- nir%*%phi
> fwd <- glm(octane ~ v)
```

The resulting MR factors $v$ are shown in Figure 7.20. The in-sample $R^2$ is around 30%. This is the combined signal available using only the *marginal* correlations (i.e., univariate correlations) between each NIR measurement and the octane.

**PARTIAL LEAST SQUARES IS AN EXTENSION OF MARGINAL REGRESSION.** Instead of stopping after running the single MR, you iterate: take the *residuals* from the first MR and repeat a second MR to predict these residuals. You can then take the

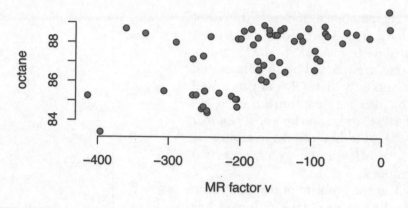

**FIGURE 7.20:** Fitted MR factors $v$ (i.e., the first PLS direction) versus octane $y$.

residuals from the second MR and repeat, continuing until you reach the minimum of $p$ and $n$.

---

**ALGORITHM 21** **Partial Least Squares (PLS)**

Begin by running MR from Algorithm 20 for $y$ on $x$. Store the MR factor as $v^1$, the 1st PLS direction, and PLS(1) forward regression fitted values as $\hat{y}^1 = \alpha + \beta_1 \cdot v^1$. Then, for $k = 2 \ldots K$, calculate the following:

- Residuals $\tilde{y}_i^{k-1} = y_i - \hat{y}_i^{k-1}$
- Loadings $\varphi_k$ via $\varphi_{kj} = \text{cor}(x_j, \tilde{y}_i^{k-1})/\text{sd}(x_j)$ and factors $v_i^k = x_i'\varphi_k$
- Fitted values $\hat{y}_i^k = \hat{y}_i^{k-1} + \beta_k v_i^k$ where $\beta_k = \text{cor}(v^k, \tilde{y}_i^{k-1})/\text{sd}(v^k)$

This yields PLS rotations $\Phi = [\varphi_1 \ldots \varphi_K]$ and factors $V = [v^1 \ldots v^K]$.

---

The PLS routine in Algorithm 21 involves a number of steps but is really very simple. We are just running marginal regression on the residuals after each PLS($k$) fit and updating the fitted values. This general procedure of taking a simple algorithm and repeatedly applying it to residuals from previous fits is called *boosting*. That is, PLS is *boosted marginal regression*. Boosting[13] is a general and powerful machine learning technique. Although we don't cover it in detail in this text (we focus on the related technique of *bagging* in Chapter 9), it is a useful way to add

---

13. Jerome H. Friedman. Greedy function approximation: a gradient boosting machine. *Annals of Statistics*, pages 1189–1232, 2001.

flexibility to simple methods, and you will likely encounter it often in your data science travels.

> If $p < n$ and you do PLS with $K = p$, then the fitted $\hat{y}_{Ki}$ will be the same as what you would get running OLS for $y$ on $x$. The PLS coefficients on each $x_{ij}$, available as $\sum_k \beta_k \varphi_{kj}$, also match the OLS coefficients. Thus, PLS provides a path of models between MR and OLS.

Whenever you are boosting, there is a potential for overfit. You should use OOS experimentation to select where the boosting should stop—i.e., to select $K$ for the PLS($K$) prediction model. Unlike with PCR, the $y$ values are used in construction of the $v_k$ factors; hence, you can't simply dump everything into `gamlr` and get a valid OOS experiment. In addition, there is no easy way to know the degrees of freedom for each PLS($K$) fit, so you can't apply tools like the AICc. You need to run an OOS experiment where PLS is run on a data subset and you evaluate predictive performance on a left-out sample.

The `textir` package in R has a `pls` function for running partial least squares, along with the usual utilities of `summary`, `plot`, and so on. We can use this to fit PLS for $K \leq 3$ on the gas data:

```
gaspls <- pls(X=nir, y=octane, K=3)
plot(gaspls)
```

Figure 7.21 shows the resulting fitted versus true values. The correlations are marked on each plot; we see that after just three iterations of boosting there is correlation of 0.99 between $y_i$ and $\hat{y}_{3i}$.

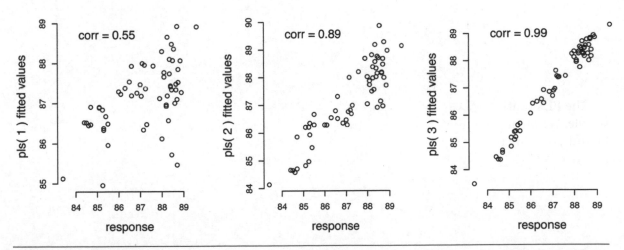

**FIGURE 7.21:** Fitted versus true values for octane PLS regressions with $K \leq 3$. Note that PLS(1) is just marginal regression, so the leftmost panel is a version of Figure 7.20.

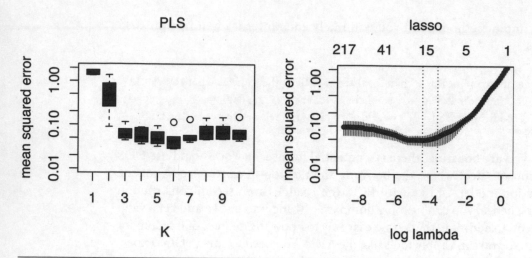

**FIGURE 7.22:** OOS prediction results for (left) PLS as a function of $K$ and (right) lasso as a function of $\lambda$.

We also run a six-fold CV routine, repeatedly fitting PLS($K$) for $K = 1 \ldots 10$ and evaluating on the left-out fold. The results are shown in Figure 7.22 and we compare against a lasso for octane regressed onto the raw NIR values. PLS performance improves from $K = 1$ to $K = 3$ and flattens for $K > 3$. While the lasso is able to obtain a comparable MSE to PLS with $K = 3$, it may be preferable to work with (and build interpretation around) three PLS factors rather than a sparse set of direct effects at different wavelengths. This interpretability is often the main advantage for PLS over a raw lasso regression.

# Text as Data

The modern business environment generates vast quantities of raw unstructured text. As the costs of storage drop and as more conversations and records move to digital platforms, we accumulate massive corpora that track communications, including customer conversations, product descriptions or reviews, news, comments, blogs, and tweets. For business decision-makers, this provides an opportunity to dive into customer relationships and understand marketplaces. The information in text is a rich complement to the more structured variables contained in a traditional transaction or customer database.

Social scientists have also woken up to the potential of such data and recent years have seen an explosion in studies that make use of text as data. See Gentzkow et al. [2017] for an overview.[1] In finance, text from financial news, social media, and company filings is used to predict asset price movements and study the causal impact of new information. In macroeconomics, text is used to forecast variation in inflation and unemployment and estimate the effects of policy uncertainty. In media economics, text from news and social media is used to study the drivers and effects of political slant. In marketing, text from advertisements and product reviews is used to study consumer decision-making. In the political economy, text from politicians' speeches is used to study the dynamics of political agendas and debate.

To analyze text, you need to transform it into data that can be input to numeric regression and factorization algorithms. This is almost always done by mapping from the raw text to counts of words or phrases. We will begin this chapter by outlining the process of *tokenization*, results of which are (very) high-dimensional $x$ matrices. These text matrices can be incorporated into your analyses via methods we've already covered in this book (e.g., via lasso regression). Indeed, working with text data is a great way to get more familiar with modern statistical learning techniques. It is

---

1. Matthew Gentzkow, Bryan Kelly, and Matt Taddy. Text-as-data. *NBER working paper* 23276, 2017.

messy but also interpretable (words have known meanings) and is high dimensional in a way that stumps classical statisticians: as you accumulate more text data, the size of the vocabulary—your model dimension—will also grow. You are never in the statistician's safe space of having many more observations than variables.

We will also cover a number of text-specific techniques, including topic modeling and multinomial inverse regression. However, the main message of this chapter is that with some standard data science tools you can tap into the information contained in messy unstructured text and use text as data in your business decisions.

## Tokenization

Raw text—the language that humans read—is an incredibly rich object. It is much more than a sum of words. Meaning is built from ordered *sequences* of words that refer to each other, often separated across sentences or paragraphs. However, the vast majority of text analyses will ignore this complexity and rely solely on *counts* for language *tokens*: words, phrases, or other basic elements. Fortunately, a huge amount of information is contained in these simple counts. The lesson of the past 30 years has been that, for prediction and classification with text, it is difficult to make effective use of any statistics other than simple word counts. This is quickly changing with the commoditization of deep learning techniques (see Chapter 10). However, for data science and business analytics the bulk of text-as-data applications will continue to incorporate word and phrase counts for the foreseeable future—token-based learning is just too fast and effective to be made redundant, especially when you don't have a huge number of documents to train against.

Consider a little Shakespeare:

> *All the world's a stage,*
> *and all the men and women merely players;*
> *they have their exits and their entrances,*
> *and one man in his time plays many parts . . .*

Powerful and poetic. What the data scientist sees is more pedestrian. For example, we might just count some key terms and represent the snippet as a numeric vector $x$:

```
world stage men women play exit entrance time
    1     1   2     1    2    1        1    1
```

This is the *bag-of-words* representation of text. More precisely, the bag-of-words representation treats documents as if they were constructed by randomly drawing words with-replacement from a bucket containing the fixed vocabulary. By summarizing a document in terms of word counts, we are throwing away all information relevant to any more complex processes of document construction. The advantage of this approach is its simplicity: you can characterize relationships between language and outside variables (e.g., authorship or sentiment) by building a model for word probabilities.

There are many possible algorithms for going from raw text to a summary token-count vector $x$. A basic recipe first removes the following:

- Overly common or rare words

- Isolated punctuation (, but not :-P) and numbers

- Common suffixes like s or ing

You then count the remaining tokens (words or other elements separated by whitespace). The reason for doing the pruning before counting is computational and statistical efficiency: you want to only store and model the tokens that are important for the task at hand.

You should strive for a light touch in each of these steps. Since you're going to be using regularization and selection techniques in your text models, you don't need to be overly worried about including too many tokens. Words that are junk for one purpose might be crucial for another. For example, overly common words like if or but are called *stop words*; the frequency of the in a document likely says little about the author's sentiment, so in many applications it can be dropped. However, in other applications these common words can indicate a specific author's writing style. The classic work of Mosteller and Wallace [1963] uses counts for common words to classify authorship for disputed federalist papers.[2] Similarly, punctuation is probably fine for removal when analyzing news articles or literature, but it provides important signals on meaning and sentiment in online corpora such as Twitter: -).

Exclusion of rare words is a necessary evil—these words are likely rich in meaning (they are rare and hence not generic) but you observe so few of them that you cannot hope to learn much about their meaning. As you accumulate more data, you can keep words that are more rare. Culling rare words is also an effective way to reduce the cost of computation. We will typically remove all words that are not in at least $N$ documents, where $N$ is some intuitive minimum threshold. It is good practice to make sure that the results don't change if you make small adjustments to this threshold.

*Stemming* is the process of cutting words to their root—for example, tax from taxing, taxes, taxation, or taxable. When you remove simple suffixes, such as s and ing, you are doing a sort of basic stemming. Many more sophisticated options are available, such as the Porter stemmer for English. However, these tools are often overly aggressive. They reduce words with distinct meaning to a shared root. As we advised

2. Frederick Mosteller and David L. Wallace. Inference in an authorship problem. *Journal of the American Statistical Association*, 58:275–309, 1963.

for the rare and common token removal, it is best to avoid cutting too much and let the statistical learning tools sort through any extra vocabulary elements.

There are many other possible tokenization steps beyond those listed here. See Gentzkow et al. [2017] or the text[3] by Jurafsky and Martin [2009] for more thorough reviews. One common strategy is to count *n*-grams, or combinations of *n* words, rather than single "unigrams" (what we've been counting thus far). For example, the Shakespeare bigrams include `world.stage`, `stage.men`, `men.women`, and `women.play`. Our knowledge of natural language leads us to expect such bigrams to be useful—`very.good` and `very.bad` are very different. However, moving from unigrams to bigrams massively increases vocabulary dimension. In practice, it is seldom worth the computational effort.

I often use Python to parse documents. Figure 8.1 shows one of my simple text cleaners. Python, especially Python 3, makes it really easy to work with non-ASCII character sets (e.g., including foreign language or emoticons). There is also a large ecosystem of tools built on top of Python that facilitate tokenization and text analysis (e.g., `gensim`). If you are working with a lot of raw text, you will likely want to add Python programming to your repertoire.

```python
import re

contractions = re.compile(r"'|-|\"")
# all non alphanumeric
symbols = re.compile(r'(\W+)', re.U)
# single character removal
singles = re.compile(r'(\s\S\s)', re.I|re.U)
# separators (any whitespace)
seps = re.compile(r'\s+')

# cleaner (order matters)
def clean(text):
    text = text.lower()
    text = contractions.sub('', text)
    text = symbols.sub(r' \1 ', text)
    text = singles.sub(' ', text)
    text = seps.sub(' ', text)
    return text
```

**FIGURE 8.1:** A basic tokenizer function written in Python. The `re.compile` lines each create text objects that are searched for and removed in the `clean(text)` function. This function will return a stream of standardized tokens separated by whitespace.

---

3. Daniel Jurafsky and James H. Martin. *Speech and Language Processing*, 2nd edition. Prentice Hall, 2009.

It is also possible to use R for tokenization. Despite being a little clunky for exotic characters and Unicode, the `tm` library wraps together a number of useful functions for text analysis and parsing. File input with `tm` works via reader functions: you use `tm` tools to define a function that scans through documents and reads their content into R. For example, we can create a reader for `pdf` files and apply it to the lecture slides from my big data course (available via the book's website).

```
# define the reader
> readerPDF <- function(fname){
+        txt <- readPDF(
+          control = list(text = "-layout -enc UTF-8"))(
+                        elem=lis$id=fname, language'en')
+        return(txt)
+    }
>
> files <- Sys.glob("/Users/taddy/project/BigData/slides/*.pdf")
> notes <- lapply(files, readerPDF)
> names(notes) <- sub (' .pdf', ", substring (files, first=37))
> names(notes) # 12 documents
[1] "01Data"          "02Regression" "03Models"       "04Treatments"
[5] "05Classification" "06Networks"   "07Clustering" "08Factors"
[9] "09Trees"          "text"          "timespace"
> writeLines(content(notes[[1]])[1]) # the cover slide
      [1] Big Data: Inference at Scale
```

The `notes` object here is a list of 11 elements, each of which contains lines of raw text from the class slides. The first line, printed earlier, is the title for the first lecture. To make life easy and avoid working with non-ASCII in R, we'll also take the step of converting to ASCII:

```
> for(i in 1:11)
>   content(notes[[i]]) <-
+   iconv(content(notes[[i]]), from ="UTF-8", to="ASCII", sub="")
```

Finally, we can apply `tm`'s `Corpus` function to convert from a generic list to a `Corpus` object called `docs`:

```
> docs <- Corpus(VectorSource(notes))
```

This brings the documents into the `tm` ecosystem.

We can now use the `tm_map` function to apply various text-cleaning operations.

```
> ## tm_map just maps some function to every document in the corpus
> docs <- tm_map(docs, content_transformer(tolower)) ## make lowercase
> docs <- tm_map(docs, content_transformer(removeNumbers)) ## remove numbers
> docs <- tm_map(docs, content_transformer(removePunctuation)) ## drop punctuation
> docs <- tm_map(docs, content_transformer(removeWords), stopwords("SMART")) # stopwords
> docs <- tm_map(docs, content_transformer(stripWhitespace)) ## clean whitespace
```

This is a more heavy-handed version of the cleaning and pruning in my Python snippet from Figure 8.1; for example, the SMART list of stop words includes many I would normally not drop:

```
> head(stopwords("SMART"))
[1] "a"     "s"  "able"  "about"  "above"  "according"
```

With only 12 documents, we need to cut liberally to keep the dimension low.

Once we have this clean text, we can convert from words to counts of words and create a *document-term-matrix* (DTM) $X$ that has a row for each document and a column for each word. Element $x_{ij}$ is the count for word $j$ in document $i$.

```
> dtm <- DocumentTermMatrix(docs)
> dtm
<<DocumentTermMatrix (documents: 11, terms: 4009)>>
Non-/sparse entries: 7062/37037
Sparsity           : 84%
Maximal term length: 39
Weighting          : term frequency (tf)
```

This matrix contains more than 4000 terms (columns). As a final pruning step, we remove terms that have a zero count in more than 75% of the documents (since we have only 11, this will remove words that don't occur in at least three lectures). This leaves us with a total of around 700 terms.

```
> dtm <- removeSparseTerms(dtm, 0.75)
> dtm
<<DocumentTermMatrix (documents: 11, terms: 680)>>
Non-/sparse entries: 3127/4353
Sparsity           : 58%
Maximal term length: 39
Weighting          : term frequency (tf)
```

That's it! You now have a *numeric* matrix $X$ that can be treated like any other high-dimensional data. For example, the three most common words (those occurring more than 100 times total) make sense for a data science course:

```
> findFreqTerms(dtm,100)
[1] "data"        "model"          "regression"
```

Or, we can look at those words whose counts are highly correlated with counts for the word Lasso:

```
> findAssocs(dtm, "Lasso", .9)
$Lasso
    players     stable     beta     experiments
      0.93       0.92     0.91            0.91
```

As described in the next section, we can also use $X$ as input to the ML techniques like lasso and PCA.

## Text Regression

Once you have the text in a numeric format, the tools you've learned from elsewhere in this book give you a powerful framework for text analysis. Indeed, you've already seen some text regression: the spam filtering example that we used to introduce logistic regression takes email content as input. This was a document classification exercise, and we used normalized text counts $f_i = x_i / \sum_j x_{ij}$ to predict whether the message was *spam* or *not-spam* via logistic regression:

$$\text{logit}\,[\text{p(spam)}] = \alpha + f'\beta.$$

This section will provide additional examples to illustrate use of generic ML tools for text analysis.

As an example dataset, consider the Congress109 data that are included in the textir R package. This data originally appear in Gentzkow and Shapiro [2010], a study on how newspapers target content to the politics of their readership.[4] The dataset summarizes the first year of the 109th Congressional Record (2005), containing all speech in that year for members of the U.S. House and Senate.

The text is already tokenized into bigrams (two-word phrases) after stopword removal and stemming (using the Porter stemmer). The matrix congress109Counts contains the number of times each phrase in a list of 1000 common tokens was used in the 109th Congress by each of the 529 members of the House and Senate. That is, each document

---

4. Matthew Gentzkow and Jesse Shapiro. What drives media slant? Evidence from U.S. daily newspapers. *Econometrica*, 78:35–72, 2010.

contains the combined transcripts for a single speaker. We can inspect counts for a few terms for two speakers:

```
> data(congress109)
> congress109Counts[c("Barack Obama", "John Boehner"),995:998]
2 × 4 sparse Matrix of class "dgCMatrix"
            stem.cel natural.ga hurricane.katrina trade.agreement
Barack Obama       .          1                20               7
John Boehner       .          .                14               .
```

Notice the effects of stemming: *stem cell* becomes 'stem.cel' and *natural gas* becomes 'natural.ga'.

In addition to these term counts, we also have information about each member of Congress in congress109Ideology:

```
> congress109Ideology[1:4,]
            name party state chamber   repshare     cs1      cs2
1     Chris Cannon    R    UT       H  0.7900621   0.534   -0.124
2  Michael Conaway    R    TX       H  0.7836028   0.484    0.051
3   Spencer Bachus    R    AL       H  0.7812933   0.369   -0.013
4   Mac Thornberry    R    TX       H  0.7776520   0.493    0.002
```

**FIGURE 8.2:** Words sized by their absolute covariance with repshapre and colored by sign: black for negative (Democrat direction) and grey for positive (Republican). This is an example of a *wordle*, which is a useful visualization tool when you need to get a bunch of words together on a plot.

The main variable of interest here will be repshare, the proportion of the two-party vote (Dem and GOP, excluding independents and third parties) obtained by George W. Bush in the 2004 presidential election for each member's constituency (district for representatives, states for senators). See Figure 8.2 for illustration of the relationship between repshare and vocabulary.

`cs1` and `cs2` are also interesting. These are essentially the first two principal component scores for each member in PCA of their voting record. The model used is slightly different but closely related to the roll-call voting PCA example in Chapter 7.

Under the assumption that the average beliefs of someone's constituents provide a signal on their own beliefs (or at least how they portray their beliefs), we can use `repshare` as a surrogate for ideology and partisanship. For example, Tom Price (R GA) says the term `death.tax` often (28 times), and he is from a congressional district that voted 70% for Bush in 2004. William Jefferson (D LA) says `estate.tax` often (32 times), and his district voted strongly against Bush (24%). If this pattern repeats itself (it does), we'd model `death.tax` as a Republican term and `estate.tax` as a Democratic term.

Gentzkow and Shapiro apply this logic to build an index of *slant* that sums across a speaker's term usage weighted by the direction of slant for each term. Their method turns out to be an instance of *marginal regression* (i.e., PLS(1); see Chapter 7). They are regressing `repshare` on speech content to build a model that connects language to partisanship. This is then used to quantify political slant in newspapers and investigate issues around partisanship and press ownership.

We can replicate their analysis using the `pls` function:

```
> x <- congress109Counts
> slant <- pls(x, congress109Ideology$repshare, K=3)
```

Figure 8.3 shows results for the first three PLS directions. The insample $R^2$ for each direction is 0.17, 0.32, and 0.43—there is a big increase with each extra dimension. Qualitatively, the second direction appears to be necessary for picking up the language associated with high-`repshare` Republicans (those likely on the right of the party).

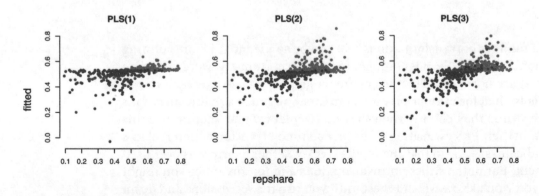

**FIGURE 8.3:** The PLS fits for repshare on relative term usage in the 1000 bigram `congress109` vocabulary. Points are colored by political party—grey for Republicans and black for Democrats.

As an alternative to PLS, we can also run a lasso regression for `repshare` on text:

```
> Lassoslant <- cv.gamlr(x, congress109Ideology)
```

Figure 8.4 shows the results of a CV experiment used to select $\lambda$ next to an OOS experiment to evaluate the number of PLS directions. We see that the lasso generally outperforms PLS here—the best PLS results are for $K$ of one or two, and OOS MSE for these is still more variable and slightly higher than for lasso under a range of $\lambda$.

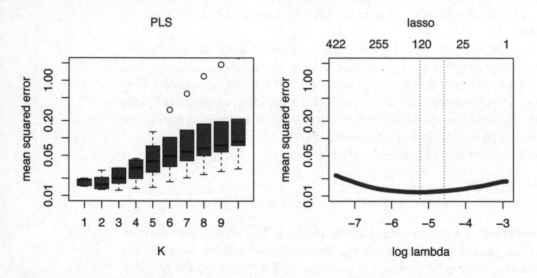

**FIGURE 8.4:** The OOS predictive performance for (left) PLS as a function of $K$ and (right) lasso as a function of $\lambda$ in prediction of `repshare` from text.

There are a number of transformations that can be applied to $X$ before running a text regression. For example, it is common to transform from raw word counts to *proportions* that are normalized by the document lengths. You divide each row of $X$ by row totals so that, for example, it doesn't matter how much a politician speaks but just which words they choose when they do (Gentzkow and Shapiro use this normalization in their PLS estimation). Another common transformation replaces $x_{ij}$ with the indicators $\mathbb{1}_{[x_{ij}>0]}$ so that the inputs track whether a term was ever used in the document. For both of these transformations and for any other you might think to use, you won't know which is best until you run the regressions and do an OOS experiment. Model building and selection proceeds the same as for nontext data: construct a set of candidate models, and use CV (or an IC) to choose from this set.

In this example, applying lasso regression on the indicators $\mathbb{1}_{[x_{ij}>0]}$ gets us the best[5] OOS fit yet: a minimum MSE of 0.012 versus 0.015 for lasso regression onto the raw $x_{ij}$. Working with this model, the CV-min selection rule returns a set of 64 nonzero $\hat{\beta}_j$ loadings. We can investigate the ten phrases most indicative of low repshare (i.e., left-leaning Democrats):

```
> names(sort(B)[1:10])
[1] "congressional.black.caucu"    "family.value"
[3] "issue.facing.american"        "voter.registration"
[5] "minority.owned.business"      "strong.opposition"
[7] "civil.right"                  "universal.health.care"
[9] "congressional.hispanic.caucu" "ohio.electoral.vote"
```

And those most predictive of high repshare (i.e., right-leaning Republicans):

```
> names(sort(-B)[1:10])
 [1] "million.illegal.alien"  "human.embryo"         "action.lawsuit"
 [4] "private.property"       "war.terror"           "look.forward"
 [7] "global.war"             "illegal.immigration"  "percent.growth"
[10] "illegal.alien"
```

Although interpretation of loadings in a lasso should be done with caution, it appears that the model is picking up issues that are indeed associated with each party.

## Topic Models

Text is super high dimensional, and there is often abundant *unlabeled* text available. For these reasons, unsupervised factor modeling is a popular and useful strategy with text data. You can fit a factor model to a giant corpus and use these factors for supervised learning on a subset of labeled documents. The unsupervised dimension reduction facilitates the supervised learning.

To study text factorization, we'll switch from politics to restaurants. We have 6166 reviews, with an average length of 90 words per review, from the now-defunct travel website we8there.com. A useful feature of these reviews is that they contain both text and a multidimensional rating on *overall* experience, *atmosphere, food, service,* and *value.* Each aspect is rated on a five-point scale, with 1 indicating terrible and 5

---

5. This is also better than the results from regressing onto counts normalized by the total amount of speech.

indicating excellent. As an example, one user submitted a glowing review for Waffle House #1258 in Bossier City, Louisiana:

> *I normally would not revue a Waffle House but this one deserves it. The workers, Amanda, Amy, Cherry, James and J.D. were the most pleasant crew I have seen. While it was only lunch, B.L.T. and chili, it was great. The best thing was the 50's rock and roll music, not to loud not to soft. This is a rare exception to what you all think a Waffle House is. Keep up the good work.*
>
> *Overall: 5, Atmosphere: 5, Food: 5, Service: 5, Value: 5.*

Another user found Sartin's Seafood in Nassau Bay, Texas, to be all-around low quality (but it must have been cheap):

> *Had a very rude waitress and the manager wasn't nice either.*
> *Overall: 1, Atmosphere: 1, Food: 1, Service: 1, Value: 5.*

Intuitively, these reviews will be constructed from a number of underlying *topics*, for example, the type of food, the quality of the restaurant, or the geographic location. The hope is that we can uncover these topics via factorization.

After cleaning and Porter stemming, following the same procedure as for the `congress109` text tokenization, we are left with a vocabulary of 2640 bigrams. For example, the first review in the document-term matrix has nonzero counts on bigrams indicating a pleasant meal at a rib joint:

```
> x <- we8thereCounts
> x[1,x[1,]!=0]
even though  larg portion  mouth water  red sauc  babi back
          1            1            1         1          1
   back rib  chocol mouss  veri satisfi
          1            1             1
```

We can apply PCA to get a factor representation of the review text. After digging through the biggest rotations in the first few factors, we find that PC1 looks like it will be big and positive for positive reviews, while PC4 will be big and negative for Italian (pizza).

```
> pca <- prcomp(x, scale=TRUE)
> tail(sort(pca$rotation[,1]))
     food great     staff veri    excel food  high recommend
    0.007386860    0.007593374    0.007629771    0.007821171
     great food     food excel
    0.008503594    0.008736181
> head(sort(pca$rotation[,4]))
pizza like  thin crust  thin crispi  deep dish  crust pizza
-0.1794166  -0.1705301   -0.1551877  -0.1531820   -0.1311161
```

For top-down interpretation, Figure 8.5 shows PC1 scores against the overall rating. Because of a long tail of negative PC1 scores, it is tough to see the relationship between PC1 and quality that seems clear from our bottom-up look at the largest rotations. As always with PCA, building interpretation around factors is a messy and difficult process.

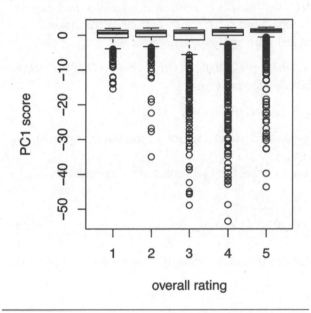

**FIGURE 8.5:** PC1 score and overall rating for we8there reviews.

---

**ALGORITHM 22** | **PCA for Big Sparse Data**

As a practical aside, note that prcomp converts x here from sparse to dense matrix storage. For really big text DTMs, which will be very sparse, this will cause you to run out of memory. A big data strategy for PCA is to first calculate the covariance matrix for $x$ and then obtain PC rotations as the *eigenvalues* of this covariance matrix. The first step can be done using sparse matrix algebra.

```
> xm <- colMeans(x)
> xx <- crossprod(x) # X´X
> xvar <- xx/nrow(x) - tcrossprod(xm) # covariance matrix
```

The rotations are then available as eigen(xvar, symmetric=TRUE)$vec. There are also approximate PCA algorithms available for fast factorization on big data. See, for example, the irlba package for R.

The approach of using PCA to factorize text was common before the 2000s. Versions of this algorithm were referred to under the label *latent semantic analysis*. However, this changed with the introduction of *topic modeling*, also known as Latent Dirichlet Allocation[6] (LDA), by Blei et al. in 2003. These authors pointed out that the squared error loss (i.e., Gaussian model) implied by PCA is inappropriate for analysis of sparse word-count data. Instead, they proposed you take the bag-of-words representation seriously and model token counts as realizations from a *multinomial* distribution. That is, they proposed topic models as a multinomial factor model.

Topic models are built on a simple document generation process:

- For each word, pick a "topic" $k$. This topic is *defined* through a probability vector over words, say, $\boldsymbol{\theta}_k$ with probability $\theta_{kj}$ for each word $j$.

- Then draw the word according to the probabilities encoded in $\boldsymbol{\theta}_k$.

After doing this over and over for each word in the document, you have proportion $\omega_{i1}$ from topic 1, $\omega_{i2}$ from topic 2, and so on.

This basic generation process implies that the full vector of word counts, $\boldsymbol{x}_i$, has a *multinomial factor distribution*:

$$\boldsymbol{x}_i \sim \mathrm{MN}(\omega_{i1}\boldsymbol{\theta}_1 + \ldots + \omega_{iK}\boldsymbol{\theta}_K, m_i). \tag{8.1}$$

Here, $m_i = \sum_j x_{ij}$ is the total document length and, for example, the probability of word $j$ in document $i$ will be $\sum_k \omega_{ik}\theta_{kj}$.

Recall our PCA factor model:

$$\mathbb{E}[\boldsymbol{x}_i] = v_{i1}\boldsymbol{\varphi}_1 + \ldots v_{iK}\boldsymbol{\varphi}_K. \tag{8.2}$$

The analogous topic model representation, implied by Equation 8.1, is

$$\mathbb{E}\left[\frac{\boldsymbol{x}_i}{m_i}\right] = \omega_{i1}\boldsymbol{\theta}_1 + \ldots + \omega_{iK}\boldsymbol{\theta}_K, \tag{8.3}$$

such that *topic score* $\omega_{ik}$ is like PC score $v_{ik}$ and $\boldsymbol{\theta}_k$ *topic probabilities* are like rotations $\boldsymbol{\varphi}_k$. The distinction is that the multinomial in Equation 8.1 implies a different loss function—a multinomial deviance—than the sums of squared errors that PCA minimizes. Also, $\boldsymbol{\omega}_i$ and $\boldsymbol{\theta}_k$ are *probabilities* so that all of these vectors are forced to sum to 1. Note that we condition on document length here so that topics are driven by relative rather than absolute term usage.

Topic models have been adopted instead of PCA for text because they tend to lead to more easily interpretable factorization. Interpretation remains subjective and messy, but a large industry of exploratory analysis has grown up around mostly plausible interpretations of fitted topic models. There are many extensions of the

---

6. David M. Blei, Andrew Y. Ng, and Michael I. Jordan. Latent Dirichlet allocation. *Journal of Machine Learning Research*, 3:993-1022, 2003.

original framework (e.g., "dynamic" models[7] where topics are allowed to change slowly in time), but the classic topic model remains a dominant tool for unsupervised dimension reduction for text.

Topic model estimation is a difficult and computationally intensive task—the optimization problem involved is much harder than that solved during PCA. However, this is a problem that many have worked on and there are plenty of efficient algorithms available. If you are working in Python, the `gensim` library implements the fast and memory-efficient *stochastic gradient descent* (SGD) routine of Hoffman et al. [2013], which streams data during estimation rather than loading it into memory as a block.[8] For R users, the `maptpx` package[9] implementing the algorithm from Taddy [2012] is a fast and stable option for data that is not too big to fit in memory.

To work with `maptpx`, you need first to migrate your sparse matrices from the `Matrix` to `slam` package formats. Fortunately, `slam` has a function to facilitate this. Once we have the DTM in the correct format, we just give it to the `topics` function from `maptpx` along with a specified $K$, the number of topics:

```
x <- as.simple_triplet_matrix(we8thereCounts)
tpc <- topics(x,K=10)
```

Here, we've fit a ten-topic model. You can also give `topics` a range of $K$ values and let it choose the best number using a *Bayes factor* (BF) criterion that is closely related to the BIC. The BF is proportional to the *posterior model probability* approximated by $\exp[-\text{BIC}]$, so whereas you want to minimize the BIC, you will want to maximize the BF.

```
> tpcs <- topics(x,K=5*(1:5))
Estimating on a 6166 document collection.
Fit and Bayes Factor Estimation for K = 5 ... 25
log BF( 5 ) = 86639.7
log BF( 10 ) = 99317.15
log BF( 15 ) = 13398.18
log BF( 20 ) = -55807.93
> dim(tpcs$omega)
[1] 6166   10
```

Given $K$ of 5, 10, 15, 20, or 25, `topics` chooses[10] the BF maximizing $K = 10$. I have generally advised against putting too much faith in this sort of selection for unsupervised models. However, since topic models are so expensive to fit, it is

7. David M. Blei and John D. Lafferty. Dynamic topic models. In *Proceedings of the 23rd international conference on Machine learning*, pages 113–120, 2006.

8. Matthew D. Hoffman, David M. Blei, Chong Wang, and John Paisley. Stochastic variational inference. *The Journal of Machine Learning Research*, 14: 1303–1347, 2013.

9. Matt Taddy. On estimation and selection for topic models. In *Proceedings of the 15th International Conference on Artificial Intelligence and Statistics (AISTATS 2012)*, 2012.

10. The software never bothered to fit $K = 25$ because the BF dropped from 10 to 15 and again from 15 to 20.

convenient to have a fast search strategy. In my experience, the BF maximization in maptpx finds $K$ that will perform well for a variety of downstream tasks, although it does sometimes tend to select $K$ smaller than we would like for storytelling purposes. If you are going to use the topics as inputs to a lasso regression, analogous to the lasso PCR, then you can use a larger $K$ and let the lasso choose the ones it needs.

Interpretation for topics proceeds the same as for PCA; you work from bottom up and top down to build a narrative. Bottom up, you look at "top" words for each topic. For this to work, you need to take care in how you order words when looking at the "top." Ordering words by topic probability, $\theta_{kj}$, will yield top words that are common in topic $k$ but, potentially, also common in other topics (especially when you've cut only a small set of stop words). Instead, the summary function in maptpx orders words by *lift*—the probability of word $j$ in topic $k$ divided by its aggregate probability:

$$\text{lift}_{jk} = \theta_{jk} / \bar{q}_j.$$

Here, $\bar{q}_j$ is the sample mean for $x_{ij}/m_i$, the average proportion of a document allocated to word $j$. This lift will be high for words that are much more common in topic $k$ than they are in general speech.

```
> summary(tpcs)
Top 5 phrases by topic-over-null term lift (and usage %):
[1] 'food veri', 'staff veri', 'food excel', 'veri good', 'excel servic' (13.2)
[2] 'over minut', 'flag down', 'wait over', 'least minut', 'sever minut' (12.2)
[3] 'alway great', 'wait go', 'never bad', 'great servic', 'alway excel' (11.4)
[4] 'enough share', 'highlight menu', 'select includ', 'until pm', 'open daili' (10.5)
[5] 'mexican food', 'italian food', 'authent mexican', 'list extens', 'food wonder' (10.4)
[6] 'veri pleasant', 'indian food', 'thai food', 'again again', 'thai restaur' (9.3)
[7] 'francisco bay', 'best kept', 'kept secret', 'best steak', 'just right' (9)
[8] 'chicago style', 'great pizza', 'best bbq', 'carri out', 'style food' (8.4)
[9] 'chees steak', 'food place', 'drive thru', 'york style', 'just anoth' (8.2)
[10] 'over drink', 'wasn whole', 'got littl', 'took seat', 'came chip' (7.4)
```

The first topic contains positive feedback and thus has the same interpretation as PC1. But the other topics seem different from and more interpretable than the factors obtained via PCA. For example, topic 2 is about having to wait and topic 3 contains positive reviews from regular customers. I suspect that topics 7 to 9 are regionally focused, perhaps on the west, midwest, and northeast.

As an example top-down view, we can compare $\omega_{ki}$ topic scores to the review ratings. Figure 8.6 shows the overall rating against the document scores in the first two topics. Compared to Figure 8.7, the positive relationship between topic 1 and overall rating is clearer here than it was for PC1. The *negative* content of topic 2 is even more explicit: most four- and five-star reviews have $\omega_{2i} < 0.1$, whereas this topic is commonly between 0.2 and 0.9 for one- to two-star reviews.

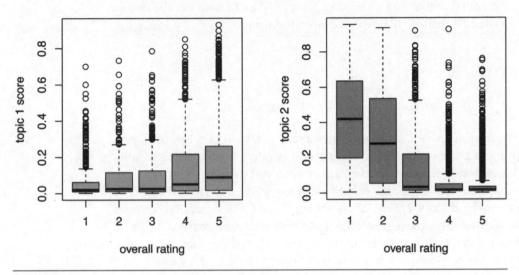

**FIGURE 8.6:** We8there overall rating against topic scores $\omega_{1i}$ and $\omega_{2i}$.

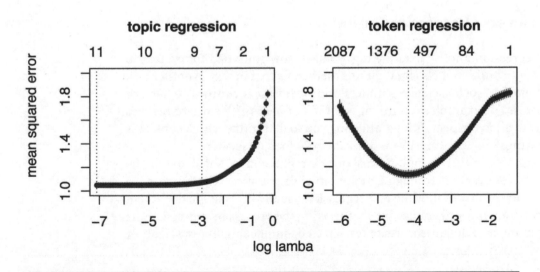

**FIGURE 8.7:** Comparison of topic regression and a lasso onto the raw token counts $x_{ij}$.

These relationships suggest a topic regression strategy for predicting review rating from text content. The scheme for topic regression works the same as the PCR in Algorithm 19: fit the topics and then use them as inputs to a lasso with AICc or CV selection.

```
> stars <- we8thereRatings[,"Overall"]
> tpcreg <- gamlr(tpcs$omega, stars, lmr=1e-3)
```

The AICc selects a model that loads on nine of ten topics.[11] We can multiply the coefficients by 0.1 to see what happens to the expected overall star rating from a 0.1 increase in $\omega_{ki}$.

```
> round(coef(tpcreg) [-1,]*.1, 1)
   1    2    3    4    5    6    7    8    9   10
 0.1 -0.4  0.0  0.0  0.0  0.1  0.1  0.0 -0.1 -0.1
```

So, for example, you drop an expected −0.4 star when a review has an extra 10% of its content coming from topic 2 (the waiting topic). As anyone who has worked in restaurants can tell you, the fastest way to unhappy (American) customers is to make them wait.

We can also compare the topic regression to a lasso where the overall rating is regressed onto raw token counts. Figure 8.7 shows results of OOS validation for each approach, and we see that the topic regression outperforms the token regression. There is a useful low-dimensional factor structure in the review text, and this factor structure is directly relevant to the response of interest: overall quality. In this case, we gain estimation efficiency by doing unsupervised dimension reduction before running the lasso.

## Multinomial Inverse Regression (MNIR)

Between text regression and topic modeling, you are now equipped to use text to predict some $y$ or to build models for latent unobserved factors in text. Another task that comes up often in social science is understanding how text connects to a *set* of related covariates. For example, you might want to connect the we8there reviews simultaneously to all five aspect ratings, allowing you to determine which content is predictive of ratings on, say, atmosphere *separate* from food or service.

For such tasks, we can turn to multinomial inverse regression (MNIR)[12] to link the text with observable covariates through a multinomial distribution. The "inverse" in MNIR comes from the fact that, while text regression usually fits a single document attribute as a function of word counts, we are inverting the process by regressing the counts on any number of document attributes. Given document attributes $v_i$ (author

---

11. In this example, we needed to drop the ratio $\lambda_T/\lambda_1$ to 0.001 (via lmr=1e-3) from its default of 0.01 to get a set of candidate models that includes low enough penalization. You will know that you need to do this if you run gamlr and find that AICc selects a model at the edge of the candidate set (i.e., at smallest penalty, $\lambda_T$). You want your model selection to choose a model in the *interior* of your candidate set.
12. Matt Taddy. Multinomial inverse regression for text analysis. *Journal of the American Statistical Association*, 108: 755–770, 2013b.

characteristics, date, beliefs, sentiment, etc.), MNIR follows the familiar generalized linear model framework. Each document $x_i$ is modeled as arising from a multinomial with a logit link onto a linear function of $v_i$:

$$x_i \sim \text{MN}(q_i, m_i) \text{ with } q_{ij} = \frac{\exp[\alpha_j + v_i'\varphi_j]}{\sum_{l=1}^{p} \exp[\alpha_l + v_i'\varphi_l]}. \tag{8.4}$$

This is the same as the multinomial logistic regression introduced in Chapter 4. Now, the number of outcome categories is the number of tokens in our text vocabulary. This can be viewed as a natural extension of topic modeling: we are keeping the multinomial model for token counts but replacing unknown topics with known attributes.

Looking again at the we8there data, we can set $v_i$ as the vector of five aspect ratings: overall, atmosphere, value, food, and service. The multinomial response will be the vector of word counts for each document, $x_i$, which implies 2640 outcome categories. This is far too many dimensions for most multinomial logistic regression algorithms (e.g., glmnet will hang and then choke). Fortunately, as discussed in Chapter 4, the distrom package is specifically designed to be efficient for these types of massive-response multinomials. It uses a Poisson distribution representation of the multinomial to distribute computation for each vocabulary element across multiple processors.

```
> cl <- makeCluster(detectCores())
> ## small nlambda for a fast example
> fits <- dmr(cl, we8thereRatings,
+             we8thereCounts, bins=5)
```

An additional (massive) computational efficiency comes from the use of the bins argument. Since sums of multinomial vectors will also have multinomial distribution, it is possible to collapse across observations when the input set is the same. That is, from a computational perspective, all reviews with (say) all four-star ratings can be treated as a single observation. Flagging bins=5 tells dmr that it can group each attribute into one of five bins. Even if the attributes can take more than bins values, for speed of estimation you might want to still do the binning and collapsing; dmr will choose bins automatically.

Figure 8.8 shows the lasso regularization paths for a selection of terms. Some terms (chicken wing and ate here) are found to be unrelated to review rating, while the others can load positively on some ratings and negatively on other ratings. For example, terribl servic (stemmed from *terrible service*) is negatively related to all aspects except food, with which it has a strong positive relationship.

```
> B[-1, "terribl servic"]
     Food   Service   Value   Atmosphere   Overall
    0.312    -1.489  -0.639       -0.333     0.000
```

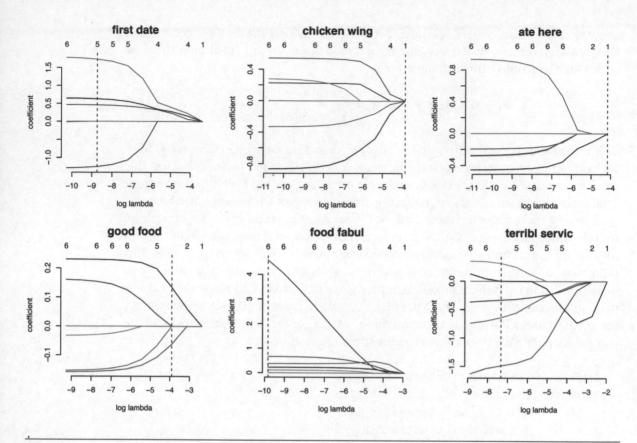

**FIGURE 8.8:** Lasso paths for a selection of the terms from the we8there reviews.

As in any multivariate regression, these are a *partial effects*: they represent the influence of one attribute after controlling for the other attributes. In the case of `terribl servic`, this term is expected to occur more often if the food rating is high *relative to what you'd expect given the other ratings*. That is, even though `terribl servic` has a negative *marginal* association with the food rating (count-to-rating correlation is −0.1), it has a positive MNIR loading for the food rating because diners will highlight it in a generally negative review if the food was not that bad (just, for example, overpriced and slow).

This is the power of MNIR—you can control for confounds in the same way that you do in a standard regression analysis. It allocates language among multiple observable influences, similar to how topic models attempt allocate language across multiple unobserved topics. Figure 8.9 shows top loadings by the size of their $|\varphi_{kj}|$ for each aspect $k$. There is a clear sorting of terms to the appropriate aspect rating, and the overall ratings are related to summaries of the experience: you "plan to return" if the experience was positive and ended up "speaking to the manager" if it was overall negative.

There is a connection between MNIR and factorization. Recall that, after the PC factor model, you obtain the PC scores by projecting the raw $x_i$ through the loadings $\varphi_k$. The same operation is used in PLS to map from marginal regressions to each PLS direction. A similar logic applies to MNIR: if you want to get a *score* for the degree to which

| *Overall* | *Food* | *Service* | *Value* | *Atmosphere* |
|---|---|---|---|---|
| plan.return | again.again | cozi.atmospher | big.portion | walk.down |
| feel.welcom | mouth.water | **servic.terribl** | around.world | great.bar |
| best.meal | francisco.bay | servic.impecc | chicken.pork | atmospher.wonder |
| select.includ | high.recomend | attent.staff | perfect.place | dark.wood |
| finest.restaur | cannot.wait | time.favorit | place.visit | food.superb |
| steak.chicken | best.servic | servic.outstand | mahi.mahi | atmospher.great |
| love.restaur | kept.secret | **servic.horribl** | veri.reason | alway.go |
| **ask.waitress** | **food.poison** | dessert.great | babi.back | bleu.chees |
| good.work | outstand.servic | **terribl.servic** | low.price | realli.cool |
| can.enough | far.best | **never.came** | peanut.sauc | recommend.everyon |
| **after.left** | food.awesom | experi.wonder | wonder.time | great.atmospher |
| come.close | best.kept | **time.took** | garlic.sauc | wonder.restaur |
| open.lunch | everyth.menu | waitress.come | great.can | love.atmospher |
| warm.friend | excel.price | servic.except | absolut.best | bar.just |
| **spoke.manag** | keep.come | **final.came** | place.best | expos.brick |
| definit.recommend | hot.fresh | new.favorit | year.alway | back.drink |
| expect.wait | best.mexican | servic.awesom | **over.price** | fri.noth |
| great.time | best.sushi | **sever.minut** | dish.well | great.view |
| chicken.beef | pizza.best | best.dine | few.place | chicken.good |
| room.dessert | food.fabul | **veri.rude** | authent.mexican | bar.great |
| price.great | melt.mouth | peopl.veri | wether.com | person.favorit |
| seafood.restaur | each.dish | **poor.servic** | especi.good | great.decor |
| friend.atmospher | absolut.wonder | **ask.check** | like.sit | french.dip |
| **sent.back** | foie.gras | real.treat | open.until | pub.food |
| ll.definit | menu.chang | **never.got** | great.too | coconut.shrimp |
| anyon.look | **food.bland** | **non.exist** | open.daili | go.up |
| most.popular | noth.fanci | **flag.down** | best.valu | servic.fantast |
| **order.wrong** | **back.time** | tabl.ask | just.great | **gas.station** |
| delici.food | food.excel | **least.minut** | fri.littl | **pork.loin** |
| fresh.seafood | worth.trip | won.disappoint | portion.huge | place.friend |

—— negative  —— positive

**FIGURE 8.9:** Big absolute loadings by aspect rating in the we8there MNIR.

text $x_i$ is associated with document attribute $k$, you can obtain the MNIR projection $z_{ik} = x_i' \varphi_k = \sum_j x_{ij} \varphi_{jk}$. These scores will contain *all of the information in $x_i$ that is relevant to $v_{ik}$.* If you know $z_{ik}$, then there is nothing more that $x_i$ can tell you about aspect $k$. Figure 8.10 shows scores against true values for overall rating; it is clear that $z_{\text{overall}}$ is rich with information about $v_{\text{overall}}$.

These MNIR projections (also called *sufficient reduction* [SR] projections) are especially useful for sorting documents according to the various attributes. Taking an example from Taddy [2015b], we consider reviews on Yelp.com for a variety of places (restaurants, hotels, landmarks). In addition to the reviewer's star rating, these reviews also come accompanied with votes from other Yelp users on the quality of the review itself. On Yelp.com you can give a review a vote as funny, useful, or cool. You can run MNIR onto these vote counts as well as a list of other variables that you would like to control for, such as the category of the review subject (e.g., restaurant, bowling alley, or both) and how long this subject has been up on Yelp.

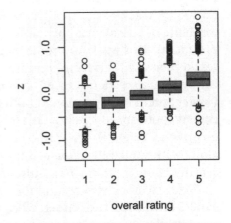

**FIGURE 8.10:** MNIR projection $z_{\text{overall}}$ against true overall review rating.

The results illustrate the usefulness of MNIR projections based on partial correlations. Sorting reviews by vote alone is not especially informative because the reviews that get a lot of votes tend to be those that are old or associated with popular subjects. For example, the funniest review by votes in the sample is a nonhumorous review of the Casa Grande national monument in Coolidge, Arizona; this is also the most useful and coolest review by votes.

In contrast, the review with highest MNIR projection $z_{funny}$ is an open letter to the restaurant that is designed to be humorous:

*Dear La Piazza al Forno: you need to talk. I don't quite know how to say this so I'm just going to come out with it. I've been seeing someone else. How long? About a year now. Am I in love? Yes. Was it you? It was. The day you decided to remove hoagies from the lunch menu, about a year ago, I'm sorry, but it really was you. . .and not me. Hey. . . wait. . . put down that pizza peel. . . try to stay calm. . . please? [Olive oil container whizzing past head] Please! Stop throwing shit at me. . . everyone breaks up on social media these days. . . or haven't you heard? Wow, what a Bitch!*

You can also normalize the SR projections by the length of review, for example, reporting $z_{ik}/m_i$. On this scale, the funniest review is *Holy Mother of God*, and the most useful review is *Ask for Nick!*.

Overall, MNIR is useful for sorting through a large number of related influences on text and for categorizing texts according to these factors. It is a complement to text regression and topic modeling. In full-scale text analysis applications, you will find yourself combining all of these tools as appropriate. For example, in Taddy [2013a], I tracked political sentiment on Twitter about candidates in the 2012 Republican presidential primaries (plus sentiment about Obama, the incumbent president). This work uses topic modeling to factorize a massive bank of unlabeled text; I then used this factor representation to guide the selection of tweets for labeling by human readers. Once I accumulated the labeled data, I used MNIR to model tweet content as a function of both generic sentiment (happy versus sad) and sentiment about specific politicians (e.g., support for Romney is not the same as being positive in general). The resulting factors are used as input to a text regression, along with some raw token counts, to train a model that can track subject-specific sentiment on Twitter. The results are shown in Figure 8.11.

Before leaving text behind for a bit, here is an important reminder that is relevant to any novice text-miner: when you introduce text data, don't forget all that you already know. If you get access to a Twitter feed, don't just naively try to use this data to predict, for example, stock prices. Instead, use the text as a complement to the existing trading system—use it to predict residuals. Text information is best as part of a larger system. Use it to fill in the pieces you don't know and to automate analysis that is expensive and time-consuming.

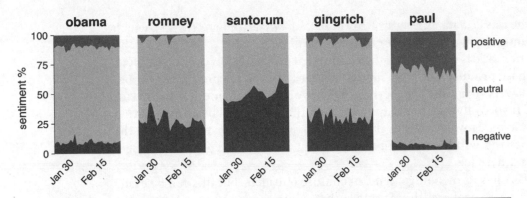

**FIGURE 8.11:** Sentiment about politicians in Twitter traffic during the 2012 Republican presidential primaries.

## Collaborative Filtering

At the beginning of this chapter, we were clear that the bag-of-words representation is a brutal oversimplification of language. However, we've seen that this simple framework can facilitate a number of powerful text analysis frameworks. The simplicity of the bag-of-words representation leads us to treat text as a series of generic counts. This implies that the tools of text analysis we've covered in this chapter should apply beyond text to any other setting that is centered on count data.

One important case is that of collaborative filtering: the task of predicting a person's future choices from their and others' past choices. A well-known example is the *Netflix problem*: Given past movie choices, what should be recommended for you to watch tonight? The data here is essentially the same as what you get for text: each user has a vector $x_i$ containing 0/1 information for what they have watched. we'd like to, for example, find underlying *genres* that collect movies watched by the same people.

I don't know what Netflix uses as a collaborative filtering scheme, and I imagine that it depends upon movie context (e.g., reviews, actors, content) as well as past transaction data. But the creative "genres" that they suggest on their platform (e.g., "darkly comedic historical drama") suggest that they are fitting some sort of a topic model and building an ex-post interpretation around the topics.

Collaborative filtering is far more general than movie recommendation. As Amazon says, "People who buy this book also bought . . ." One way to approach the problem is to run a ton of logistic lasso regressions—one for each product (movie) on to every other product. This is actually not a bad idea, *if* you have the massive computing resources that it requires. A lower fidelity but more computationally feasible alternative is the classic data mining strategy of *market basket analysis* (MBA), which searches efficiently through the data for *association rules*.

An association rule is a case where the conditional probability of product A given you also purchase product B is high—much higher than the *unconditional* probability for product A. For example, perhaps when you buy *beer*, you need *chips* for the munchies. If you only ever buy chips after beer, then there will be an association rule: beer → chips. However, if you always buy chips regardless of beer, then the probability of chips will be high, but this is *not* an association rule because beer doesn't make a difference.

That's it. MBA has its own lingo that can confuse outsiders, but this can be easily translated into basic probabilities. Suppose that chips are purchased 10% of the time in general, but 50% of the time when the consumer grabs beer. You then have a beer → chips association rule.

- The *support* for chips is 10%. This is p(chips).

- The *confidence* of this rule is 50%. This is p(chips|beer).

- The rule *lift* is 5: 50% is 5 times higher than 10%. This is

$$\frac{p(\text{chips}|\text{beer})}{p(\text{chips})} = \frac{p(\text{chips},\text{beer})}{p(\text{beer})\,p(\text{chips})},$$

the increase in the joint probability relative to what you'd expect if chips and beer were independent.

Association rules with high lift are most useful because they tell you something you don't already know.

There's no deep theory around association rules. You just scan the product pairings to find interesting high-lift and high-confidence rules. To illustrate, we'll switch from movies and beer to music. We have data from last.fm, an online radio service. For each of 15,000 users, we have the playlist of their recent listening session.

```
> head(lastfm)
user                    artist sex country
1  1     red hot chili peppers   f Germany
2  1  the black dahlia murder    f Germany
3  1                goldfrapp    f Germany
4  1          dropkick murphys    f Germany
5  1                le tigre     f Germany
```

To find a set of association rules in R, you can use the apriori function from the arules package. There is a whole ecosystem around the arules package, serving the world of market basket analysts. To use it, you need to use arules to get the data into a certain special `basket` format, but after these manipulations, the package is easy to use. Here, we fit the association rules on the lastfm data and return those of high lift and confidence.

```
> library(arules)
> playlists <- split(x=lastfm$artist, f=lastfm$user)
> playlists <- lapply(playlists, unique)
> playtrans <- as(playlists, "transactions")
>
> # find rules with support > .01 & confidence >.5 & length (# artists) <= 3
> musicrules <- apriori(playtrans,
+     parameter=list(support=.01, confidence=.5, maxlen=3))
> inspect(subset(musicrules, subset=lift > 5))
    lhs                          rhs             support      confidence   lift
1   {t.i.}                    => {kanye west}    0.01040000   0.5672727    8.854413
2   {the pussycat dolls}      =>{rihanna         0.01040000   0.5777778    13.415893
4   {sonata arctica}          => {nightwish}     0.01346667   0.5101010    8.236292
5   {judas priest}            => {iron maiden}   0.01353333   0.5075000    8.562992
20  {led zeppelin, the doors} => {pink floyd}    0.01066667   0.5970149    5.689469
21  {pink floyd, the doors}   => {led zeppelin}  0.01066667   0.5387205    6.802027
```

We've discovered that listeners of Judas Priest are nine times more likely to listen to Iron Maiden and that listeners of *both* Led Zeppelin and The Doors are six times more likely to dig Pink Floyd.

Association rules can give you some useful insights, but they are limited to comparisons between pairs or small sets of products. The algorithm also remains fairly slow by modern standards. Instead, we can look to our wider toolbox. Topic modeling is one tool that is especially useful for collaborative filtering. The multinomial response model works well with binary choice data, and once you have fitted topic scores you can suggest new products of high probability in whatever topics it appears your user favors. This is an example of a standard and robust ML tool (topic modeling) having immediate applicability in a business setting where many people are still using much older technology (market basket association rules).

Using `maptpx`, we find that on this data it again (coincidentally) chooses $K = 10$ topics, or rather genres. The top "words" in each topic/genre are now musical artists. When we sort the artists by their genre lift, we see top artists that are much more likely for listeners of a specific genre than they are for the general listening public.

```
> lastfm <- read.csv("lastfm.csv", colClasses=rep("factor",4))
> # convert to slam sparse matrix
> x <- simple_triplet_matrix(i=as.numeric(lastfm$user),
    j=as.numeric(lastfm$artist), v=rep(1,nrow(lastfm)),
```

```
        nrow = nlevels(lastfm$user), ncol = nlevels (lastfm$artist),
             dimnames = list (levels(lastfm$user), levels(lastfm$artist)))
> summary( tpcs <- topics (x, K=5*(1:5)) )
```

```
Top 5 phrases by topic-over-null term lift (and usage %):
[1]  'equilibrium', 'hypocrisy', 'turisas', 'norther', 'bloodbath' (13.6)
[2]  'of montreal', 'animal collective', 'sufjan stevens', 'broken social scene', 'andrew bird' (12.5)
[3]  'jordin sparks', 'the pussycat dolls', 'leona lewis', 'rihanna', 'kelly clarkson' (11.1)
[4]  'aerosmith', 'dire straits', 'lynyrd skynyrd', 'led zeppelin', 'eric clapton' (10.2)
[5]  'charlie parker', 'captain beefheart & his magic band', 'billie holiday', 'chet baker' (9.5)
[6]  'the pigeon detectives', 'kaiser chiefs', 'dirty pretty things', 'the fratellis' (9.1)
[7]  'comeback kid', 'the bouncing souls', 'chiodos', 'a day to remember', 'underoath' (8.9)
[8]  'enya', 'garbage', 'pidzama porno', 'hey', 'skinny puppy' (8.8)
[9]  'nas', 'j dilla', 'common', 'talib kweli', 'notorious b.i.g.' (8.7)
[10] 'ferry corsten', 'paul van dyk', 'above & beyond', 'armin van buuren', 'tiesto' (7.6)
```

Genre 1 appears to be metal, 2 is indy rock, 3 is pop, 4 is classic rock, and so on. These top-lift artists could be great recommendations for listeners who score high in each genre (i.e., have large $\omega_{ik}$). The artists are rare enough to not be on the listener's radar, but from their shared-genre interest we expect that the listener will enjoy the music.

## Word Embedding

We close this chapter with some exciting new methods in natural language processing that have come out of work in deep learning. *Word embedding* was originally motivated as a technique for dimension reduction on the inputs to a deep neural network. As outlined in Chapter 10, such initial dimension reduction is a key part of the success of contemporary ML systems. However, word embedding turns out to be valuable in its own right: it imposes a spatial structure on words, making it possible for those studying language to reason about distances between meanings and consider the algebra behind combinations of words in documents.

In the original deep learning context, embedding layers replace each word with a vector value, such that, for example, *hotdog* becomes the location [1, –5, 0.25] in a three-dimensional embedding space (this is just for illustration; embedding spaces are typically of more than 100 dimensions). Compare this to the standard "one-hot" or bag-of-words representation, where *hotdog* would be represented as a binary vector that is as long as there are words in the vocabulary, say, $p$. This binary vector will have $p - 1$ zeros and a one in the *hotdog* dimension. The word embedding has translated the language representation from a large binary space to a smaller real-valued (and much richer) space.

The basic idea of word embedding is related to concepts covered in our earlier discussions of factor modeling. In those contexts, we looked at ways to "embed" documents in a vector space—representing each document $i$ either as a vector of topic weights $\boldsymbol{\omega}_i$ or as a vector of PCA scores $\boldsymbol{v}_i$. This gives a reduced dimension representation of the document. Instead of $p$-dimensional bag-of-words representations, you get $K \ll p$ dimensional factor (topic) representations. Word embedding takes a similar approach to dimension reduction, but on the words themselves rather than on the document as a whole.

There are a variety of different embedding algorithms—as many as there are different architectures for deep neural networks. The most common and general embeddings are built around *word co-occurrence matrices*. This includes the popular Glove[13] and Word2Vec[14] frameworks. In this class of methods, the first step is to define a notion of co-occurrence. For example, in the common skip-gram formulation, with a "window size" of $b$, two words co-occur if they appear within the same sentence and within $b$ words of each other. For a vocabulary size $p$, this leads to a sparse $p \times p$ co-occurrence matrix where each $[i, j]$ entry is the number of times that words $i$ and $j$ co-occur. Call this matrix $\boldsymbol{C}$. A word embedding algorithm seeks to approximate $\boldsymbol{C}$ as the product of two lower-dimensional matrices:

$$C \approx UV'. \tag{8.5}$$

Here, $\boldsymbol{U}$ and $\boldsymbol{V}$ are each $p \times K$ dimensional dense and real valued matrices. $K$ is the dimension of the embedding space; hence, $K \ll p$ and both $\boldsymbol{U}$ and $\boldsymbol{V}$ are very tall and thin matrices. Each row of $\boldsymbol{U}$ and of $\boldsymbol{V}$—say, $\boldsymbol{u}_j$ and $\boldsymbol{v}_j$—is then a $K$-dimensional embedding of the $j$th word. The implication of Equation 8.3 is

$$c_{ij} \approx \boldsymbol{u}_i'\boldsymbol{v}_j = \sum_{k=1}^{K} u_{ik}v_{jk}, \tag{8.6}$$

such that these embeddings summarize the *meaning* of words inasmuch as their inner product—a standard measure of *distance* in linear algebra—defines how much you expect them to co-occur.

One way to find $\boldsymbol{U}$ and $\boldsymbol{V}$ is to solve Equation 8.5 is through the singular value decomposition (SVD). This is a core algorithm in linear algebra that can also be used, for example, in finding the eigenvalues and eigenvectors of square symmetric matrices (and hence in calculating principal components). In practice, most of the software embedding solutions use alternatives to SVD that are designed to deal with the high amount of sparsity in $\boldsymbol{C}$ (since most words never co-occur in limited windows for standard corpora).

13. Jeffrey Pennington, Richard Socher, and Christopher Manning. Glove: Global vectors for word representation. In *Proceedings of the 2014 Conference on Empirical Methods in Natural Language Processing (EMNLP)*, pages 1532–1543, 2014.

14. Tomas Mikolov, Ilya Sutskever, Kai Chen, Greg S. Corrado, and Jeff Dean. Distributed representations of words and phrases and their compositionality. In *Advances in Neural Information Processing Systems*, pages 3111–3119, 2013.

Under many algorithms, especially when co-occurrence is symmetric,[15] *U* and *V* will be mirror images of each other. Thus, it is standard to take one of these vectors—say, $u_j$—as the single embedding *location* for word *j*. As mentioned at the outset, these *locations* were originally viewed as an intermediate output—as a processing step for inputs to a deep neural network. However, social scientists and linguists have discovered that the *space* of word locations contains rich information about the language of the documents used to train the embedding. For example, the Word2Vec authors emphasized the possibility of algebra in the embedding space: if you take the vector for *Paris*, subtract *France*, and add *Italy*, then you get a location near to the coordinates of the vector for *Rome*. From a data scientific perspective, the word embeddings open up the option of taking advantage of word order and context in prediction tasks. As one example, Taddy [2015a] describes a simple Bayesian classifier built around word2vec embeddings and compares this classifier to other techniques we've covered in this chapter.

One example that nicely illustrates the potential of embedding is the work of Bolukbasi et al. [2016].[16] In this work, the authors trained a standard word2vec embedding algorithm on the Google News corpora of news articles. They look at the differences between established *gender* words (for example, the vector for *man* minus the vector for *woman*, or *father* minus *mother*) to establish an axis in the embedding space that spans from masculinity to femininity. They then calculate the location along this axis for a large number of terms that should be gender-neutral. For example, Figure 8.12 shows professional titles that end up on the extremes of this male-versus-female axis. It is clear that the embedding space has *learned*—from how the words are used in news articles—that these professions are stereotypically viewed as female and male occupations.

| Extreme *she* | Extreme *he* |
| --- | --- |
| 1. homemaker | 1. maestro |
| 2. nurse | 2. skipper |
| 3. receptionist | 3. protege |
| 4. librarian | 4. philosopher |
| 5. socialite | 5. captain |
| 6. hairdresser | 6. architect |
| 7. nanny | 7. financier |
| 8. bookkeeper | 8. warrior |
| 9. stylist | 9. broadcaster |
| 10. housekeeper | 10. magician |

**FIGURE 8.12:** Figure taken from Bolukbasi et al. [2016] showing occupational titles that are at the extremes of the estimated male-versus-female axis of an embedding space trained on Google News.

Beyond pointing out the chauvinism of journalists, the authors highlight the fact that ML algorithms trained on this data will adopt the same biases. The idea of bias in AI resulting from bias in training data is an important issue that the industry is struggling to grapple with. In this case, they suggest a clever solution: you take all of the words that *should* be gender neutral and *subtract* from their embedding vectors the estimated gender direction. In the same way that subtracting France from Paris got you to a location that was generically associated with "capital city," this algebra should move these occupations to a location that is no longer gender biased. Indeed, the authors

---

15. The co-occurrence matrices need not be symmetric. For example, you can define co-occurrence windows with different lengths before and after each word. In that case, you will have unique *directional* embedding information in each of *U* and *V*. But the common approaches are all symmetric.
16. Tolga Bolukbasi, Kai-Wei Chang, James Y. Zou, Venkatesh Saligrama, and Adam T. Kalai. Man is to computer programmer as woman is to homemaker? Debiasing word embeddings. In *Advances in Neural Information Processing Systems*, pages 4349–4357, 2016.

demonstrate that ML algorithms trained on these de-biased vectors do a substantially better job of answering questions that demand gender-neutral answers.

There are a number of different software solutions for fitting embeddings. Google released the *C*-code for word2vec, and it has been wrapped for use in a number of languages, including R. The `text2vec` package implements Glove and other embedding algorithms, and the authors have provided a number of vignettes demonstrating their usage. If you are willing to work in Python, there are many options, including fast and memory-efficient implementation as part of the `gensim` library (which also provides a number of demonstration notebooks). Although we will not work through code details in this text, word embedding is now a common enough procedure that you should not have trouble finding an implementation that suits your computing environment and data scale.

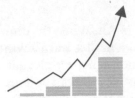

# Nonparametrics

## 9

All of the regressions that we have worked with up until now are *parametric*. They place restrictions on how the inputs can influence the response, for example forcing the relationship to act through a linear model. This is called *parametric analysis* because these models have parameters and you fit a model to the data by optimizing parameters.

*Nonparametric* regression algorithms make fewer assumptions about the relationship between $x$ and $y$. In their purest form, these algorithms will learn the true relationship between $x$ and $y$ as you observe more data, regardless of what this truth looks like. As you accumulate data, your predictions get arbitrarily close to the truth. Such *fully nonparametric* techniques place no assumptions on the data-generating process other than *independence*[1] between observations. This chapter will introduce regression (and classification) trees and forests as fully nonparametric regression methods that have found successful application in business data science.

Recalling what you've learned elsewhere in this text, you should expect that the flexibility gained through a nonparametric approach will lead to overfit unless it is combined with some type of regularization. Unfortunately, penalized-deviance and CV-selection *do not* work for regularization of nonparametric regressions—the fitted objects are *unstable*, and small data jitter will lead to wildly different predictive performances. Fortunately, you can both stabilize and regularize with a technique called *bagging*,[2] which when applied to trees leads to random forests. This strategy is also sometimes called *model averaging*; it is a necessary ingredient in practical nonparametrics.

---

1. Independence between observations is an important but often unmentioned requirement for fully nonparametric procedures. When it fails, these procedures will tend to be outperformed by parametric procedures that do account for dependence, even if they do so in a way that is somewhat misspecified.
2. Leo Breiman. Heuristics of instability and stabilization in model selection. *The Annals of Statistics*, 24: 2350–2383, 1996.

Bagging is great, but it can help you only so much. When the dimension gets too big, the super flexibility of nonparametrics makes it hard to learn anything useful. You should be cautious about using fully nonparametric regressions outside of settings where you have much more data than dimensions (i.e., you can be nonparametric only when $p \ll n$). A good rule of thumb is that you want $p < n/4$. In higher-dimensional problems, we instead tend to work with *semiparametric* methods that combine targeted nonparametric flexibility with parametric restrictions that encourage stability and dimension reduction. At the end of this chapter we'll touch briefly on *Gaussian processes*, a relatively intuitive semiparametric procedure. And in Chapter 10, on AI, we'll introduce deep neural networks as a semiparametric method that plays a starring role in contemporary ML. However, there are a *ton* of real data applications where $p$ is big but $n$ is much bigger; in these settings, you should consider forests and other tree-based methods as your default prediction[3] tool.

## Decision Trees

A decision tree is a logical system for mapping from inputs to outcomes. Trees are *hierarchical*: you use a series of ordered steps (decision nodes) to come to a conclusion.

Tree-logic uses a series of steps to come to a conclusion. Figure 9.1 shows a simple example for the process of deciding whether to bring an umbrella to work: each implies a split on the forecast data available (from either a weather report or current conditions), and the final decisions—the *leaf nodes*—are based upon rain predictions conditional upon these splits. The tree nodes have a parent – child structure: every node except the root ("wake up") has a parent, and every node except the leaves has two children. The trick to building an effective decision tree is to have the sequence of decision nodes combine for good final choices.

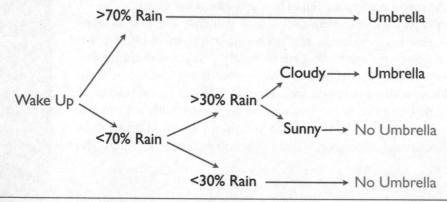

**FIGURE 9.1:** A cartoon decision tree.

---

3. They can also be good tools for inference; see the "Causal Trees" section.

At the core of a decision tree is a regression model. You have inputs $x$ (forecast, current conditions) and an output of interest $y$ (the amount or probability of rain). The decision (umbrella?) is made by combining the predictive distribution for $y$ with a utility function, for example, on the competing inconveniences of carrying an umbrella and getting wet. The trees act like a game of mousetrap. You drop your $x$ covariates in at the top, and each decision node bounces you either left or right. Finally, you end up in a leaf node that contains the data subset defined by these decisions (splits). The following is an example tree structure that uses our familiar regression notation:

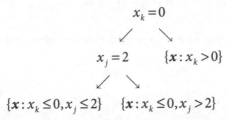

The *prediction rule* at each leaf—the predicted $\hat{y}$—is the average of the sample $y$ values that end up in that leaf. In this example tree, $\hat{y}$ for the bottom-left leaf would be the average of all $y_i$ values such that $x_{ik} \leq 0$ and $x_{jk} \leq 2$. For example, if the response is a real number, then $\hat{y}$ is just a simple average. If the response is categorical, such that each $y_i$ is a vector of zeros and a one indicating the observed category, then the leaf average $\bar{y}$ will be the proportion of observations in each category for that leaf.

To build such trees, you need an algorithm that takes previous $[x, y]$ pairs and automatically constructs a useful set of splitting rules. The goal will be to minimize a *loss function*. The loss functions for trees look the same as the *deviance* functions that we've been using as objectives for parametric regression modeling. For example, if the response is a real number, then you can fit your "regression" tree to minimize the sum-squared error $\Sigma_{i=1}^{n} (y_i - \hat{y}_i)^2$. For a classification problem, you can fit your tree to minimize the multinomial deviance $-\Sigma_{i=1}^{n}\Sigma_{k=1}^{K} y_{ik} \log(\hat{y}_{ik})$. As a historical quirk, for classification most tree software implementations instead minimize "Gini impurity" $\Sigma_{i=1}^{n} \hat{y}_{ik} (1 - \hat{y}_{ik})$, a measure of the multinomial variance. You don't really need to worry about this—both Gini loss and multinomial deviance lead to similar fits, and both work fine for classification.

In the language of this text, all trees are regression trees—it is just the loss function that changes. However, the tree literature tends to use "regression" for the specific scenario of real valued outputs. I'll adopt that lingo here.

As in any regression estimation, from linear to multinomial models, we are fitting regressions to minimize a loss function on the response. However, instead of being based on $x'\beta$, the predicted $\hat{y}$ are now defined through splitting via thresholds on dimensions of $x$. The full space of possible splitting rules is impossibly large (all possible orders of all possible splits), so we need an efficient search algorithm. As we've done previously, we'll use *greedy* forward search—we'll construct splits sequentially and recursively.

Given a *parent* node containing data $\{x_i, y_i\}_{i=1}^n$, the optimal split is location $x_{ij}$—dimension $j$ on observation $i$—that makes the *child* sets as *homogeneous* in response $y$ as possible. These child sets are denoted as

$$\text{left: } \{x_k, y_k : x_{kj} \leq x_{ij}\} \qquad \text{and} \qquad \text{right: } \{x_k, y_k : x_{kj} > x_{ij}\}.$$

For a regression tree with squared error loss, this means that you would want to minimize the function:

$$\sum_{k \in \text{left}} (y_k - \bar{y}_{\text{left}})^2 + \sum_{k \in \text{right}} (y_k - \bar{y}_{\text{right}})^2. \tag{9.1}$$

The classification and regression tree[4] (CART) algorithm of Breiman et al. [1984] is the dominant method for fitting trees. It proceeds by iteratively choosing splits to minimize "node impurities."

---

**ALGORITHM** | **23 CART**

For each node, beginning with the root containing the full sample:

1. Determine the single error minimizing split for this data sample—location $x_{ij}$ that minimizes the loss across children, as in Equation 9.1.

2. Split this parent node into the left and right children.

3. Apply steps 1 and 2 to each child node.

This continues *recursively* until you reach a leaf node of some prespecified minimum size (e.g., stop splitting when there are fewer than, say, 10 observations in each leaf).

---

In addition to leaf size, many implementations include alternative stopping rules around a minimum loss improvement. I find it simple and transparent to use the single leaf-size stopping rule.

---

4. Leo Breiman, Jerome Friedman, Richard Olshen, and Charles Stone. *Classification and Regression Trees*. Chapman & Hall/CRC, 1984.

To fit CART trees, you can use the `tree` library in R. The syntax is essentially the same as for `glm`.

```
mytree = tree (y ~ x1 + x2 + x3 ..., data=mydata)
```

There are a few other useful arguments, all of which adjust the stopping rules.

- `mincut` is the minimum size for a new child.

- `mindev` is the minimum (proportion) deviance improvement for proceeding with a new split.

In many applications, you will want to lower `mindev` from its default of `mindev=0.01`, which stops splitting if there is a less than 1% improvement in loss. This is an overly high bar for many applications. I often use `mindev=0` so that leaf size is the only stopping rule. To understand the results, you can call `print`, `summarize`, and `plot` (with `text` to get something readable) on the fitted object.

As an introductory example, recall the NBC data from Chapter 7. Instead of looking at the pilot surveys, we'll instead look at predicting the show genre (comedy, reality, or drama) from the viewer demographics. These demographics include percent of viewership for each show that falls in a number of categories defined by region, race, and how the household consumes TV.

```
> nbc <- read.csv("nbc_showdetails.csv")
> genre <- nbc$Genre
> demos <- read.csv("nbc_demographics.csv", row.names=1)
> round(demos[1:4, 11:17])
```

|  | WIRED.CABLE.W.PAY | WIRED.CABLE.W.O.PAY | DBS.OWNER |
|---|---|---|---|
| Living with Ed | 36 | 44 | 20 |
| Monarch Cove | 31 | 40 | 29 |
| Top Chef | 43 | 34 | 23 |
| Iron Chef America | 44 | 30 | 26 |

|  | BROADCAST.ONLY | VIDEO.GAME.OWNER | DVD.OWNER | VCR.OWNER |
|---|---|---|---|---|
| Living with Ed | 0 | 66 | 98 | 90 |
| Monarch Cove | 0 | 55 | 94 | 74 |
| Top Chef | 0 | 51 | 92 | 78 |
| Iron Chef America | 0 | 57 | 94 | 84 |

For illustration, we allow CART to split down to single-show leaves.

```
> genretree <- tree(genre ~ ., data=demos, mincut=1)
> genretree
node), split, n, deviance, yval, (yprob)
      * denotes terminal node
```

```
1) root 40 75.800 Drama/Adventure ( 0.475 0.425 0.100 )
 2) CABLE.W.O.PAY < 28.6651 22 33.420 Drama/Adventure (0.73 0.09 0.18)
  4) VCR.OWNER < 83.749 5  6.730 Situation Comedy (0.00 0.40 0.60) *
  5) VCR.OWNER > 83.749 17  7.606 Drama/Adventure (0.941 0.000 0.059)
   10) TERRITORY.EAST.CENTRAL < 16.4555 16  0.000 Drama/Adventure(1 0 0)*
   11) TERRITORY.EAST.CENTRAL > 16.4555 1  0.000 Situation Comedy(0 0 1)*
 3) CABLE.W.O.PAY > 28.6651 18 16.220 Reality (0.16667 0.83333 0)
   6) BLACK < 17.2017 15  0.000 Reality ( 0 1 0 ) *
   7) BLACK > 17.2017 3  0.000 Drama/Adventure ( 1 0 0 ) *
```

The printed output for the `tree` object shows a series of decision nodes and the proportion in each genre at these nodes, down to the leaves. The (`yprob`) output for each node shows the average 0/1 category membership vector, with $k = 1$ for `Drama/Adventure`, $k = 2$ for `Reality`, and $k = 3$ for `Situation Comedy`. In this case, all but one of the tree leaves contain only a single genre; the exception is node 4, containing two reality shows and three comedies.

Trees are easiest to understand in a *dendrogram* plot—a diagram of internal splits, ending in leaf-node decisions. To get this in R you need two steps: first `plot` the tree outline and second add the `text`.

```
> plot(genretree, col=8, lwd=2)
> text(genretree)
```

Figure 9.2 shows the resulting image. The genre at each leaf node is that with highest probability in that node. You can alternatively call `text (genretree, label="yprob")` to get the full set of class probabilities for each leaf.

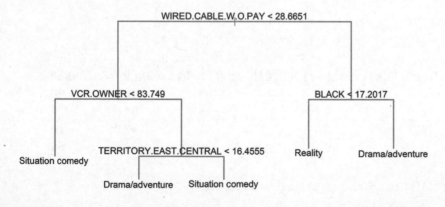

**FIGURE 9.2:** Dendrogram for the CART fit to classify show genre from viewer demographics (% membership in various demographic categories). The noted parent splitting condition (e.g., BLACK<17.2) is true for the left child and false for the right child.

Moving to an example with real-valued response (i.e., a "regression tree"), we consider predicting *projected engagement* (PE) from *ratings* and *genre*. Recall that PE measures how much a viewer is able to recall from the show in a post-viewing survey. To make our life easy when plotting, we'll create our own design matrix by turning it into a group of numeric variables (otherwise the `text` function gives funny labels for our factor input, genre).

```
> x <- as.data.frame(model.matrix(PE ~ Genre + GRP, data=nbc)[,-1])
> names (x) <- c("reality", "comedy", "GRP")
> nbctree <- tree(nbc$PE ~ ., data=x, mincut=1)
```

Figure 9.3 shows the results. Since the input space is so simple here (one continuous input and one factor input), we can visualize the response surface. Figure 9.3 illustrates the translation from the dendrogram to the predicted $\hat{y}$ values for each show. Note the automatic interaction detection; for example, the relationship between GRP and PE depends upon genre.[5]

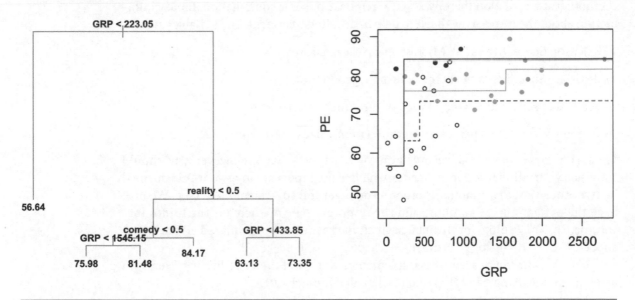

**FIGURE 9.3:** CART fit to predict projected engagement (PE) from the gross ratings (GRP) and genre. The tree dendrogram is on the left, and on the right we plot GRP against observed and fitted PE with the shows colored by genre (black for comedy, grey for drama, white for reality).

---

5. As a historical note, automatic interaction detection (AID) was an original motivation for building decision trees, and older algorithms have AID in their name (e.g., CHAID).

This is powerful technology: given enough data, trees will fit nonlinear means and interaction effects without you having to specify them in advance. Moreover, nonconstant variance is no problem: for regression trees you can have a completely different error variance in different parts of the input space. This all contrasts with the standard parametric regression formulation, $y = x'\beta + \varepsilon$, where you need to pick the design $x$ in advance and $\varepsilon$ has a single shared variance, say, $\sigma^2$. This is why we call CART a *fully nonparametric* regression method.

To avoid overfit in practice, you need to somehow constrain the flexibility of CART. One approach is to apply the usual selection routine: build a *path* of candidate models and apply CV. Candidate CART models are ordered through a pruning process: fit an overgrown tree (deeper than you think will work well for prediction) and prune it backward by iteratively removing the leaf splits (those right above the leaf nodes) that yield the lowest in-sample error reduction. This reversal of the CART growth process yields a set of candidate trees, and you can use cross validation to choose the best model from this set (tools like AICc don't apply because there is no good estimate of degrees of freedom for trees).

As an illustrative example, we'll consider biopsy data for $n = 97$ prostate cancer tumors. After a tumor has been detected, there are many possible treatment options: chemotherapy, radiation therapy, surgical removal, or some combination. Biopsy information about the tumor is available to help in deciding treatment. The variables are:

- Gleason Score (gleason): Microscopic pattern classes

- Prostate Specific Antigen (lpsa): Protein production

- Capsular Penetration (lcp): Reach of tumor into gland lining

- Benign Prostatic Hyperplasia Amount (lbph): Size of prostate

lpsa, lcp, and lbph are all recorded on log scale in the data. However, you should convince yourself that it doesn't matter whether the inputs are logged or transformed in any other way that maintains order—you'll get the equivalent CART fit. We also have the patient age as an input, and the response to be predicted is the tumor logvolume, lcavol (unlike for the inputs, since you're minimizing squared errors it *does* affect CART fit if you log the response variable).

This CV pruning procedure is implemented as part of the tree library. We begin by fitting a tree using mincut=1 and R's default mindev=0.01.

```
> pstree <- tree(lcavol ~., data=prostate, mincut=1)
```

Figure 9.4 shows the overgrown (i.e., overly deep) tree. The cv.tree function takes this fitted tree object and executes the CV pruning routine over a specified $K$ folds. The resulting object contains OOS deviance for trees of each candidate size (number of leaf nodes) along the pruning path (Figure 9.5). In this case, we see that the tree of size 3 has the lowest OOS error.

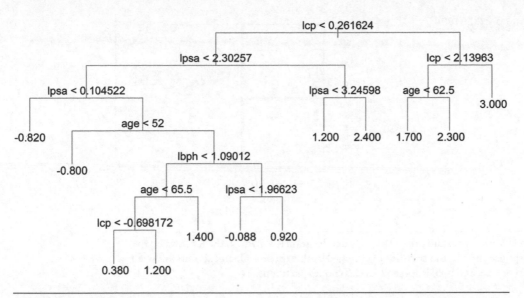

**FIGURE 9.4:** Overgrown tree for the prostate cancer biopsy data. Leaf node labels are the mean log tumor volume.

```
> cvpst <- cv.tree(pstree, K=10)
> cvpst$size
 [1]  12 11  8  7  6  5  4  3  2 1
> round (cvpst$dev)
 [1]  80 77 77 77 78 75 75 74 88 135
> plot (cvpst$size, cvpst$dev, xlab="size", ylab="OOS Error")
```

This indicates that the tree with three leaves is "best." To obtain this tree, we use the prune.tree function with best=3.

```
pstcut <- prune.tree(pstree, best=3)
```

This pstcut is then itself a new tree object—the tree in Figure 9.6. CV has selected PSA and penetration as the only influential variables, and PSA matters only for low-penetration tumors. We see that tumor size tends to increase with penetration but that there are some large tumors with low penetration when PSA is high.

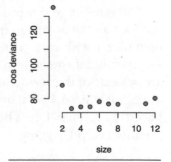

**FIGURE 9.5:** OOS deviance (mean squared error) against tree size for trees along the pruning path for the prostate cancer biopsy tree from Figure 9.4.

## Random Forests

Trees seem great. And they are, *if* you can tame their flexibility and avoid overfit. Unfortunately, the CV routine that we just described does not work reliably in practice. It

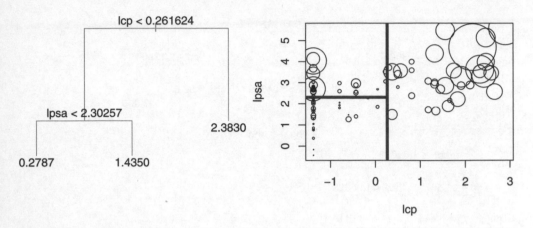

**FIGURE 9.6:** Pruned 3-node prostate tumor tree. The dendrogram is shown on the left, and on the right we see the response surface and partitioning implied by this three-node tree. Points are sized proportional to tumor size, and bold lines show the leaf nodes partitions.

suffers from the same instability issues that we highlighted for subset selection and forward stepwise regression. When prediction rules are highly variable across the model path—here, the iteratively pruned trees—the CV estimates of OOS performance will vary dramatically across samples. This means that the model choice and predictions will have high variance, leading to a large average squared prediction error.

As we cited in Chapter 3, Leo Breiman[6] was among the first to highlight the problems of using CV selection on nonstable models. In that regularization chapter, we were able to *stabilize* the path of candidate models by adding a penalty on coefficient size. This stability is the key to the success of the lasso. However, with tree models there are no coefficients to penalize, and we can't apply this regularization strategy.

The solution to this problem is the technique of *bagging*, for "bootstrap aggregating." Recall the bootstrap from Chapter 1: you rerun your algorithm (e.g., regression) on multiple with-replacement samples of the data to mimic the sampling uncertainty for the full-data fit. Following this logic, the *mean* fit across bootstrap samples is then an estimate of the *average* model fit. If you have a procedure that is *unbiased* (e.g., on average it will work well) but has high sampling variance, then it would follow that the bootstrap mean will be a better model to use than the full-sample data fit. This is the premise behind bagging.

There is also a Bayesian interpretation of bagging based on the Bayesian interpretation of the bootstrap (e.g., in Rubin [1988] or Chamberlain and Imbens [2003]). This holds that the bootstrap sample is an approximation to the posterior distribution for the optimal regression fit and that the bootstrap mean approximates the posterior mean. Bagging is thus *model averaging*, and all of the good stability properties of Bayesian inference follow.

6. Leo Breiman. Heuristics of instability and stabilization in model selection. *The Annals of Statistics*, 24:2350–2383, 1996.

Bagging works best when the individual models are simple but flexible so that you can quickly fit many *unbiased* (but overfit) models. CART trees are a perfect candidate. Indeed, the bagging of CART trees is the essence of the celebrated *random forest*[7] (RF) algorithm of Breiman [2001]. RFs fit CART trees on with-replacement samples of the data, and the resulting prediction rule is the *average* of the predictions from each tree in the bootstrap sample. These RFs are an industrial workhorse for large-scale flexible regression—they require almost no tuning, and nothing performs better out of the box on big data prediction problems. Every time that you use the Internet, it is likely that a some portion of your online experience has been tuned using an RF-based prediction rule.

The full RF algorithm fits a variation of CART on each bootstrap sample: instead of choosing each greedy split location optimally across all inputs, it chooses optimally across *a random sample of inputs*. Unlike the bagging process, this extra randomization does not have a clear theoretical basis or interpretation. However, intuitively it provides some amount of extra regularization by forcing the greedy splitting algorithm to avoid always splitting variables in a similar order. In empirical work, we've found that this input randomization is useful in small samples (i.e., if $p \approx \sqrt{n}$ or bigger) but that it can damage performance if you have large $n$. This would support its interpretation as extra regularization.

---

**ALGORITHM 24** **Random Forest (RF)**

Suppose $B$ is the bootstrap size (i.e., the number of trees in the forest). For $b = 1 \ldots B$:

1. Sample with-replacement $n$ observations from the data.

2. Fit a CART tree—say, $\mathcal{T}_b$—to this sample.

   (a) Alternatively, fit randomized CART with input variables for each greedy split a random draw from the full input set.

This results in a set of trees $\mathcal{T}_1 \ldots \mathcal{T}_B$. The forest predictions are the average of individual tree predictions. If $\hat{y}_{fb}$ is the prediction for $x_f$ from tree $\mathcal{T}_b$, then the random forest prediction is $\hat{y}_f = \frac{1}{B}\sum_b \hat{y}_{fb}$.

---

For classification problems, some RF implementations have trees vote on the response rather than average. That is, each tree contributes its highest probability response class and $\hat{y}_f$ is the proportion of vote for each class. The bagging theory suggests it is preferable to have $\hat{y}_f$ the average of class *probabilities* $\hat{y}_{fb}$.

---

7. Leo Breiman. Random forests. *Machine Learning*, 45:5–32, 2001.

To build intuition about random forests, let's consider a simple one-dimensional regression problem. The "motorcycle data" contained in the MASS package are 133 measurements of acceleration on a motorcycle rider's helmet in the moments after a head-on collision (we assume that this is data from crash-test dummies). As a regression problem, input $x$ is time-since-impact and response $y$ is acceleration. Figure 9.7 shows the data and CART fit. Even though this is a simple 1-D regression, it illustrates the flexibility of CART: the tree is able to follow a nonlinear mean with highly variable noise (e.g., noise at impact is low relative to the noise after whiplash).

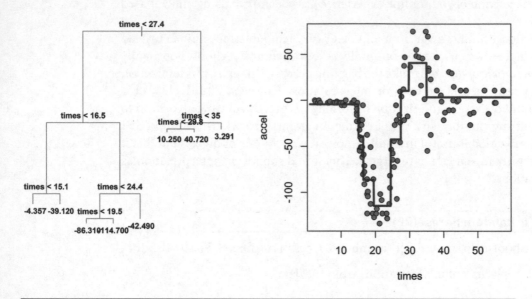

**FIGURE 9.7:** CART fit for the motorcycle data. The dendrogram on the left corresponds to the prediction surface on the right.

Each tree in a random forest is instead fit to a resample of the data. Figure 9.8 illustrates this procedure: each bootstrap sample leads to a slightly different CART fit as the more heavily weighted observations (those resampled more times) pull on the response surface. Figure 9.9 shows how the sampled CART fits accumulate and aggregate—for a forest with many trees, the average becomes a smooth (or mostly smooth) surface even though the constituent trees all imply jagged prediction surfaces. We recall here the Bayesian interpretation of a forest as a posterior over trees, such that the distribution of bootstrap CART fits is the distribution for your "best" tree fit. Notice the adaptive uncertainty bounds in Figure 9.9: there is little uncertainty about $\mathbb{E}[y|x]$ at the edges of the time grid, but large amounts of uncertainty during the backward-forward acceleration in the middle.

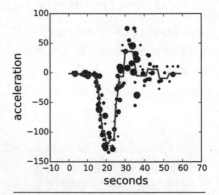

**FIGURE 9.8:** A bootstrap sampled CART fit. The points are sized proportional to the number of times they occur in the with-replacement sample, and the line shows the resulting CART fit.

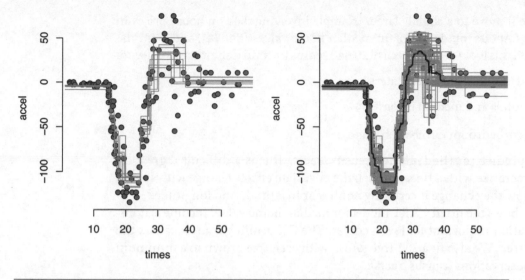

**FIGURE 9.9:** Bootstrap resampled CART fits for the motorcycle data. The left panel shows 10 fits, and the right shows 100 fits plus their mean in bold.

These figures illustrate how the mechanics of averaging act to regularize and avoid overfit. Individual trees might be optimized to noise, but *by definition* this noisy overfit will not be repeated across many of the resampled CART fits (otherwise it is real structure and not just noise). The noise in the individual fits thus averages out after aggregation, and only the persistent structure survives. This is the massive power of model averaging: it can be used to stabilize and regularize arbitrary algorithms. This strategy features commonly in ML, under many names such as ensemble learning, Bayesian model averaging, or bagging. The basic idea is always the same: aggregate many models to eliminate the noise.

How many trees do you want in your forest? As for the original bootstrapping procedure, the answer is: as many as you can get. There is no drawback from including more trees. Each additional tree helps you get a better estimate of the true sampling mean—the mean for an infinite number of bootstrap resamples—that is your best guess at the true response surface. However, as with any sampling procedure, there are diminishing returns for additional trees. Out-of-sample predictive performance tends to improve quickly with the first several trees and then flatten out as you add more. For example, Figure 9.10 shows that OOS performance for the motorcycle regression improves little beyond that of the 100 tree forest.

Fitting forests in R is easy with the `ranger` package, which uses essentially the same syntax as the `glm` and `tree` functions.[8]

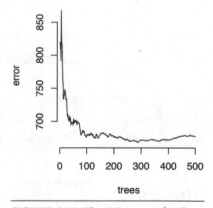

**FIGURE 9.10:** The OOS error for the motorcycle regression as a function of the number of trees in the forest. This error is calculated on a single random test sample of 33 of the 133 observations.

---

8. `ranger` is a much faster implementation of the original `randomForest` package.

To illustrate, we'll move to a slightly larger example involving data on house prices in California. The `CAhousing` data contain median home values (`MedVal`, and from the prices you can tell this is old data) for each of 20,640 census tracts in California, along with:

- Latitude and longitude of tract centers

- Population totals and median income

- Average room/bedroom numbers, home age

The goal is to predict `log(MedVal)` for census tracts. This is a difficult regression surface to characterize with a linear model: the covariate effects change with spatial location, and how they change is certainly nonlinear in latitude and longitude.[9]

Figure 9.11 shows the fitted CART model for median home value. Income is dominant, with location important for low incomes. The CV pruning routine favors the plotted 12-leaf tree. We also fit a 200-tree forest, with each tree grown to a minimum leaf size of 25 observations (census tracts):

```
> carf <- ranger(logMedVal ~ ., data=CAhousing,
+    write.forest=TRUE, num.tree=200, min.node.size=25,
     importance="impurity")
```

The disadvantage of moving from a tree to a forest is that you lose the single-tree interpretability of Figure 9.11. However, there are statistics of "variable importance" that can be used to gain some limited insight. With the argument `importance="impurity"`, `ranger` tracks each $\mathcal{T}_b$'s predictive performance on the *out-of-bag* sample—the observations that

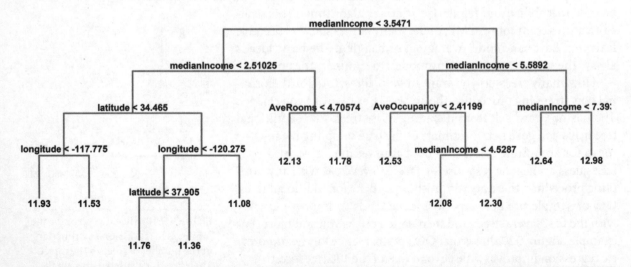

**FIGURE 9.11:** CART for CA housing. Income and home prices (the leaf labels) are expressed in units of $10,000.

9. We are making things artificially hard for a linear model here by not including region and census track effects as dummy variables. You can think of the tree methods as automatically learning these geographic factors.

were not included in the $b$th resample. These errors are paired with information about which variables are split upon in each tree. This yields a `variable.importance` statistic: the increase in error that occurs when that variable is *not* used to define tree splits. We can sort variables by their importance for our house price example:

```
> sort(carf$variable.importance, decreasing=TRUE)
    medianIncome         latitude         longitude      AveOccupancy
      2354.6238         981.3186          932.0298          607.6977
        AveRooms  housingMedianAge         AveBedrms        households
        574.0029         213.4008          166.4089          122.2114
      population
        106.6222
```

The most important variable is median income, followed by geographic location. This matches up with the first few splits in the CART tree of Figure 9.11. It is a bit surprising that occupancy rates are the next most important input; this variable must feature commonly on deep splits in the bootstrap sample trees. However, I caution against putting too much weight on variable importance statistics—there are lots of things happening in the forest, and it is of limited utility to try to interpret the "importance" of a variable without understanding how it acts on the response.

Figure 9.12 shows in-sample residuals for the tree and forest, along with those from lasso on a linear design that interacts latitude and longitude with each other and with all other inputs. The in-sample residuals are largest for this linear model, followed by CART and then by RF. The RF residuals are much smaller than for the other two methods—large errors have disappeared apart from a few underestimates around Los Angeles and the San Francisco Bay Area. The RF is not overfitting; this in-sample fit corresponds to a real out-of-sample improvement in predictive performance. Figure 9.13 shows the OOS log errors for each regression, and we see that the RFs are a persistent large improvement over the other methods.

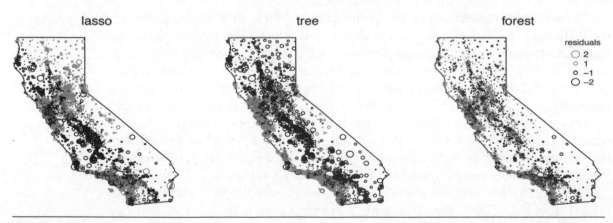

**FIGURE 9.12:** In-sample residuals for the California home values for lasso, CART, and RF fitted regressions. These images were created using the `maps` package, which is one of the many tools in R for plotting and analyzing spatial data.

**RANDOM FORESTS ARE A BIG DATA TECHNIQUE.** It just might not seem that way when fitting them on your laptop. Without making use of parallelization, the sequential fitting of trees will take a long time. However, forests are all about big data! They work on massive distributed datasets and can be deployed on industrial scale. You just need to make use of the parallel and partitioned computing ideas that we introduced at the end of Chapter 4. To close this section on RFs, we'll outline the techniques necessary for deploying them at Internet scale.

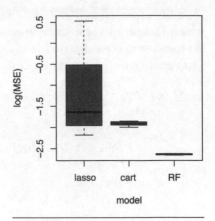

**FIGURE 9.13:** Out-of-sample performance over ten random folds for the California housing regressions.

First, if you ran the 200-tree RF for the California housing regression, you would have noticed that it took much longer than running CART—perhaps even 200 times longer. However, each of these trees could have been fit *at the same time* if you had enough available processors. Indeed, the `ranger` library automatically uses all of your cores for parallel processing—that is, you were probably parallel computing even if you didn't know it. The `num.threads` argument specifies the number parallel tree-fitting processes (threads), and the default of `num.threads=NULL` chooses as many threads as you have cores. Moving from one to four threads decreases my compute time by half to one-third.

```
> system.time(carf <- ranger(logMedVal ~ ., data=CAhousing, num.threads=1, ...
   user system elapsed
   8.75   0.03   8.92
> system.time(carf <- ranger(logMedVal ~ ., data=CAhousing, num.threads=4, ...
   user system elapsed
  13.00   0.04   3.50
```

In these printouts the `elapsed` number corresponds to the actual wall-clock time spent waiting. The speed-up is less than a factor of 4 because of the considerable overhead involved in copying data across the four compute cores.

The overhead created by data copy points to the problem with this type of basic parallelization: no matter how many cores you can get, you will be limited by the communication cost of data transfer. Even worse, if the data are very big, then it can be impossible to fit them into the working memory of a single processing unit. In that case, full parallelization becomes infeasible and RFs are hopelessly slow. In industry, engineers have developed a number of work-arounds to deal with this issue of memory limits. One common strategy is to replace the with-replacement sampling of RFs with subsampling: each tree is fit to a without-replacement sample of size smaller than *n* (small enough to fit on a single core). This leads to what I call a *subsampling forest*, in which each tree has been fit to a small random data subset.

*This is a really bad idea.* Subsampling forests tend to have sharply worse predictive performance than RFs. Understanding why this happens gets to the heart of nonparametrics. Methods such as trees lead to increasingly complex surfaces as you give them more data. The idea of RFs is to take advantage of this nonparametric adaptivity while using bootstrap aggregation to avoid overfit. If you replace the bootstrapping with subsampling, then you are starving your nonparametric learners (the trees) of the data that they need to perform well.

While working with eBay, a group of us noticed a prediction performance decrease because of a switch from full RFs to subsampling forests. This motivated us to formalize a simple alternative called *empirical Bayesian forests*[10] (EBF; the Bayesian name is due to theory derived from a Bayesian bootstrap, but it is not important in practice). The algorithm is based on a simple observation: when you have a large dataset, the *tops* (or trunks—the first few splits) of the trees in a forest are mostly similar.[11]

For example, fitting CART to the California housing data down to a minimum leaf size of 3500 observations results in the *trunk* shown in Figure 9.14. After fitting an RF to the same data, a comparison across trees in the forest shows that they all have a trunk structure similar to that of Figure 9.14. In particular, that *exact* trunk occurs 62% of the time. The second most common trunk, occurring 28% of the time, differs only in that it splits on median income again instead of on housing median age. Thus, 90% of the posterior weight is on trees that split on income twice and then latitude. Moreover, a striking 100% of trees have first two splits on median income. Figure 9.15 shows the locations of these first two splits: each split-location is concentrated around the trunk split in Figure 9.14.

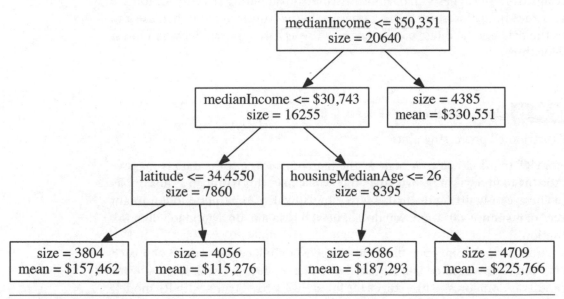

**FIGURE 9.14:** The trunk of the California housing tree that results when fitting with a minimum leaf size of 3500 (out of 20,640 total census tracts).

10. Matt Taddy, Chun-Sheng Chen, Jun Yu, and Mitch Wyle. Bayesian and empirical Bayesian forests. In *Proceedings of the 32nd International Conference on Machine Learning*, 2015.
11. This is true only for the version of RFs where all variables are always available for splitting, but that is the preferred approach when you have large *n*.

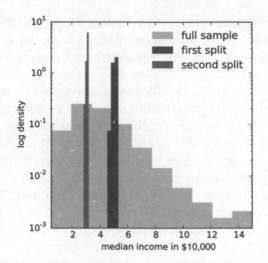

**FIGURE 9.15:** The distribution of median income and of the first two split locations for trees in the housing forest.

This trunk stability occurs after only 20,000 observations. The stability increases dramatically for the millions-plus observation datasets encountered in industrial big data settings. This all suggests an obvious distributed computing strategy for forests: since the trunks in the forest are all the same, just fit the trunk once and then use it to partition the data and facilitate parallelization. This is the empirical Bayesian forest (EBF) algorithm.

---

**ALGORITHM 25**  **Empirical Bayesian Forest (EBF)**

Given $K$ distributed processing units:

- Fit a CART trunk down to $K$ nodes—the trunk *branches*. If the data is massive (i.e., too big to fit on a single machine), then you can fit this trunk on a subsample. Since you are only fitting the first few tree splits, which correspond to dominant sources of response variation, you do not need big data to do a good job of trunk estimation.
- This trunk defines a mapper function in the MapReduce algorithm: `map` each observation to its allocated trunk branch and then `reduce` on each branch by fitting a full random forest. This returns the fitted EBF: a fixed trunk with RF models at each branch.

---

The result is a sort of hybrid CART-RF object, with fixed initial splits and a bootstrap sample of trees for deeper structure. Since the hypothetical (potentially infeasible) full sample RF has the same trunk for most trees, this EBF will lead to similar predictions. In the California housing example, an EBF with the trunk of Figure 9.14 has 2% worse predictive performance than the full sample RF, compared with 10% worse for a subsampling forest of comparable computational cost. For large datasets the results are more dramatic; Taddy et al. [2015] show EBFs 1% to 4% worse than a full RF on examples where the subsampling forests are 12% to 38% worse.

In massive data environments, simple but efficient strategies like Algorithm 25 allow you to crunch more data faster. And more data always wins: even though an EBF does a bit worse than a full RF on the same dataset, an EBF with more data will give better predictions than a small-sample RF. For prediction tasks, never reduce the amount of data you can work with to fit some fancy but computationally costly model—you're better off with a simple but flexible model fit to as much data as you can get your hands on.

## Causal Trees

Random forests and trees are commonly viewed as pure prediction tools—they are supervised ML procedures for predicting a future that is mostly like the past. However, trees have recently found application in causal inference settings. In particular, it turns out that tree-based models are great tools for modeling heterogeneous treatment effects (HTEs; see also Chapter 6).

We'll focus on a basic setting of binary treatment, $d = 0$ or 1, and assume that treatment has been randomized. That is, you are fitting HTEs after a standard AB experiment. The conditional average treatment effect (CATE) of interest is then the difference between conditional expected response for the treatment and control groups given covariates $x$:

$$\gamma(x) = \mathbb{E}[y|d = 1, x] - \mathbb{E}[y|d = 0, x]. \tag{9.2}$$

Given the results of an AB test, one way to estimate HTEs is to simply fit two functions to predict $y$ from $x$—one for the treatment group and one for the control group—and use the difference between these two fitted predictors as the estimate for $\gamma(x)$. This is the approach taken in, for example, the work of Jennifer Hill [2011][12]. For each treatment group, Hill fits Bayesian additive regression trees[13] (BART), a model that regresses $y$ onto a set of shallow trees constructed from $x$. Since this is a fully Bayesian regression method, and because the two samples are independent, she is able to get a full posterior for $\gamma(x)$ simply by differencing the two BART objects.

---

12. Jennifer Hill. Bayesian nonparametric modeling for causal inference. *Journal of Computational and Graphical Statistics*, 20:217–240, 2011.

13. Hugh A. Chipman, Edward I. George, and Robert E. McCulloch. BART: Bayesian additive regression trees. *The Annals of Applied Statistics*, 4:266–298, 2010.

Athey and Imbens [2016] show that in many cases you can do better in modeling HTEs by targeting them directly rather than looking at the difference of two treatment-specific functions. Their causal tree[14] (CT) framework is a simple extension of the usual CART algorithm. Instead of choosing splits to minimize impurity (e.g., the SSE), you choose the tree splits to *maximize* the squared difference between estimated treatment effects in each child node. Algorithm 26 outlines the full routine.

---

**ALGORITHM 26** | **Causal Tree (CT)**

Given a set of $[d_i, x_i, y_i]$ observations in node $\eta$ of a tree, the estimated treatment effect is

$$\hat{\gamma}_\eta = \bar{y}_{\eta 1} - \bar{y}_{\eta 0}. \tag{9.3}$$

Here, $\bar{y}_{\eta d}$ is the sample mean of observations in node $\eta$ with treatment status $d$. CT uses the same greedy recursive strategy as CART. Given a node, you split into left and right children on the variable observation $x_{ij}$ that maximizes

$$\sum_{k \in \text{left}} \hat{\gamma}^2_{\text{left}} + \sum_{k \in \text{right}} \hat{\gamma}^2_{\text{right}}. \tag{9.4}$$

This splitting continues until you hit a minimum number of observations *from each treatment group* in a node; these terminal nodes are the leaves of the causal tree.

---

Algorithm 26 is more precisely what Athey and Imbens refer to as their *adaptive* CT algorithm. Their preferred *honest* version of the estimator uses two samples to fit the tree: one for determining the tree splits and a second that is used to re-estimate the treatment effects within each leaf *conditional* upon this tree structure. This has the advantage that it allows you to derive approximately Gaussian sampling distributions around the leaf estimates (either $\hat{y}_\eta$ for CART or $\hat{\gamma}_\eta$ for CT).[15] But beyond this "honest" adaptation, CTs follow the same philosophy as CART: very simple leaf estimates are combined with partitioning on $x_i$ to create complicated surfaces.

---

14. Susan Athey and Guido Imbens. Recursive partitioning for heterogeneous causal effects. *Proceedings of the National Academy of Sciences*, 113:7353–7360, 2016.

15. The same two-sample procedure can be used to get honest CART in prediction problems. The disadvantage of such honesty is that you are using less data for determining the best tree splits, and this can to lead to point estimates that perform slightly worse. The trade of precision for honesty is usually worthwhile in causal treatment effect modeling, but this will not always be true for pure prediction problems. Note also that this type of sample splitting is the basis of the orthogonal ML algorithm from Chapter 6.

Athey and Imbens [2016] provide the `causalTree` R package for implementing CTs. It is based upon the `rpart` package, which can be used to fit standard CART models. To illustrate the CT algorithm, let's revisit the Oregon Health Insurance Experiment (OHIE) from Chapter 5. Recall that we were interested in observing the treatment effect of randomly selected eligibility for Medicaid on the probability that someone visits a primary-care physician (PCP) at least once a year. The treatment variable is `selected`, indicating whether a person's household was selected for eligibility, the response variable is binary `doc_any_12m`, and for covariates we have a set of results from a survey on subject demographics.

> See Chapter 6 for a lasso analysis of HTEs in this experiment.

The basic `causalTree` algorithms are designed for perfectly randomized experiments. In the original OHIE analysis, the randomization was corrupted by the fact that if anyone from a household was selected, then the whole house was eligible for enrollment. It would be best to control for the number of people in each household when comparing treatment and control groups, and you can do this in the `causalTree` package using *propensity weights* (see discussion on propensities in Chapter 6). However, controlling for `numhh` made little difference in the original analysis, and for simplicity, here we will treat the randomization as perfect. Thus, repeating results from earlier, the overall average treatment effect on the probability that a patient sees a doctor in the next 12 months is around 0.06 (a six percentage point increase).

```
> ybar <- tapply(P$doc_any_12m, P$selected, mean)
> ybar ['1'] - ybar['0']
          1
0.05746606
```

The causal tree syntax is similar to that of `glm`; you provide a regression formula and a data frame. You need also to specify a treatment variable (*d*) and some algorithm parameters. Here, we will ask for the causal tree algorithm of Algorithm 26 with honest splitting (i.e., sample splitting). In addition, we specify the minimum leaf size as 2000 observations. This yields a short tree, with splits for a few major sources of heterogeneity.

```
> ct <- causalTree(P$doc_any_12m ~ ., data=X, treatment=P$selected,
+       split.Rule = "CT", split.Honest=TRUE, minsize=1000)
```

Figure 9.16 shows the resulting tree fit. As might be suspected, a number of the splits are on income: `hhinc_pctfpl_12m` is household income as a percentage of the federal poverty line. For example, for those who make enough money to be at or above the poverty rate (`hhinc_pctfpl_12m >= 97`), eligibility for Medicaid actually *decreases* the probability that they see a PCP. Possibly, for these subjects Medicaid is replacing a private insurance option that makes it easier to visit a doctor. On the other hand, for those who make less than 60% of the poverty line, the treatment effect is greater than 0.1, and as high as 0.15 for women in small household born after 1966.

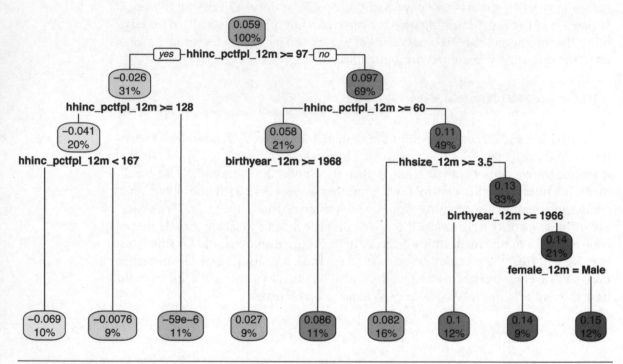

**FIGURE 9.16:** Fitted causal tree for the Oregon Health Insurance Experiment. Each node shows its treatment effect estimate and percentage of total data.

Athey and Imbens describe CV algorithms for pruning CTs. However, as was the case with CART, CTs are unstable prediction rules, and CV selection for tree depth is not advisable (it will yield different trees on different samples and give high-variance results). Instead, for many real applications, you can do as we have here: fit a single shallow tree that gives you a handful of the largest sources of heterogeneity. You might want to know the best way to partition your customers into, say, four segments of differing sensitivity to marketing. In that case, you don't need to worry about overfit and can simply fit a shallow four-leaf tree.

For more complex HTE modeling, you should look beyond single CTs and make use of a forest algorithm. Athey et al. [2017b] detail a generalized random forest (GRF) framework that includes ensembles of CTs and they provide the grf package for implementation of these methods. As was the case for RFs, GRFs are most appropriate when the input dimension (here, the dimension of potential sources of heterogeneity) is low relative to the sample size (e.g., $p < \sqrt{n}$ is a rule of thumb). For higher-dimensional inputs, you can get better results by using lasso-type linear estimators (i.e., interacting treatment with other inputs in a linear model, as we did in Chapter 6 as an extension of orthogonal ML). This is also a hot area of research in the ML community and there are a variety of *semi-parametric* methods being developed to predict HTEs. For example, the framework of Hartford et al. [2017] uses deep neural networks to model HTEs in an instrumental variables setting (and can thus also be applied to study randomized trials). As causal inference becomes a more important topic in ML, expect faster and better HTE prediction algorithms.

## Semiparametrics and Gaussian Processes

Although this chapter is about nonparametrics, everything we have discussed so far makes use of a single technology—trees. This is for good reason; among nonparametric regression methods, nothing is faster, is more robust, and performs better off-the-shelf than ensembles of trees. But we haven't even covered the full breadth of tree frameworks. The most important alternative class of tree-based algorithms, beyond random forests, is built around gradient boosting machines[16] (GBMs). These GBMs make use of the boosting procedure that we introduced in Chapter 7 as the basis for partial least squares. They iteratively estimate a sequence of shallow trees, each trained to predict the residuals of the previous tree. This leads to a prediction rule that combines many simple (and stable) trees.[17] In practice, I have found RFs easier to work with at massive scale than GBMs because of the robustness of bagging as a mechanism for avoiding overfit (GBMs require some sort of CV to choose when to stop boosting). However, there are many examples of successful industrial-scale GBM deployments, and if you find yourself with colleagues who favor boosting over forests, you don't need to worry.

One class of common alternatives to tree-based methods are *sieve* estimators that represent functions via *basis expansions*—sums of approximating functions. Sieve estimators remain popular with classical economists and statisticians because they are relatively easy to study mathematically. A sieve takes the following form:

$$\mathbb{E}[y \mid x] = \sum_{k=1}^{K} \omega_k \psi_k(x). \tag{9.5}$$

Here, $K$ increases with the amount of data that you have available. For example, a polynomial series has $\psi_k(x) = (x'\beta_k)^k$. *Wavelets* are a class of basis functions that satisfy nice mathematical properties; Vidakovic and Mueller [1994] provide a user-friendly overview.

---

16. Jerome H. Friedman. Greedy function approximation: A gradient boosting machine. *Annals of Statistics*, pages 1189–1232, 2001.
17. The BART algorithm of Chipman et al. [2010] is a successful Bayesian analog of GBMs.

And *shallow* neural networks (the sort that were popular in the 1980s and 90s) can be written as a series estimator like that in Equation 9.5.[18]

One other nonparametric framework of note is that of support vector machines (SVMs). These resemble sieves in that they involve basis expansion, but the expansions are used as input to discriminant classifiers rather than as function approximations. SVM algorithms are interesting theoretically,[19] but in practice they are unstable and difficult to tune. I and others[20] attribute their sustained popularity in some application areas (e.g., finance) to an ignorance of alternatives. Again, if you want nonparametric regression and are interested in practical prediction performance, trees are your tool.

However, nonparametric regression is not always (or even often) the best approach to prediction. Trees and splines are extremely flexible—with enough data they can approximate arbitrarily complex functions. However, this comes at the price of *instability*: nonparametric regression methods have very high sampling variance and are sensitive to noise in the data. They are susceptible to overfit, and techniques such as bagging can only help so much. This is the famous "bias versus variance" trade-off: nonparametric regression methods have little or no bias (they can represent any functional form), but this inevitably yields high variance estimates. As has been mentioned elsewhere, a decent rule of thumb is that you should have $p < \sqrt{n}$ for nonparametric regression to be a high-performing option.

For high-dimensional inputs, a great option is to use the regularized linear regression methods emphasized throughout this book. However, there is also a middle ground between nonparametrics and linear models. *Semiparametric* methods mix flexible function approximation with restrictive domain-specific structure. You might combine a flexible mean function approximation with strong distributional assumptions—for example, additive $\varepsilon \sim N(0, \sigma^2)$ errors or a multinomial sampling model (e.g., the bag-of-words model for text).

Much of contemporary ML relies upon semiparametric *kernel* methods that *smooth* predictions across observations that are "near" each other. A kernel is a mathematical abstraction for defining distance between two input vectors, and you can use domain knowledge to help inform which observations are near or far from each other. Thus, in a simple example, $\hat{y}(x_s)$ and $\hat{y}(x_t)$ will be similar if $x_s$ and $x_t$ are nearby according to the fitted kernel, and this kernel can be given application-specific structure.

In Chapter 10, we will describe how contemporary *deep* neural networks are semiparametric regression tools. They make use of restrictive kernel smoothing on the inputs—e.g., smoothing ("convolution") across neighboring pixels in images or across words that are estimated to be near to each other in meaning. The innovation of deep learning is that the outputs of this kernel smoothing, which are typically of much

---

18.  Kurt Hornik, Maxwell Stinchcombe, and Halbert White. Multilayer feedforward networks are universal approximators. *Neural Networks*, 2:359–366, 1989.

19.  Vladimir Vapnik. *The Nature of Statistical Learning Theory*. Springer, 1996.

20.  Kevin Patrick Murphy. *Machine Learning: A Probabilistic Perspective*. MIT Press, 2012.

lower dimension than the original covariates, are used as inputs something that looks like the sieve estimator of Equation 9.5. This combination of restrictive dimension reduction with flexible basis expansion has been widely successful. It powers much of the modern industrial machine learning.

> The line between semi- and nonparametrics is fuzzy. There are kernel regression algorithms with data-dependent kernels that are as flexible as standard sieves, and there are restrictive sieve algorithms that impose high degrees of smoothness. In fact, you can draw a theoretical equivalence between almost any sieve estimator and a kernel method that gives the same predictions. The distinction we're drawing is on common implementation of these frameworks; ML applications of kernel methods typically use domain-specific knowledge to guide the structure of smoothing across observations.

**GAUSSIAN PROCESSES (GPs),** which are a powerful modeling framework in their own right, serve as a more transparent illustration of kernel methods. GPs are relatively simple models that smooth predictions across observations according to distances between the original inputs—say, $x_s$ and $x_t$ as earlier. This is in contrast to the deep neural network models which first project from raw inputs to low-dimensional spaces (think of methods like PCA) and calculated distances in these lower dimensions. In the language of modern ML, the GPs are "shallow."[21] However, these simple models are extremely useful and commonly deployed, especially in applications involving spatial data or physical systems. We'll briefly introduce GPs to close this chapter; look to Rasmussen and Williams [2006][22] for a more detailed overview.

Consider a standard regression setup, with inputs $x$ and response $y$. A Gaussian process models the responses at two locations as draws from a multivariate normal (i.e., Gaussian) distribution:

$$\begin{bmatrix} y_s \\ y_t \end{bmatrix} \sim N\left( \mathbf{0}, \sigma^2 \begin{bmatrix} 1 & \kappa(x_s, x_t) \\ \kappa(x_t, x_s) & 1 \end{bmatrix} \right). \tag{9.6}$$

Here, $\kappa(x_s, x_t)$ is the *kernel function*. That is, $\kappa(x_s, x_t)$ defines the *correlation* between the corresponding responses, $\text{cor}(y_t, y_s)$.[23] For example, the common *exponential* kernel function has

$$\kappa(x_s, x_t) = \exp\left[ -\sum_j \frac{(x_{sj} - x_{tj})^2}{\delta_j} \right]. \tag{9.7}$$

---

21. Of course, ML researchers such as Damianou and Lawrence [2013] have also developed deep GP models.
22. C.E. Rasmussen and C.K.I. Williams. *Gaussian Processes for Machine Learning*. MIT Press, 2006.
23. Their *covariance* is $\sigma^2 \kappa(x_s, x_t)$.

Here, correlation decreases with the exponentiated Euclidean distance between entries of the input vectors. *Range* parameters, the $\delta_j$, allow for different units of distance in different input coordinates. The end result is a function of smoothly decaying dependence between responses, $y_t$ and $y_s$, as a function of distance between inputs. Note that $\kappa(\cdot, \cdot)$ produces values between 0 and 1 (you can't have negative dependence under this kernel) and that $\kappa(\boldsymbol{x}_i, \boldsymbol{x}_i) = 1$ (the correlation between every observation and itself is 1).

It might seem strange to have a regression method without an explicit mean function: the mean in Equation 9.6 is zero, regardless of input coordinates.[24] However, the *conditional* distribution for $y_s$ given $y_t$ will have a nonzero mean. Properties of the Gaussian distribution imply that, under the model in Equation 9.6, the conditional distribution is

$$ y_s \mid y_t \sim \mathrm{N}\left(y_t \kappa(\boldsymbol{x}_s, \boldsymbol{x}_t), \sigma^2[1 - \kappa(\boldsymbol{x}_s, \boldsymbol{x}_t)^2]\right). \tag{9.8} $$

Here, the distribution for $y_s$ is a function of the value of its neighbor, $y_t$. The mean for $y_s$ is a linear function of $y_t$, and the conditional variance for $y_s$ is *smaller* than the unconditional variance, $\sigma^2$. This is the essence of kernel regression: predictions at new inputs are combinations of the existing observations, with combination weights that depend upon the distance between new and existing input locations.

In a full data example, you have $n$ total sample observations—all of which are assumed jointly drawn from a multivariate Gaussian. In addition, it is prudent[25] to add a positive *nugget g* to diagonals of the covariance matrix; otherwise, the rule in Equation 9.8 implies perfect interpolation (zero variance) at already observed $\boldsymbol{x}$ locations. The resulting GP covariance matrix is then

$$ \sigma^2 \begin{bmatrix} 1+g & \kappa(\boldsymbol{x}_1, \boldsymbol{x}_2) & \kappa(\boldsymbol{x}_1, \boldsymbol{x}_3) & \cdots & \kappa(\boldsymbol{x}_1, \boldsymbol{x}_n) \\ \kappa(\boldsymbol{x}_2, \boldsymbol{x}_1) & 1+g & \kappa(\boldsymbol{x}_2, \boldsymbol{x}_3) & \cdots & \kappa(\boldsymbol{x}_2, \boldsymbol{x}_n) \\ \vdots & & & & \vdots \\ \kappa(\boldsymbol{x}_n, \boldsymbol{x}_1) & \kappa(\boldsymbol{x}_n, \boldsymbol{x}_2) & \cdots & \kappa(\boldsymbol{x}_n, \boldsymbol{x}_{n-1}) & 1+g \end{bmatrix}. \tag{9.9} $$

Under the multivariate version of the conditioning rule in Equation 9.8, this covariance matrix can then be used to combine observed responses, $\boldsymbol{y}$, to predict the response at any new input locations.

To fit GPs in R, you can make use of the `laGP` package.[26] This package was developed to implement algorithms for fitting *approximate* GPs on massive datasets

---

24. It is common to have nonzero means in GPs, but they are unnecessary for many applications.

25. Robert B. Gramacy and Herbert K.H. Lee. Cases for the nugget in modeling computer experiments. *Statistics and Computing*, 22(3):713–722, 2012.

26. Robert B. Gramacy. lagp: Large-scale spatial modeling via local approximate gaussian processes in R. *Journal of Statistical Software* (available as a vignette in the laGP package), 2015.

(which is great, because you can keep using laGP as you scale to larger applications) but also provides fast and robust routines for fitting standard GPs. Detailed examples are provided in Gramacy [2015] and in the package documentation.

We will illustrate using the motorcycle data from earlier in this chapter. Recall that the (univariate) input is the time since crash impact and the response is the acceleration of the rider's helmet.

```
library(MASS)
x <- mcycle[,1,drop=FALSE]
y <- mcycle[,2]
```

laGP works by first doing some prework to get a rough guess at the kernel parameters, the nugget g and the range $\delta$ (which it calls d). We then use these pre-estimates to initialize a newGP—an in-memory object that exists as part of the back-end infrastructure of laGP (all coded in C, which is why the package is fast and robust).

```
> library(laGP)
> ## get parameters
> d <- darg(NULL, x)
> g <- garg(list(mle=TRUE), y)
> ## initialize (dK=TRUE saves info you need in estimation)
> gpi <- newGP(x, y, d=d$start, g=g$start, dK=TRUE)
```

Finally, we take this initialized model and the pre-estimates and use the jmleGP function to fit the GP parameters (jmle for "joint" MLE, indicating estimation of both $g$ and $\delta$).

```
> print(jmleGP(gpi, drange=c(d$min, d$max), grange=c(g$min, g$max)))
          d         g tot.its dits gits
1 54.92436 0.2485222      91   28   63
```

The gpi object is now updated with the correct parameter estimates (the print-out shows these estimates and the time they required). The resulting prediction surface is shown in Figure 9.17.

The models we've fit here are the simplest form of GPs. There are plenty of extensions, for example, to allow for different correlation structures or error variances in different parts of the input space (for example, note that true motorcycle variances are much smaller at early time points and that the homoskedastic error structure yields too-wide uncertainty bounds in this region). The treed Gaussian process[27] (TGP)

---

27. Robert B. Gramacy and Herbert K.H. Lee. Bayesian treed gaussian process models with an application to computer modeling. *Journal of the American Statistical Association*, 103(483): 1119–1130, 2008.

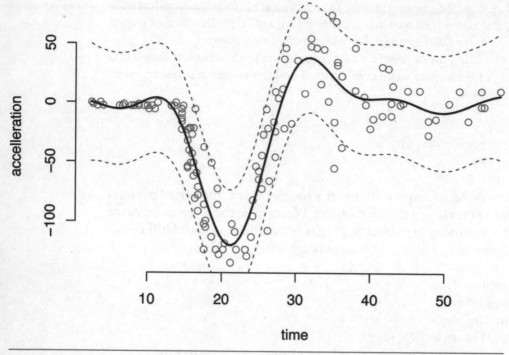

**FIGURE 9.17:** Basic stationary GP fit to the motorcycle data (mean and 95% prediction interval).

algorithm is one that should appeal to readers of this chapter—it combines trees with GPs by using CART partitioning with a GP regression model at each leaf node. This allows you to get away with using shallower trees (since the GPs can model structure at the leaves) and hence leading to more stable prediction rules. The tgp package for R implements these TGP models, and you can look to Gramacy [2007] and Gramacy and Taddy [2010] for lengthy vignettes illustrating its capabilities.

# Artificial Intelligence

## 10

Throughout this book, we have covered the wide variety of new ways that companies are using data to optimize their businesses. Variously called the big data or data science revolution, the rise of this type of analysis over the past decade has been characterized by massive amounts of data, including unstructured and nontraditional data like text and images, and the use of fast and flexible machine learning algorithms in analysis.

With recent improvements in deep neural networks (DNNs) and related methods, application of high-performance ML algorithms has become more *automatic* and robust to different data scenarios. That has led to the rapid rise of an artificial intelligence (AI) that works by combining many ML algorithms together—each targeting a straightforward prediction task—to solve complex problems.

In this final chapter, we will stretch away from today's business data science to describe a framework for thinking about this new ML-driven AI. Having an understanding of the pieces that make up these systems and how they fit together is important for those who will be building businesses around this technology. Having some clear and hype-free definitions around AI should help you understand the requirements for successful AI and anticipate the change that it is bringing.

## What Is AI?

Figure 10.1 shows a breakdown of AI into three major and essential pieces. A full end-to-end AI solution—what we sometimes call a *system of intelligence*—is able to

# AI = Domain Structure + Data Generation + General Purpose ML

| Business Expertise | Reinforcement Learning | Deep Neural Nets |
| Structural Econom[etr]ics | Big Data Assets | Video/Audio/Text |
| Relaxations and Heuristics | Sensor/Video Tracking | OOS + SGD + GPUs |

**FIGURE 10.1:** Business AI systems are self-training structures of ML predictors that automate and accelerate human tasks.

ingest human-level knowledge (e.g., via machine reading and computer vision) and use this information to automate and accelerate tasks that were previously performed only by humans. It is necessary to have a well-defined task structure to engineer against, and in a business setting this structure is provided by business and economic domain expertise. You need a massive bank of data to get the system up and running and a strategy to continue generating data so that the system can respond and learn. Finally, you need machine learning routines that can detect patterns in and make predictions from the unstructured data. This section will work through each of these pillars, and in later sections we dive in detail into deep learning models, their optimization, and data generation.

Notice that we are explicitly separating ML from AI here. This is important: these are different but often confused technologies. ML can do fantastic things, but it is basically limited to predicting a future that looks mostly like the past. These are tools for pattern recognition. In contrast, an AI system is able to solve complex problems that have been previously reserved for humans. It does this by breaking these problems into a bunch of simple prediction tasks, each of which can be attacked by a "dumb" ML algorithm. AI *uses* instances of machine learning as components of the larger system. These ML instances need to be organized within a structure defined by domain knowledge, and they need to be fed data that helps them complete their allotted prediction tasks.

This is not to downplay the importance of ML in AI. In contrast to earlier attempts at AI, the current instance of AI is *ML-driven*. ML algorithms are implanted in every aspect of AI, and in this chapter we describe the evolution of machine learning toward status as a general-purpose technology. This evolution is the main driver behind the current rise of AI. However, ML algorithms are building blocks of AI within a larger context.

To make these ideas concrete, consider an example AI system from the Microsoft-owned company Maluuba that was designed to play (and win!) the video game *Ms. Pac-Man* on Atari.[1] Figure 10.2 illustrates the system. The player moves *Ms. Pac-Man* on this game "board," gaining rewards for eating pellets while making sure to avoid getting eaten by one of the adversarial "ghosts." The Maluuba researchers were able

---

1. Harm van Seijen, Mehdi Fatemi, Joshua Romoff, Romain Laroche, Tavian Barnes, and Jeffrey Tsang. Hybrid reward architecture for reinforcement learning. *arXiv:1706.04208*, 2017.

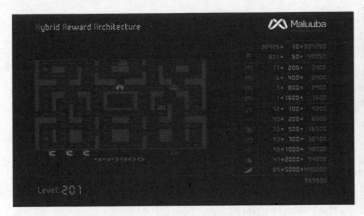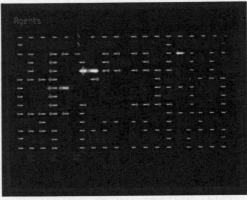

**FIGURE 10.2:** Screenshots of the Maluuba system playing *Ms. Pac-Man*. On the left, you see the game board, containing a maze for Ms. Pac-Man and the ghosts. On the right, the authors have assigned arrows showing the current direction for Ms. Pac-Man that is advised by different locations on the board, each corresponding to a distinct deep neural network. The full video is at `https://youtu.be/zQyWMHFjewU`.

to build a system that learned how to master the game, achieving the highest possible score and surpassing human performance.

A common misunderstanding of AI imagines that, in a system like Maluuba's, the player of the game *is* a deep neural network. That is, the system works by swapping out the human joy-stick operator for an artificial DNN "brain." That's not how it works. Instead of a single DNN that is tied to the *Ms. Pac-Man* avatar (which is how the human player experiences the game), the Maluuba system is broken down into 163 component ML tasks. As illustrated on the right panel of Figure 10.2, the engineers have assigned a distinct DNN routine to each cell of the board. In addition, they have DNNs that track the game characters: the ghosts and, of course, Ms. Pac-Man herself. The direction that the AI system sends Ms. Pac-Man at any point in the game is then chosen through consideration of the advice from each of these ML components. Recommendations from the components that are close to Ms. Pac-Man's current board position are weighted more strongly than those of currently remote locations. Hence, you can think of the ML algorithm assigned to each square on the board as having a simple task to solve: when Ms. Pac-Man crosses over this location, which direction should she go next?

Learning to play a video or board game is a standard way for AI firms to demonstrate their current capabilities. The Google Deep-Mind system AlphaGo,[2] which was constructed to play the fantastically complex board game Go, is the most prominent of such demonstrations. The system was able to surpass human capability, beating

2. David Silver, Aja Huang, Chris J Maddison, Arthur Guez, Laurent Sifre, George Van Den Driessche, Julian Schrittwieser, Ioannis Antonoglou, Veda Panneershelvam, Marc Lanctot, et al. Mastering the game of go with deep neural networks and tree search. *Nature*, 529:484–489, 2016.

the world champion, Lee Sedol, four matches to one at a live-broadcast event in Seoul, South Korea, in March 2016. Just as Maluuba's system broke *Ms. Pac-Man* into a number of composite tasks, AlphaGo succeeded by breaking Go into an even larger number of ML problems: "value networks" that evaluate different board positions and "policy networks" that recommend moves. The key point here is that while the composite ML tasks can be attacked with relatively generic DNNs, the full combined system is constructed in a way that is highly specialized to the structure of the problem at hand.

In Figure 10.1, the first listed pillar of AI is *domain structure*. This is the structure that allows you to break a complex problem into composite tasks that can be solved with ML. The reason that AI firms choose to work with games is that such structure is explicit: the rules of the game are codified. This exposes the massive gap between playing games and a system that could replace humans in a real-world business application. To deal with the real world, you need to have a theory as to the rules of the relevant game. For example, if you want to build a system that can communicate with customers, you might proceed by mapping out customer desires and intents in such a way that allows different dialogue-generating ML routines for each. Or, for any AI system that deals with marketing and prices in a retail environment, you need to be able to use the structure of an economic demand system to forecast how changing the price on a single item (which might, say, be the job of a single DNN) will affect optimal prices for other products and behavior of your consumers (who might themselves be modeled with DNNs).

The success or failure of an AI system is defined in a specific *context*, and you need to use the structure of that context to guide the architecture of the AI. This is a crucial point for businesses hoping to leverage AI and economists looking to predict its impact. As we will detail in this section, machine learning in its current form has become a *general-purpose technology*.[3] These tools are going to get cheaper and faster over time because of innovations in the ML itself and above and below in the AI technology stack (e.g., improved software connectors for business systems above, and improved computing hardware like GPUs below). ML has the potential to become a cloud computing commodity.[4] In contrast, the domain knowledge necessary to combine ML components into an end-to-end AI solution will not be commoditized. Those who have expertise that can break complex human business problems into ML-solvable components will succeed in building the next generation of business AI—technology that can do more than just play games.

In many of these scenarios, social science will have a role to play. Science is about putting structure and theory around phenomena that are observationally incredibly complex. Economics, as the social science closest to business, will often be relied upon to provide the rules for business AI. And since ML-driven AI relies upon measuring rewards and parameters inside its context, *econometrics* will play a key role in bridging

---

3. Timothy Bresnahan. General purpose technologies. *Handbook of the Economics of Innovation*, 2:761–791, 2010.

4. Amazon, Microsoft, and Google are all starting to offer basic ML capabilities such as transcription and image classification as part of their cloud services. The prices for these services are low and mostly matched across providers.

between the assumed system and the data signals used for feedback and learning. The work will not translate directly. You need to build systems that allow for a certain margin of error in the ML algorithms. Those economic theories that apply for only a narrow set of conditions—e.g., at a knife's edge equilibrium—will be too unstable for AI. This is why we mention relaxations and heuristics in Figure 10.1. There is an exciting future here where social scientists can contribute to AI engineering, and both AI and social science will advance as we learn what recipes do or do not work for business AI.

Beyond ML and domain structure, the third pillar of AI in Figure 10.1 is *data generation*. We're using the term *generation* here, instead of a more passive term like *collection*, to highlight that AI systems require an active strategy to keep a steady stream of new and useful information flowing into the composite learning algorithms. In most AI applications there will be two general classes of data: fixed-size data assets that can be used to train the models for generic tasks, and data that is actively generated by the system as it experiments and improves performance. For example, in learning how to play *Ms. Pac-Man*, the models could be initialized on a bank of data recording how humans have played the game. This is the fixed-size data asset. This initialized system then starts to *play* the game of *Ms. Pac-Man*. Recalling that the system is broken into a number of ML components, as more games are played, each component is able to experiment with possible moves in different scenarios. Since all of this automated, the system can iterate through a massive number of games and quickly accumulate a wealth of experience.

For business applications, you should not underestimate the advantage of having large data assets to initialize AI systems. Unlike board or video games, real-world systems need to be able to interpret a variety of extremely subtle signals. For example, any system that interacts with human dialogue must be able to understand the general domain language before it can deal with specific problems. For this reason, firms that have large banks of human interaction data (e.g., social media or a search engine) have a technological advantage in conversational AI systems. However, this data just gets you started. The context-specific learning starts happening when, after this "warm start," the system begins interacting with real-world business events.

The general framework of ML algorithms actively choosing the data that they consume is referred to as *reinforcement learning* (RL).[5] It is a hugely important aspect of ML-driven AI. In some narrow and highly structured scenarios, researchers have built "zero-shot" learning systems where the AI is able to achieve high performance after starting without any static training data. For example, in subsequent research, Google DeepMind has developed the AlphaGoZero[6] system that uses zero-shot learning replicate their earlier AlphaGo success. Noting that the RL is happening on the level of individual ML tasks, we can update our description of AI as being composed of many *RL-driven* ML components.

---

5. This is an old concept in statistics. In previous iterations, parts of reinforcement learning have been referred to as the sequential design of experiments, active learning, and Bayesian optimization.
6. David Silver, Julian Schrittwieser, Karen Simonyan, Ioannis Antonoglou, Aja Huang, Arthur Guez, Thomas Hubert, Lucas Baker, Matthew Lai, Adrian Bolton, et al. Mastering the game of go without human knowledge. *Nature*, 550:354–359, 2017.

As a complement to the work on reinforcement learning, there is a lot of research activity around AI systems that can simulate "data" to appear as though it came from a real-world source. This has the potential to accelerate system training, replicating the AI successes in video and board games where experimentation is virtually costless (just play the game, nobody loses money or gets hurt). Generative adversarial networks[7] (GANs) are schemes where one DNN is simulating data and another is attempting to discern which data is real and which is simulated. For example, in an image-tagging application, one network will generate captions for the image while the other network attempts to discern which captions are human versus machine generated. If this scheme works well enough, then you can build an image tagger while minimizing the number of dumb captions you need to show humans while training.

Finally, AI is pushing into physical spaces. For example, the Amazon Go concept promises a frictionless shopping-checkout experience where cameras and sensors determine what you've taken from the shelves and charge you accordingly. These systems are as data intensive as any other AI application, but they have the added need to translate information from a physical to a digital space. They need to be able to recognize and track both objects and individuals. Current implementations appear to rely on a combination of object-based data sources, via sensor and device networks (i.e., the Internet of Things [IoT]) and video data from surveillance cameras. The object-based sensor data has the advantage that it is well structured and tied to objects, but the video data has the flexibility to look in places and at objects that you didn't know to tag in advance. As computer vision technology advances and as the camera hardware adapts and decreases in cost, we should see a shift in emphasis toward unstructured video data. We've seen similar patterns in AI development, for example, as use of raw conversation logs increases with improved machine reading capability. This is the progress of ML-driven AI toward general-purpose forms.

## General-Purpose Machine Learning

The piece of AI that gets the most publicity—so much so that it is often confused with all of AI—is *general-purpose* machine learning. Regardless of this slight overemphasis, it is clear that the recent rise of deep neural networks (DNNs; see the "Deep Learning" section) is a main driver behind growth in AI. These DNNs have the ability to learn patterns in speech, image, and video data (as well as in more traditional structured data) faster, and more automatically, than ever before. They provide new ML capabilities and have completely changed the workflow of an ML engineer. However, this technology should be understood as a rapid evolution of existing ML capabilities rather than as a completely new object.

---

7. Ian Goodfellow, Jean Pouget-Abadie, Mehdi Mirza, Bing Xu, David Warde-Farley, Sherjil Ozair, Aaron Courville, and Yoshua Bengio. Generative adversarial nets. In *Advances in Neural Information Processing Systems*, pages 2672–2680, 2014.

As discussed in the introduction and throughout this book, machine learning is the field that thinks about how to *automatically* build robust predictions from complex data. ML is single-mindedly focused on the goal of maximizing predictive performance on new unseen data. This clear focus, and the ability to *test* performance through validation on left-out data, has allowed ML to quickly push new levels of performance, speed, and automation. The specific ML techniques used include lasso regularized regression, tree algorithms and ensembles of trees (e.g., random forests), and neural networks. These techniques have found application in business problems, under such labels as "data mining" and, more recently, "predictive analytics." Driven by the fact that many policy and business questions require more than just prediction, practitioners have added an emphasis on inference and incorporated ideas from statistics. Their work, combined with the demands and abundance of big data, coalesced together to form the loosely defined field of data science—the topic of this book.

The push of ML into the general area of business analytics has allowed companies to gain insight from high–dimensional and unstructured data. This is only possible because the ML tools and recipes have become robust and usable enough that they can be deployed by nonexperts in computer science or statistics. That is, they can be used by people with a variety of quantitative backgrounds who have domain knowledge for their business use case. Similarly, the tools can be used by economists and other social scientists to bring new data to bear on scientifically compelling research questions. The general usability of these tools has driven their adoption across disciplines. They come packaged as quality software and include validation routines that allow the user to observe how well their fitted models will perform in future prediction tasks.

The latest generation of ML algorithms, especially the deep learning technology that has exploded since around 2012,[8] has increased the level of *automation* in the process of fitting and applying prediction models. This new class of ML is the *general-purpose ML* (GPML) that we reference in the rightmost pillar of Figure 10.1. The first component of GPML is deep neural networks: models made up of *layers* of nonlinear transformation *node* functions, where the output of each layer becomes input to the next layer in the network. We will describe DNNs in more detail below, but for now it suffices to say that they make it faster and easier than ever before to find patterns in unstructured data. They are also highly modular. You can take a layer that is optimized for one type of data (e.g., images) and combine it with other layers for other types of data (e.g., text). You can also use layers that have been pretrained on one dataset (e.g., generic images) as components in a more specialized model (e.g., a specific recognition task).

Specialized DNN architectures are responsible for the key GPML capability of working on human-level data: video, audio, and text. This is essential for AI because it allows these systems to be installed on top of the same sources of knowledge that humans are able to digest. You don't need to create a new database system (or have an

8. Alex Krizhevsky, Ilya Sutskever, and Geoffrey E. Hinton. Imagenet classification with deep convolutional neural networks. In *Advances in Neural Information Processing Systems*, pages 1097–1105, 2012.

existing standard form) to feed the AI; rather, the AI can live on top of the chaos of information generated through business functions. This capability helps to illustrate why the new AI, based on GPML, is so much more promising than previous attempts at AI. Classical AI relied on hand-specified logic rules to mimic how a rational human might approach a given problem.[9] This approach is sometimes nostalgically referred to as GOFAI, or "good old-fashioned AI." The problem with GOFAI is obvious: solving human problems with logic rules requires an impossibly complex cataloging of all possible scenarios and actions. The system designer must to know in advance how to translate complex human tasks into deterministic algorithms.

The new AI doesn't have this limitation. For example, consider the problem of creating a virtual agent that can answer customer questions (e.g., "Why won't my computer start?"). A GOFAI system would be based on hand-coded dialog trees: if a user says X, answer Y, and so on. To install the system, you'd need to have human engineers understand and explicitly code for all of the main customer issues. In contrast, the new ML-driven AI can simply ingest all of the existing customer-support logs and learn to replicate how human agents have answered customer questions in the past. The ML allows the system to infer support patterns from human conversations. The installation engineer just needs to start the DNN fitting routine.

This gets to the last bit of GPML highlighted in Figure 10.1, the tools that facilitate model fitting on massive datasets: out-of-sample (*OOS*) validation for model tuning, stochastic gradient descent (*SGD*) for parameter optimization, and graphical processing units (*GPUs*) and other computer hardware for massively parallel optimization. Each of these pieces is essential for the success of large-scale GPML. Although they are commonly associated with deep learning and DNNs (especially SGD and GPUs), these tools have developed in the context of many different ML algorithms. The rise of DNNs over alternative ML modeling schemes is partly because, through trial and error, ML researchers have discovered that neural network models are especially well suited to engineering within the context of these available tools.[10]

As we've covered throughout this book, OOS validation is a basic idea: you choose the best model specification by comparing predictions from models estimated on data that was not used during the model "training" (fitting). This can be formalized as a crossvalidation routine: you split the data into K "folds" and then K times fit the model on all data but the Kth fold and evaluate its predictive performance (e.g., mean squared error or misclassification rate) on the left-out fold. The model with optimal average OOS performance (e.g., minimum error rate) is then deployed in practice.

ML's wholesale adoption of OOS validation as the arbitrator of model quality has freed the ML engineer from the need to *theorize* about model quality. Of course, this can create frustration and delays when you have nothing other than "guess-and-test" as a method for model selection. But, increasingly, the requisite model search is not being

9. John Haugeland. *Artificial Intelligence: The Very Idea*. MIT Press, 1985.

10. Yann LeCun, Léon Bottou, Yoshua Bengio, and Patrick Haffner. Gradientbased learning applied to document recognition. *Proceedings of the IEEE*, 86: 2278–2324, 1998.

executed by humans: it is done by additional ML routines. This happens either explic-itly, in *AutoML*[11] frameworks that use simple auxiliary ML to predict OOS performance of the more complex target model, or implicitly by adding flexibility to the target model (e.g., making the tuning parameters part of the optimization objective). The fact that OOS validation provides a clear target to optimize against—a target that, unlike the in-sample likelihood, does not incentive overfit—facilitates automated model tuning. It removes humans from the process of adapting models to specific datasets.

SGD optimization will be less familiar to most readers, but it is a crucial part of GPML. This class of algorithms allows models to be fit to data that is observed in only small chunks: you can train the model on a *stream* of data and avoid having to do *batch* computations on the entire dataset. This lets you estimate complex models on massive datasets. For subtle reasons, the engineering of SGD algo-rithms also tends to encourage robust and generalizable model fits (i.e., use of SGD discourages overfit).

Finally, the GPUs: specialized computer processors have made massive-scale ML a reality, and continued hardware innovation will help push AI to new domains. Deep neural network training with stochastic gradient descent involves massively *parallel* computations: many basic operations executed simultaneously across parameters of the network. Graphical processing units were devised for calculations of this type, in the context of video and computer graphics display where all pixels of an image need to be rendered simultaneously, in parallel. Although DNN training was originally a side use case for GPUs (i.e., as an aside from their main computer graphics mandate), AI applications are now of primary importance for GPU man-ufacturers. Nvidia, for example, is a GPU company whose rise in market value has been driven by the rise of AI.

The technology here is not standing still. GPUs are getting faster and cheaper every day. We are also seeing the deployment of new chips that have been designed from scratch for ML optimization. For example, field-programmable gate arrays (FPGAs) are being used by Microsoft and Amazon in their data centers. These chips allow precision requirements to be set dynamically, thus efficiently allocating resources to high-precision operations and saving compute effort when you need only a few decimal points (e.g., in early optimization updates to the DNN parameters). As another example, Google's tensor processing units (TPUs) are specifically designed for algebra with "tensors," a mathematical object that occurs commonly in ML.[12]

One of the hallmarks of a general-purpose technology is that it leads to broad industrial changes, both above and below where that technology lives in the supply chain. This is what we are observing with the new general-purpose ML. Below, we can see that chip makers are changing the type of hardware they create to suit these

11. Matthias Feurer, Aaron Klein, Katharina Eggensperger, Jost Springenberg, Manuel Blum, and Frank Hutter. Efficient and robust automated machine learning. In *Advances in Neural Information Processing Systems*, pages 2962–2970, 2015.
12. A tensor is a multidimensional extension of a matrix—that is, a matrix is another name for a two-dimensional tensor.

DNN-based AI systems. Above, GPML has led to a new class of ML-driven AI products. As we seek more real-world AI capabilities—self-driving cars, conversational business agents, intelligent economic marketplaces—domain experts in these areas will need to find ways to resolve their complex questions into structures of ML tasks. This is a role that economists and business professionals should embrace, where the increasingly user-friendly GPML routines become basic tools of their trade.

## Deep Learning

We've stated that deep neural networks are a key tool in GPML, but what exactly are they? And what makes them *deep*? In this section, we will give a high-level overview of these models. This is not a user guide. For that, you might want to look to the excellent recent textbook[13] by Goodfellow, Bengio, and Courville. This is a rapidly evolving area of research, and new types of neural network models and estimation algorithms are being developed at a steady clip. The excitement in this area, and considerable media and business hype, makes it difficult to keep up to date. Moreover, the tendency of ML companies and academics to proclaim every incremental change as "completely brand new" has led to messy literature that is tough for newcomers to navigate. But there is a general structure to deep learning, and a hype-free understanding of this structure should give you insight into the reasons for its success.

Neural networks are simple models. Indeed, their simplicity is a strength because basic patterns facilitate fast training and computation. The model has linear combinations of inputs that are passed through nonlinear activation functions called *nodes* (or, in reference to the human brain, neurons). A set of nodes taking different weighted sums of the same inputs is called a *layer*, and the output of one layer's nodes becomes input to the next layer. This structure is illustrated in Figure 10.3. Each circle here is a node. Those in the input (furthest left) layer typically have a special structure; they are either raw data or data that has been processed through an additional set of layers (e.g., convolutions as we'll describe in a moment). The output layer gives the predictions. In a simple regression setting, this output could just be $\hat{y}$, the predicted value for some random variable $y$, but DNNs can be used to predict all sorts of high-dimensional objects. As it is for nodes in input layers, output nodes also tend to take application-specific forms.

Nodes in the interior of the network have a "classical" neural network structure. Suppose that $\eta_{hk}(\cdot)$ is the $k$th node in interior layer $h$. This node takes as input a weighted combination of the output of the nodes in the previous layer of the network, layer $h - 1$, and applies a *nonlinear* transformation to yield the output. For example, the ReLU (for "rectified linear unit") node is by far the most common functional form used today; it simply outputs the maximum of its input and zero, as shown in

---

13. Ian Goodfellow, Yoshua Bengio, and Aaron Courville. *Deep Learning*. MIT Press, 2016.

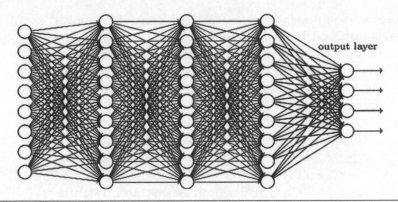

**FIGURE 10.3:** A five-layer network, adapted from Nielsen [2015].

Figure 10.4.[14] Suppose $z_{ij}^{h-1}$ is the output of node $j$ in layer $h - 1$ for observation $i$. Then the corresponding output for the $k$th node in the $h$th layer can be written as

$$z_{ik}^h = \eta_{hk}\left(\omega'_h z_i^{h-1}\right) = \max\left(0, \sum_j \omega_{hj} z_{ij}^{h-1}\right). \tag{10.1}$$

Here, $\omega_{hj}$ are the network *weights*. For a given network architecture—the structure of nodes and layers—these weights are the parameters that are updated during network training.

Neural networks have a long history. Work on these types of models dates back to the mid-twentieth century, e.g., including Rosenblatt's perceptron.[15] This early work was focused on networks as models that could mimic the actual structure of the human brain. In the late 1980s, advances in algorithms for *training* neural networks[16] opened the potential for these models to act as general pattern recognition tools rather than as a toy model of the brain. This led to a boom in neural network research, and methods developed during the 1990s are at the foundation of much of deep learning today.[17] However, this boom ended in bust. Because of the gap between promised and realized results (and enduring difficulties in training networks on massive datasets) from the late 1990s, neural networks became just one ML method among many. In applications, they were supplanted by more robust

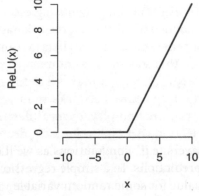

**FIGURE 10.4:** The ReLU function.

14. In the 1990s, people spent much effort choosing among different node transformation functions. More recently, the consensus is that you can just use a simple and computationally convenient transformation (like ReLU). If you have enough nodes and layers, the specific transformation doesn't really matter, so long as it is nonlinear.

15. Frank Rosenblatt. The perceptron: A probabilistic model for information storage and organization in the brain. *Psychological review*, 65:386, 1958.

16. David E. Rumelhart, Geoffrey E. Hinton, Ronald J. Williams, et al. Learning representations by back-propagating errors. *Cognitive Modeling*, 5(3):1, 1988.

17. Sepp Hochreiter and Jürgen Schmidhuber. Long short-term memory. *Neural Computation*, 9(8):1735–1780, 1997; and Yann LeCun, Léon Bottou, Yoshua Bengio, and Patrick Haffner. Gradient-based learning applied to document recognition. *Proceedings of the IEEE*, 86: 2278–2324, 1998.

tools such as random forests, high-dimensional regularized regression, and a variety of Bayesian stochastic process models.

In the 1990s, one tended to add network complexity by adding *width*. A couple of layers (e.g., a single hidden layer was common) with a large number of nodes in each layer were used to approximate complex functions. Researchers had established that such "wide" learning could approximate arbitrary functions[18] if you were able to train on enough data. The problem, however, was that this turns out to be an inefficient way to learn from data. The wide networks are *flexible*, but they need a ton of data to tame this flexibility. In this way, the wide nets resemble traditional *nonparametric* statistical models like series estimators. Indeed, near the end of the 1990s, Radford Neal showed that certain neural networks converge toward Gaussian processes, a classical statistical regression model, as the number of nodes in a single layer grows toward infinity.[19] It seemed reasonable to conclude that neural networks were just clunky versions of more transparent statistical models.

What changed? A bunch of things. Two nonmethodological events are of primary importance: we got much more data (big data) and computing hardware became much more efficient (GPUs). But there was also a crucial methodological development: networks went *deep*. This breakthrough is often credited to 2006 work by Geoff Hinton and coauthors[20] on a network architecture that stacked many *pretrained* layers together for a handwriting recognition task. In this pretraining, interior layers of the network are fit using an *unsupervised* learning task (i.e., dimension reduction of the inputs) before being used as part of the supervised learning machinery. The idea is analogous to that of principal components regression: you first fit a low-dimensional representation of $x$ and then use that low-dimensional representation to predict some associated $y$. Hinton's scheme allowed researchers to train deeper networks than was previously possible.

This specific type of unsupervised pretraining is no longer viewed as central to deep learning. However, Hinton's paper opened many people's eyes to the potential for deep neural networks: models with many layers, each of which may have different structure and play a very different role in the overall machinery. That is, a demonstration that one *could* train deep networks soon turned into a realization that one *should* add depth to models. In the following years, research groups began to show empirically and theoretically that depth was important for learning efficiently from data.[21] The *modularity* of a deep network is key: each layer of functional structure plays a specific role, and you can swap out layers like Lego blocks when moving across data applications. This allows for fast application-specific model development and also for *transfer learning* across models. An internal layer from a network that has been trained for one type of image recognition problem can be used to hot-start a new network for a different computer vision task.

18. Kurt Hornik, Maxwell Stinchcombe, and Halbert White. Multilayer feedforward networks are universal approximators. *Neural Networks*, 2:359–366, 1989.

19. Radford M. Neal. *Bayesian Learning for Neural Networks*, volume 118. Springer Science & Business Media, 2012.

20. Geoffrey E. Hinton, Simon Osindero, and Yee-Whye Teh. A fast learning algorithm for deep belief nets. *Neural Computation*, 18(7):1527–1554, 2006.

21. Yoshua Bengio, Yann LeCun, et al. Scaling learning algorithms towards AI. *Large-Scale Kernel Machines*, 34(5):1–41, 2007.

Deep learning came into the ML mainstream with a 2012 paper by Krizhevsky, Sutskever, and Hinton[22] that showed their DNN was able to smash current performance benchmarks in the well-known ImageNet computer vision contest. Since then, the race has been on. For example, image classification performance has surpassed human abilities[23], and DNNs are now able to both recognize images and generate appropriate captions.[24]

The models behind these computer vision advances all make use of a specific type of *convolution* transformation. The raw image data (pixels) goes through multiple convolution layers before the output of those convolutions is fed into the more classical neural network architecture of Equation 10.1 and Figure 10.3. Figure 10.5 shows a basic image convolution operation: a *kernel* of weights is used to combine image pixels in a local area into a single output pixel in a (usually) lower- dimensional output image. So-called convolutional neural networks[25] (CNNs) illustrate the strategy that makes deep learning so successful: it is convenient to stack layers of different specializations, such that image-specific functions (convolutions) can feed into layers that are good at representing generic functional forms. In a contemporary CNN, typically you will have multiple layers of convolutions feeding into ReLU activations and, eventually, into a *max pooling* layer constructed of nodes that output the maximum of each input matrix.[26] For example, Figure 10.6 shows the simple architecture used in Hartford et al. [2017] for a task that mixed digit recognition with (simulated) business data.

$$
\begin{array}{|c|c|c|}
\hline
A & B & C \\
\hline
D & E & F \\
\hline
G & H & I \\
\hline
\end{array}
\;\star\;
\begin{array}{|c|c|}
\hline
\omega_1 & \omega_2 \\
\hline
\omega_3 & \omega_4 \\
\hline
\end{array}
\;=\;
\begin{array}{|c|c|}
\hline
\omega_1 A + \omega_2 B + \omega_3 D + \omega_4 E & \omega_1 B + \omega_2 C + \omega_3 E + \omega_4 F \\
\hline
\omega_1 D + \omega_2 E + \omega_3 G + \omega_4 H & \omega_1 E + \omega_2 F + \omega_3 H + \omega_4 I \\
\hline
\end{array}
$$

**FIGURE 10.5:** A basic convolution operation. The pixels $A$, $B$, etc., are multiplied and summed across kernel weights $\omega_k$. The kernel here is applied to every $2 \times 2$ submatrix of the "image."

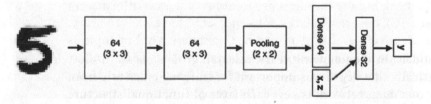

**FIGURE 10.6:** The simple architecture used in Hartford et al. [2017]. Variables $x, z$ contain structured business information (e.g., product IDs and prices) that is mixed with images of handwritten digits in the network.

22. Alex Krizhevsky, Ilya Sutskever, and Geoffrey E. Hinton. Imagenet classification with deep convolutional neural networks. In *Advances in Neural Information Processing Systems*, pages 1097–1105, 2012.
23. Kaiming He, Xiangyu Zhang, Shaoqing Ren, and Jian Sun. Deep residual learning for image recognition. In *Proceedings of the IEEE Conference on Computer Vision and Pattern Recognition*, pages 770–778, 2016.
24. Andrej Karpathy and Li Fei-Fei. Deep visual-semantic alignments for generating image descriptions. In *Proceedings of the IEEE Conference on Computer Vision and Pattern Recognition*, pages 3128–3137, 2015.
25. Yann LeCun, Yoshua Bengio, et al. Convolutional networks for images, speech, and time series. *The Handbook of Brain Theory and Neural Networks*, 3361: 1995.
26. CNNs are a huge and interesting area. The textbook by Goodfellow et al. [2016] is a good place to learn more.

This is a theme of deep learning: the models use early-layer transformations that are specific to the input data format. For images, you use CNNs. For text data, you need to *embed* words into a vector space. This can happen through a simple word2vec transformation,[27] as we discussed in Chapter 8, or through a long short-term memory (LSTM) architecture[28]—models for sequences of words or letters that essentially mix a hidden Markov model (long) with an autoregressive process (short). And there are many other variants, with new architectures being developed every day.[29]

One thing should be clear: there is a lot of *structure* in DNNs. These models are *not* similar to the sorts of nonparametric regression models used by statisticians, econometricians, and in earlier ML. They are *semi-parametric*. Consider the cartoon DNN in Figure 10.7. The early stages in the network provide dramatic, and often linear, dimension reduction. These early stages are highly parametric: it makes no sense to take a convolution model for image data and apply it to, say, consumer transaction data. The output of these early layers is then processed through a series of classical neural network nodes, as in Equation 10.1. These later network layers work like a traditional nonparametric regression: they expand the output of early layers to approximate arbitrary functional forms in the response of interest. Thus, the DNNs combine restrictive dimension reduction with flexible function approximation. The key is that both components are learned jointly.

**FIGURE 10.7:** A cartoon of a DNN, taking as input images, structured data $x_1 \ldots x_{big}$, and raw document text.

We've covered only a tiny part of the area of deep learning. There is a ton of exciting new material coming out of both industry and academia. For a glimpse of what is happening in the field, browse the latest proceedings of neural information processing systems (NeurIPS), the premier ML conference, at `https://NeurIPS.cc`. You'll see quickly the massive breadth of research. One currently hot topic is on uncertainty quantification for deep neural networks. Another is on understanding how imbalance in training data leads to potentially biased predictions. Topics of this type are gaining prominence as DNNs are moving away from academic competitions and into real-world applications. As the field grows and DNN model construction moves from a scientific to an engineering discipline, we'll see more need for this type of research that tells us when and how much we can trust the DNNs.

27. Tomas Mikolov, Ilya Sutskever, Kai Chen, Greg S. Corrado, and Jeff Dean. Distributed representations of words and phrases and their compositionality. In *Advances in Neural Information Processing Systems*, pages 3111–3119, 2013.
28. Sepp Hochreiter and Jürgen Schmidhuber. Long short-term memory. *Neural Computation*, 9(8):1735–1780, 1997.
29. For example, the new *Capsule* networks of Sabour et al. [2017] replace the max-pooling of CNNs with more structured summarization functions.

Stochastic Gradient Descent

To give a complete view of deep learning, we need to describe the one algorithm that is relied upon for training all of the models: stochastic gradient descent. SGD optimization is a twist on gradient descent (GD), the previously dominant method for minimizing any function that you can differentiate. Given a minimization objective $\mathcal{L}(\Omega)$, where $\Omega$ is the full set of model parameters, each iteration of a gradient descent routine updates from current parameters $\Omega_t$ as follows:

$$\Omega_{t+1} = \Omega_t - C_t \nabla \mathcal{L} \big|_{\Omega_t}. \tag{10.2}$$

Here, $\nabla \mathcal{L} \big|_{\Omega t}$ is the gradient of $\mathcal{L}$ evaluated at the current parameters, and $C_t$ is a projection matrix that determines the size of the steps taken in the direction implied by $\nabla \mathcal{L}$.[30] We have the subscript $t$ on $C_t$ because this projection can be allowed to update during the optimization. For example, Newton's algorithm uses $C_t$ equal to the matrix of objective second derivatives, $\nabla^2 \mathcal{L} \big|_{\Omega_t}$.

It is often stated that neural networks are trained through "backpropagation," which is not quite correct. Rather, they are trained through variants of gradient descent. Back-propagation,[31] or *backprop* for short, is a method for calculating gradients on the parameters of a network. In particular, backprop is just an algorithmic implementation of the chain rule from calculus. In the context of the simple neuron from Equation 10.1, the gradient calculation for a single weight $\omega_{hj}$ is

$$\frac{\partial \mathcal{L}}{\partial \omega_{hj}} = \sum_{i=1}^{n} \frac{\partial \mathcal{L}}{\partial z_{ij}^{h}} \frac{\partial z_{ij}^{h}}{\partial \omega_{hj}} = \sum_{i=1}^{n} \frac{\partial \mathcal{L}}{\partial z_{ij}^{h}} z_{ij}^{h-1} \mathbb{1}_{\left[ 0 < \Sigma_j \omega_{hj} z_{ij}^{h-1} \right]}. \tag{10.3}$$

Another application of the chain rule can be used to expand $\partial \mathcal{L} / \partial z_{ij}^{h}$ as $\partial \mathcal{L} / \partial z_{ij}^{h+1} \times \partial z_{ij}^{h+1} / \partial z_{ij}^{h}$, and so on, until you have written the full gradient as a product of layer-specific operations. The directed structure of the network lets you efficiently calculate all of the gradients by working backward layer by layer, from the response down to the inputs. This recursive application of the chain rule and the associated computation recipes make up the general backprop algorithm.

In statistical estimation and ML model-training, $\mathcal{L}$ typically involves a loss function that *sums* across data observations. For example, assuming an $\ell_2$ (ridge) regularization penalty on the parameters, the *minimization* objective corresponding to regularized likelihood maximization over $n$ independent observations $z_i$ (e.g., $z_i = [x_i, y_i]$ for regression) can be written as

$$\mathcal{L}(\Omega) \equiv \mathcal{L}(\Omega; \{d_i\}_{i=1}^{n}) = \sum_{i=1}^{n} \left[ -\log \mathrm{p}(z_i \mid \Omega) + \lambda \| \Omega \|_2^2 \right]. \tag{10.4}$$

30. If $\Omega = [\omega_1 \cdots \omega_p]$, then $\nabla \mathcal{L}(\Omega) = [\partial \mathcal{L} / \partial \omega_1 \cdots \partial \mathcal{L} / \partial \omega_p]$. The *Hessian* matrix, $\nabla^2 \mathcal{L}$, has elements $[\nabla^2 \mathcal{L}]_{jk} = \partial \mathcal{L}^2 / \partial \omega_j \partial \omega_k$.
31. David E. Rumelhart, Geoffrey E. Hinton, Ronald J. Williams, et al. Learning representations by back-propagating errors. *Cognitive Modeling*, 5(3):1, 1988.

Here, $\| \Omega \|_2^2$ is the sum of all squared parameters in $\Omega$. More generally, $\mathcal{L}(\Omega; \{z_i\}_{i=1}^n)$ can consist of any loss function that involves summation over observations. For example, to model predictive uncertainty, we often work with quantile loss. Define $\tau_q(x; \Omega)$ as the *quantile function*, parametrized by $\Omega$, that maps from covariates $x$ to the $q$th quantile of the response $y$:

$$p\big(y < \tau_q(x; \Omega) \mid x\big) = q. \tag{10.5}$$

You fit $\tau_q$ to minimize the regularized quantile loss function (again assuming a ridge penalty):

$$\mathcal{L}(\Omega; \{d_i\}_{i=1}^n) = \sum_{i=1}^n \Big[\big(y_i - \tau_q(x_i; \Omega)\big)\big(q - \mathbb{1}_{[y_i < \tau_q(x_i; \Omega)]}\big) + \lambda \| \Omega \|_2^2\Big]. \tag{10.6}$$

The common "sum of squared errors" criterion, possibly regularized, is another loss function that fits this pattern of summation over observations.

In all of these cases, the gradient calculations required for the updates in Equation 10.2 involve sums over all $n$ observations. That is, each calculation of $\nabla \mathcal{L}$ requires an order of $n$ calculations. For example, in a ridge-penalized linear regression where $\Omega = \beta$, a vector of regression coefficients, the $j$th gradient component is

$$\frac{\partial \mathcal{L}}{\partial \beta_j} = \sum_{i=1}^n \Big[(y_i - x_i'\beta)x_j + \lambda \beta_j\Big]. \tag{10.7}$$

The problem for massive datasets is that when $n$ is really big, these calculations become prohibitively expensive. The issue is aggravated when, as it is for DNNs, $\Omega$ is high dimensional and there are complex calculations required in each gradient summand. GD is the best optimization tool that we have, but it becomes computationally infeasible for massive datasets.

The solution is to replace the actual gradients in Equation 10.2 with *estimates* of those gradients based upon a subset of the data. This is the SGD algorithm. It has a long history, dating back to the Robbins-Munro[32] algorithm proposed by a couple of statisticians in 1951. In the most common versions of SGD, the full-sample gradient is simply replaced by the gradient on a smaller subsample. Instead of calculating gradients on the full-sample loss, $\mathcal{L}(\Omega; \{d_i\}_{i=1}^n)$, we descend according to subsample calculations,

$$\Omega_{t+1} = \Omega_t - C_t \nabla \mathcal{L}(\Omega; \{d_{i_b}\}_{b=1}^B)\big|_{\Omega_t}. \tag{10.8}$$

---

32. Herbert Robbins and Sutton Monro. A stochastic approximation method. *The Annals of Mathematical Statistics*, pages 400–407, 1951.

Here, $\{d_{i_b}\}_{b=1}^{B}$ is a *mini-batch* of observations with $B \ll n$. The key mathematical result behind SGD is that, so long as the sequence of $C_t$ matrices satisfy some basic requirements, the SGD algorithm will converge to a local optimum whenever $\nabla\mathcal{L}(\Omega; \{d_{i_b}\}_{b=1}^{B})$ is an *unbiased* estimate of the full sample gradient.[33] That is, SGD convergence relies upon the following:

$$\mathbb{E}\left[ \frac{1}{B} \nabla\mathcal{L}(\Omega; \{d_{i_b}\}_{b=1}^{B}) \right] = \mathbb{E}\left[ \frac{1}{n} \nabla\mathcal{L}(\Omega; \{d_i\}_{i=1}^{n}) \right] = \mathbb{E}\,\nabla\mathcal{L}(\Omega; d). \tag{10.9}$$

Here, the last term refers to the *population* expected gradient—that is, the average gradient for observation $d$ drawn from the true data-generating process.

To understand why SGD is so preferable to GD for machine learning, it helps to discuss how computer scientists think about the *constraints* on estimation. Statisticians and economists tend to view sample size (i.e., lack of data) as the binding constraint on their estimators. In contrast, in many ML applications the data is practically unlimited and continues to grow during system deployment. Despite this abundance, there is a fixed computational budget (or the need to update in near-real-time for streaming data), such that you can execute only a limited number of operations when crunching through the data. Thus, in ML, the binding constraint is the amount of computation rather than the amount of data.

SGD trades faster updates for a slower per-update convergence rate. As explained in a 2008 paper by Bousquet and Boutteau,[34] this trade is worthwhile when the faster updates allows you to expose your model to more data than would otherwise be possible. To see this, note that the mini-batch gradient $B^{-1}\nabla\mathcal{L}(\Omega; \{d_{i_b}\}_{b=1}^{B})$ has a much higher variance than the full-sample gradient, $n^{-1}\nabla\mathcal{L}(\Omega; \{d_i\}_{i=1}^{n})$. This variance introduces noise into the optimization updates. As a result, for a fixed data sample $n$, the GD algorithm will tend to take far fewer iterations than SGD to get to a minimum of the *in-sample* loss, $\mathcal{L}(\Omega; \{d_i\}_{i=1}^{n})$. However, in DNN training you don't really care about the in-sample loss. You want to minimize future prediction loss—that is, you want to minimize the *population* loss function $\mathbb{E}\,\mathcal{L}(\Omega; d)$. And the best way to understand the population loss is to see as much data as possible. Thus, if the variance of the SGD updates is not too large, it is more valuable to spend computational effort streaming through extra data than to spend it on minimizing the variance of each individual optimization update.

This is related to an important high-level point about SGD: the nature of the algorithm is such that engineering steps taken to improve *optimization* performance will tend to also improve *estimation* performance. The same tweaks and tricks that lower

---

33. You can actually get away with biased gradients. In Hartford et al. [2017], we find that trading bias for variance can actually improve performance. But this is tricky business, and in any case the bias must be kept very small.
34. Olivier Bousquet and Léon Bottou. The tradeoffs of large scale learning. In *Advances in Neural Information Processing Systems*, pages 161–168, 2008.

the variance of each SGD update will lead to fitted models that generalize better when predicting new unseen data. The "train faster, generalize better" paper by Hardt, Recht, and Singer[35] explains this phenomenon within the framework of algorithm stability. For SGD to converge in fewer iterations means that the gradients on new observations (new mini-batches) are approaching zero more quickly. That is, faster SGD convergence means by definition that the model fits are generalizing better to unseen data. Contrast this with full-sample GD, for example, for likelihood maximization: faster convergence implies only quicker fitting on the current sample, potentially overfitting for future data. A reliance on SGD has made it relatively easy for deep learning to progress from a scientific to engineering discipline. Faster is better, so the engineers tuning SGD algorithms for DNNs can just focus on convergence speed.

On the topic of tuning SGD, real-world performance is sensitive to the choice of $C_t$, the projection matrix in Equation 10.8. For computational reasons, this matrix is usually diagonal (i.e., it has zeros off of the diagonal) such that entries of $C_t$ dictate the *step-size* in the direction of each parameter gradient. SGD algorithms have often been studied theoretically under a single step-size, such that $C_t = \delta_t I$ where $\delta_t$ is a scalar and $I$ is the identity matrix. Unfortunately, this simple specification will under-perform and even fail to converge if $\delta_t$ is not going toward zero at a precise rate.[36] Instead, practitioners make use of algorithms where $C_t = [\delta_{1t} \ldots \delta_{pt}] I$, with $p$ the dimension of $\Omega$, and each $\delta_{jt}$ is chosen to approximate $\partial^2 \mathcal{L} / \partial \omega_j^2$, the corresponding diagonal element of the Hessian matrix of loss-function second derivatives (i.e., what would be used in a Newton's algorithm). The ADAGRAD paper[37] provides a theoretical foundation for this approach and suggests an algorithm for specifying $\delta_{jt}$. Most deep learning systems make use of ADAGRAD-inspired algorithms, such as ADAM[38], that combine the original algorithm with heuristics that have been shown empirically to improve performance.

Finally, there is another key trick to DNN training: *dropout*. This procedure, proposed by researchers[39] in Hinton's lab at the University of Toronto, involves introduction of random noise into each gradient calculation. For example, Bernoulli dropout replaces current estimates $\omega_{tj}$ with $\tilde{\omega}_{tj} = \omega_{tj} \xi_{tj}$ where $\xi_{tj}$ is a Bernoulli random variable with $p(\xi_{tj} = 1) = c$. Each SGD update from Equation 10.8 then uses these parameter values when evaluating the gradient:

$$\Omega_{t+1} = \Omega_t - C_t \nabla f \left( \Omega; \{d_{ib}\}_{b=1}^{B} \right)\big|_{\tilde{\Omega}_t}. \tag{10.10}$$

Here, $\tilde{\Omega}_t$ is the noised-up version of $\Omega_t$, with elements $\tilde{\omega}_{tj}$.

35. Moritz Hardt, Ben Recht, and Yoram Singer. Train faster, generalize better: Stability of stochastic gradient descent. In *International Conference on Machine Learning*, pages 1225–1234, 2016.
36. Panagiotis Toulis, Edoardo Airoldi, and Jason Rennie. Statistical analysis of stochastic gradient methods for generalized linear models. In *International Conference on Machine Learning*, pages 667–675, 2014.
37. John Duchi, Elad Hazan, and Yoram Singer. Adaptive subgradient methods for online learning and stochastic optimization. *Journal of Machine Learning Research*, 12:2121–2159, 2011.
38. Diederik Kingma and Jimmy Ba. Adam: A method for stochastic optimization. In *3rd International Conference on Learning Representations (ICLR)*, 2015.
39. Nitish Srivastava, Geoffrey E. Hinton, Alex Krizhevsky, Ilya Sutskever, and Ruslan Salakhutdinov. Dropout: A simple way to prevent neural networks from overfitting. *Journal of Machine Learning Research*, 15(1):1929–1958, 2014.

Dropout is used because it has been observed to yield model fits that have lower out-of-sample error rates (so long as you tune $c$ appropriately). Why does this happen? Informally, dropout acts as a type of implicit regularization. An example of explicit regularization is parameter penalization: to avoid overfit, the minimization objective for DNNs almost always has a $\lambda \|\Omega\|_2^2$ ridge penalty term added to the data-likelihood loss function. Dropout plays a similar role. By forcing SGD updates to ignore a random sample of the parameters, it prevents overfit on any individual parameter.[40] More rigorously, it has recently been established[41] that SGD with dropout corresponds to a type of "variational Bayesian inference." That means that dropout SGD is solving to find the posterior *distribution* over $\Omega$ rather than a point estimate.[42] As interest grows around uncertainty quantification for DNNs, this interpretation of dropout is one option for bringing Bayesian inference into deep learning.

## Reinforcement Learning

As the final section on the elements of deep learning, let's consider how these AI systems generate their own training data through a mix of experimentation and optimization. Reinforcement learning (RL) is the common term for this aspect of AI. RL is sometimes used to denote specific algorithms, but we are using it to refer to the full area of active data collection.

The general problem can be formulated as a reward maximization task. You have some policy or "action" function, $d(x_t; \Omega)$, that dictates how the system responds to "event" $t$ with characteristics $x_t$. The event could be a customer arriving on your website at a specific time, a scenario in a video game, and so on. After the event, you observe "response" $y_t$, and the reward is calculated as $r(d(x_t; \Omega), y_t)$. During this process you are accumulating data and *learning* the parameters $\Omega$, so you can write $\Omega_t$ as the parameters used at event $t$. The goal is that this learning converges to some optimal reward-maximizing parametrization, say $\Omega^*$, and that this happens after some $T$ events where $T$ is not too big—i.e., so that you minimize *regret*:

$$\sum_{t=1}^{T} \left[ r(d(x_t; \Omega^*), y_t) - r(d(x_t; \Omega_t), y_t) \right]. \tag{10.11}$$

---

40. This seems to contradict the earlier discussion about minimizing the variance of gradient estimates. The distinction is that we want to minimize variance because of noise in the data, but here we are introducing noise in the parameters *independent* of the data.

41. Alex Kendall and Yarin Gal. What uncertainties do we need in Bayesian deep learning for computer vision? *arXiv:1703.04977*, 2017.

42. It is a strange variational distribution, but basically the posterior distribution over $\Omega$ becomes that implied by $W$, with elements $\omega_j$ multiplied by random Bernoulli noise.

This is a general formulation. We can map it to some familiar scenarios. For example, suppose that the event $t$ is a user landing on your website. You would like to show a banner advertisement on the landing page, and you want to show the ad that has the highest probability of getting clicked by the user. Suppose that there are $J$ different possible ads you can show, such that the action $d_t = d(x_t; \Omega_t) \in \{1, \ldots, J\}$ is the one chosen for display. The final reward is $y_t = 1$ if the user clicks the ad and $y_t = 0$ otherwise.[43]

This specific scenario is a *multi-armed bandit* (MAB) setup, so named by analogy to a casino with many slot machines of different payout probabilities (the casino is the bandit). In the classic MAB (or simply *bandit*) problem, there are no covariates associated with each ad and each user, such that you are attempting to optimize toward a single ad that has highest click probability across all users. That is, $\omega_j$ is $p(y_t = 1 \mid d_t = j)$, the generic click probability for ad $j$, and you want to set $d_t$ to the ad with highest $\omega_j$. There are many different algorithms for bandit optimization. They use different heuristics to balance *exploitation* with *exploration*. A fully exploitive algorithm is greedy: it always takes the currently estimated best option without any consideration of uncertainty. In the simple advertising example, this implies always converging to the first ad that ever gets clicked. A fully exploratory algorithm always randomizes the ads, and it will never converge to a single optimum. The trick to bandit learning is finding a way to balance between these two extremes.

A classic bandit algorithm, and one that gives solid intuition into RL in general, is Thompson sampling.[44] Like many tools in RL, Thompson sampling uses Bayesian inference to model the accumulation of knowledge over time. The basic idea is simple: at any point in the optimization process you have a probability distribution over the vector of click rates, $\boldsymbol{\omega} = [\omega_1 \ldots \omega_j]$, and you want to show each ad $j$ in proportion to the probability that $\omega_j$ is the largest click rate. That is, with $y^t = \{y_s\}_{s=1}^t$ denoting observed responses at time $t$, you want each ad's selection probability to be equal to the posterior probability that it is the best choice:

$$p\left(d_{t+1} = j\right) = p\left(\omega_j = \max\{\omega_k\}_{k=1}^J \mid y^t\right). \tag{10.12}$$

Since the probability in Equation 10.12 is tough to calculate in practice (the probability of a maximum is not an easy object to analyze), Thompson sampling uses Monte Carlo estimation. You draw a sample of ad-click probabilities from the posterior distribution at time $t$,

$$\boldsymbol{\omega}_{t+1} \sim p(\boldsymbol{\omega} \mid y^t), \tag{10.13}$$

---

43. This application, on the news website MSN.com with headlines rather than ads, motivates much of the RL work in Agarwal et al. [2014].
44. William R. Thompson. On the likelihood that one unknown probability exceeds another in view of the evidence of two samples. *Biometrika*, 25:285–294, 1933.

and set $d_{t+1} = \text{argmax}_j\, \omega_{t+1j}$. For example, suppose that you have a Beta(1, 1) prior on each ad's click rate (i.e., a uniform distribution between zero and one). At time $t$, the posterior distribution for the $j$th ad's click rate is

$$p(\omega_j | d^t, y^t) = \text{Beta}\left(1 + \sum_{s=1}^{t} \mathbb{1}_{[d_s=j]}\, y_s,\; 1 + \sum_{s=1}^{t} \mathbb{1}_{[d_s=j]}(1 - y_s)\right). \tag{10.14}$$

A Thompson sampling algorithm draws $\omega_{t+1j}$ from Equation 10.14 for each $j$ and then shows the ad with highest sampled click rate.

Why does this work? Think about scenarios where an ad $j$ would be shown at time $t$—in other words, when the sampled $\omega_{tj}$ is largest. This can occur if there is a lot of uncertainty about $\omega_j$, in which case high probabilities have nontrivial posterior weight, or if the expected value of $\omega_j$ is high. Thus, Thompson sampling will naturally balance between exploration and exploitation. There are many other algorithms for obtaining this balance. For example, Agarwal et al. [2014] survey methods that work well in the *contextual* bandit setting where you have covariates attached to events (such that action-payoff probabilities are event-specific). The options considered include $\varepsilon$-greedy search, which finds a predicted optimal choice and explores within a neighborhood of that optimum, and a bootstrap-based algorithm that is effectively a nonparametric version of Thompson sampling.

Another large literature looks at so-called Bayesian optimization.[45] In these algorithms, you have an unknown function $r(x)$ that you'd like to maximize. This function is modeled using some type of flexible Bayesian regression model, e.g., a Gaussian process. As you accumulate data, you have a posterior over the "response surface" $r(x)$ at all potential input locations. Suppose that, after $t$ function realizations, you have observed a maximal value $r_{\max}$. This is your current best option, but you want to continue exploring to see whether you can find a higher maximum. The Bayesian optimization update is based on the *expected improvement* statistic:

$$\mathbb{E}[\max(0, r(x) - r_{\max})]. \tag{10.15}$$

This is the posterior expectation of improvement at new location $x$, thresholded below at *zero*. The algorithm evaluates Equation 10.15 over a grid of potential $x$ locations, and you choose to evaluate $r(x_{t+1})$ at the location $x_{t+1}$ with highest expected improvement. Again, this balances exploitation with exploration: the statistic in Equation 10.15 can be high if $r(x)$ has high variance or a high mean (or both).

These RL algorithms are all described in the language of optimization, but it is possible to map many learning tasks to optimization problems. For example, the term *active learning* is usually used to refer to algorithms that choose data to minimize

---

45. For example, Matt Taddy, Herbert K.H. Lee, Genetha A. Gray, and Joshua D. Griffin. Bayesian guided pattern search for robust local optimization. *Technometrics*, 51(4):389–401, 2009.

some estimation variance (e.g., the average prediction error for a regression function over a fixed input distribution). Suppose $f(x; \Omega)$ is the regression function, attempting to predict response $y$. Then the *action* function is simply prediction, $d(x; \Omega) = f(x; \Omega)$, and the optimization goal could be to minimize the squared error—i.e., to maximize $r(d(x; \Omega), y) = -(y - f(x; \Omega))^2$. In this way, active learning problems are special cases of the RL framework.

From a business and economic perspective, RL is interesting (beyond its obvious usefulness) for assigning a *value* to new data points. In many settings, the rewards can be mapped to actual monetary value (e.g., in the advertising example where the website receives revenue-per-click). RL algorithms assign a dollar value to data observations. There is a growing literature on markets for data, including the "data-is-labor" proposal in Lanier [2014]. It seems useful for future study in this area to take account of how currently deployed AI systems assign relative data value. As a high-level point, the valuation of data in RL depends upon the *action* options and potential *rewards* associated with these actions. The value of data is defined only in a specific context.

The bandit algorithms described earlier are vastly simplified in comparison to the type of RL that is deployed as part of a deep learning system. In practice, when using RL with complex flexible functions like DNNs, you need to be careful to avoid overexploitation and early convergence.[46] It is also impossible to do a comprehensive search through the super high-dimensional space of possible values for the $\Omega$ that parametrizes a DNN. However, approaches such as that in van Seijen et al. [2017] and Silver et al. [2017] show that if you impose *structure* on the full learning problem, then it can be broken into a number of simple composite tasks, each of which is solvable with RL. As we discussed earlier, there is an undeniable advantage to having large fixed data assets that you can use to hot-start the AI (e.g., data from a search engine or social media platform). But the exploration and active data collection of RL is essential when tuning an AI system to be successful in specific contexts. These systems are taking actions and setting policy in an uncertain and dynamic world. As statisticians, scientists, and economists are well aware, without constant experimentation it is not possible to learn and improve.

## AI in Context

This chapter provided a primer on the key ingredients of AI. We have also been pushing some general points. First, the current wave of ML-driven AI should be viewed as a new class of products growing up around a new general-purpose technology: large-scale, fast, and robust machine learning. AI is not machine learning, but general

---

46. Volodymyr Mnih, Koray Kavukcuoglu, David Silver, Andrei A. Rusu, Joel Veness, Marc G. Bellemare, Alex Graves, Martin Riedmiller, Andreas K. Fidjeland, Georg Ostrovski, Stig Petersen, Charles Beattie, Amir Sadik, Ioannis Antonoglou, Helen King, Dharshan Kumaran, Daan Wierstra, Shane Legg, and Demis Hassabis. Human-level control through deep reinforcement learning. *Nature*, 518(7540):529–533, 2015.

purpose ML—specifically, deep learning—is the electric motor of AI. These ML tools are going to continue to get better, faster, and cheaper. Hardware and big data resources are adapting to the demands of DNNs, and self-service ML solutions are available on all of the major cloud computing platforms. Trained DNNs might become a commodity in the near-term future, and the market for deep learning could get wrapped up in the larger battle over market share in cloud computing services.

Second, we are still waiting for true end-to-end business AI solutions that drive a real increase in productivity. AI's current "wins" are mostly limited to settings with high amounts of explicit structure, such as board and video games.[47] This is changing, as companies like Microsoft and Amazon produce semi-autonomous systems that can engage with real business problems.[48] But there is still much work to be done, and the advances will be made by those who can impose structure on these complex business problems. That is, for business AI to succeed, you need to combine the GPML and big data with people who know the rules of the "game" in their business domain.

Finally, all of this will have significant implications for the role of science in industry. The economists, social scientists, and finance professionals are the people who can provide structure and rules around messy business scenarios. For example, a good structural econometrician[49] uses economic theory to break a complex question into a set of *measurable* (i.e., identified) equations with parameters that can be estimated from data. In many settings, this is *exactly* the type of workflow required for AI. The difference is that, instead of being limited to basic linear regression, these measurable pieces of the system will be modeled via DNNs that can actively experiment and generate their own training data. The next generation of economists and business scientists needs to be comfortable in knowing how to apply economic theory to obtain such structure and how to translate this structure into recipes that can be automated with ML and RL. Just as big data led to data science, a discipline combining statistics and computer science, moving from business data science to business AI will require interdisciplinary pioneers who can combine economics, statistics, and machine learning.

---

47. An exception to this is web search, which is a compelling real-world problem that has been effectively solved through AI.

48. As another example of AI moving into new domains, at the end of 2017 researchers from Carnegie Mellon built an AI system to beat human champions of Texas Hold 'em poker. Poker has explicit rules, but unlike Go or *Ms. Pac-Man*, it is a game of uncertainty and *imperfect* information. Brown and Sandholm [2017] use game theory to break a poker game into various subproblems.

49. For example, Daniel McFadden. Econometric models for probabilistic choice among products. *Journal of Business*, pages S13–S29, 1980; James J. Heckman. Sample selection bias as a specification error (with an application to the estimation of labor supply functions), 1977; and Angus Deaton and John Muellbauer. An almost ideal demand system. *The American Economic Review*, 70:312–326, 1980.

# BIBLIOGRAPHY

Alberto Abadie, Alexis Diamond, and Jens Hainmueller. Synthetic control methods for comparative case studies: Estimating the effect of California's tobacco control program. *Journal of the American Statistical Association*, 105(490):493–505, 2010.

Alberto Abadie and Javier Gardeazabal. The economic costs of conflict: A case study of the Basque country. *The American Economic Review*, 93(1):113–132, 2003.

Alekh Agarwal, Daniel Hsu, Satyen Kale, John Langford, Lihong Li, and Robert Schapire. Taming the monster: A fast and simple algorithm for contextual bandits. In *International Conference on Machine Learning*, pages 1638–1646, 2014.

H. Akaike. Information theory and the maximum likelihood principle. In B.N. Petrov and F. Csaki, editors, *2nd International Symposium on Information Theory*. Akademiai Kiado, 1973.

Joshua D. Angrist, Kathryn Graddy, and Guido W. Imbens. The interpretation of instrumental variables estimators in simultaneous equations models with an application to the demand for fish. *The Review of Economic Studies*, 67:499–527, 2000.

Joshua D. Angrist, Guido W. Imbens, and Donald B. Rubin. Identification of causal effects using instrumental variables. *Journal of the American Statistical Association*, 91:444–455, 1996.

Joshua D. Angrist and Jörn-Steffen Pischke. *Mostly Harmless Econometrics*. Princeton University Press, 2009.

Susan Athey. Beyond prediction: Using big data for policy problems. *Science*, 355:483–485, 2017.

Susan Athey, Mohsen Bayati, Nikolay Doudchenko, Guido Imbens, and Khashayar Khosravi. Matrix completion methods for causal panel data models. *arXiv: 1710.10251*, 2017a.

Susan Athey and Guido Imbens. Recursive partitioning for heterogeneous causal effects. *Proceedings of the National Academy of Sciences*, 113:7353–7360, 2016.

Susan Athey, Julie Tibshirani, and Stefan Wager. Generalized random forests. *arXiv: 1610.01271v3*, 2017b.

Eric Bair, Trevor Hastie, Paul Debashis, and Robert Tibshirani. Prediction by supervised principal components. *Journal of the American Statistical Association*, 101:119–137, 2006.

Alexandre Belloni, Victor Chernozhukov, and Christian Hansen. Inference on treatment effects after selection among high-dimensional controls. *The Review of Economic Studies*, 81:608–650, 2014.

Yoshua Bengio and Yann LeCun. Scaling learning algorithms towards AI. In *Large-Scale Kernel Machines*, MIT Press, 2007.

Y. Benjamini and Y. Hochberg. Controlling the false discovery rate: A practical and powerful approach to multiple testing. *Journal of the Royal Statistical Society, Series B*, 57:289–300, 1995.

Steven Berry, James Levinsohn, and Ariel Pakes. Automobile prices in market equilibrium. *Econometrica*, 63:841–890, 1995.

Christopher Bishop. *Pattern Recognition and Machine Learning*. Springer, 2006.

Tom Blake, Chris Nosko, and Steve Tadelis. Consumer heterogeneity and paid search effectiveness: A large-scale field experiment. *Econometrica* 83:155–174, 2014.

David M. Blei and John D. Lafferty. Dynamic topic models. In *Proceedings of the 23rd International Conference on Machine learning*, pages 113–120, 2006.

David M. Blei, Andrew Y. Ng, and Michael I. Jordan. Latent Dirichlet allocation. *Journal of Machine Learning Research*, 3:993–1022, 2003.

Tolga Bolukbasi, Kai-Wei Chang, James Y. Zou, Venkatesh Saligrama, and Adam T. Kalai. Man is to computer programmer as woman is to homemaker? Debiasing word embeddings. In *Advances in Neural Information Processing Systems*, pages 4349–4357, 2016.

Olivier Bousquet and Léon Bottou. The tradeoffs of large-scale learning. In *Advances in Neural Information Processing Systems*, pages 161–168, 2008.

Leo Breiman. Heuristics of instability and stabilization in model selection. *The Annals of Statistics*, 24:2350–2383, 1996.

Leo Breiman. Random Forests. *Machine Learning*, 45:5–32, 2001.

Leo Breiman, Jerome Friedman, Richard Olshen, and Charles Stone. *Classification and Regression Trees*. Chapman & Hall/CRC, 1984.

Timothy Bresnahan. General-purpose technologies. *Handbook of the Economics of Innovation*, 2:761–791, 2010.

Kay H. Brodersen, Fabian Gallusser, Jim Koehler, Nicolas Remy, Steven L. Scott. Inferring causal impact using Bayesian structural time-series models. *The Annals of Applied Statistics*, 9:247–274, 2015.

Noam Brown and Tuomas Sandholm. Superhuman AI for heads-up no-limit poker: Libratus beats top professionals. *Science*, 359:418–424, 2017.

Carlos M. Carvalho, Hedibert F. Lopes, and Robert E. McCulloch. On the long run volatility of stocks. *Journal of the American Statistical Association*, 113:1050–1069, 2018.

G. Chamberlain and G.W. Imbens. Nonparametric applications of Bayesian inference. *Journal of Business and Economic Statistics*, 21:12–18, 2003.

Victor Chernozhukov, Denis Chetverikov, Mert Demirer, Esther Duflo, Christian Hansen, Whitney Newey, and James Robins. Double/debiased machine learning for treatment and structural parameters. *The Econometrics Journal*, 21:1-68, 2017a.

Victor Chernozhukov, Matt Goldman, Vira Semenova, and Matt Taddy. Orthogonal machine learning for demand estimation: High dimensional causal inference in dynamic panels. *arXiv:1712.09988*, 2017b.

Hugh A. Chipman, Edward I. George, and Robert E. McCulloch. BART: Bayesian Additive Regression Trees. *The Annals of Applied Statistics*, 4:266–298, 2010.

Richard K. Crump, V. Joseph Hotz, Guido W. Imbens, and Oscar A. Mitnik. Dealing with limited overlap in estimation of average treatment effects. *Biometrika*, 96:187–199, 2009.

Andreas Damianou and Neil Lawrence. Deep Gaussian processes. In *Artificial Intelligence and Statistics*, pages 207–215, 2013.

Anthony Christopher Davison and David Victor Hinkley. *Bootstrap Methods and Their Application*. Cambridge University Press, 1997.

Jeffrey Dean and Sanjay Ghemawat. MapReduce: Simplified data processing on large clusters. In *Proceedings of Operating Systems Design and Implementation*, pages 137–150, 2004.

Angus Deaton and John Muellbauer. An almost ideal demand system. *The American Economic Review*, 70:312–326, 1980.

John J. Donohue and Steven D. Levitt. The impact of legalized abortion on crime. *The Quarterly Journal of Economics*, 116:379–420, 2001.

John Duchi, Elad Hazan, and Yoram Singer. Adaptive subgradient methods for online learning and stochastic optimization. *Journal of Machine Learning Research*, 12:2121–2159, 2011.

Bradley Efron. Bayesian inference and the parametric bootstrap. *The Annals of Applied Statistics*, 6:1971–1997, 2012.

Matthias Feurer, Aaron Klein, Katharina Eggensperger, Jost Springenberg, Manuel Blum, and Frank Hutter. Efficient and robust automated machine learning. In *Advances in Neural Information Processing Systems*, pages 2962–2970, 2015.

Amy Finkelstein, Sarah Taubman, Bill Wright, Mira Bernstein, Jonathan Gruber, Joseph P. Newhouse, Heidi Allen, Katherine Baicker, and Oregon Health Study Group. The Oregon health insurance experiment: Evidence from the first year. *The Quarterly Journal of Economics*, 127:1057–1106, 2012.

David A. Freedman. On regression adjustments in experiments with several treatments. *The Annals of Applied Statistics*, 2:176–196, 2008.

Jerome H. Friedman. Greedy function approximation: A gradient boosting machine. *Annals of Statistics*, pages 1189–1232, 2001.

Alan E. Gelfand and Adrian F.M. Smith. Sampling-based approaches to calculating marginal densities. *Journal of the American Statistical Association*, 85(410): 398–409, 1990.

Andrew Gelman, John B. Carlin, Hal S. Stern, David B. Dunson, Aki Vehtari, and Donald B. Rubin. *Bayesian Data Analysis*, 3rd edition. Chapman & Hall 2014.

Matthew Gentzkow and Jesse Shapiro. What drives media slant? Evidence from U.S. daily newspapers. *Econometrica*, 78:35–72, 2010.

Matthew Gentzkow, Bryan Kelly, and Matt Taddy. Text-as-data. *NBER working paper 23276*, 2017.

Matthew Gentzkow, Jesse M. Shapiro, and Matt Taddy. Measuring polarization in high-dimensional data: Method and application to congressional speech. *NBER working paper 22423*, 2016.

Ian Goodfellow, Jean Pouget-Abadie, Mehdi Mirza, Bing Xu, David Warde-Farley, Sherjil Ozair, Aaron Courville, and Yoshua Bengio. Generative adversarial nets. In *Advances in neural information processing systems*, pages 2672–2680, 2014.

Ian Goodfellow, Yoshua Bengio, and Aaron Courville. *Deep Learning*. MIT Press, 2016.

Robert B. Gramacy. laGP: Large-scale spatial modeling via local approximate Gaussian processes in R. *Journal of Statistical Software* (available as a vignette in the laGP package), 2015.

Robert B. Gramacy. tgp: An R package for Bayesian nonstationary, semiparametric non-linear regression and design by treed Gaussian process models. *Journal of Statistical Software*, 19:1–46, 2007.

Robert B. Gramacy and Matt Taddy. Categorical inputs, sensitivity analysis, optimization and importance tempering with tgp version 2, an R package for treed Gaussian process models. *Journal of Statistical Software*, 33:1–48, 2010.

Robert Gramacy, Matt Taddy, and Sen Tian. Hockey performance via regression. In *Handbook of Statistical Methods for Design and Analysis in Sports*, 2015.

Robert B. Gramacy and Herbert K.H. Lee. Bayesian treed Gaussian process models with an application to computer modeling. *Journal of the American Statistical Association*, 103(483):1119–1130, 2008.

Robert B. Gramacy and Herbert K.H. Lee. Cases for the nugget in modeling computer experiments. *Statistics and Computing*, 22(3):713–722, 2012.

Ian Hacking. *The Emergence of Probability*. Cambridge University Press, 1975.

J. Hahn, P. Todd, and W. Van der Klaauw. Evaluating the effect of an antidiscrimination law using a regression-discontinuity design. *NBER Working Paper* 7131, 1999.

Moritz Hardt, Ben Recht, and Yoram Singer. Train faster, generalize better: Stability of stochastic gradient descent. In the proceedings of the *International Conference on Machine Learning*, pages 1225–1234, 2016.

Jason Hartford, Greg Lewis, Kevin Leyton-Brown, and Matt Taddy. Deep IV: A flexible approach for counterfactual prediction. In the proceedings of the *International Conference on Machine Learning*, pages 1414–1423, 2017.

Trevor Hastie, Robert Tibshirani, and Jerome Friedman. *The Elements of Statistical Learning*, 2nd edition. Springer, 2009.

John Haugeland. *Artificial Intelligence: The Very Idea*. MIT Press, 1985.

Kaiming He, Xiangyu Zhang, Shaoqing Ren, and Jian Sun. Deep residual learning for image recognition. In *Proceedings of the IEEE conference on computer vision and pattern recognition*, pages 770–778, 2016.

James J. Heckman. Sample selection bias as a specification error (with an application to the estimation of labor supply functions). *Econometrica* 47:153–161, 1977.

Jennifer Hill. Bayesian Nonparametric Modeling for Causal Inference. *Journal of Computational and Graphical Statistics*, 20:217–240, 2011.

Geoffrey E. Hinton, Simon Osindero, and Yee-Whye Teh. A fast learning algorithm for deep belief nets. *Neural Computation*, 18:1527–1554, 2006.

Stephen J. Hoch, Byung-Do Kim, Alan L. Montgomery, and Peter E. Rossi. Determinants of store-level price elasticity. *Journal of marketing Research*, pages 17–29, 1995.

Sepp Hochreiter and Jürgen Schmidhuber. Long short-term memory. *Neural computation*, 9:1735–1780, 1997.

Peter D. Hoff. *A first course in Bayesian statistical methods*. Springer Science & Business Media, 2009.

Matthew D. Hoffman, David M. Blei, Chong Wang, and John Paisley. Stochastic variational inference. *The Journal of Machine Learning Research*, 14:1303–1347, 2013.

Kurt Hornik, Maxwell Stinchcombe, and Halbert White. Multilayer feedforward networks are universal approximators. *Neural Networks*, 2:359–366, 1989.

Clifford M. Hurvich and Chih-Ling Tsai. Regression and time series model selection in small samples. *Biometrika*, 76:297–307, 1989.

Guido Imbens and Thomas Lemieux. Regression discontinuity designs: A guide to practice. *Journal of Econometrics*, 142:615–635, 2008.

Guido Imbens and Donald Rubin. *Causal Inference in Statistics, Social, and Biomedical Sciences*. Cambridge University Press, 2015.

Gareth James, Daniela Witten, Trevor Hastie, and Robert Tibshirani. *An Introduction to Statistical Learning*. Springer, 2013.

Daniel Jurafsky and James H. Martin. *Speech and Language Processing*, 2nd edition. Prentice Hall, 2009.

Andrej Karpathy and Li Fei-Fei. Deep visual-semantic alignments for generating image descriptions. In *Proceedings of the IEEE Conference on Computer Vision and Pattern Recognition*, pages 3128–3137, 2015.

Alex Kendall and Yarin Gal. What uncertainties do we need in Bayesian deep learning for computer vision? *arXiv:1703.04977*, 2017.

Diederik Kingma and Jimmy Ba. Adam: A method for stochastic optimization. In the proceedings of the *3rd International Conference on Learning Representations (ICLR)*, 2015.

Keith Knight and Wenjiang Fu. Asymptotics for lasso-type estimators. *Annals of Statistics*, pages 1356–1378, 2000.

Alex Krizhevsky, Ilya Sutskever, and Geoffrey E. Hinton. Imagenet classification with deep convolutional neural networks. In *Advances in neural information processing systems*, pages 1097–1105, 2012.

Jaron Lanier. *Who Owns the Future*. Simon & Schuster, 2014.

Yann LeCun and Yoshua Bengio. Convolutional networks for images, speech, and time series. In *The Handbook of Brain Theory and Neural Networks*, 1995.

Yann LeCun, Léon Bottou, Yoshua Bengio, and Patrick Haffner. Gradient-based learning applied to document recognition. *Proceedings of the IEEE*, 86:2278–2324, 1998.

S.D. Levitt and S.J. Dubner. *Freakonomics*. William Morrow, 2005.

Daniel McFadden. Econometric models for probabilistic choice among products. *Journal of Business*, 53:S13–S29, 1980.

Tomas Mikolov, Ilya Sutskever, Kai Chen, Greg S. Corrado, and Jeff Dean. Distributed representations of words and phrases and their compositionality. In *Advances in Neural Information Processing Systems*, pages 3111–3119, 2013.

Volodymyr Mnih, Koray Kavukcuoglu, David Silver, Andrei A. Rusu, Joel Veness, Marc G. Bellemare, Alex Graves, Martin Riedmiller, Andreas K. Fidjeland, Georg Ostrovski, Stig Petersen, Charles Beattie, Amir Sadik, Ioannis Antonoglou, Helen King, Dharshan Kumaran, Daan Wierstra, Shane Legg, and Demis Hassabis. Human-level control through deep reinforcement learning. *Nature*, 518:529–533, 2015.

Stephen L. Morgan and Christopher Winship. *Counterfactuals and Causal Inference*, 2nd edition. Cambridge University Press, 2015.

Frederick Mosteller and David L. Wallace. Inference in an Authorship Problem. *Journal of the American Statistical Association*, 58:275–309, 1963.

Kevin Patrick Murphy. *Machine Learning: A Probabilistic Perspective*. MIT Press, 2012.

Radford M. Neal. *Bayesian learning for neural networks*, Springer, 2012.

Michael A. Nielsen. *Neural Networks and Deep Learning*. Determination Press, 2015.

John Novembre, Toby Johnson, Katarzyna Bryc, Zoltan Kutalik, Adam R. Boyko, Adam Auton, Amit Indap, Karen S. King, Sven Bergmann, Matthew R. Nelson, Matthew Stephens, and Carlos D. Bustamante. Genes mirror geography within Europe. *Nature*, 456: 98–101, 2008.

J. Pearl. *Causality*. Cambridge University Press, 2009.

Jeffrey Pennington, Richard Socher, and Christopher Manning. Glove: Global vectors for word representation. In *Proceedings of the 2014 Conference on Empirical Methods in Natural Language Processing (EMNLP)*, pages 1532–1543, 2014.

Dale J. Poirier. Bayesian interpretations of heteroskedastic consistent covariance estimators using the informed Bayesian bootstrap. *Econometric Reviews*, 30: 457–468, 2011.

Dimitris N. Politis, Joseph P. Romano, and Michael Wolf. *Subsampling*. Springer, 1999.

Keith T. Poole. *Spatial Models of Parliamentary Voting*. Cambridge University Press, New York, 2005.

C.E. Rasmussen and C.K.I. Williams. *Gaussian Processes for Machine Learning*. MIT Press, 2006.

Herbert Robbins and Sutton Monro. A stochastic approximation method. *The Annals of Mathematical Statistics*, 22:400–407, 1951.

K. Roeder and L. Wasserman. Practical Bayesian density estimation using mixtures of normals. *Journal of the American Statistical Association*, 92:894–902, 1997.

Frank Rosenblatt. The perceptron: A probabilistic model for information storage and organization in the brain. *Psychological Review*, 65:386, 1958.

D. Rubin. Using the SIR algorithm to simulate posterior distributions by data augmentation. In J.M. Bernardo, M.H. DeGroot, and D.V. Lindley, A.F.M. Smith, editors, *Bayesian Statistics 3*. Oxford University Press, 1988.

David E. Rumelhart, Geoffrey E. Hinton, Ronald J. Williams. Learning representations by back-propagating errors. *Cognitive Modeling*, 5:1, 1988.

Sara Sabour, Nicholas Frosst, and Geoffrey E. Hinton. Dynamic routing between capsules. In *Advances in Neural Information Processing Systems*, pages 3857–3867, 2017.

David Silver, Aja Huang, Chris J. Maddison, Arthur Guez, Laurent Sifre, George Van Den Driessche, Julian Schrittwieser, Ioannis Antonoglou, Veda Panneershelvam, Marc Lanctot, et al. Mastering the game of go with deep neural networks and tree search. *Nature*, 529:484–489, 2016.

David Silver, Julian Schrittwieser, Karen Simonyan, Ioannis Antonoglou, Aja Huang, Arthur Guez, Thomas Hubert, Lucas Baker, Matthew Lai, Adrian Bolton, et al. Mastering the game of go without human knowledge. *Nature*, 550:354–359, 2017.

Nitish Srivastava, Geoffrey E. Hinton, Alex Krizhevsky, Ilya Sutskever, and Ruslan Salakhutdinov. Dropout: A simple way to prevent neural networks from overfitting. *Journal of Machine Learning Reseach*, 15:1929–1958, 2014.

Matt Taddy. On estimation and selection for topic models. In *Proceedings of the 15th International Conference on Artificial Intelligence and Statistics*, 2012.

Matt Taddy. Measuring political sentiment on Twitter: Factor optimal design for multinomial inverse regression. *Technometrics*, 55:415–425, 2013a.

Matt Taddy. Multinomial inverse regression for text analysis. *Journal of the American Statistical Association*, 108:755–770, 2013b.

Matt Taddy. Document classification by inversion of distributed language representations. In *Proceedings of the Conference of the Association for Computational Linguistics*, 2015a.

Matt Taddy. Distributed multinomial regression. *The Annals of Applied Statistics*, 9:1394–1414, 2015b.

Matt Taddy, Chun-Sheng Chen, Jun Yu, and Mitch Wyle. Bayesian and empirical Bayesian forests. In *Proceedings of the 32nd International Conference on Machine Learning*, 2015.

Matt Taddy, Matt Gardner, Liyun Chen, and David Draper. Nonparametric Bayesian analysis of heterogeneous treatment effects in digital experimentation. *Journal of Business and Economic Statistics*, 34:661–672, 2016a.

Matt Taddy, Herbert K.H. Lee, Genetha A. Gray, and Joshua D. Griffin. Bayesian guided pattern search for robust local optimization. *Technometrics*, 51:389–401, 2009.

Matt Taddy, Hedibert Lopes, and Matt Gardner. Scalable semiparametric inference for the means of heavy-tailed distributions. *arXiv:1602.08066*, 2016b.

William R. Thompson. On the likelihood that one unknown probability exceeds another in view of the evidence of two samples. *Biometrika*, 25:285–294, 1933.

Panagiotis Toulis, Edoardo Airoldi, and Jason Rennie. Statistical analysis of stochastic gradient methods for generalized linear models. In Proceedings of the *International Conference on Machine Learning*, pages 667–675, 2014.

Harm van Seijen, Mehdi Fatemi, Joshua Romoff, Romain Laroche, Tavian Barnes, and Jeffrey Tsang. Hybrid reward architecture for reinforcement learning. *arXiv:1706.04208*, 2017.

Vladimir Vapnik. *The Nature of Statistical Learning Theory*. Springer, 1996.

Hal R. Varian. Online ad auctions. *The American Economic Review*, 99:430–434, 2009.

W.N. Venables and B.D. Ripley. *Modern Applied Statistics with S*, 4th edition. Springer, 2002.

Brani Vidakovic and Peter Mueller. Wavelets for kids. Technical report, Instituto de Estadística, Universidad de Duke, 1994.

Ganapathy Vidyamurthy. *Pairs Trading: Quantitative Methods and Analysis*, volume 217. John Wiley & Sons, 2004.

Wei Wang, David Rothschild, Sharad Goel, and Andrew Gelman. Forecasting elections with non-representative polls. *International Journal of Forecasting*, 31(3): 980–991, 2015.

Wei Wang, David Rothschild, Sharad Goel, and Andrew Gelman. High-frequency polling with nonrepresentative data. In *Political Communication in Real Time*. Routledge, 2016.

Halbert White. A heteroskedasticity-consistent covariance matrix estimator and a direct test for heteroskedasticity. *Econometrica*, 48:817–838, 1980.

Cristen J. Willer, Ellen M. Schmidt, Sebanti Sengupta, Gina M. Peloso, Stefan Gustafsson, Stavroula Kanoni, Andrea Ganna, Jin Chen, Martin L Buchkovich, Samia Mora, et al. Discovery and refinement of loci associated with lipid levels. *Nature Genetics*, 45:1274–1285, 2013.

H. Wold. Soft Modeling by Latent Variables: The nonlinear iterative partial least squares approach. In *Perspectives in Probability and Statistics, Papers in Honour of M.S. Bartlett*. Academic Press, 1975.

Hui Zou, Trevor Hastie, and Robert Tibshirani. On the degrees of freedom of the lasso. *The Annals of Statistics*, 35:2173–2192, 2007.

# INDEX

## H

## I

## J

# ABOUT THE AUTHOR

**Matt Taddy** was a professor of econometrics and statistics from 2008–2018 at the University of Chicago Booth School of Business, where he developed their data science curriculum. He has also worked in a variety of industry positions, including as a principal researcher at Microsoft and a research fellow at eBay. He left Chicago in 2018 to join Amazon as a vice president.